Aging in Nonhuman Primates

Malysh, subject of a uniquely comprehensive case report on aging in the rhesus macaque. Malysh, whose name in Russian means "Little One" or "Little Man," was among the first group of monkeys imported to the Soviet primate center at Sukhumi in 1927. In his early years he participated in a series of experiments demonstrating that monkeys are resistant to the kinds of cognitive stressors that ordinarily produce experimental neurosis in dogs. Malysh fathered 75 offspring and was 27 years old when he died. This photograph was taken just before his death in 1950.

Aging in Nonhuman Primates

DOUGLAS M. BOWDEN, Editor

Regional Primate Research Center
and Department of Psychiatry and Behavioral Sciences,
University of Washington,
Seattle, Washington.

Van Nostrand Reinhold
Primate Behavior and Development Series

 VAN NOSTRAND REINHOLD COMPANY
NEW YORK   CINCINNATI   ATLANTA   DALLAS   SAN FRANCISCO
LONDON   TORONTO   MELBOURNE

Van Nostrand Reinhold Company Regional Offices:
New York   Cincinnati   Atlanta   Dallas   San Francisco

Van Nostrand Reinhold Company International Offices:
London   Toronto   Melbourne

Library of Congress Catalog Card Number: 79-10269
ISBN: 0-442-20734-4

Manufactured in the United States of America

Published by Van Nostrand Reinhold Company
135 West 50th Street, New York, NY 10020

Published simultaneously in Canada by Van Nostrand Reinhold Ltd.

15 14 13 12 11 10 9 8 7 6 5 4 3 2 1

Library of Congress Cataloging in Publication Data

Main entry under title:

Aging in nonhuman primates.

   Includes index.
   1. Aging.   2. Primates—Physiology.   3. Age factors
in disease.   I. Bowden, Douglas M
QP86.A365   599'.8'04372   79-10269
ISBN 0-442-20734-4

Van Nostrand Reinhold Primate Behavior and Development Series

AGING IN NONHUMAN PRIMATES, edited by Douglas M. Bowden

CAPTIVITY AND BEHAVIOR: Primates in Breeding Colonies, Laboratories, and Zoos, edited by J. Erwin, T. Maple and G. Mitchell

ORANGUTAN BEHAVIOR, by Terry L. Maple

GORILLA BEHAVIOR, by Terry L. Maple

CHIMPANZEE BEHAVIOR, by Terry L. Maple

BEHAVIORAL SEX DIFFERENCES IN NONHUMAN PRIMATES, by G. Mitchell

Contributors

Tai Akera*
Department of Pharmacology, Michigan State University, East Lansing, Michigan 48824

P. Arce
Department of Environmental Health, University of Washington, Seattle, Washington 98195

John E. Aschenbrenner*
Department of Basic Health Sciences, Division of Anatomy, North Texas State University Health Science Center, Texas College of Osteopathic Medicine, Fort Worth, Texas 76107

Nobuhisa Baba*
Departments of Pathology and Radiology, Ohio State University College of Medicine, Columbus, Ohio 43210

Peter B. Baker
Departments of Pathology and Radiology, Ohio State University College of Medicine, Columbus, Ohio 43210

*Collaborating Investigator

Steven I. Baskin*
Department of Pharmacology, The Medical College of Pennsylvania, Philadelphia, Pennsylvania 19129

Peter H. Blake
Regional Primate Research Center, University of Washington, Seattle, Washington 98195

E. S. Boatman*
Department of Environmental Health, University of Washington, Seattle, Washington 98195

Douglas M. Bowden*
Regional Primate Research Center, and Department of Psychiatry and Behavioral Sciences, University of Washington, Seattle, Washington 98195

John T. Boyce
Department of Pathology, University of Washington, Seattle, Washington 98195

Theodore M. Brody
Department of Pharmacology and Toxicology, Michigan State University, East Lansing, Michigan 48824

Elizabeth M. Burns*
College of Nursing, University of Illinois Medical Center, Chicago, Illinois 60612

Philip Chin
Department of Medicine, New York University School of Medicine, New York, New York 10016

Donna Cohen*
Department of Psychiatry and Behavioral Sciences, University of Washington, Seattle, Washington 98195

Lynn E. Comerford
College of Nursing, University of Illinois Medical Center, Chicago, Illinois 60612

Carl Eisdorfer
Department of Psychiatry and Behavioral Sciences, University of Washington, Seattle, Washington 98195; and Acting Director, Institute on Aging, University of Washington, Seattle, Washington 98195

Margaret N. Farquhar*
Center for Inherited Diseases, Department of Medicine, Division of Medical Genetics, University of Washington, Seattle, Washington 98195

Ralph T. Geer
Department of Anesthesia, University of Pennsylvania School of Medicine, Philadelphia, Pennsylvania 19104

W. E. Giddens, Jr.*
Regional Primate Research Center and Department of Pathology, School of Medicine, University of Washington, Seattle, Washington 98195

Charles E. Graham*
Yerkes Regional Primate Research Center, Emory University, Atlanta, Georgia 30322

Daniel R. Hanson
Division of Medical Genetics, University of Washington, Seattle, Washington 98195

William R. Hazzard*
Department of Medicine and Northwest Lipid Research Clinic, University of Washington School of Medicine, Seattle, Washington 98195

Marvin L. Jones*
Zoological Society of San Diego, San Diego, California 92112

Beverly K. Kariya
Department of Pathology, University of Washington, Seattle, Washington 98195

Zebulon V. Kendrick
Department of Pharmacology, The Medical College of Pennsylvania, Philadelphia, Pennsylvania 19129

David L. Kleinberg*
Department of Medicine, New York University School of Medicine, New York, New York 10016; and Medical Research Service, New York Veterans Administration Hospital, New York, New York 10010

O. Ray Kling*
Department of Gynecology and Obstetrics, University of Oklahoma College of Medicine, Oklahoma City, Oklahoma 73190

Glenn H. Knitter
Regional Primate Research Center, University of Washington, Seattle, Washington 98195

Vincent G. Kokich*
Department of Orthodontics, School of Dentistry, University of Washington, Seattle, Washington 98195

Kathleen J. Kosky
Center for Inherited Diseases, Department of Medicine, Division of Medical Genetics, University of Washington, Seattle, Washington 98195

Thomas W. Kruckeberg
College of Nursing, University of Illinois Medical Center, Chicago, Illinois 60612

John Claude Krusz*
Department of Pharmacology, The Medical College of Pennsylvania, Philadelphia, Pennsylvania 19129

Andras G. Lacko*
Department of Biochemistry, Texas College of Osteopathic Medicine; and Center for Studies in Aging, North Texas State University, Denton, Texas 76203

K. Y. Lei*
Nutrition Program, College of Agriculture and Home Economics, Agricultural and Forestry Experiment Station, Mississippi State University, Mississippi State, Mississippi 39762

Pete E. Lestrel*
Dental Research Unit, Veterans Administration Hospital, Sepulveda, California 91343

Lisa A. Litvin
Department of Anesthesia, University of Pennsylvania School of Medicine, Philadelphia, Pennsylvania 19104

D. Luchtel
Department of Environmental Health, University of Washington, Seattle, Washington 98195

Bryan E. Marshall*
Department of Anesthesia, University of Pennsylvania School of Medicine, Philadelphia, Pennsylvania 19104

C. J. Martin*
Institute of Respiratory Physiology, Virginia Mason Research Center, Seattle, Washington 98101

George M. Martin*
Department of Pathology, University of Washington, Seattle, Washington 98195

Peter E. Maxim*
Department of Psychiatry and Behavioral Sciences and Regional Primate Research Center, University of Washington, Seattle, Washington 98195

Thomas H. McNeill
Department of Neurology, University of Rochester School of Medicine, Rochester, New York 14642

Benjamin C. Moffett
Department of Orthodontics, School of Dentistry, University of Washington, Seattle, Washington 98195

Robert N. Moore*
Department of Orthodontics, School of Dentistry, and Department of Anatomy, School of Medicine, West Virginia University Medical Center, Morgantown, West Virginia 26506

Charles F. Mueller
Departments of Pathology and Radiology, Ohio State University College of Medicine, Columbus, Ohio 43210

Kalidas Nandy*
Geriatric Research, Education and Clinical Center, Veterans Administration Hospital, Bedford, Massachusetts 01730; and Department of Anatomy and Neurology, Boston University Medical School, Boston, Massachusetts 02215

Gordon R. Neufeld
Department of Anesthesia, University of Pennsylvania School of Medicine, Philadelphia, Pennsylvania 19104

Charles E. Ogburn*
Department of Pathology, University of Washington, Seattle, Washington 98195

Gilbert S. Omenn*
Center for Inherited Diseases, Department of Medicine, Division of Medical Genetics, University of Washington, Seattle, Washington 98195

K. K. Pump
Department of Medicine, University of British Columbia, Vancouver, B.C.

James J. Quattrochi
Departments of Pathology and Radiology, Ohio State University College of Medicine, Columbus, Ohio 43210

Ernest W. Retzlaff*
Department of Biomechanics, College of Osteopathic Medicine, Michigan State University, East Lansing, Michigan 48824

Russell Ross*
Department of Pathology, University of Washington, Seattle, Washington 98195

Harvey Schiller*
Department of Laboratory Medicine, University of Washington, Seattle, Washington 98195

R. A. Seifert
Department of Pathology, University of Washington, Seattle, Washington 98195

Peter A. Shapiro*
Department of Orthodontics, School of Dentistry, University of Washington, Seattle, Washington 98195

Celia D. Sladek
Departments of Neurology and Anatomy, University of Rochester School of Medicine, Rochester, New York 14642

John R. Sladek, Jr.*
Department of Anatomy, University of Rochester School of Medicine, Rochester, New York 14642

Lynne T. Smith
Division of Medical Genetics, University of Washington, Seattle, Washington 98195

Robert A. Steiner*
Departments of Physiology & Biophysics and Obstetrics & Gynecology, and Regional Primate Research Center, University of Washington, Seattle, Washington 98195

William H. Stone*
Laboratory of Genetics and Wisconsin Regional Primate Research Center, University of Wisconsin, Madison, Wisconsin 53706

Cheryl Teets
Department of Psychiatry and Behavioral Sciences, University of Washington, Seattle, Washington 98195

Jean Todd
Department of Medicine, New York University School of Medicine, New York, New York 10016

Elise Torczynski*
Ophthalmic Pathology Laboratory, Department of Ophthalmology, College of Medicine, University of South Florida, Tampa, Florida 33612

Vijaya K. Vijayan*
Department of Human Anatomy, University of California School of Medicine, Davis, California 95616

Patricia Walker
Department of Anatomy, University of Rochester School of Medicine, Rochester, New York 14642

M. R. Warner*
Meredith Mosle Laboratory for Cancer Research, Department of Obstetrics and Gynecology, and Department of Cell Biology, Baylor College of Medicine, Houston, Texas 77030

Joan Witkin*
Department of Anthropology, Columbia University, New York, New York 10027

Satoshi Yamamoto
Department of Pharmacology, Michigan State University, East Lansing, Michigan 48824

David M. Young*
Department of Veterinary Science, Montana State University, Bozeman, Montana 59717

L. C. Young
Nutrition Program, College of Agriculture and Home Economics, Agricultural and Forestry Experiment Station, Mississippi State University, Mississippi State, Mississippi 39762

Foreword

Robert N. Butler, M.D.,
Director, National Institute on Aging

Because of its recent emergence as a field of scientific study and its relation to all major areas of biomedical investigation, research on aging requires an integrative approach. Often, however, it is not possible or practical to study the complex biological, psychological, and social processes of aging using human subjects. The nonhuman primate is uniquely well suited for such studies because of its close phylogenetic relationship to the human. However, the use of nonhuman primates in aging research has been extremely limited owing to their long life spans compared with those of most other commonly used laboratory animals; husbandry and veterinary care requirements; limited availability; and a lack of baseline biological, behavioral, and actuarial characteristics beyond reproductive age.

In many respects, these limitations are the basic justification for the development of this publication. Nonhuman primates should be used only when they are appropriate and necessary for investigations of aging processes relevant to the human. One important use of the nonhuman primate addressed in this publication is as a validation model for less expensive, shorter-lived species such as the rat.

Although the information provided in this book enhances our understanding of the nonhuman primate as a model for human aging, it should also remind us of how much we have to learn. We still cannot always distinguish between the effects of aging and those of disease. We do not know how captivity and controlled diet affect research results. The list of areas in which our knowledge is incomplete is long, and the supply of nonhuman primates for study is limited. One way to mitigate the expense and short supply of animals is to establish tissue banks and encourage collaboration among scientists working with non-human primates. Another means to advance the state of our knowledge on animal models of aging is to carefully characterize nonhuman primates and develop acceptable primate or other relevant models for studies of cognition, social behavior, menopause, and benign hyperplasia of the prostate, to name but a few. The contributions in these areas provide vital information that will be invaluable to present and future research on aging. Therefore, the National Institute on Aging is particularly pleased to have been instrumental in support-ing the development of the studies and the body of information contained in this book.

Preface

For the individual, aging is a disease—the ultimate disease of his mortal existence. For most species, however, aging simply represents the approaching completion of one experiment in adaptation. Death is the point at which the species consolidates its gains, its energy shifting to a new generation.

For our own species, with its highly developed appetite for knowledge, aging and death are intriguing prey. How is it, asks *Homo sapiens*, that the fruit fly completes its duty as an organism in hours, whereas others of us require the better part of a century? What prevents each creature from living out the maximal lifespan of its species? What are the pros and cons of extending this lifespan? Some of these questions are philosophical and invite reflection on the accumulated wisdom of generations. Other questions are theoretical and require synthesizing scientific information already available. Still other questions demand the collection of new facts. This book is devoted to the last strategy, to the gathering of new knowledge. In this endeavor some answers will be found in fruit flies, some in ourselves and some in our closest relatives, the nonhuman primates.

DOUGLAS M. BOWDEN

Contents

Skeletal System

1

Aging Research in Nonhuman Primates

Douglas M. Bowden
Department of Psychiatry and Behavioral Sciences and
Regional Primate Research Center,
University of Washington SJ-50,
Seattle, Washington

Marvin L. Jones
San Diego Zoo,
San Diego, California

Our knowledge of aging in the nonhuman primates is extremely limited. As recently as 1974, the authors of a review article on animal models in aging research (10) found too little information on nonhuman primates to merit discussion. A 1978 bibliography listing all publications since 1940 in which primate aging was the focus of interest, or even in which individual aged animals were mentioned, comprised only 148 references (4). Very few of the reports involved the study of more than one or two animals that could reasonably be regarded as being in the last third of the lifespan of their species. Many of them are discussed in the appropriate chapters which follow. The purpose of this chapter is to review current knowledge and theories regarding the variation in longevity among different primate genera and to explore several potential strategies for optimizing the use of aging nonhuman primates in biomedical research.

Man is the only primate for whom we have estimates of lifespan based on sufficient numbers of individuals to be considered accurate. Nevertheless, information on the maximum lifespan in various genera of nonhuman primates is accumulating, and some general patterns have begun to emerge. Current knowledge regarding the maximum lifespan of various nonhuman primate species is summarized in Figure 1-1. It is based largely on longevity statistics from primate collections throughout the world compiled since 1941 by M.L.J. In 1958, a mimeographed listing was distributed to a number of zoos and individuals with

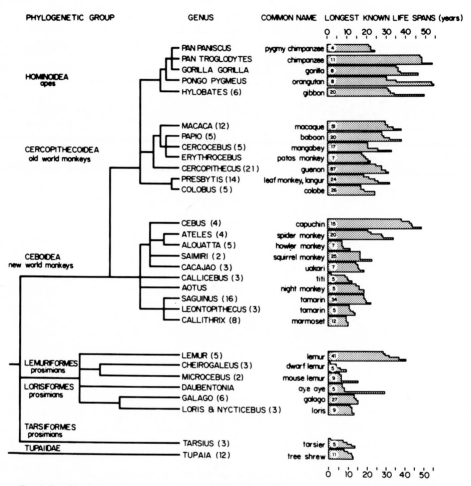

Fig. 1-1. Maximum longevity records of 30 major primate genera. Phylogenetic relationships adapted from Simpson (22), Sarich and Cronin (21) and Cutler (7) are represented by the branching diagram at left. Ages of the 5 oldest individuals of a given genus or species recorded as of November 1977 are represented in horizontal histograms at right. Numbers in parentheses represent the number of species comprising the genus (17).

the data available at that time. This formed the basis for many of the records cited by Crandall in 1964 (5). A summary of updated records published in the *Laboratory Primate Newsletter* in 1962 became the reference quoted by Napier and Napier in 1967 (17). The data presented here are drawn from the compilation updated in the fall of 1977. They are more extensive than those previously reported, partly because living animals reported earlier have grown older, and, even more so, because a number of collections from which information was previously lacking have made their records available for analysis. Based now on information from some 100 zoological collections and research institutions and on records going back to the turn of the century, it includes longevity data on about 600 individual animals of some 150 species representing all of the major genera of primates.

The lifespans have been estimated conservatively in that, with few exceptions the recorded age represents the time in captivity. Thus, the ages of animals captured in the wild are underestimated by their age at entry into captivity; the ages of those still living are underestimated by the time they will continue to live. Three of the great apes' ages have been increased by as much as 5 years based upon estimated age at entry, and the ages of 6 Old World monkeys have been increased by as much as 3 years on the same basis. Each of the horizontal bars in Figure 1-1 is a histogram representing the ages of the 4 or 5 longest-lived individuals of a particular genus. The number at the left end of each histogram indicates the number of individuals for which data are available, i.e., from which the oldest were selected.

In drawing conclusions from the figure, one must bear in mind that, while it represents the current state of knowledge, it is certain to change in future years as more animals are maintained for longer periods of time. One can gain some impression of the fragility of generalizations based on this summary by recognizing that in the 15 years since the last summary was compiled the maximum recorded lifespan of the average genus has increased by 8 years. As data from more collections have become available and animals identified earlier have grown older, the increases for particular genera have ranged from 0 to 25 years, or as much as 800%. While future increases may not be as great, one has little reason to doubt that further changes of significant magnitude will occur in coming years. With these reservations in mind, it is of interest to consider generalizations that can be made about the data currently available.

The longest lived nonhuman primates are the great apes (chimpanzee, gorilla, and orangutan). To date, no member of these species has been reported to live longer than half the maximal human lifespan of 110-115 years (18). Considering the small number and relatively recent establishment of facilities for maintaining old apes, however, it is not likely that we have had an opportunity to observe the maximum lifespan of these creatures. Female chimpanzees in captivity continue to menstruate into the fifth decade of life (Chapter 16, this volume). If menopause occurs in this species as in the human female and our more distant cousins, the Old World monkeys, we may expect that the maximal lifespan of chimpanzees will prove to be 6-7 or more decades rather than the 5.5 decades indicated in Figure 1-1.

It is impossible to say whether there are marked differences in maximal lifespan among the apes. The pygmy chimpanzee appears shortlived according to present information, but only 4 individuals are reported. The maximum lifespan is no doubt longer than such limited data indicate. Still, an ape with a lifespan comparable to that of most Old World monkeys would be a very valuable species for aging research, and more lifespan information on the pygmy chimpanzee should be obtained.

The shortest maximal lifespans among primates occur among the New World monkeys and Prosimians. No doubt some of the short lifespans illustrated here reflect small numbers of observations in animals that are very difficult to maintain in captivity, e.g., the howler monkey, dwarf lemur, and tarsier. The data that suggest the lifespans of such animals as the mouse lemur, tamarin, marmoset, galago, and loris are limited to 1 or 2 decades are more extensive, however, and probably more reliable.

An interesting feature of all of the 4 major groups of primates is the heterogeneity of maximum lifespan within the group. Such heterogeneity, together with knowledge of the phylogenetic relations among species and the fossil evidence regarding chronology of species differentiation, gives some indication of the rate at which longevity has evolved as a genetic characteristic among the primates (7). For instance, today's capuchins and marmosets (New World monkeys) descended from a common ancestor that lived about 30 million years ago. Since that time, the longevities of the 2 genera have diverged to the point at which the maximum longevity of one is approximately 4 times that of the other. On the basis of this kind of observation, Sacher (19), Cutler (6) and others have concluded that the genetic mechanism controlling the longevity of a species must be relatively simple. Most of the increase in human maximum lifespan, which is now approximately twice that of our nearest cousins, the chimpanzees, has probably occurred in the last 2 million years. Such a rapid rate of divergence in a genetic characteristic suggests that a relatively small number of gene substitutions, perhaps only a few hundred, were required to accomplish the remarkable differentiations in longevity and other characteristics that distinguish us from the great apes (20).

In recent years several investigators have directed research toward identifying metabolic processes that are under simple genetic control yet sufficiently pervasive in their effects as to be capable of determining how long the organism survives. Enzymes that protect the genome against deterioration, or that protect the organism against the immediate consequences of deterioration of the genome, are good candidates.

Deoxyribonucleic acid (DNA) is the molecular substrate of the genome. One enzyme that may contribute to deterioration of DNA is the mixed function oxidase that converts harmless substances, such as the polycyclic hydrocarbons, into mutagens, i.e., into chemicals capable of altering the structure of DNA molecules and thus degrading the genetic code. The activity level of the enzyme, or enzymes, performing this function has been measured in tissues from a variety of different species and has been found to correlate inversely with the lifespan of the species (16). Thus, some species may live longer than others because they do not metabolize otherwise neutral substances into chemicals that degrade the genome.

Another line of study has demonstrated a direct correlation between species longevity and the activity of an enzyme involved in the repair of damaged DNA (12). Exposure of cells to ultraviolet light can produce breaks in DNA molecules that are detrimental to a number of cell functions including cell division. Measures of the rate and amount of DNA repair in cells cultured from a variety of mammals, ranging from the mouse to the elephant, have shown that the greater the DNA repair capability, the longer lived the species. Regulation of the enzyme activity responsible for DNA excision repair is of particular interest in primate aging, because the relationship of this enzymatic function to longevity has been demonstrated to hold within the Order Primates (13). The observation that DNA excision repair is greater in man than in great apes, and greater in great apes than monkeys (Figure 1-2), suggests that changes in regulation of this enzyme or enzyme system may account for some of the difference in longevity between man and his nearest relatives.

Other enzymatic functions, genetic regulation of which may influence species longevity have to do with protection of the organism against the effects of deterioration in other cell components as well as, perhaps, the genome. Superoxide free radicals, which occur as a by-product of normal metabolism, can be transformed within the cell into hydroxy free radicals. Hydroxy free radicals are extremely toxic oxidizing agents that can alter cellular structure and impair function by changing the structure of proteins and other molecular components of the cell. Superoxide dismutase is an enzyme which protects against this sequence of events by converting the superoxide free radicals into neutral metabolites before they can be hydroxylated. The activity levels of protective enzymes like superoxide dismutase are genetically regulated and may be a factor in determining the longevity of species (9). Evidence now accumulating indicates that the lifespan potential of different primate species, including man, correlates with the activity level of superoxide dismutase characteristic of the species. Such a correlation has not been found between mouse species with different longevities, suggesting that this enzyme may play a more important role in determining differences in longevity among primates than among species more distantly related to man (R. Cutler, personal communication).

Finally, variation in the effectiveness of the mechanism for eliminating the abnormal proteins that result from unrepaired damage to the genome may account for variation in longevity among some species. A fundamental property

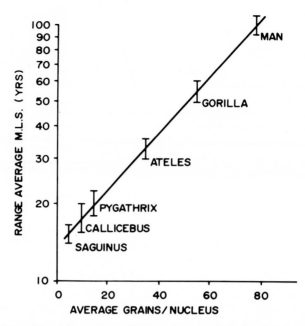

Fig. 1-2. Relationship of longevity to DNA excision repair in 6 primate species including man. Average grains/nucleus is a measure of unscheduled DNA synthesis in cultured skin fibroblasts in which the DNA has been damaged by exposure to ultraviolet light (12). In this case, unscheduled DNA synthesis reflects DNA excision repair. M.L.S. = maximum life span. Range bars indicate confidence interval for M.L.S. of the species. (Graph courtesy of R. W. Hart, K. Y. Hall and C. Albrightson.)

of animal and bacterial cells is the ability to degrade proteins that deviate from normal conformations (11). Failure of this degradative system could lead to a fatal accumulation of faulty proteins, which are the basic structural and functional components of the cell. If species vary in their genetic regulation of this protective function, one might expect that those in which it is more efficient would have longer lifespans than those in which it is less efficient.

In summary, differences in longevity among primates may be attributable to a limited number of protective processes that all primates share, but the expression of which varies among species. The search for processes that can play such a role and efforts to correlate their levels of expression with species longevity is currently a very active area in primate aging research.

Questions asked in aging research generally fall into two categories. Investigations like the ones discussed above deal with aging as a normal biological process common to animals of all species above a certain level of complexity. The other category has to do with senescence and the pathology of aging as sources of suffering and economic burden in human society. Biological aging is not totally dissociable from the pathology of aging because one facet of biological aging is an increase in vulnerability to the diseases and functional impairments that constitute the pathological aspect of aging (15). Nevertheless, the questions typically posed and the appropriate research strategies for answering them tend to be different in these two spheres of inquiry. A considerable portion of the ambiguity and argument that arise in any detailed discussion of the "relevance" of animal models to aging research can be avoided by identifying the kind of question to be answered.

Questions about the *biology* of aging, such as what determines rate of senescence and whether senescence occurs independently in different organs or is paced by deterioration of one system, clearly require the comparative study of a wide range of species. Before we can accept one or another view as an accurate description of the underlying mechanism(s) of biological aging, we must obtain information on a variety of mammals and other vertebrates. The understanding of broad biological issues of this kind requires study of representatives of several genera in different taxonomic orders if we are to be convinced of the generality of findings across species. For some studies on the genetics of longevity, it is important to have several closely related species of different longevities, but all relatively short-lived, plentiful, and having extensive background information already in the literature.

Questions regarding the *pathology* of aging, on the other hand, tend to focus directly on problems of human aging. The goals of research in this sphere are defined in terms of preventing or curing diseases and social problems of elderly humans. The answers lie in basic understanding of human physiology and behavior, and require the study of animals in which the functions disrupted during aging are similar enough to those of man to make it likely that interpretation of findings will be applicable to man. The range of species sharing processes that are sufficiently identical to make their disruption mimic diseases of man is considerably narrower than the range suitable for studying the principles of biological aging. For example, only a limited number of closely related primate species exhibit the kind of reproductive cycle seen in the human female. Thus, in animal studies of menopausal problems, primate species with a menstrual cycle similar to that of the human are much more likely to yield results relevant to humans than are other primate or nonprimate species with a different kind of reproductive cycle. We are just in the early stages of identifying the questions regarding the pathology of aging that are particularly appropriate for study in nonhuman primates.

One can argue theoretically that any question about the pathology of aging that cannot for ethical reasons be studied in members of our own species should be studied in other primates; their genetic similarity makes it most likely that the phenomenon of interest will be similar to that of the human and the findings applicable to man. There are, however, several very practical arguments against total acceptance of this approach. The answers to many important questions require study of organisms through several generations, or at least through the lifespan of one generation. Nonhuman primates, with lifespans ranging from 10 to 50 years or more, are not suitable subjects. Furthermore, in the foreseeable future, the number of old monkeys and apes available for study will be too small to meet the needs of large numbers of investigators. Estimating the number of such animals currently in the United States to be a few hundred at most, the number of potential subjects is considerably less than the number of potential investigators. If we are to make optimal use of this small, valuable scientific resource, we must differentiate questions that can be effectively studied in other species from questions that can be answered only by studying another primate (3).

One important use of nonhuman primates in aging research is to validate other animal models, i.e., to determine in what respects aging phenomena discovered in less expensive, more plentiful species are representative of aging in primates and, thus, potentially relevant to human aging. A good example of this application of the primate model is seen in Chapter 23 of this volume. Investigators studying the mechanism of the age-related increase in toxicity of the cardiac glycosides had gathered evidence through a long sequence of studies in rats, guinea pigs and other animals that drugs like digitalis, which is very important for treating heart disease in older people, may exercise their toxic effects through action on the heart and/or on the nervous system. In the study reported here, Baskin *et al.* found that, while the kinetics of interaction of the drug with sodium-potassium ATPase from the primate spinal cord was similar to that in the rat, interaction kinetics with the enzyme from the heart were different in the two species. Such findings suggest that while the rat may be an appropriate model for pursuing the study of neural toxicity of the cardiac glycosides, other species may be more appropriate for studying its toxic effects on cardiac tissue. Another example of using the primate to validate a less expensive model is seen in Chapter 8 where Omenn *et al.* demonstrated that in the macaque, as in the mouse, the uptake of serotonin by platelets is a one-component process, whereas the uptake by brain synaptosomes is a two-component process. Both of these studies illustrate one strategy for conserving nonhuman primates as research subjects, namely to use them periodically to validate the clinical relevance of less expensive models, the bulk of study being done on species genetically further removed from man, but more plentiful as research subjects.

Some aspects of the pathology of aging can only be studied in man or closely related species. These range from studies of isolated enzymes to whole functional systems that have developed in primates and are not found in other phylogenetic orders. An example in the first category is the dimer of apolipo-protein-A-2, a serum protein that may play a role in human atherosclerosis and is not found in any genus more distant from man than the great apes (8, 2). Examples of extensive functional systems that distinguish primates, including man, from other phylogenetic orders are the mechanism of female reproductive cyclicity (Chapter 16, this volume) and the neural systems that mediate socio-emotional behavior and complex cognitive function in primates (Chapters 4 and 5).

Identifying questions for which primates are the only appropriate subjects of study is one strategy that will make best use of the limited number of available subjects. Another strategy that can conserve the population of aged subjects is based on the recognition that many problems of the elderly occur in younger people as well and can be studied in young animals. The processes that ultimately lead to many of the cardiovascular, skeletal, behavioral and other problems of old age begin many years before their clinical sequelae become problems for the geriatrician. The osteoporosis of aging, intimal fibrosis of the coronary arteries, and increase in brain reactive antibodies are just a few of the changes reported in this volume to be significantly more advanced in 20-y.o. than in 10-y.o. macaques. Experiments designed to analyze the etiology of such differences or to manipulate them by nutritional, pharmacological, or other interventions may better be performed on animals in a middle age range than on older animals in which the phenomena of primary interest may be complicated by secondary changes or by advanced age-related disorders in other organ systems. Once the existence of a particular clinical condition has been identified in a sample of senescent individuals of a particular species, further research may be pursued in much younger, more plentiful animals.

Some questions require the study of old animals, i.e., subjects in the third trimester of the lifespan. For example, menopause has only been observed in macaques judged to be well over 20 y.o. (14 and Chapter 16, this volume). It would be wise to use the old animals available in such a way as to maximize the number of useful studies that can be performed. One way of increasing the number of old animals available for study may be to develop more efficient methods of determining the ages of animals in captivity. As mentioned earlier, the only current means of estimating the age of an elderly macaque is to have a reliable estimate of its age at entry and to know how long it has lived in captivity. Because age estimates obtained by most institutions 10 and 20 years ago were not sufficiently detailed to be reliable for animals over 3 to 5 y.o., an animal must have been in captivity for 15 or more years to be reliably classified as 20 y.o. or older today. The results of several studies reported in this volume sug-gest the feasibility of estimating the ages of animals that have been in captivity for much shorter periods of time. Such indices as the percent cortical area of the second metacarpal (Chapter 27), serum level of brain reactive antibodies (Chapter 10), and tactile corpuscle density in skin of the finger tip (Chapter 14), appear to change sufficiently rapidly with aging in the pigtail macaque to provide the basis for a battery of measures that could be used to identify old animals that would otherwise go unidentified in our research colonies.

Another way to reduce the problem of short supply is to assure multiple use of the aged animals available. With care to avoid incompatible experimental manipulations, numerous studies can be performed on the same animals over extended periods of time. Even in the context of the present project, which was organized primarily to provide tissues and body fluids to a large group of investigators in a short period of time, it was possible to carry out several small studies evaluating such functions as cognition, social interactions, and hormonal response to restraint stress in most of the animals before they were sacrificed.

Yet another way to achieve multiple use is to preserve specimens for subsequent, unanticipated studies, fixing them for light and electron microscopy or freezing them for biochemical analysis. The project described in this volume provided specimens to some 45 investigators at more than 20 institutions. While the results of many studies are described in the following pages, sufficient material for at least an equal number of studies remains in the hands of the investigators and can be expected to result in further characterization of aging in the pigtail macaque as more analyses are completed.

Multiple use of aged animals for compatible studies not only helps to circumvent the scarcity problem, but provides an opportunity to look for correlations among variables that an individual investigator would be unable, or unlikely, to measure on his own. The present project produced some intriguing correlations that would not have been detected in a comparable set of studies if different investigators had studied different animals. The correlation between osteoporosis and serum copper level (Chapter 28), the correlation of the corticosteroid stress response with serum HDL-cholesterol level (Chapter 19), relation of gonadotroph degranulation in the pituitary to the triiodothyronine/thyroxine ratio (Chapter 15), and the correlation between mammary dysplasias and serum androgen levels (Chapter 18) are a few examples of unanticipated, potentially significant findings that would not have been made were it not for the multiple use of subjects.

The long lifespans of the nonhuman primate species most widely used in laboratory research, e.g., the macaques, baboons, and squirrel monkey, will continue to be an obstacle for a number of the studies one would like to perform in a nonhuman primate. Genetic studies that require controlled breeding through several generations cannot help but be unwieldy in species where the gestation period is 5–7 months, time to sexual maturity is 2 to 5 years, and median lifespan is on the order of decades. Studies requiring that measurements be made at several points in the lifespan of the same animal may benefit from the kinds of mixed longitudinal and cross-sectional experimental designs that have been developed for human studies (1). However, another relatively unexplored strategy for circumventing the longevity problem is to identify primate species that are sufficiently close to man phylogenetically to have advantages over other animal models currently in use, yet sufficiently short-lived to permit studies that are not feasible in the commonly used primate models.

The data in Figure 1-1 suggest that, to a certain extent, the more distant the genus is from man, the greater the likelihood of its having a short lifespan. The heterogeneity of maximum lifespans within the major primate groups, however, suggests that it may not be necessary to go as far as the tree shrew, or even the Prosimians to find species with lifespans approximating those of the shortest-lived primates. There are 27 species of tamarins and marmosets, two genera of New World monkeys some of which may have lifespans as short as those of the galago and loris, two short-lived Prosimian genera.

By what strategy, short of maintaining a number of individuals from each species for 10 years, are we likely to identify the ones of particularly short lifespan? One approach might be to take advantage of the correlation between maximal longevity and various morphological, physiological, and biochemical characteristics of mammalian species that have been worked out in recent years (12, 19, 7). Using the technique of multiple regression analysis, Sacher (20) has derived an equation based on four physical characteristics of the species to predict the maximal lifespan of individuals of that species:

$$L = 8E^{0.6} S^{-0.4} M^{-0.5} 10^{0.025 T_b}$$

where L is lifespan (months), E is brain weight (grams), S is body weight (grams), M is resting metabolic rate (cal/g-hr), and T_b is body temperature (°C). The relationship defined in the equation accounts for 85% of the lifespan variance in a wide variety of mammalian species including rodents, carnivores, ungulates, and primates. Levels of mixed function oxidases, DNA excision repair, superoxide dismutase, and other enzymes known to correlate with lifespan may also find practical application in identifying the primate species closest to man with the shortest maximum longevity. The degree of resolution one can expect in applying these methods to species within the genus rather than across genera is unknown, but they may be capable in a short time of providing useful information that, otherwise, would take decades to obtain.

In summary, application of the concept that the nonhuman primate can play a significant role in answering the theoretical questions of biological aging and in solving the practical problems posed by the pathology of human aging is relatively new. The expense, scarcity, and longevity of the primate species customarily used in laboratory research are obstacles to their assuming that role. As we examine them more closely, however, there is reason for optimism that those obstacles can be overcome.

REFERENCES

1. Baltes, P. B. (1968): Longitudinal and cross-sectional sequences in the study of age and generational effects. *Human Development*, 11: 145–171.
2. Blaton, V., Vercaemst, R., Vandecasteele, N., Carter, H., and Peeters, H. (1974): Isolation and partial characterization of chimpanzee plasma high density lipoproteins and their apolipoproteins, *Biochemistry*, 13(6), 1127–1134.
3. Bowden, D. M.: Nonhuman primates in aging research. In: *Proceedings of XIth International Congress of Gerontology*, August 1978, Tokyo (in press).
4. Caminiti, B. (1978): *The Aged Nonhuman Primate: A Bibliography*. Primate Information Center, Regional Primate Research Center, University of Washington, Seattle.
5. Crandall, L. S. (1964): *Management of Wild Mammals in Captivity*. Chicago and London; University of Chicago Press.
6. Cutler, R. G. (1975): Evolution of human longevity and the genetic complexity governing aging rate. *Proceedings of the National Academy of Sciences USA*, 72: 4664–4668.
7. Cutler, R. G. (1976): Evolution of longevity in primates. *J. Human Evolution*, 5: 169–202.
8. Edelstein, C., Chang, T. M., and Scanu, A. M. (1976): The serum high density lipoproteins of Macacus rhesus. *J. Biol. Chem.*, 248: 7653–7660.
9. Fridovich, I. (1975): Superoxide dismutase. *Ann. Rev. Biochem.*, 44: 147–159.
10. Getty, R. and Ellenport, C. R. (1974): Laboratory animals in aging studies. *Meth. Anim. Exp.*, 5: 41–179.
11. Goldberg, A. L. and St. Johns, A. C. (1976): Intracellular protein degradation in mammalian and bacterial cells. Part II. *Ann. Rev. Biochem.*, 45: 747–803.
12. Hart, R. W. and Setlow, R. B. (1974): Correlation between deoxyribonucleic acid excision-repair and lifespan in a number of mammalian species. *Proc. Nat. Acad. Sci. USA*, 71: 2169–2173.
13. Hart, R. W., Hall, K. Y., Albrightson, C., and Sacher, G. A.: Evaluation of longevity and DNA repair processes in mammals. In: *Proceedings of the International Congress of Gerontology*, August 1978, Tokyo (in press).
14. Hodgen, G. D., Goodman, A. C., O'Connor, A., and Johnson, D. K. (1977): Menopause in rhesus monkeys: model for study of disorders in the human climacteric, *Am. J. Obstet. Gynec.*, 127: 581–584.
15. Ludwig, F. C.: The biology of aging and modern medicine. *Interciencia*, 2: 275–280, 1977.
16. Moore, C. J., Schwartz, A. G.: Inverse correlation between species life span and capacity of cultured fibroblasts to convert benzo(a)pyrene to water soluble metabolites, *Exp. Cell Res.* (in press, 1978).
17. Napier, J. R. and Napier, P. H. (1967): *A Handbook of Living Primates*. New York; Academic Press.
18. Rockstein, M., Chesky, J., Sussman, M. (1977): Comparative biology and evolution of aging. In: *Handbook of the Biology of Aging*, C. E. Finch and L. Hayflick (Eds.), pp. 3–34, New York; Van Nostrand, Reinhold.

19. Sacher, G. A. (1975): Maturation and longevity in relation to cranial capacity in hominid evolution. In: *Primate Functional and Morphological Evolution*, R. Tuttle (ed.), The Hague; Mouton.

20. Sacher, G. A. (1978): Longevity, aging and death: An evolutionary perspective. *The Gerontologist*, **18**: 112–119.

21. Sarich, V. M. and Cronin, J. E. (1976): Molecular systematics of the primates. In: *Molecular Anthropology*, M. Goodman and R. E. Tashian (Eds.), pp. 141–170, New York; Plenum Press.

22. Simpson, G. G., (1945) *The Principles of Classification and a Classification of Mammals*, Bulletin of the American Museum of Natural History, Vol. 85, New York.

2
Observations from Sukhumi

B. A. Lapin, R. I. Krilova, G. M. Cherkovich, and N. S. Asanov
Institute of Experimental Pathology and Therapy,
Academy of Medical Sciences, Sukhumi, USSR

INTRODUCTION

In light of efforts to increase longevity and prevent the onset of senescent changes associated with old age, it is necessary to study all aspects of aging, i.e., to determine the location, nature, and timing of changes in physiological functions during senescence. Ten years ago gerontologists did not favor monkeys over other animals as experimental models for aging research (20), but today many investigators stress the need to study the problems of senescence in animals that are phylogenetically close to man. Data on aging processes in monkeys are scarce, as it is practically impossible to watch animals from adulthood to senescence in the wild, and in captivity monkeys seldom reach old age because of their use in terminal experiments. However, the development of breeding groups in large monkey colonies now makes it possible to study longevity, the length of the reproductive period, the onset of menopause in females, and morphological changes in the process of natural aging.

The primate breeding station at Sukhumi was established in 1927. Although we have not conducted special studies in gerontology, we have over the years accumulated data in a number of areas important for characterizing aging in nonhuman primates. These data relate particularly to the longevity of monkeys in captivity, normal morphological changes with age, and pathology of aged monkeys.

LONGEVITY AND CAUSES OF DEATH

The animals at Sukhumi live in a temperate climate with relatively distinct seasons. They are, for the most part, maintained in outdoor compounds attached to shelters which provide protection from wind and precipitation. Moderate periods of subfreezing weather are not uncommon during the winter. Until recently, all animals received a daily diet of unprocessed foods consisting of fruit and vegetables (550 to 600 g), sugar (35 g), oil (10 to 15 g), bread and grain (350 g), milk (200 g), and nuts or sunflower seeds (140 g). In recent years, some animals have been maintained on monkey chow (350 g) in a pellet form similar to that commonly used in the United States.

A summary of longevity data obtained for 5 species at the Sukhumi colony over the past 50 years is presented in Table 2-1. Five animals have lived beyond 30 years of age; 19 have lived 26 to 30 years; and 53 have lived 20 to 25 years; 4 animals in the 24- to 27-y.o. range were still alive in 1978. The baboon that is now 27 y.o. shows marked signs of senile cachexia. The best documented maximum lifespans include one female baboon who lived 31.5 years, 3 macaques (1 male and 2 females) who lived 25 to 27 years, and a female green monkey who lived 30 years. These data came from animals that were either born in the Sukhumi colony or entered the colony before 3.5 years of age as judged by weight and other characteristics.

Aged monkeys have a characteristic appearance (Frontispiece and Figure 2-1). Their skin is wrinkled and flaccid with prominent twisted sclerotic vessels on the abdomen and extremities. Joint contractures, baldness, decreased motor activity, muscular atrophy, loss of teeth, and atrophy of alveolar processes of the jaw (Figure 2-2) are also apparent. In the process of aging, human body weight de-

Table 2-1. Species and Sex of Monkeys Surviving More than 20 Years at the Sukhumi Colony. Numbers in Parentheses Represent the Number of Animals in the Category that Were Born in Captivity.

Age (years)	20–25		26–30		Over 30	
Sex	Male	Female	Male	Female	Male	Female
Baboons						
P. hamadryas	3(3)	16(15)	—	11(9)	1(0)	4(3)
P. anubis	—	3(1)	—	—	—	—
Macaques						
M. mulatta	6(2)	18(4)	3(0)	3(1)	—	—
M. nemestrina	1(1)	1(1)	—	—	—	—
Green Monkeys						
C. aethiops	3(0)	2(0)	—	2(1)	—	—

Fig. 2-1.   External appearance of female *P. hamadryas* estimated to be 31 y.o.

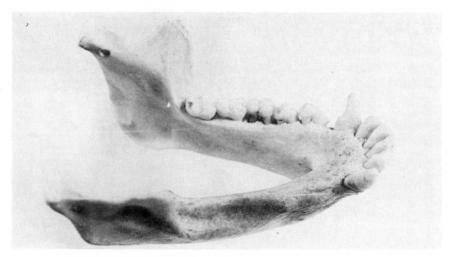

Fig. 2-2.   Loss of teeth, osteoporosis and atrophy of alveolar processes of mandible in a 25-y.o. *M. mulatta.*

Table 2-2. Loss of Weight with Age in *P. hamadryas*
(Mean ± Standard Deviation; n = 10).

Age (years)	10	18–22	25–30
Weight (kg)	15.3 ± 7.0	17.3 ± 1.9	11.8 ± 0.76

creases owing to muscular atrophy (9). The same is true of nonhuman primates, particularly *Papio hamadryas*, which gradually gain weight until 18 to 20 years of age and rapidly lose it after age 25 (Table 2-2). In *Macaca mulatta* weight loss is not so great, and some monkeys even gain weight due to obesity. Similar changes in the external appearance of a *M. mulatta* at 24 years have been reported by Wisniewski and Terry (22). In addition to other characteristics of aging, it had gray hair on its head, chest and upper arms; we have never observed this phenomenon.

The causes of death of 73 animals over 20 y.o. are summarized in Table 2-3: 54 died spontaneously and 19 were sacrificed, most of them for experimental reasons. The most extensive data relate to *P. hamadryas* (32 deaths, 25 of them spontaneous) and *M. mulatta* (29 deaths, 17 of them spontaneous). Many of the animals, including those sacrificed, exhibited degenerative or pathological changes in several organ systems. In this respect old monkeys greatly resemble aged humans. The broad spectrum of pathology is described below. Table 2-3 relates only to pathology or events that resulted in death of the animal.

The most common causes of spontaneous death in all species were lesions or disorders of the digestive system. These included enteritis or colitis in 18, pancreatic disease in 3, senile cachexia in 3, and cholelithiasis in 1. The second most common cause of death was pulmonary disease, namely, pneumonia. In 4 of the 11 cases, pneumonia coexisted with colitis at the time of death. The cause of death in these cases was ambiguous; to that extent, attribution to the

Table 2-3. Causes of Death in 73 Monkeys over 20 y.o.

Cause of Death	P. hamadryas	P. anubis	M. mulatta	M. nemestrina	C. aethiops	Total
Circulatory	2	–	1	1	–	4
Respiratory	4	–	6	–	1	11
Digestive	13	–	7	1	4	25
Reproductive	2	1	2	–	1	6
Neoplastic	2	2	–	–	1	5
Other	2	–	1	–	–	3
Sacrifice	7	–	12	–	–	19
Total	32	3	29	2	7	73

Table 2-4. Tumors in Monkeys Over 20 y.o.

Species	Sex	Age (years)	Years in Captivity	Tumor
P. hamadryas	M	23	23	adenocarcinoma of the common bile duct
P. hamadryas	F	29	29	adenocarcinoma of the common bile duct
P. hamadryas	F	29	29	lipoma of the abdominal wall
P. hamadryas	F	31	31	gastric leiomyoma
P. anubis	F	20	8	metastatic ovarian reticulosarcoma
P. anubis	F	20	16	metastatic renal reticulosarcoma
M. mulatta	F	21	19	cervical polyp
M. mulatta	F	20	20	mammary fibroadenoma, insuloma of pancreas, colloid goiter
M. mulatta	F	20	16	gastric polyp, cervical polyp
M. mulatta	F	22	22	gastric polyp
M. nemestrina	F	22	22	cervical polyp
C. aethiops*	F	30	28	metastatic cervical carcinoma; duodenal cylindroma; colonic neurilemmoma

*9-10-dimethyl-1-2benzanthracen was inserted into the tibia of this animal 24 years prior to death.

pulmonary category was arbitrary. The deaths attributed to reproductive disorders resulted from perinatal complications: placental retention, hemorrhage, and postpartum endometritis and sepsis. All 6 deaths in this category occurred in animals less than 25 y.o. Deaths attributed to circulatory failure resulted from postinfarctional myocardial fibrosis in 2 animals, diffuse myocardial fibrosis secondary to myocarditis in 1, and basilar artery thrombosis secondary to atherosclerosis in 1. The 5 fatal neoplasms included 2 bile duct adenocarcinomas, a cervical carcinoma, and reticulosarcomas of the ovary and kidney. Other causes of death in 3 animals were trauma, sepsis, and strangulated hernia.

The following sections describe the degenerative and pathological changes found in the 73 animals over 20 y.o. The types of tumors observed are noted in Table 2-4.

CARDIOVASCULAR SYSTEM

Atherosclerotic changes in the cardiovascular system have been well studied in aging primates (13). A summary of findings from necropsies on 31 animals over 20 y.o. is presented in Table 2-5. Signs of atherosclerosis were demonstrable in virtually every animal (Figure 2-3). Moderate to severe signs were present in about half of the animals. As in man, the frequency and severity of lesions were correlated with age. The most extensive lesions in younger (20 to 25 y.o.) animals were seen in *Cercopithecus aethiops*; and the severity of lesions may be greater in *P. hamadryas* than in *M. mulatta*. In *P. hamadryas* and *C. aethiops*,

Table 2-5. Degree of Atherosclerotic Lesions and Myocardial Fibrosis in Monkeys Over 20 y.o.

Age (years)	Sex	Aortic Segment			Cerebral Arteries	Coronary Arteries	Myocardial Fibrosis	
		Arch	Thoracic	Abdominal			Focal	Diffuse
Papio hamadryas								
20	M	+	–	+	–	++	–	–
20	F	–	–	+	–	–	–	–
20	M	–	–	+	–	–	–	–
23	M	+	–	++	–	–	–	–
24	F	++	–	+++	++	++	–	–
24	F	+	–	+	+	++	–	–
25	F	+++	–	++	–	+	–	–
28	F	+	–	+	–	–	–	+
29	F	+	–	++	–	–	–	+
30	F	+	+	++	–	–	–	+
30	M	+	++	+++	–	–	–	–
32	F	++	+	+++	–	–	–	+
Papio anubis								
20	F	+	–	+	–	–	–	–
20	F	++	+	++	–	–	–	–
Macaca mulatta								
20	M	+	+	+	–	+	–	+
20	F	+	–	+–	–	–	–	+
20	F	–	–	+–	–	–	–	–
21	F	+	–	+	–	–	–	–
22	M	+	–	+	–	–	–	+
22	F	+	–	+	–	–	–	–
22	M	+	–	+	–	–	–	–
22	F	–	+	++	–	–	–	–
23	M	++	++	++	–	+	+	–
25	M	–	–	+–	–	–	–	+
27	M	++	–	+++	–	+	–	–
27	F	++	+	+++	+	++	–	+
Macaca nemestrina								
22	F	+	–	–	–	–	+	–
Cercopithecus aethiops								
20	F	+++	+++	+++	–	+++	+	–
20	M	+	++	+++	–	++	–	–
20	F	–	–	+++	–	–	–	–
30	F	+	+	++	–	–	–	+

Code for atherosclerotic changes
+++ Severe widespread atherosclerosis with great number of calcified plaques.
 ++ Moderate atherosclerosis with fibrous plaques in restricted areas.
  + Single fibrous plaques and yellow streaks.
 +– Yellow streaks.
  – No atherosclerotic changes.

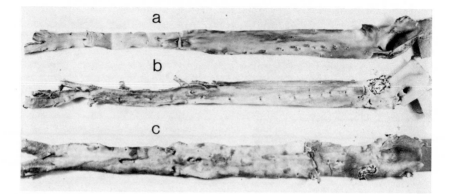

Fig. 2-3. Atherosclerosis of the aorta (Sudan stain). (a) Scattered plaques in thoracic aorta of 20-y.o. *M. mulatta*. (b) Lesions of aortic arch, abdominal aorta, and both iliac arteries in 20-y.o. *C. aethiops*. (c) Atherosclerotic lesion of all parts of aorta from *P. hamadryas* estimated to be 30 y.o.

aortic intima sometimes constituted one-third, or even one-half, of the thickness of the wall. In all species studied, as in man, the most frequent and severe lesions were in the abdominal aorta and aortic arch, with decreasing frequency and severity in the thoracic aorta, coronary arteries, and cerebral arteries. No sex difference was detected.

Age-related changes observed in the myocardium included hypertrophy of myocardial fibers and diffuse thickening of connective tissue, particularly around vessels. Atrophy of cardiac muscle fibers was apparent in cachexic monkeys. In obese monkeys, muscular tissue was replaced by adipose tissue not only in subepicardial layers, but within the wall itself.

Myocardial fibrosis was also a frequent finding. It was noted in 18 monkeys, 13 of which are presented in Table 2-5; it caused cardiac failure and death in 3 animals. Three animals had macrofocal lesions with large scars (Figure 2-4) in the left ventricular wall and interventricular septum. The other 15 developed varying degrees of diffuse interstitial fibrosis. Some of these animals were hypertensive. In most cases, diffuse interstitial fibrosis was regarded as resulting from coronary insufficiency. Two animals exhibited signs of myocarditis which may have given rise to the fibrosis. In general, the atherosclerotic changes observed in the coronary arteries of monkeys at Sukhumi were not severe enough to be regarded as mechanical blocks to coronary circulation, and the presence or absence of myocardial fibrosis did not correlate with the severity of coronary atherosclerosis (Table 2-5). The 3 animals with large focal lesions were of different species. The 22-y.o. *M. nemestrina* (Table 2-5) with large focal post-infarctional scarring and no sign of coronary artery disease is described in detail elsewhere (13). The 23-y.o. *M. mulatta* was known to be hypertensive and was

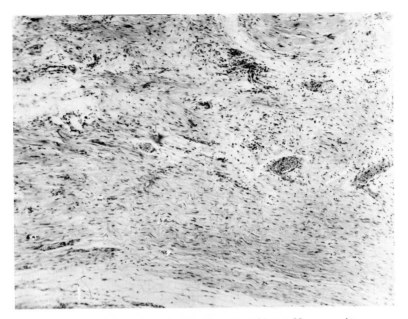

Fig. 2-4.   Gross scar in the heart muscle of 22-y.o. *M. nemestrina*.

found at autopsy to have pallid, dense scarring of the anterior and posterior walls of the left ventricle and septum. The 20-y.o. *C. aethiops* developed coronary insufficiency and infarction of the posterior wall of the left ventricle; unlike the others, she had marked atherosclerosis of the coronary vessels. She died not of her heart disease, however, but of postpartum hemorrhage.

The fact that old monkeys develop cardiac pathology indicative of coronary insufficiency without atherosclerosis of the coronary arteries suggests that coronary insufficiency can be conditioned by functional disorders of the coronary circulation. Several cases have been reported in which histologically confirmed infarctions seemed to result from functional disturbances of coronary vasomotor activity in the course of stressful studies of experimental neurosis (5, 14).

Electrocardiogram (ECG) changes in some 20-y.o. monkeys were similar to those observed in old people. As in man, a shift of the QRS axis to the left occurs in old monkeys (12). Figure 2-5 shows recordings from 4 baboons and 5 rhesus monkeys with significant decrease in the voltage of all ECG waves (11, 15, 16). While we have observed ECG evidence of left bundle branch block and coronary insufficiency (Figure 2-6), the ECG findings in these monkeys also did not correlate with the severity of coronary atherosclerosis. Both the ECGs and electro-encephalograms (EEGs) in old monkeys are characterized by low voltage compared with those of younger monkeys (Figure 2-15). Thus, the ECG

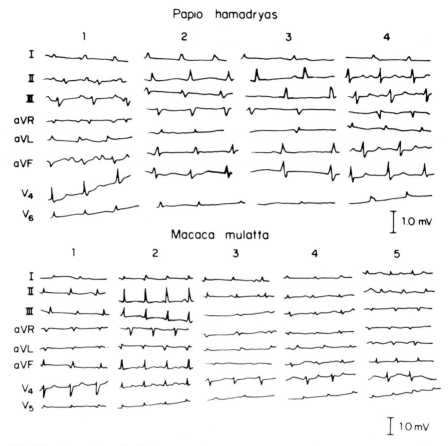

Fig. 2-5. Low voltage ECG's in 4 *P. hamadryas* and 5 *M. mulatta*, all 20 y.o. MV = 1.0 cm.

voltage decrease may reflect a general phenomenon of attenuated biopotentials reflecting reduced metabolic activity in depolarizing cells of older animals. Reduced intensity of oxidation and phosphorylation with increasing age impair myocardial contractility, especially the isometric phase (4, 8). As a result, intense muscular or emotional activity can lead to pronounced myocardial hypoxia. The increased incidence of myocardial decompensation in old age may reflect decreased oxidative processes. An absence of ECG changes in some old monkeys may account for their longevity. Such is observed in man; some people over 100 y.o. show no significant ECG changes (11, 15).

Valvular changes were seen in 11 of the aged monkeys (8 *P. hamadryas* and 3 *M. mulatta*). As in man, the lesions included fibrosis of the connective tissue

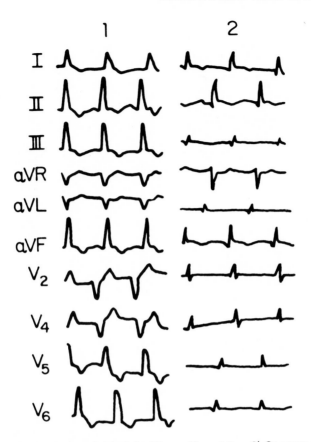

Fig. 2-6. 1) Left bundle branch block in 20-y.o. *M. mulatta*. 2) Coronary insufficiency in 25-y.o. *P. hamadryas*. MV = 1.0 cm.

layer, total valvular collagenization (mainly proximal areas), focal valvular sclerosis and subendothelial thickening sometimes leading to disfiguration of the cusp. Endocardial sclerosis was a frequent finding. The etiology of the valvular changes is unknown. They occurred in 16% of old animals. In some cases, valvular defects were extreme and reminiscent of those seen in post rheumatic heart disease. A female *P. hamadryas* exhibited mitral valvular insufficiency (Figure 2-7) and a male developed marked deformation and insufficiency of the tricuspid valve with fibrosis in the bicuspid and tricuspid valves. Two cases were most likely caused by endocarditis. A rhesus monkey that died of colitis and pneumonia showed thickening and deformation of the mitral cusps with partial adhesions at the base; valvular insufficiency and stenosis of the left venous

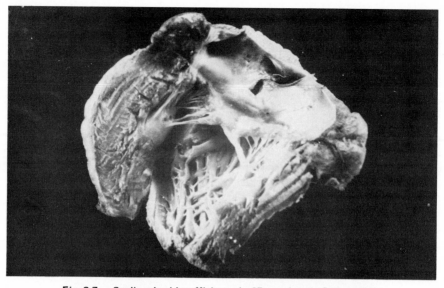

Fig. 2-7.   Senile mitral insufficiency in 25-y.o. female *P. hamadryas*.

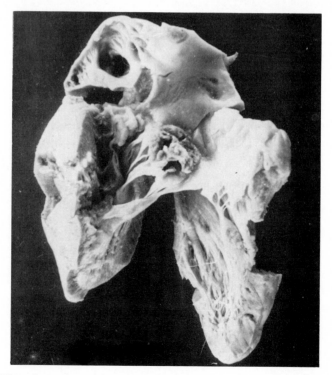

Fig. 2-8.   Ulcerative polyp with endocarditis involving the mitral valve in 27-y.o. male *M. mulatta*.

orifice were noted.   A severe valvular defect in one 27-y.o. *M. mulatta* was caused by sepsis or resulted from ulcerative polypoid endocarditis (Figure 2-8). Microscopic examination revealed marked leukocytic infiltration of the valve, especially at superficial necrotic sites, where fibrin deposition and purulent infiltration of the tissue were noted.

RESPIRATORY SYSTEM

Some changes in the respiratory system may be regarded as phenomena of physiological aging.   Emphysema was observed in 9 animals.   In their lungs, the elastic fibers were thin, elongated, and disorderly, lacking the elastic matrix characteristic of younger animals.   Four of these animals had subpleural bullae, sufficiently confluent in some areas to constitute bullous emphysema.

Atrophy of supporting collagenous elastic structures in the trachea and bronchi, and atrophy of bronchial glands were noted.   Impairment of bronchial drainage due to the atrophy of supporting collagenous and elastic structures may contribute to the increased frequency of pulmonary lesions in old monkeys (Table 2-3).

Anthracosis of the parenchyma and of lymphatic glands in the hilus also occurred.   Deposits of coal dust were noted in the alveolar septa, around the bronchi and especially around the vessels (Figure 2-9), both extracellularly and in the

Fig. 2-9.   Pulmonary emphysema and anthracosis in 20-y.o. female *M. mulatta*.   Hematoxylin and eosin, ✕60.

cytoplasm of macrophages.   Fibrosis was very seldom observed around such deposits.

DIGESTIVE SYSTEM

Age changes in the digestive system were overshadowed by pathological changes in about one-third of the animals, both experimental and intact.   In the remaining animals, atrophy of the gastric and intestinal mucosa seemed to develop with age (Figure 2-10).   Glands and crypts were sparse and mild sclerotic changes were noted in the submucosa.   Intestinal lymphoid tissue was markedly atrophic. A degree of muscular atrophy and thickening of collagenous fibers seemed to predispose to intestinal atony and distention.   The most common intestinal lesions were attributable to *Shigella* infection; *Salmonella* infection was very rare.

Several noninfectious diseases of the digestive system were noted including cholelithiasis, polycystic disease of the liver and pancreas, hepatic cirrhosis, and tumors.

Cholelithiasis is rare in monkeys.   Small soft greenish-black inclusions were found in the gallbladder and hepatic bile ducts of an asymptomatic 20-y.o. *P.*

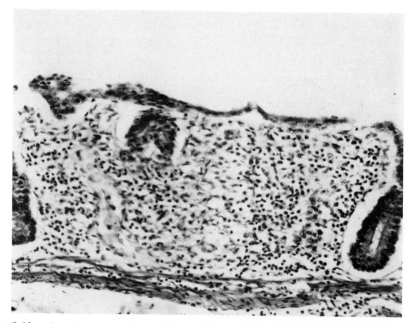

Fig. 2-10.   Atrophy of colonic mucosa in 20-y.o. female *M. mulatta*.   Hematoxylin and eosin, X60.

anubis that died of a malignant tumor. Another 20-y.o. baboon (*P. hamadryas*) developed acute cholecystic disease that clinically resembled ileus; the animal died during surgery. Necropsy revealed large rounded light-gray gallstones 0.5 cm in diameter, consisting of cholesterol (65%) and calcium salts (35%). The gallbladder was distended and chronically inflamed. Similar stones occluded the pancreatic duct. Necrosis and extensive hemorrhage were found in the pancreas, omentum and left perirenal area.

The most common hepatic lesion was polycystic disease. Grossly this condition was characterized by swelling and protrusion of cysts beneath the capsule (Figure 2-11). It occurred in 11 animals, 9 of them *P. hamadryas*. Histologically, the cyst wall was composed of a thin connective tissue matrix lined by a mononuclear prismatic or cuboidal epithelium similar to the bile duct epithelium. There were no signs of inflammation. Combinations of hepatic, pancreatic and renal polycystic disease were a frequent finding. Such changes have been seen in different age groups. Nevertheless they are much more frequent in old animals. It is also possible that the hepatic lesions were bile duct retention cysts. Congenital origin of this lesion cannot be ruled out.

Fig. 2-11.   Multiple hepatic cysts in 21-y.o. female *P. hamadryas*.

Seven animals developed cystic lesions in the pancreas. The pancreatic cysts were composed of a thin connective tissue capsule lined by a single layer of epithelium. No inflammation was present. Papillary protrusions and multiple cavities gave certain areas the appearance of cystic papillary adenomas. The exocrine tissue of the gland was compressed by the multiple cysts and atrophic. Three of the animals died of a disease that clinically resembled diabetes, although the diagnosis had not been supported by laboratory investigations. One of these had bilateral cataracts and gangrenous lesions on the tail. All three suffered from ulcerative stomatitis, alopecia, cachexia, and seizures. Polycystic disease of the pancreas and liver appeared to be the cause of death. Amyloidosis involving the islets of Langerhans was observed in 3 monkeys. Again, insufficient clinical data were available to determine whether they were diabetic. Diabetes due to amyloidosis of the insular part of the pancreas has been reported in nonhuman primates (10, 19).

Biliary cirrhosis was noted in 4 animals of different species. In 2 cases it developed secondary to infiltration of the large bile ducts by adenocarcinoma.

Half of the 16 neoplasms found in old animals were associated with the digestive system (Table 2-4). Adenocarcinoma of the major bile ducts similar to that seen in man occurred in 2 *P. hamadryas*. The clinical signs included hepato-

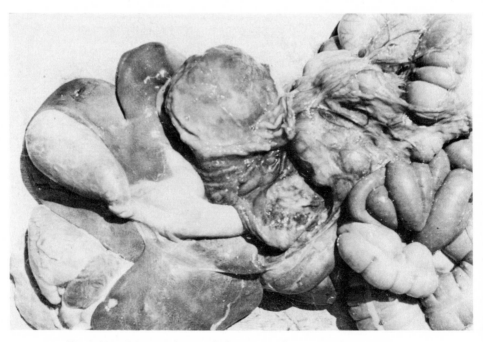

Fig. 2-12.   Adenocarcinoma of bile duct in 23-y.o. male *P. hamadryas*.

megaly, jaundice, loss of muscular tone, proteinuria, choluria, acholic stools, anorexia, and emaciation culminating in death. Necropsy findings were similar in the two animals. The tumors (Figure 2-12) invaded along the common bile ducts to the duodenal papilla. They were not metastatic. Infection of intra- hepatic and extrahepatic bile ducts gave rise to purulent inflammation and cho- langitic cirrhosis.

Gastric polyps (adenopapillomas) were noted in two animals, a subserous gastric leiomyoma 1 cm in diameter was found in one animal, and an insuloma 0.3 cm in diameter was found in the pancreas of one animal. The latter monkey had a mammary fibroadenoma and colloid goiter as well. Another monkey (*C. aethiops*) had multiple tumors of different kinds, one of which was a cylin- droma adherent to the duodenum.

RENAL SYSTEM

Glomerular sclerosis and moderate sclerosis of perivascular spaces in the kidneys were common in the old animals. In 5 cases (4 *P. hamadryas* and 1 *M. mulatta*), sclerosis produced gross changes reminiscent of wrinkled kidney syndrome in man. Collagenous scars were found on the kidneys of 3 monkeys. Proliferation of connective tissue, small cysts and glomerular sclerosis and hyalinization were noted. All severe cases of nephrosclerosis were accompanied by sclerosis of the abdominal aorta and of the orifices of the renal arteries, suggesting an inter- relation between the 2 processes.

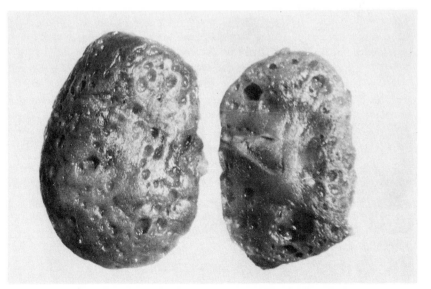

Fig. 2-13.   Renal cysts in a female *P. hamadryas* estimated to be 31 y.o.

Nine *P. hamadryas* and 2 *M. mulatta* had renal cysts of variable size (Figure 2-13). Small (less than 1 cm in diameter), and containing transparent yellowish fluid, they occurred both separately and in association with nephrosclerosis and multiple cysts of the liver and pancreas. They were lined by tubular epithelium with a basal membrane and connective tissue matrix. Such cysts were much less common in younger monkeys. They retained fluid and, in combination with cysts in the liver and pancreas, may reflect a congenital abnormality.

A renal reticulosarcoma that metastasized to the pelvic and inguinal lymph nodes was found in one *P. anubis*.

REPRODUCTIVE SYSTEM

Data on reproductive functions of monkeys in captivity must be evaluated carefully because of a number of artificially imposed conditions that influence social relationships. Despite these factors, it is apparent that the old animals show changes in reproductive function with age (Figure 2-14). Maximum fertility is generally achieved by female *P. hamadryas* at 6 years and by males at 11 to 12 years. Decline of sexual function in females begins at about 14 years, and in males toward the end of life. There are great individual variations in the age at which female fertility begins to decline and sexual cycles begin to change (Table 2-6). The fertility period is somewhat longer in *P. hamadryas* than in *M. mulatta*. Pregnancies decline after 15 to 18 years in *P. hamadryas*, and after 13 to 17 years in *M. mulatta*. The onset of menstrual irregularity or menopause occurred in the mid-20s in most *P. hamadryas*, as opposed to the early 20s in most *M. mulatta*. Pregnancies after age 18 are often complicated and end in abortion. The 6 females listed in Table 2-3 as dying of reproductive disorders succumbed to postpartum complications. The reproductive ability of males begins to decline after 25 to 28 years. The number of conceptions from a male *P. hamadryas* declined precipitously from 23 to 27 per year in his mid-20s to 11, 3, and 0 per year in his 28th, 29th and 30th years.

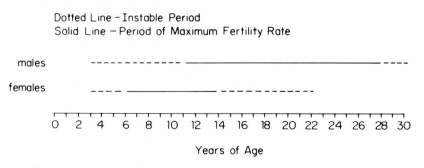

Fig. 2-14.   Changes in fertility with age in *P. hamadryas* males and females.

Table 2-6. Reproductive Function in Female Monkeys over 20 y.o.

Age (years)	Age at Last Pregnancy	Duration of Reproductive Period	Age at Onset of Sexual Cycle Disorders
P. hamadryas			
21	18	14	20
22	22	18	22
22	15	10	21
23	19	16	20
23	19	15	22
24	17	13	sc
24	18	14	24
25	20	17	25
25	19	16	25
28	19	16	21
29	20	16	24
29	22	18	26
29	22	17	23
30	22	17	24
31	17	13	25
31	22	19	24
32	21	18	26
M. mulatta			
20	13	10	sc
20	17	12	sc
21	17	13	sc
22	16	11	18
22	—	—	22
22	—	—	20
25	17	12	23
27	13	10	27

sc = still cycling

Morphological changes seen in the reproductive organs of old animals included bilateral ovarian cysts (4 animals, more common in *M. mulatta*) and atrophy with moderate sclerosis of the uterus.

Polyps of the cervix were the most frequent type of female genital tumor. They were composed of solid collagenous tissue, with scattered smooth muscle fibers, covered with columnar epithelium forming a great number of deep crypts that intruded into the body of the polyp. The crypts expanded here and there to form cystic cavities with mucus in the lumen. A squamous cell carcinoma of the cervix that metastasized to the lymph nodes of the pelvis, mesentery and omentum was found in one *C. aethiops*. A metastatic reticulosarcoma the size of a walnut was found in the right ovary of a *P. anubis* (13). The same type of tissue was found in the broad ligament of the uterus, lymph nodes along the aorta, and axillary lymph nodes.

IMMUNE SYSTEM

Age changes in the immune system included atrophy of the thymus, spleen, and lymph nodes. The thymus was replaced by adipose tissue in obese animals or by a sclerotic layer of connective tissue on the anterior epicardial surface. It was impossible to determine the borders or weight of the thymus in these animals. Microscopic investigation in *M. mulatta* revealed islands of lymphoid tissue in shapeless lobules separated by large strands of connective tissue and adipose tissue. Lymphocytic involution was even more pronounced in *P. hamadryas*. Only small accumulations of lymphoid cells were found. Scattered thymic corpuscles were found in *M. mulatta* but not in *P. hamadryas*.

Considerable atrophic change was also noted in the spleen. The weight was low, particularly in cachexic animals. In *P. hamadryas*, capsular hyalinization was a frequent finding. The connective tissue matrix was increased, the number of follicles markedly decreased, and germinal centers were almost absent from the white pulp. The walls of central arteries were sclerosed and hyalinized. Such involutional changes were most pronounced in *P. hamadryas* and *C. aethiops*. Lymphatic atrophy was noted in all animals but was not always accompanied by reduced splenic weight because of hyperemia and hypertrophy of the connective tissue in other areas. Atrophy of lymph nodes, especially peripheral ones, was also noted. The connective tissue stroma was increased, number of follicles decreased, and germinal centers were seen only in scattered nodules. The cortical layer was narrowed at the expense of the marginal, intermediate, and medullary sinuses which were relatively enlarged. Small lymphocytes predominated over reticular and younger lymphoid cells. Lymphatic atrophy was also noted in the intestines and lungs.

NERVOUS SYSTEM

Only one study has included a systematic attempt to relate behavioral changes to brain pathology in an old nonhuman primate, a male *M. mulatta* which was studied from 21 to 27 years of age (1). Changes in the conditioned responses included a 59 to 70% decrease in appropriate responses to stimuli. Inhibition of inappropriate responses was particularly deficient. While differential responses that had been elaborated previously were not affected, it was difficult to elaborate new inhibitory responses. Necropsy revealed senile plaques in the brain typical of old age. Argentophilic plaques, 30 to 50 per visual field, were distributed in the cerebral cortex, white matter, hippocampus, and subcortical ganglia. Brizzee (3) has reported reduced brain weight and decrease in the cortical neuronal cell packing density in cortical areas 1, 3 and 4 and an increase in the glial cell packing density in 18- to 20-y.o. *M. mulatta*. Senile plaques have been observed in the brain of two anthropoid species (21).

In a behavioral study of 6 old (23 to 27 years) and 5 young (8 to 13 years) *P. hamadryas*, each animal was put into a large chamber for training to produce

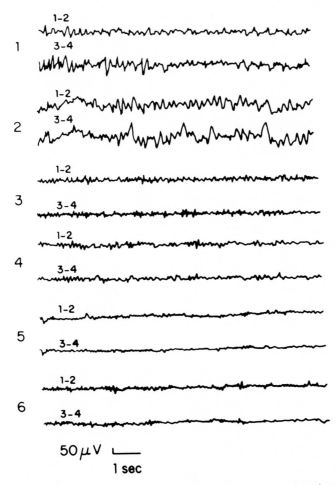

Fig. 2-15. Comparison of EEG's in infant, juvenile and old monkeys. 1) 1-mo-old *M. mulatta*; 2) 1-mo-old *P. hamadryas*; 3) 2-y.o. *M. mulatta*; 4) 2-y.o. *P. hamadryas*; 5) 21-y.o. *M. mulatta*; 6) 21-y.o. *P. hamadryas*.   Upper tracings (1-2), left fronto-occipital leads; lower tracings (3-4), right fronto-occipital leads.

Table 2-7. EEG Rhythmic Driving Response to Different Frequencies of Light Flashes in Monkeys Over 14 y.o.

Age (years)	Species	Sex	Frequency of Light Flashes per Sec			
			5	10	15	20
14	M. mulatta	F	+	+	+	+
14	M. mulatta	F	+	+	−	−
14	M. mulatta	F	−	−	−	−
15	M. mulatta	F	+	+	+	+
18	M. mulatta	F	+	+	−	−
19	M. mulatta	F	+	+	+	+
19	M. mulatta	F	+	−	−	−
19	M. mulatta	F	−	−	−	−
21	M. mulatta	M	−	−	−	−
21	P. hamadryas	F	−	−	−	−

+ Clear rhythmic driving response.
− No driving response.

a particular motor response for food reward. The old monkeys were less active in the unfamiliar environment than the young monkeys. They soon began to take food, while the young monkeys were restless, agitated, jumped about the chamber walls, and refused to eat. This activity impeded elaboration of the appropriate behavior, so that elaboration of conditioned responses was more rapid in old monkeys.

The EEG was studied in 12 old monkeys. In *P. hamadryas* and *M. mulatta* over 20 y.o. the amplitudes of waves of all frequencies, using fronto-occipital leads, were decreased (Figure 2-15). The dynamics of rhythmic driving responses to light flash frequencies of 5, 10, 15 and 20/sec, recorded on the EEG of the occipital area of the cortex, was also studied (Table 2-7). In general, 19- to 21-y.o. *M. mulatta* and *P. hamadryas* seldom exhibited driving responses to these frequencies. Monkeys 14 to 15 y.o. most often showed driving to the lower frequencies (5 and 10/sec), but failed to exhibit driving at the higher frequencies. However, individual variation occurred. For instance, one 14-y.o. animal showed no driving at any flash frequency while one 19-y.o. showed driving at all frequencies. Young monkeys (6 to 12 y.o.) developed rhythmic driving responses quite well.

MUSCULOSKELETAL SYSTEM

Though obesity occurs in some animals, a degree of cachexia is typical of most aged *P. hamadryas*. Marked cachexia was noted in half of the 20- to 25-y.o. animals, and in almost all animals over 30 y.o. In 3 it seemed to be the cause of death.

In *M. mulatta*, changes in nutritional status were less pronounced. Some animals gained weight and became obese, and others lost weight, but their weight loss was not as great as in *P. hamadryas*. Muscular atrophy was observed in both obese and cachexic animals. In a few animals (4 *P. hamadryas*, 1 *M. mulatta*) muscular atrophy and atony resulted in abdominal hernias. Such lesions are very rare in monkeys, being confined largely to old multiparous females. All of the hernias occurred along the linea alba with perforation of striate musculature of the abdominal wall. Most contained omentum and were reducible. In one *P. hamadryas*, strangulation of a liver-containing hernial sac led to hepatic necrosis, hemorrhage and death. Skeletal changes seen in some *P. hamadryas* and *M. mulatta* included calcification of cartilaginous costal segments, dystrophy of the cartilage on weight-bearing articular surfaces, and osteoporosis, particularly of the vertebral column. Worn teeth and atrophy of alveolar processes (Figure 2-2) were frequent findings. In one *P. hamadryas*, a disorder of calcium metabolism resulted in calcinosis of the myocardium and stomach.

DISCUSSION

The data presented here demonstrate the prevalence of involutional processes in old monkeys. As in humans, the time of onset of different aging changes varies from individual to individual. Some 20-y.o. baboons and macaques show no typical signs of senescence, while others develop them much earlier. There is often no correlation between manifestations of aging in different systems. Senile changes in the reproductive organs do not necessarily correlate with the signs of menopause (2), and severity of senile changes in central nervous system function and cardiac performance does not always correlate with manifestations of myocardial fibrosis and atherosclerosis of blood vessels, nor does the severity of atherosclerosis always correlate with age. It should be noted that these observations were conducted on captive monkeys, so they may differ from phenomena obtained in the wild. Less favorable conditions can occur in captivity due to stress, so lifespan and the reproductive period may be shortened and age changes may develop in a different pattern than is characteristic of the species in the wild.

Nevertheless, certain generalizations can be drawn and are worthy of note. While old monkeys suffer from the same diseases as young monkeys, the general profile of pathology differs (6, 13). Complications of pregnancy and tumor incidence are much higher in aged monkeys; the disease spectrum within individual animals is wider, lesions are more advanced, and, in some cases, death is caused by general weakening of physiological functions, organic atrophy and cachexia. Increased incidence of atherosclerotic arterial lesions in old monkeys is undeniable. The process is most pronounced in *C. aethiops* and *P. hamadryas*. The incidence of cardiac lesions believed to be caused by coronary insufficiency is also high; however, there is no direct correlation between this process and coronary atherosclerosis. In monkeys, as apparently in man, vasomotor functional factors acting in association with metabolic factors contribute to the pathogenesis of coronary insufficiency.

The incidence of tumors, particularly of malignant neoplasms, is clearly higher in older than in younger monkeys. The finding of 16 tumors, 5 of which were malignant, in 12 of 73 animals over 20 y.o. represents an incidence twice as high as in monkeys ranging from 10 to 20 y.o. and 6 to 10 times as high as in monkeys under 10 y.o. As a rule, malignant tumors in old monkeys are accompanied by clinical signs of toxicity and acute cachexia. The observation of multiple tumors in some animals agrees with reports by others (7, 18). We think that increased tumor incidence in old monkeys, as in man, is conditioned by the weakening of immune mechanisms with age. Impairment of immune mechanisms may also contribute to the increase in reproductive lesions in older females.

ACKNOWLEDGMENTS

Preparation of this manuscript was supported in part by National Institutes of Health grants RR00166 and AG62145 to the University of Washington.

REFERENCES

1. Alexandovskaya, M. M., and Shirkova, G. I. (1960): Histological and functional changes in the central nervous system of an old monkey (*M. mulatta*). *Trudy Instituta Vysshei Nervnoi Deiatel'nosti: Seria Fiziolog.*, 5: 238–249.
2. Bourne, G. H. (1975): The aging process. *Yerkes Newslet.*, 12: 6–10.
3. Brizzee, K. R. (1975): Gross morphometric analyses and quantitative histology of the aging brain. In: *Neurobiology of Aging: An Interdisciplinary Life-span Approach*, edited by J. M. Ordy and K. R. Brizzee, pp. 401–423. New York; Plenum Press.
4. Chebotariov, D. F., and Frolkis, V. V. (1967): *Cardiovascular System in Aging.* Moscow; Medicine Press.
5. Cherkovich, G. M., and Lapin, B. A. (1973): Modelling of neurogenic disease in monkeys. In: *Nonhuman Primates and Medical Research*, edited by G. H. Bourne, pp. 307–327. New York; Academic Press.
6. Fiennes, R. N., Lapin, B. A., Dzhikidze, E. K., and Yakovleva, L. A. (1972): The respiratory and alimentary systems. In: *Pathology of Simian Primates, Part I*, edited by R. N. Fiennes, pp. 671–710 Basel; Karger.
7. Fox, H. (1934): Subjects of pathological interest. *Rep. Lab. Comp. Path.*, 16: 17–30.
8. Frolkis, V. V. (1969): The cardiovascular system. In: *Osnovi gerontologii*, edited by D. F. Chebotariov, N. B. Mankovsky, and V. V. Frolkis, pp. 165–202. Moscow; Medicine Press.
9. Fudel-Osipova, S. I. (1969): Neuro-muscular system. In: *Osnovi gerontologii*, edited by D. F. Chebotariov, N. B. Mankovsky, and V. V. Frolkis, pp. 128–139. Moscow; Medicine Press.
10. Howard, C. F., and Palotay, J. L. (1975): Spontaneous diabetes mellitus in *Macaca cyclopis* and *Mandrillus leucophacus*. Case Reports. *Lab. Anim. Sci.*, 25: 191–196.

11. Kakiashvili, D. S. (1973): Cardiovascular and respiratory system in elderly, old and aged people of Abkhazia. Sukhumi Press.
12. Kokaya, G. Ya. (1958): ECG of healthy monkeys of different age and species. Dissertation, Institute of Experimental Pathology and Therapy, AMS-USSR, Sukhumi.
13. Lapin, B. A., and Yakovleva, L. A. (1963): *Comparative Pathology in Monkeys.* Springfield, Ill.; Thomas.
14. Miminoshvili, D. I. (1960): Experimental neuroses in monkeys. In: *Theoretical and Practical Problems of Medicine and Biology in Experiments on Monkeys*, edited by I. A. Utkin, pp. 53–68. New York; Pergamon Press.
15. Morosov, K. A. (1962): Functional state of myocardial tissue in elderly and old people. *Kardiologia, USSR*, 4: 52–58.
16. Olbrich, O., and Woodford-Williams, E. (1953): The normal precordial electrocardiogram in the aged. *J. Gerontol.*, 8: 40–55.
17. Ratcliffe, H. L. (1940): Familial occurrence of renal carcinoma in rhesus monkeys *(Macaca mulatta)*. *Am. J. Pathol.*, 16: 619–624.
18. Seibold, H. R., and Wolf, R. H. (1973): Neoplasms and proliferative lesions in 1065 nonhuman primate necropsies. *Lab. Anim. Sci.*, 23: 533–539.
19. Sheldon, W. G., and Gleiser, C. A. (1971): Amyloidosis of the islets of Langerhans in a crab-eating monkey *(Macaca fascicularis)*. *Vet. Pathol.*, 8: 16–18.
20. Sulkin, N. M. (1968): The needs of the gerontologist for laboratory animals. *Lab. Anim. Gerontol. Res.*, Washington, D. C., 1–7.
21. Terry, R. D., and Wisniewski, H. M. (1974): Some structural and chemical aspects of the aging nervous system. *Scand. J. Clin. Lab. Invest.*, 34, Suppl. 141: 13–15.
22. Wisniewski, H. M., and Terry, R. D. (1973): Reexamination of the pathogenesis of the senile plaque. In: *Progress in Neuropathology*, Vol. II, edited by H. M. Zimmerman, pp. 1–26. New York; Grune and Stratton.

3

The Macaca Nemestrina Project '77: Design and Procedures

Douglas M. Bowden, Peter H. Blake, Cheryl Teets, and Glenn H. Knitter

Department of Psychiatry and Behavioral Sciences and
Regional Primate Research Center, University of Washington,
Seattle, Washington

INTRODUCTION

Most of the studies reported in this volume resulted from a project carried out in 1976 and 1977 to evaluate aging in the pigtail macaque (*Macaca nemestrina*). The project was sponsored by the National Institute on Aging and involved 40 collaborating investigators at 26 research institutions. It was a cross-sectional study involving monkeys in 3 age groups—young, mature, and old adults—with more than 250 physical, physiological, and behavioral measures made quantitatively and many more qualitative examinations of as many of the subjects as possible. The chapters in this volume integrate the results of the pigtail project with previous findings in other primate species. The goal is to provide a basis for comparing aging in monkeys with aging in other species to aid investigators in selecting an animal model for studying problems of aging in man.

SUBJECTS

Old monkeys of known age are a small, heterogeneous, widely distributed resource. Because the age of macaques over 5 y.o. cannot be reliably estimated, accurate identifications of subjects over 20 y.o. is limited to animals that have been in captivity for at least 15 years and for which weight at entry is known.

Few such animals exist. The oldest animals in this study were assembled from 5 sources: The Department of Psychiatry, Downstate Medical Center, New York, and the Wisconsin, Oregon, Yerkes and Washington Regional Primate Research Centers.   Thus, the animals were originally obtained from different parts of Southeast Asia and maintained under varied housing conditions for different purposes during the decade and a half before they entered this project. As much information as possible was obtained regarding differences in past history of the animals. It was distributed to the collaborating investigators, and, where possible, comparisons were made between subgroups of different backgrounds to determine whether such factors as subspecies, treatment history, and parity influenced the characteristics under study.

The basic subject sample of the project consisted of 19 pigtail macaques (Figures 3-1 and 3-2). Because the exact ages of animals born in the wild could not be determined, their ages were conservatively estimated by adding the number of years in captivity to an estimated age at entry. The latter was derived from age-weight curves compiled from 1900 pigtail macaques in the Medical Lake Colony of the University of Washington Regional Primate Research Center. Estimates based on weights up to 5 kg (4.5 y) were considered accurate to ±1 year. By attributing an entry age of 5 y.o. to animals over 5 kg at entry, a conservative estimate of the animal's minimum possible current age was obtained. Animals were then assigned to 3 age groups referred to throughout this volume as the 4-y.o., 10-y.o., and 20-y.o. groups. By the criteria used, the 6 animals in the 20-y.o. group were at least 20–22 y.o., and several may have been much older. The 10 animals in the 10-y.o. group were estimated to be 10 ± 2 y.o. with the possible exception of #72399 described below; those in the 4-y.o. group were 4 ± 0.5 y.o. All except 2 of the animals were females; of the 2 males, 1 was 10 y.o. and 1 was 20 y.o.

Animal #72399, a female, was assigned to the 10-y.o. group on the basis of the conservative criteria outlined above. She was the only member of that group whose weight at entry exceeded 5 kg, and thus for whom the age at entry may have been seriously underestimated. Several investigators found evidence that this may have been the case. Her ovaries showed follicular depletion with a high proportion of atretic follicles (Chapter 16). The index of bone thinning (Chapter 27), and the pattern of serum lipoproteins (Chapter 22) were both consistent with her being much older than the others in her age group. At the same time, her measures on a variety of other characteristics fell well within the range of the other animals in the 10-y.o. group. To maintain the integrity of the experimental design, all of the statistics reported in this volume were calculated with #72399 in the 10-y.o. group. In instances where the possible misclassification may have seriously influenced an investigator's findings, the implications are discussed in the appropriate chapter.

Fig. 3-1. Ten-year-old *Macaca nemestrina*. The animals in the upper half of the figure were of the subspecies *M. n. nemestrina*; those in the lower half were of the subspecies *M. n. leonina*. All were females except the male in the upper right corner. Animal numbers: top: 72399, 69256, 70546; bottom: 76274, 76203.

Two subspecies of pigtail macaque were represented in the study, *M. neme-strina nemestrina* and *M. nemestrina leonina*. *M. n. nemestrina* is a subspecies of larger animals found primarily in Indonesia; *M. n. leonina* is a subspecies of smaller animals found primarily on the Thai peninsula. Individual animals were identified with one or the other subspecies by physical features including adult weight, crown color, cheek hair, and cranial x-ray (2). Subjects of both subspecies were represented in the 10-y.o. and 20-y.o. groups. Comparison of the sub-species with regard to the great majority of characteristics measured in the project revealed a few differences but no indication of subspecies differences in

Fig. 3-2.   Twenty-year-old *Macaca nemestrina*. The animals in the upper half of the figure were of the subspecies *M. n. nemestrina*; those in the lower half were of the subspecies *M. n. leonina*. All were females except the male in the upper right corner. Animal numbers: top: 75026, 57240, 67350; bottom: 76199, 76201.

those characteristics which varied with age. On this basis, data from the two subspecies were combined in most of the studies.

Some of the animals in the 10-y.o. and 20-y.o. groups had been maintained for many years at research institutions where isoniazid was administered daily for prophylaxis against tuberculosis. The drug was discontinued for at least 6 mo prior to sacrifice of these animals. Comparisons between their data and data from animals never exposed to isoniazid were made for most of the characteristics that might be considered sensitive to its effects; no differences were found. Again, data from animals in these 2 subgroups were combined in all studies.

In addition to the basic sample of 19 pigtail macaques some specimens were obtained from other old macaques that died before or during the project and from which suitable tissues could be obtained. These included 8 pigtail macaques 12.5 to 20 y.o. and 2 male longtail macaques (*M. fascicularis*), 1 10 y.o. and 1 20 y.o.

INVESTIGATORS

Collaborating investigators for the project (see Contributors, this volume) were identified through an announcement of the availability of specimens from aged macaques placed in the *NIH Guide* by the National Institute on Aging. The specimens were provided to investigators after agreement on several important aspects of the project. The analyses of all specimens were to be carried out with the investigator blind to the ages of the animals. If time or expense prevented an investigator from analyzing specimens from all of the animals, a list of trios of animal codes was provided such that each trio included an animal from each age group matched for subspecies, sex and weight at maturity; the investigator then limited his study to those trios. Each investigator agreed to contribute a copy of his measurements on individual animals to a common data bank. When the results were submitted to the data bank, the age code was provided to the investigator. Each investigator further agreed to write a report of his findings suitable for publication in this book.

One potential scientific strength of the project was the opportunity for investigators studying related variables to look for relationships that would be impossible to explore in a noncollaborative study. Thus, they were encouraged to make use of the central data base and to integrate others' findings into their own reports. To ensure that every investigator received due credit for his findings and was able to determine the proper use of his data before they appeared in published form, several collaborative principles were adopted. No investigator would cite another's findings in the book without his having reviewed and consented to the citation; and no investigator would cite publicly or publish another's results before the book went to press. Ultimately, more than half of the investigators contributing to the book did so as coauthors of chapters in which their findings were integrated and reported jointly.

PROCEDURE

During the first six months of the project the animals were assembled and housed in individual cages in a single room in the Division of Animal Medicine at the University of Washington. They had *ad libitum* access to Purina Monkey Chow #25 (Table 3-1) from noon to 5:00 p.m. daily. This was supplemented with fruit and with continuous access to water. Two animals (#71336 and #75026)

Table 3-1. Diets of *M. nemestrina* for Six Months Prior to Sacrifice.

Purina Monkey Chow	
Crude protein not less than	25.0%
Crude fat not less than	5.0%
Crude fiber not more than	3.5%
Added minerals not more than	3.0%
Ash not more than	6.0%

Ingredients: Ground yellow corn, soybean meal, ground wheat, corn gluten meal, dried skimmed milk, animal fat preserved with BHA, sucrose, brewers' dried yeast, salt, dehydrated alfalfa meal, vitamin B_{12} supplement, riboflavin supplement, calcium pantothenate, niacin, choline chloride, menadione dimethylpyrimidinol bisulfite (source of vitamin K activity), folic acid, pyridoxine hydrochloride, thiamin, ascorbic acid, vitamin A supplement, D activated animal sterol (source of vitamin D_3), vitamin E supplement, iron oxide, iron sulfate, manganese sulfate, calcium iodate, calcium carbonate, dicalcium phosphate, manganous oxide, copper oxide, cobalt carbonate, zinc oxide.

Gerbers High Protein Cereal

Ingredients: Soya, Oat, and Wheat Flours, Soya Oil, Calcium Carbonate, Soya Lecithin, Electrolyte Iron, Niacinamide, Riboflavin, Thiamin Mononitrate.

with chronic diarrhea and poor appetite received a diet of Gerbers High Protein Cereal (Table 3-1), apple juice, bananas and other fruit. Menstrual cycles were charted on the basis of daily observations of the females for vaginal discharge on the animal or in the cage. Other presacrifice procedures included physical measurements, testing of cognitive and social behavior, test of cortisol response to acute restraint, intravenous administration of tetracycline for bone labeling, x-ray of the skull, and venipuncture to obtain blood for a variety of studies. These procedures were scheduled so that behavioral measures were obtained on different days and by different personnel than invasive or stress measures.

All venipunctures were done between 8:00 a.m. and noon. The animal was anesthetized with ketamine (10 mg/kg intramuscularly) except when blood was to be drawn for cortisol and prolactin determinations. In the latter cases, blood was drawn from the restrained, awake animal within 4 min of the investigator's entry into the animal room. No more than 100 cc of blood was drawn from a given animal over a 4-mo period, and no more than 30 cc per animal was drawn in any 2-week period.

In many studies, the most important advantage of an animal model over the human model is the opportunity to obtain fresh tissues and body fluids from healthy subjects. The sacrifice procedure was designed on this principle. A 7-person team performed the sacrifice and disposition of tissues; it included 2 surgeons, 2 surgical assistants, a tissue processor, a bag sealer and a record keeper. The sacrifice was done according to the protocol presented in Table 3-2. The

Table 3-2. Sacrifice Protocol.

Animal # _____   Sex _____   Date _____

TIME*

_____ Anesthetic: ketamine, 10 mg/kg, IM; atropine 0.2 mg

_____ Shave back, head, thorax, abdomen, inguinal areas

_____ Weight _____ kg

_____ Blood for CBC, 2cc, purple top tube

_____ Blood for Hb, 4-6cc, purple top tube (Marshall—42)

_____ Blood for plasma, 5-7cc, purple tube (Marshall—43)

_____ Blood for electrolytes, 10cc, red top tube

_____ Blood for platelets, 10-15cc, purple tube (Omenn—3)

_____ Ketamine boost if indicated (5mg/kg)

_____ Administer anesthetic (Nembutal, _____ mg, IV)

_____ Prep head, chest, abdomen, flanks; Phisohex, 70% ETOH

_____ Right breast (Warner—68)

STERILE GLOVES

_____ Left breast, sterile (Kleinberg—56)

_____ Perfuse left eye, 0.1 cc McDowell's fixative

_____ Reflect scalp leaving 1 mm × 2 mm strip on p-p suture

_____ Score p-p suture

_____ Craniotomy leaving calvarium in place

SURGEON A

_____ Calvarium (Retzlaff—64)

_____ Left frontal pole (Burns—51)

_____ Left occipital pole (Burns—52)

_____ Left cortex (Omenn—6)

_____ Left caudate (Omenn—93)

_____ Left cerebellum (Nandy—83)

_____ Right cerebellum (Vijayan—67 & 94)

_____ Left brainstem (Sladek—72)

_____ Right pituitary (Aschenbrenner—73)

_____ Left eye (Torczynski—21)

_____ Skull (Kokich—20)

SURGEON B
STERILE GLOVES

_____ Laparotomy

_____ Left adrenal (Moore—89 & 90)

_____ Remove anterior chest wall

_____ Clamp trachea

_____ Remove head

_____ Thoracic aorta sterile; distal $\frac{1}{3}$ (Ross—15); middle $\frac{1}{3}$ (Martin—14)

_____ proximal $\frac{1}{3}$ (Ross—15)

_____ Heart apex, 10 g (Akera—81)

_____ Heart base (Baba—77)

_____ Lungs, sterile for dissection

_____ Abdominal aorta & iliacs, sterile; peripheral third and iliacs: (Ross—17); proximal $\frac{2}{3}$ (Martin—16)

END STERILITY
USE RINSED INSTRUMENTS

_____ Liver, 15 g from right lobe (Lei—57)

_____ Tail of pancreas, 10 g (Lei—59)

_____ Esophagus, 10 g (Lei—60)

_____ Right kidney (Lei—58)

END RINSED INSTRUMENTS

_____ Right adrenal (Moore—91 & 92)

_____ Reproductive tract (Graham—82)

_____ Viscera remains (Giddens—32)

_____ Iliac crest, two 5 mm × 10 mm, (Young—33)

_____ Spinal cord (Baskin—79)

_____ Left femur, 5cm shaft (Young—27)

_____ Left femur, two 5mm x-sec from distal shaft (Young—28)

_____ Left femur, two halves distal end (Young—29)

RINSED INSTRUMENTS

_____ Left gastrocnemius (Lei—97)

_____ Left tibia (Lei—63)

_____ X-ray hands and feet (Witkin—1)

_____ Right great toe (Witkin—103)

_____ Right thumb (Witkin—104)

_____ Right index finger (Witkin—125)

*Time is in minutes relative to cardiorespiratory arrest. Names of investigators and specimen numbers appear in parentheses. Only specimens reported in this book are included.

animal was anesthetized with ketamine in the home cage, weighed, and the head and trunk were shaved. It was delivered to the operating room where blood was drawn for several studies. Nembutal was administered and when the animal was in Stage 3, Plane 4 anesthesia, as judged by loss of the corneal reflex, the surgical excision of specimens began. Insofar as possible, specimens that could be removed without endangering the life of the animal were taken first; other specimens intended for tissue culture, immediate biochemical analysis or electron microscopy were taken next; and specimens for light microscopy, delayed biochemical analysis, routine pathology or x-rays were taken last.

The surgeons, one working on the head, the other on the trunk, and both under the direction of the record keeper, removed specimens in a manner appropriate to the intended use, e.g., by sterile technique or with instruments rinsed in saline. Each surgeon passed the specimen to a surgical assistant who located a prepared label bearing the animal number, date, recipient, investigator's name, specimen number, and directions for preserving and shipping the specimen. The assistant passed the specimen and label to the processor who followed directions on the label. In general, specimens for culture were placed in 50-cc plastic vials of medium provided by the investigator. Specimens for biochemical analysis were frozen on prefrozen, prelabeled 2 X 3 inch glass slides on a block of dry ice and under a petri dish cover. After freezing they were sealed in a plastic bag (Scotchpak, Kapak Ind., Bloomington, Minn.). Specimens for light microscopy were sealed in a plastic bag containing at least 15 times their volume of 10% buffered formalin or McDowell's fixative (3) (4% commercial formaldehyde, 1% glutaraldehyde, prepared with a 200-mOsm phosphate buffer). The latter was adequate for most applications except those requiring that shrink artifact be homogeneous throughout the block. It was excellent for electronmicroscopy but exceedingly poor for cerebral cortex intended for cell counts and marginally adequate for light microscopy of renal cortex. Specimens intended for electron microscopy were diced in 1-mm cubes before fixation. Some specimens were bagged in Bouin's fixative or ethanol as specified by the investigator. The plastic bag containing frozen or fixed tissue was passed with its label to the sealer who heat-sealed it (package sealer by Kapak Ind., Bloomington, Minn.), stapled the label to it, and placed it on ice, dry ice, or in an open container at ambient temperature until the sacrifice was completed. The remains of the carcass were sealed in a container of formalin.

During the procedure, the record keeper noted on the protocol the time at which each step was completed and a calculation of the time specimens were taken relative to cardiorespiratory arrest (Table 3-2). In most cases, cardiorespiratory arrest did not occur before thoracotomy and clamping of the trachea. All tissues for culture or for which immediate fixation was essential were obtained within 20 to 30 min of cardiorespiratory arrest, and the sacrifice was completed in 40 to 55 min.

Most specimens were delivered locally or shipped to investigators the day of the sacrifice. Those to be shipped were placed in rigid plastic containers of the kind used for refrigerating meal left-overs and packed with prefrozen artificial ice (Blue Ice (R)), dry ice, or wadded newspaper in 12 × 16 × 8 inch boxes. The boxes were made of styrofoam $\frac{3}{4}$ inch thick (Tempress Inc., Seattle, WA) surrounded by a corrugated cardboard box and lined with aluminum foil. Preliminary testing showed that these boxes, loaded with 20 lbs of dry ice, maintained an internal temperature close to $-20°C$ for more than 72 hours.

Two or 3 animals were sacrificed on a given day. Enclosed with every shipment were (a) biographical information on each animal including species, sex, source, weight (maximum adult weight and weight at sacrifice), breeding history, nature of previous experiments to which the animal had been assigned and a summary of diseases and treatments; age information was omitted, (b) a specimen log for each kind of specimen updating the cumulative list of samples provided to the investigator in terms of animal number and date, (c) a copy of the protocol for each sacrifice to provide information regarding such factors as anesthesia and times specimens were taken relative to cardiorespiratory arrest, and (d) a questionnaire regarding the condition of the specimens when received by the investigator, e.g., adequacy of specimen size, fixation, and packing and shipping procedures. The first sacrifice in the study was restricted to 1 animal to test the entire procedure.

All fresh and frozen specimens were shipped by air. The recipient was notified by telephone of the shipping company, airline, airbill number, flight number, and expected time of arrival. We quickly found that, if a shipment did not arrive on schedule, the recipient could pursue the matter more effectively than the sender. Specimens were generally in the hands of the recipients within 24 to 36 hours.

Each investigator studied and reported findings on the materials he received according to protocols appropriate to his own discipline and interests. All investigators, including those engaged in studies of gross and microscopic anatomy, were encouraged to scale their observations in a manner appropriate for parametric or nonparametric statistical analysis. Data from all of the collaborating investigators were entered into the CLINFO computer operated by the Clinical Research Center at the University of Washington. This computer system was developed by the Division of Research Resources of the National Institutes of Health to simplify the acquisition and analysis of large volumes of diverse clinical data. It was used to test all variables for relation to age and to explore possible relationships between variables studied by different investigators.

To analyze for age effects data on every variable were plotted as a scattergram against age group (see for example, Figure 28-1). A linear regression coefficient and significance level were calculated (e.g., Table 11-1). If a significance level of $p < .05$ was obtained, t-tests were performed to compare the mean values of all possible combinations of the age-groups taken two at a time (e.g., Table 10-1). If the data were not suitable for parametric analysis, they were subjected to Fischer's exact probability test for age-group effects (e.g., Table 16-2). This analysis was performed on a PDP-1115 computer (Digital Equipment Corporation), in the Department of Psychiatry and Behavioral Sciences, University of Washington. Comparisons between potentially related variables were obtained in the form of scatter plots and linear regressions. Copies of all analyses were provided to all investigators whose data were involved in the analyses. The interpretation and scientific judgment as to whether the findings merited inclusion in the reports in this volume were the responsibility of the chapter authors. Assistance in literature search was provided in the form of a bibliography on aging in nonhuman primates published by the Primate Information Center (1).

ACKNOWLEDGMENTS

The subjects of this study were obtained through the generous cooperation of the Oregon, Wisconsin, Yerkes, and Washington Regional Primate Research Centers and Dr. Leonard Rosenblum of Downstate Medical Center, State University of New York. Drs. Richard A. Holm and Gene P. Sackett provided the age-weight curves used to estimate ages, and Dr. Donald C. Martin consulted on the approach to statistical analysis. Ms. Ann Lescher and Mr. James Cruver contributed photographs of the subjects. Ms. Kathleen Schmitt assisted greatly in preparing the manuscripts for publication. Ms. Phyllis Wood, Ms. Patricia Clausen, Ms. Patricia Manning, and Drs. John Boyce, Ellis Giddens, and Daris Swindler all contributed essential services to the successful outcome of the project. This research was supported in part by grants and contracts RR00166, RR52177, RR00374, and AG72145 from the National Institutes of Health to the University of Washington.

REFERENCES

1. Caminiti, B. (1978) *The Aged Nonhuman Primate: A Bibliography.* Primate Information Center, Regional Primate Research Center, University of Washington.
2. Fooden, J. (1975) Taxonomy and evolution of liontail and pigtail macaques (Primates: Cercopithecidae). *Fieldiana Zoology* **67**: 1–169.
3. McDowell, E. M. and Trump, B. G. (1976) Histologic fixatives suitable for diagnostic light and electron microscopy. *Archives of Pathology and Laboratory Medicine*, **100**: 405–414.

4

Cognition

Donna Cohen, Carl Eisdorfer, and Douglas M. Bowden
Department of Psychiatry and Behavioral Sciences, and
Regional Primate Research Center, School of Medicine,
University of Washington, Seattle, Washington;
and
Geriatric Research Educational and Clinical Center,
Veterans Administration Hospitals,
Seattle and American Lake, Washington

INTRODUCTION

The scientific literature on cognition and aging in nonhuman primates is limited. To our knowledge, the first report of a longitudinal study was from Sukhumi (1) (see Chapter 2, this volume). It described a single male rhesus macaque (*Macaca mulatta*) studied up to 27 years of age. The authors reported that in its last years the animal became less proficient in discrimination learning and stimulus reversal tasks and failed to withhold responses during operant extinction. In recent years a 24-year longitudinal study of a small group of rhesus macaques has demonstrated that in their third decade of life they show an increase in reaction time (10), deficits in long-term memory (19), and increased stereotypy in spontaneous behavior patterns (16).

In the present study, we tested for differences in cognitive performance in pigtail macaques (*M. nemestrina*). Because rapid pacing in learning tasks is associated with poor performance in the aged human (6, 11, 12, 21), we adopted a behavioral test battery designed to evaluate unpaced learning performance.

METHODS

Sixteen female *M. nemestrina* (4 20-y.o., 9 10-y.o. and 3 4-y.o. animals) were housed in individual cages in a small animal care facility. There was no record that the monkeys had ever been trained in any cognitive procedure. Testing was done in a Wisconsin General Test Apparatus (WGTA) in a separate room (17). Every subject participated in cognitive test sessions for 5 consecutive days each week until sacrifice. The study was initiated with the first session in which the animal attended to the test apparatus sufficiently for its learning performance to be evaluated. It comprised 4 experiments.

Adaptation

The monkey learned to reach through the cage bars to lift the lid of a 4-cm square gray box to obtain a food reward. The box was baited on every trial. Twenty-five trials were conducted daily until the monkey quickly opened the box and took the food reward in 24 of 25 consecutive trials.

Color Discrimination Learning

Formal learning began with 25 color discrimination trials daily. A blue and a yellow box were presented simultaneously. For a given animal, the reward was always in the same color box; the right or left position of the box was changed randomly from trial to trial using a computer-generated random position sequence. The monkey was allowed to respond to only one box during each trial. The criterion for learning was 24 correct responses in 25 trials.

Color Discrimination Reversal

Reversal training began the day after the monkey met the criterion for discrimination learning. The procedure was identical to that for learning, except that the color of the reward box was reversed.

Learning Set and Response Inhibition

[Modified Hamilton Search Problem (22)]. This experiment was carried out in two phases. In Phase 1, *set making*, four identical boxes with closed lids were presented in each trial. A different box was baited with food for 25 consecutive trials according to a computer-generated random sequence for 5 consecutive days. In each trial, the appropriate box was baited before the blind was raised, and the monkey was allowed to open boxes until the food was located. An efficient search strategy (opening each box in succession) would require an average number of 2.5 openings/trial to find the food. The experimenter recorded the order in which the boxes were opened. Then we determined the average number of boxes opened per trial, the predictability of each monkey's sequence of responses, and the box each monkey was least likely to open first. In Phase II, *set breaking*, the least preferred box was always baited with food for at least 5 days, 25 trials per day, and the experimenter recorded only the number of responses per trial. We then determined the average number of responses per trial and the total number of trials required to meet the criterion of 5 consecutive correct first choices. Separate analyses of variance were used to test for age group differences in all measures of adaptation and learning performance.

RESULTS

Despite the limitations imposed by the small sample, competing experimental demands (semiweekly catching and blood drawing for other studies), and the short amount of time available for the entire study, several age-related trends emerged. There were significant age differences in days required for adaptation (F = 12.4, p = 0.004); the 20-y.o. animals took an average of 6 days to reach criterion performance compared with averages of 3 days for 10-y.o. and 2 days for 2 4-y.o.'s who reached criterion (Figure 4-1). In the color discrimination task, the old macaques took an average of 12 days to reach criterion performance, compared with an average of 5 days for the other two groups. No age differences

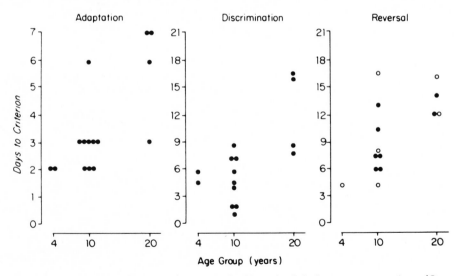

Fig. 4-1. Adaptation: Number of days required by animals in 3 age groups to adapt. (One 4-y.o. subject did not adapt.) Discrimination: Number of days required by animals in 3 age groups to reach criterion performance on the blue-yellow discrimination task. Reversal: Number of days of reversal training for monkeys in 3 age groups. Open circles indicate animal did not complete training because of scheduling constraints.

Table 4-1. Performance of Pigtail Macaques in Two Age Groups on the
Learning Set and Response Inhibition Task.

| Age Group and Name | Set-Making | | Set-Breaking | | Days of Testing | % Correct First Choices* |
	Mean Choices to Reward	± Latency (sec)	Mean Choices to Reward	± Latency (sec)		
20 y.o.						
Toad	2.5	2.6	1.9	1.8	10	80
Fang	3.6	5.6	2.1	4.5	8	56
Attila	2.5	2.0				
10 y.o.						
Vitamins	2.4	4.0	2.5	2.3	3	50
Bambi	2.4	3.8	2.4	3.1	9	82
Toots	2.5	3.1	1.8	2.9	13	82
Neu	2.3	3.2	1.3	0.6	2	82
Pip	2.3	3.7				
Oop	2.5	2.0				
Cecilia	2.5	2.7				

*Scores of 80% or better mean that the animal was able to recognize its least-preferred box, which contained the reward during the set-breaking phase.

emerged, however, when several other measures besides days-to-criterion were evaluated in relation to age using analysis of variance. Neither mean latencies, nor percent correct responses on the first and last days of both discrimination and reversal learning, were significantly different in the old and young monkeys.

The sacrifice schedule severely affected the outcome of the reversal training. Of the 4 20-y.o. macaques, 2 reached criterion in 12 and 14 days, 1 failed to reach criterion after 16 days, and 1 was sacrificed after 12 days of training. Of the 9 10-y.o. animals, 1 failed to reach criterion performance after 17 days, and 2 were sacrificed after 3 and 8 days of training. The remaining 7 animals averaged 8 days to criterion. Neither of the 2 4-y.o. monkeys learned the reversal task before they were sacrificed.

Except for 1 20-y.o. monkey, all of the animals used efficient search strategies in Phase I of the Hamilton Search task. Only 6 animals (2 20-y.o. and 4 10-y.o.) reached the set-breaking phase of the Hamilton Search task. Of these, 1 20-y.o. and 3 10-y.o. animals reached criterion (Table 4-1).

DISCUSSION

Our findings indicate that once they begin to attend to the test apparatus, older female pigtail macaques adapt more slowly than younger ones to an unfamiliar test, and require more trials to learn a color discrimination. While based on a small sample, the findings are consistent with some of the results of similar work with rhesus macaques (*M. mulatta*) (9). However, Lapin *et al.* (Chapter 2) cite an experiment in which older (23–27 y.o.) hamadryas baboons (*P. hamadryas*) learned more rapidly than younger (8–13 y.o.) ones. The difference was attributed to hyperactivity of the younger animals in the large test chamber which prevented their attending to the conditioning task. Except for 1 4-y.o. that failed to adapt, such activity was not characteristic of animals in our study. The reason for the contrast between their behavior and that of the baboons merits investigation; it may relate to the size of the test chamber, the sex of the subjects, or the species. To the extent that hyperactivity occurred initially in our study, its effect on learning measures was minimized by initiating data collection with the first session in which the animal attended to the training apparatus. Perhaps such a procedure would unmask similar age-related learning differences in the baboon.

Bartus, Fleming, and Johnson (personal communication) working with rhesus macaques found marked impairment of reversal learning and of a delayed response test of short-term memory in a 17-y.o. and older group, compared with a 3- to 5-y.o. group. They found, however, no consistent age-related impairment in discrimination learning. The reason for the discrepancy between their results and ours is unclear. Again, we are inclined to believe that it relates more to differences in experimental technique or age of the subjects than to species differences in cognitive change with age.

Discriminating saturations of blue and green is more difficult and declines more rapidly with age in rhesus macaques than discriminating saturations of red and yellow (9). One might question whether such a phenomenon influenced the learning of the pigtail monkeys in this study. Our subjects, however, were not required to discriminate color saturation, and a blue or yellow box was assigned randomly as the constant reward location for each monkey during color discrimination learning. Monkeys assigned the yellow reward did not acquire discrimination more rapidly than monkeys assigned the blue reward.

Continued investigation of cognitive functioning during development and aging is warranted in both nonhuman and human primates to assess individual differences in cognitive variability and to evaluate factors that may account for performance changes. The observations in these monkeys corroborate observations in human populations. There is wide variation between and within individuals. The results of numerous longitudinal investigations of middle-aged and older human populations do not support the simple hypothesis of a progressive general loss of intellectual ability with advancing age (2, 3, 13, 18). Instead, several recent long-term studies have identified fundamental conceptual and practical difficulties in the study of age-related changes in man: the need for appropriate tests to measure cognition in the aged; the influence of variables such as initial ability, education, socioeconomic status (13, 18); cohort and time of measurement effects (2); stress and response patterns under paced conditions (3, 13).

In contrast, the limited literature on cognition in nonhuman primates suggests age-related impairment at least in the cognitive processes examined. Davis' (10) unique longitudinal lifespan study of rhesus macaques is uncontaminated by many of the factors that are ordinarily confounded with age in human studies, such as cohort and time of testing effects and socioeconomic status. Although the findings reported here and by others (1; Bartus *et al.*, pers. comm.) are consistent with the age trends published by Davis and his colleagues, considerably more research is needed to evaluate the etiology or pathogenesis of cognitive change in the aging monkey.

It still remains to be carefully determined whether cognitive and behavioral impairment occur as a natural course of advancing age (a primary process) or are the result of pathological (secondary) processes (14). Our data concerning cognitive changes during development and aging in man suggest that being old, and being old and sick, lead to different changes. We are attempting to develop biobehavioral models of cognitive impairment evaluating the roles of genetic, cardiovascular, endocrine, immunologic, and other somatic factors that may mediate age- and pathology-related changes in cognition (4, 14, 15, 18).

A critical weak link in the future development of biobehavioral models of cognitive change is the lack of appropriate tools for the microanalysis of cognition in the aged. Most of the studies on cognition and aging in humans use tests designed for populations other than the elderly, such as psychometric tests developed to predict school success in children or to provide aptitude profiles for educational and occupational applications (3, 13, 20). Their use with the elderly, for whom normative data are lacking, is naive (8). Appropriate tests for the assessment of the elderly who demonstrate tremendous variability in performance, as well as the cognitively impaired elderly whose communication skills are markedly compromised, have not been developed (5). Although neuropsychological tests, developed primarily to evaluate cognitive impairment in patients with traumatic, neoplastic, vascular, or degenerative lesions in specific brain areas, have been used widely in the aged (again without being standardized), such tests rely heavily upon perceptual and motor skills. Vision, hearing, and other sensory systems change with age, and impaired sensory-motor functioning makes cognition difficult to evaluate. Recent reviews have emphasized that the use of cognitive models based on current theories of information processing may provide a more rational approach to test hypotheses of age-related decline (5, 7, 20). Many of the learning and memory deficits found in human and nonhuman primates are readily conceptualized and tested in terms of such models.

In our view, there are two requirements for an improved understanding of cognitive change in aging humans: (a) we need to refine measures of specific component processes and mediators of cognitive functioning, and within the limitations imposed by human research, determine which ones are most subject to change in the aging human; and (b) we need an animal model that exhibits changes in the same or similar functions during aging. On the basis of these pilot data, we are developing an automated battery to assess homologous cognitive functions, e.g., exploratory behavior, motivation, discrimination learning, and vigilance in human and nonhuman primates. The nonhuman primate model will not only allow straightforward tests of hypotheses relating cognitive functioning to age, health, and life experiences, but will allow testing of the efficacy of behavioral and pharmacological interventions in reversing dysfunction.

One important result of developing a monkey model is that it will permit us to study psychoactive drug effects on cognitive impairment in aged animals and analyze the neural mechanisms of those effects. Such studies have seldom been done in the aged, but may improve our understanding of brain changes underlying cognitive impairment. Adequate studies of this kind are impossible in human subjects for several reasons, including ethical and legal limitations, the control that must be exercised over the subject's daily activities, and availability of tissues for biologic assay. Rodents are not adequate for such studies because their brain structure and cognitive abilities are so different that comparison with age-related cognitive phenomena in man is extremely tenuous. Nonhuman primates are much preferred for such studies, and the species of choice is the macaque because of its size, cost, and availability and because of the growing body of evidence that macaques exhibit cognitive changes with aging that merit investigation in the human.

ACKNOWLEDGMENTS

This research was supported in part by the Geriatric Research Educational and Clinical Center of the Seattle/American Lake Veterans Administration Hospitals and by grants RR00166, RR52177 and AG62145 from the National Institutes of Health to the University of Washington. We thank Ms. Ann Lesher and Ms. Cheryl Teets for their help in this study.

REFERENCES

1. Aleksandrovskaia, M. M., and Shirkova, G. I. (1960): Morfologicheskie i funktsional'-nye izmeneniia tsentral'noi nervnoi sistemy u staroi obeziany (Makaka rezus). *Trudy Instituta Vysshei Nervnoi Deiatel'nosti*, 5: 238–249.
2. Baltes, P. B., and Lavouvie, G. V. (1973): Adult development of intellectual performance: description, explanation, and modification. In: *The Psychology of Adult Development and Aging*, edited by C. Eisdorfer and M. P. Lawton, pp. 157–219. Washington, D.C.; American Psychological Association.

3. Botwinick, J. (1977) Intellectual abilities. In: *Handbook of the Psychology of Aging*, edited by J. E. Birren and K. W. Schaie. New York; Van Nostrand.

4. Cohen, D. (1976): A behavioral-chromosome relationship in the elderly: A critical review of a biobehavioral hypothesis. *Exp. Aging Res.*, **2**: 271–287.

5. Cohen, D., and Eisdorfer, C. (1979): Cognitive theory and the assessment of change in the elderly. In: *Psychiatric Symptoms and Cognitive Loss in the Elderly*, edited by A. Raskin and L. Jarvik. New York; Hemisphere.

6. Cohen, D., and Wilkie, F. (in press): Sex differences in cognition among the aged. In: *Determinants of Sex-Related Differences in Cognitive Functioning*, edited by M. Wittig and A. Peterson. New York; Academic Press.

7. Craik, F. J. M. (1977): Age differences in human memory. In: *Handbook of the Psychology of Aging*, edited by J. E. Birren and K. W. Schaie. New York; Van Nostrand.

8. Crook, T. (1977): Issues related to psychometric assessment of treatment of effects in the aged. Geriatric Assessment Workshop, in press.

9. Davis, R. T. (1974): *Monkeys as Perceivers*. New York; Academic Press.

10. Davis, R. T., and Ruggiero, F. T. (1973): Memory in monkeys as a function of preparatory interval and pattern complexity of matrix displays. *Amer. J. Phys. Anthro.*, **38**: 573–578.

11. Eisdorfer, C. (1968): Arousal and performance: Experiments in verbal learning and a tentative theory. In: *Human Behavior and Aging: Recent Advances in Research and Theory*, edited by G. Talland. New York; Academic Press.

12. Eisdorfer, C. (1965): Verbal learning and response time in the aged. *J. Genet. Psychol.*, **107**: 15–22.

13. Eisdorfer, C. (1975): Intelligence and Cognition in the aged. In: *Behavior and Adaptation in Late Life*, edited by E. Busse and C. Pfeiffer.

14. Eisdorfer, C., and Cohen, D. (in press): The cognitively impaired elderly: differential diagnosis. In: *Clinical Gerontology*, edited by M. Storandt, I. Siegler and M. F. Elias. New York; Plenum.

15. Eisdorfer, C., Cohen, D., and Buckley, C. (in press). Serum immunoglobulins and cognition in the impaired elderly. In: *Proceedings of the Workshop Conferences on Alzheimer's Disease, Senile Dementia, and Related Disorders*. New York; Raven Press.

16. Fitts, S. S. (1976): Behavior stereotype and social disengagement: A descriptive study of aging in nonhuman primates. Unpublished dissertation, Washington State University.

17. Harlow, H. F. (1959): The development of learning in the rhesus monkey. *Am. Sci.*, **47**: 458.

18. Jarvik, L. F., and Cohen, D. (1973): A biobehavioral approach to intellectual changes with aging. In: *The Psychology of Adult Development and Aging*, edited by C. Eisdorfer and M. P. Lawton. Washington, D.C.; American Psychological Association.

19. Medin, D. L., O'Neil, P., Smeltz, E., and Davis, R. T. (1973): Age differences in retention of concurrent discrimination problems in monkeys. *J. Gerontol.*, **28**: 63–67.

20. Rabbitt, P. M. (1977): Changes in problem solving ability in old age. In: *Handbook of the Psychology of Aging*, edited by J. E. Birren and K. W. Schaie. New York; Van Nostrand.

21. Witte, K. L. (1975): Paired-associate learning in young and elderly adults as related to presentation rates. *Psychol. Bull.*, **82**: 975–985.

22. Zimmerman, R. R., and Torrey, C. C. (1965): Ontogeny of learning. In: *Behavior of Nonhuman Primates*, Vol. 2, edited by A. M. Schrier, F. Stollnitz, and H. Harlow. New York; Academic Press.

5

Social Behavior

Peter E. Maxim

Department of Psychiatry and Behavioral Sciences, and
Regional Primate Research Center,
University of Washington, Seattle, Washington

INTRODUCTION

Until recently, studies of social interaction of nonhuman primates failed to consider the effects of aging on the status or role of individuals in the group. Nevertheless, studies on social interaction of normal adult monkeys now provide baseline data from which to trace change in social facility that may occur in the aging monkey. Similarly, species variability in complexity of social organization provides several culture-free models of possible relations between social organization and the specific role of the aging animal.

Social Organization

Irrespective of type of social group organization, male and female primates have particular functions when alone or in a group. Males maintain spacing between neighboring troops, reduce internal competition by driving out younger males, defend against predators, and direct troop movements. Females have functions dominated by infant care: protect the infant, socialize the juvenile and determine the status of the juvenile and young adult. These roles are further differentiated according to social structure.

Eisenberg *et al.* (13) classified nonhuman primate social groups into five types:

1) solitary species, 2) parental family, 3) unimale troop, 4) age-graded male troop, and 5) multimale troop.

In the solitary species, which include nocturnal pottos, lorises and lemurs, and diurnal orangutans, the social group contains only the mother and her dependent offspring—an infant and one or two juveniles. The parental family, seen in the callithricidae (marmosets), *Indri* lemur and gibbons, consists of a bonded adult pair and their immediate offspring. Almost nothing is known of the role of the aged animal in these two types of social structure.

The structure of the remaining three classes is based on increasing adult male tolerance of other males.

In the unimale troop, seen in cebidae, cercopithecidae, colobus and patas monkeys, the mandrill, and gelada and hamadryas baboons, the dominant male maintains a harem and tolerates some closeness to other males who also have harems. Hamadryas and gelada harems have affiliative differences that affect the role of aging animals. Gelada males develop dominant-submissive but not affiliative bonds with females, while the females gradually develop strong inter-female ties. As the latter ties lead to female coalitions the aging males' dominance weakens. The success of younger males' attempts to drive an older male from the group depends on whether the female coalition follows the younger male (12). Older males can remain on the periphery if they submit to the younger dominant one, but ejection is common as solitary males are frequently found (4). Aging females seem to retain their rank through long-standing affiliation with other females, and often act as "aunts," cuddling, carrying and disciplining others' infants (3). Hamadryas females, on the other hand, do not develop affiliative bonds with one another, only dominant-submissive relations. Instead, the adult male develops both affiliative and dominance bonds with his females, and also develops affiliative bonds with males of neighboring units (22). Thus, the aging male, rather than the aging female, finds the social system of ranks and affiliations supporting him. The aging female must fall in rank, unsupported by the harem, as she becomes less interesting to the male.

The age-graded male troop, seen in squirrel and toque monkeys, langurs, several cercopithecidae and gorillas, is run by a few adult males who tolerate larger numbers of younger males within the group, though the ratio of males to females is still less than 1:1. Adult affiliative bonds are of three roughly equal types: male-male, male-female, and female-female. Adult males do not tolerate each other close to their females but they easily form affinity relationships when females are not present. Females associate matrilinearly and develop individual dominant-submissive relations but no linear hierarchy. Sexually active females are generally dominant to both younger and older females and maintain their rank through direct aggression. Aging females are the most active in leading troop movements, in defending troop territory from other troops, and attacking predators (5). Nevertheless, their weakening affiliative ties and increasing submission to young adult females lead to solitary existence as they are constantly displaced from preferred food sources, roosting sites and social interaction (5, 19). Aging male langurs are frequently forceably ejected from the troop by all-male bands who may drive out all other young male members as well (30). Once the aging male is away from the females, he easily develops affinity ties in all-male groups. Thus, though aging monkeys of both sexes lose rank they continue to maintain some social position in groups of the same sex through affiliative bonds.

Among gorillas, movement in and out of a band seems to be very casual in that older animals of both sexes may split off in solitary pursuits for days or weeks and rejoin with little ceremony. Schaller (29) reported that older silverback males may drop somewhat in rank but they still rank higher than younger blackback males or juveniles. Old females frequently act as aunts in a group, helping to care for young juveniles.

Thus, in both unimale and age-graded male social structures, aging animals maintain status through affiliative bonds. Those who have only had dominance relations become progressively isolated.

In multimale troops a number of adult males form a dominance hierarchy but tolerate animals of all ages and both sexes in the group. Both males and females have a well-developed dominance hierarchy and both sexes frequently form coalitions within the group to maintain status. This social structure characterizes two species of lemur (*Propithecus verrauxi* and *Lemur catta*), various species of macaque including *Macaca mulatta*, *M. fuscata*, *M. radiata*, *M. nemestrina* and *M. fascicularis*, various species of baboon including *Papio ursinus*, *P. cynocephalus* and *P. anubis*, and chimpanzee (*Pan satyrus*). These multimale groups have many features of human social organization, including kinship ties, genealogy, behavioral tradition, and maternal care as a determinant of future social status (17, 32).

Matrilineal genealogies play an important role in the eventual status of both males and females in most multimale macaque social groups. Young males obtain their initial rank from that of their mothers, who defend them in encounters with other males whose mothers have lower rank (28). The male's dependent rank ends at about 5 years of age when he moves to the troop periphery with his peers, where he frequently encounters aging males who have become increasingly isolated from the group center but have not dropped markedly in rank (1). Over the next 4 to 5 years he may advance or decline in rank through direct aggressive encounters. Undoubtedly his maternally derived dependent rank biases the outcome of such encounters with his peers, but any rank change with elders is effected through direct aggression, either alone or with other males. The many affinity ties that the aging male develops with peers and younger rising males probably keep him from becoming as peripheral as in other organizational structures.

Young female monkeys also obtain their mothers' rank within the female hierarchy. In *M. mulatta* and probably most *M. fuscata* groups they do not rise above their mothers (21, 28), but in *M. fascicularis* Angst (1) found that 50% of daughters ranked higher than their mothers. He notes that kinship ties preserve the rank of aging females and only senile females drop in rank. A female's rank is partly related to her association with infants since middle-aged, high ranking females are attracted to babies and accept low rank females with babies while rejecting older females without them (1). Bernstein (3) has reported aunt behavior by biologic aunts among *M. nemestrina*, which probably helps them maintain affiliative ties and slows their movement to the periphery.

Maternal lineage is also important in chimpanzee communities (31). Offspring start out with their mothers' rank, and later as adults they help her maintain rank by intervening in encounters.

In the multimale primate social structure, then, the aging female maintains status by her aunt behavior, by her progeny (particularly if they also are of high rank), and by lifetime affiliative ties with peers. The aging male maintains status through continuing affiliative ties with peers and by developing new ones with young adults as they move into the central area of the troop.

Both age-graded and multimale classes seem to support aging animals in greater numbers, since several studies report more than occasional sightings of older animals. In the male age-graded structure of the toque monkey (*M. sinica*) Dittus (11) reported that old males constituted 31/1000 and senile males, 6/1000 members while old females averaged 109/1000 and senile females, 58/1000 members. Similarly, Blaffer-Hrdy (5) found no old males in Hanuman langur troops, but old females constituted 7% of the adult female cohort. A major problem in assessing the role of aging monkeys in wild groups is determining their age. In almost all studies thus far mentioned, the authors do not say how they assign age. Dittus (11) relied on observable body changes and general activity: old monkeys were defined as those who showed wrinkled facial skin, loosening of skin folds near eyes, lips, and cheeks, hair loss on tail and dullness of fur, while senile monkeys additionally were lethargic or showed signs of illness. Unfortunately these changes do not correlate well with age in monkeys reared from birth or with radiographic bone indices. Thus, detailed future studies of aging animals in relatively natural habitats can be accurately done only with groups whose individuals have been followed for long periods of time. At present this limits available study populations to those in Japan and Cayo Santiago, Puerto Rico.

Roles and Mechanisms Determining Status of
Aging Human and Nonhuman Primates

In the current political climate of an increasingly vocal and powerful aging human population, studies on aging frequently start from the questions, "What are aged people for; what is their 'function' in society," 'function' being equated with worth. The analysis of roles in nonhuman primate social systems often seems to be couched in terms equating function with value, although such discussion is generally framed in terms of evolutionary fitness.

It seems clear that aging monkeys have been identified in greatest numbers in species whose social organization goes beyond immediate family ties and includes both male and female affinity ties, linear dominance hierarchies, and kinship ties. With such complexity of social structure, the aging animal's role can include defense of territory against other groups, defense against predation, determination of troop movement, aunt behavior, and knowledge about ways to cope with infrequently occurring problems. Several investigators suggest that older animals may also function as reservoirs of information about rare but important events such as leading the troop to a waterhole outside its normal boundaries (22). Propagation of new food habits within the troop clearly occurs faster when information comes from high ranking members (18). If the faster rate of physical growth reported in offspring of highest ranking lineages (28) is due to better nutrition, and is translated into greater longevity, then social structures that retain aging monkeys at a higher rank are well suited for providing important but infrequently needed information.

Eisenberg *et al.* (13) point out, however, that the multimale system in which role differentiations are most developed is not typical of terrestrial primates. The evolution of group structure seems to have been influenced by two factors, food gathering and defense against predation. The unimale and age-graded male systems developed in rain forest and savanna ecosystems, where social structure was influenced by food gathering. The multimale macaque and baboon social structures developed in environments where increased predation pressure was more successfully met by group mobbing than by rapid dispersal and distraction displays. Predation may be an important selective pressure maintaining individual fitness within the group and may particularly affect the role of the increasingly peripheral aging monkey (5). On the other hand, some investigators point out the difficulty of documenting the frequency of predation in various species and argue that predation is so infrequent as to be an insufficient explanation for the development of complex roles and hierarchies in primates (1, 11, 29).

Moving from the evolutionary context to the individual animal, one can identify intragroup mechanisms capable of supporting some aspects of complex hierarchical systems in terms of physical and social reinforcement (23). For example, dominant animals are rewarded by freedom of movement, freedom from aggression provided they display proper behavior, and all troop members are rewarded with predictability in social interaction. Again, however, such explanations run into difficulty when applied to many primate groups (21, 29, 31), and several investigators have recently complained of inaccuracy and overemphasis on the concept of dominance hierarchies to explain social structure (see reviews refs 14, 15). As noted above, affiliative ties, rather than coercion, seem to increase longevity of rank. Nevertheless, the dominant-submissive stratification of social organization does seem to be a common determinant of social structure in large nonhuman and human social groups.

One is tempted to extrapolate from the interplay between primate group structure and differentiation of roles for the aging nonhuman primate to analogous interplay between human societal structure and the role of the aging individual. However, the degree to which the role for the aging individual may be defined in a group is related to his potential influence on the group and this in turn is partly a function of his longevity in that role. In this sense, roles of aging nonhuman primates cannot adequately serve as models for the role of aging humans. If one uses the point of cessation of menstruation as the onset of aging then it is clear that the longevity of the aging human in modern times exerts an influence on human groups that cannot be matched in other primate species. Using Cutler's (10) estimations of maximum lifespan potential one finds that in rhesus and toque monkeys, langurs, and chimpanzees, an individual is in an aged role for only about 5 years, whereas humans with a lifespan potential of 110 years can be in the aged role for more than 50 years. Social forces that either help or hinder development of roles for the aging nonhuman primate are thus probably only precursors to the more complex forces bearing on the role in human groups.

Movement of the Individual into the Aged Role

While the attention given to the evolutionary basis for the emergence of aged roles in primates is not great, even less attention has been given to the more easily studied question of the factors that determine when individuals move into the aged role. What is the relation between change in the individuals' behavior and change in his social position as he ages? Is the shift from the mature adult role into an aged role forced by other members of the group or does the disengagement process originate in the individual? Descriptions of social structures in terms of hierarchical systems maintained primarily by aggressive interchanges suggest that loss of status and gradual isolation are imposed by the aggression of other monkeys. Carpenter (7) and others, however, have noted that the individual in a stable group seldom has to use aggressive behaviors to maintain his status. This fact, coupled with affiliative ties, should maintain his adult status into senility. Indeed, one might expect to find that the aging monkey develops significant inability to respond to the normal range of social interactions before other monkeys become aware of his social deficiency. This loss might be combined with a voluntary peripheralization as the animal becomes disinterested or unable to cope with other animals.

The brief study described below used a scale of pigtail macaque social behaviors

Table 5-1. Social Behavior Scale for *Macaca nemestrina.*

Attack	3.60	Ignore	0.0
Hit	2.80	Len	−0.15
Mount	2.30	Lipsmack	−0.60
Threaten	2.25	Look Away	−0.80
Anogenital Explore	2.05	Show Neck	−1.10
Approach	1.60	Crouch	−1.90
Stare	0.90	Present	−1.95
Branch Shake	0.70	Walk Away	−2.00
Earflick	0.10	Grimace	−3.25
Ah Grimace	0.05	Flee	−4.10
Pace	0.05		

For behavior definitions and derivation of scale values see Maxim, 1978.

(Table 5-1) designed to quantify the appropriateness as well as the degree of change in social behavior under various conditions, including advancing age (24, 25). Monkeys typically interact by producing strings of behaviors called chains, which are preceded and followed by at least 15 sec of no interaction. The set of behaviors produced by each monkey within a chain is called a half-chain. A study of interactions in 120 pairs of adult *M. nemestrina* showed that an individual signifies dominance by producing a half-chain of behaviors with positive scale values averaging 2.5 or more, subdominance by a half-chain with positive behaviors and one negative behavior whose overall sum is greater than 2.5, submission by behaviors with negative scale values having an average sum of −2.65 or less, and friendliness by mixing positive and negative behaviors serially. All friendly half-chains have a mean of −0.04.

Empirically, these four types of half-chain occur as seven combinations, or classes, of chain. Four classes account for 97% of chains: dominant/submissive, i.e., behaviors in the half-chain of the dominant monkey are all dominant and those of the submissive monkey are all submissive; friendly/friendly, i.e., the half-chains of both monkeys are mixtures of dominant and submissive categories; dominant/friendly, i.e., the behaviors of the dominant monkey are all dominant and those of the other monkey are a mixture of dominant and submissive; friendly/submissive, i.e., the half-chain of one monkey is a mixture of dominant and submissive and that of the other monkey is all submissive. Three other classes are uncommon: dominant/dominant, subdominant/submissive and subdominant/friendly.

In this study the scale was used to determine whether older pigtail females were showing signs of social disengagement as measured by decreased frequency of interaction with other females of the same age group or decreased interaction with younger adult females compared with interaction normally seen between young adult females. The data were also analyzed to determine whether the old females showed decreased flexibility in the variability of their social interaction chains, and whether their social behavior was appropriate to behavior produced by the other monkey.

METHODS

Four pigtail macaque females over 20 y.o. (A, B, C, D) were paired with one another and with at least 1 of 4 younger adult females 9 to 11 y.o. (Y1, Y2, Y3, Y4). Between observation sessions, the animals were individually caged in the same room where they could see and hear one another. The monkeys were introduced in pairs into a 1.2 X 1.2 X 2.4 m cage equipped with food, water and several plastic toys; the observer sat in front of the long plexiglas viewing wall. Observations of each pair were made in 2 30-min sessions at least 1 week apart and all behaviors were recorded at 15-sec intervals on scored check sheets.

The values of behaviors in half-chains from each animal were summed at 45-sec intervals and plotted graphically. From previous work (25), we found that adult monkeys show a typical sequence of interactions when first placed together. During the first few minutes both animals engage in dominance behaviors. This frequently escalates to a fight and then a dominant-submissive relationship is established. Once this occurs and the submissive monkey appropriately mirrors the dominance behavior of her pairmate by quantitatively equivalent submissive behavior, the behavioral interaction shifts into establishing friendly or affiliative bonds, culminating in grooming and sitting together. The appropriateness of this mirroring behavior can be assessed by computing a deviation score for the pair at 45-sec intervals. This score is the arithmetic sum of the behaviors of both monkeys. In previous work (25) we found that the overall mean deviation score per 30-min session based on 40 pairings between young adult pigtail females was 0.23, with a range of -0.47 to 0.93. The deviation score when applied to new subjects of this species reflects the extent to which animals interact appropriately. Abnormally submissive behavior on the part of one results in consistent negative deviation scores for the pair; abnormally aggressive or dominant behavior leads to consistently positive scores. In addition to graphic representation of the data, the total number of behavior chains, the mean score of each half-chain, and the frequencies of different classes of chains were determined for each session.

RESULTS

Due to scheduling constraints, observations were limited to 5 different pairings between 20-y.o. females and 6 different pairings between 20-y.o. and 10-y.o.

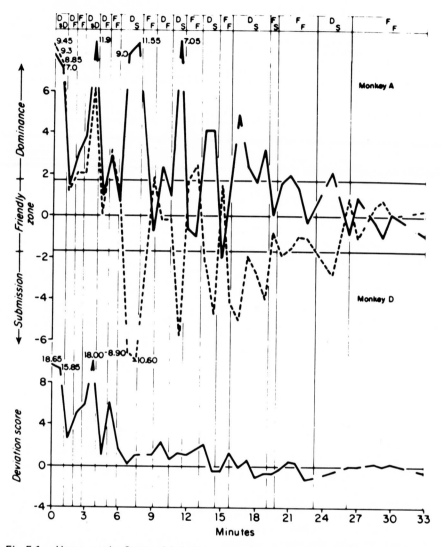

Fig. 5-1. Upper graph: Summed behavior categories of dominant female monkey A are plotted at 45-sec intervals as a solid line on the dominance-submission dimension, those of the submissive female D as a dotted line (D/sD = dominant/subdominant, D/S = dominant/submissive; D/F = dominant/friendly; F/F = friendly/friendly; F/S = friendly/submissive. Lower graph: Deviation score reflects the degree to which the behavior of one monkey is equal and opposite in sign (appropriately submissive) to behavior of the other monkey.

females. Thus, each old female was paired with another old female for 2 sessions, 2 old females (B and C) were paired twice with 1 10-y.o. female, and 2 (A and D) were each paired with 2 young females.

The interaction between old females A and D (Figure 5-1) exemplifies the pattern seen in most pairings. Figure 5-2, showing the interaction between old fe-

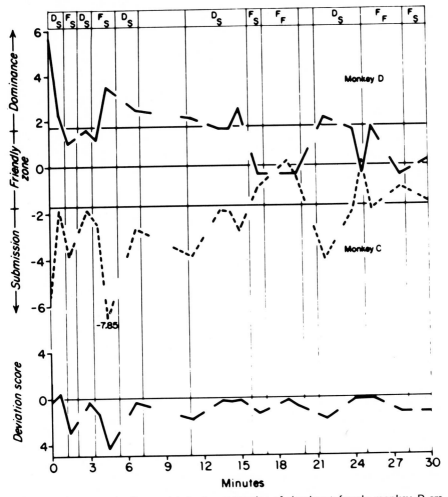

Fig. 5-2. Upper graph: Summed behavior categories of dominant female monkey D are plotted at 45-sec intervals as a solid line on the dominant-submissive dimension, those of submissive female monkey C are plotted as a dotted line. Consistent negative deviation score reflects excessive submissive responding by monkey C.

males C and D, exemplifies an abnormal relationship that monkey C established in all pairs. The interaction in Figure 5-1 shows the same degree of variability in class of chains, in chain scores, and in appropriateness of relationship as was seen in younger adult female pairings. Figure 5-2, however, illustrates how monkey C consistently and inappropriately showed negative submissive behavior. This behavior caused a consistent depression of the deviation score throughout the session (Figure 5-2) and aberrant values in the summary statistics presented in Tables 2 and 3. Tables 5-2 and 5-3 summarize the overall interaction between each of the 20-y.o. females, when paired with other 20-y.o. and with 10-y.o. animals. Except for pairings with monkey C, the number of behavior chains observed per 30-min session was about the same for all pair types (Table 5-2), and they approximated those found between young adult pairs (25). The overall mean deviation score, the distribution of chain classes, and the mean score for each half-chain in a class were similar for all pairs except those involving old female monkey C. Monkey C interacted less with other monkeys and in her interactions, with both old and young adult females, she showed inappropriately submissive behavior as reflected in deviation scores consistently below - 0.47, the lower limit of normal. When each pairing was analyzed for distribution of chain classes (Table 5-3), all pairings involving monkey C had markedly decreased friendly-friendly chains and correspondingly increased friendly-submissive chains. The inappropriateness of these submissive responses was further noted in monkey C's abnormally high half-chain submissive scores in the friendly-submissive chains of every pairing.

Table 5-2. Number of Interactions and Overall Mean Deviation Scores.

	OLD vs. OLD				
Monkey Pair	A vs. B	A vs. D	A vs. C	B vs. C	D vs. C
Dominant Monkey	A	D	A	B	D
Number of chains/session	33	24	22	29	22
Mean deviation score/session	0.02	0.61	−0.94	−0.53	−1.06

	OLD vs. YOUNG				
Monkey Pair	A vs. Y1	A vs. Y2	B vs. Y3	C vs. Y4	D vs. Y1	D vs. Y2
Dominant Monkey	A	A	Y3	Y4	D	Y2
Number of chains/session	38	28	34	20	28	44
Mean deviation score/session	0.34	−0.24	−0.07	−0.47	−0.19	−0.27

Table 5.3 Frequencies of Different Classes of Interaction and Mean Half-Chain Score Values.

	% Distribution of Chains by Class				Mean Half-Chain Scores			
	D/S	F/F	F/S	D/F	D/S	F/F	F/S	D/F
Norm: average of 40 young adult female pairs (from ref. 25)	37	38	5	19	2.79 −2.59	0.75 −0.79	1.63 −2.05	1.90 −1.25
Monkey Pair			Old vs. Old *M. nemestrina*					
A vs. B	48	48	–	4	2.16 −2.30	0.15 −0.10	– –	1.92 −0.18
A vs. D	27	54	–	19	1.38 −0.85	−0.05 1.33	– –	1.53 −1.55
A vs. C	45	20	35	–	2.01 −3.45	0.05 −1.0	1.01 −3.43	– –
B vs. C	61	23	12	4	3.25 −3.80	0.05 −0.25	2.4 −6.15	2.02 −1.75
D vs. C	50	27	23	–	2.05 −2.62	−0.03 −1.51	0.09 −2.56	– –
			Old vs. Young Adult *M. nemestrina*					
A vs. Y1	45	54	1	–	1.8 −2.4	−0.83 −0.66	2.01 −2.05	– –
A vs. Y2	48	48	–	4	1.13 −1.98	−0.58 −1.55	– –	1.95 −1.60
B vs. Y3	46	31	–	23	3.04 −3.19	−1.14 0.41	– –	2.27 −2.28
C vs. Y4	37	17	45	–	1.6 −1.9	−0.82 −1.33	0.02 −1.93	– –
D vs. Y1	36	46	–	18	2.85 −2.90	−0.15 −0.84	– –	1.7 −2.0
D vs. Y2	74	11	–	15	2.03 −2.66	0.1 0.2	– –	2.22 −1.14

D/S = dominant/submissive chains; F/F = friendly/friendly chains; F/S = friendly/submissive chains; D/F = dominant/friendly chains; − = none observed.

DISCUSSION

The results indicate that many older female pigtail macaques continue to show appropriate patterns of social interaction with peers and with younger monkeys. They also show that the social behavior scale can be used to identify and monitor the kind of deviation in social behavior exhibited by one of the old subjects, monkey C. Much more information of a longitudinal nature would be needed to trace the etiology of such deviation. Monkeys A, B and D had been in captivity for 20 years and were around 2 y.o. when caught in the wild. Thus they were at least 22 y.o. when studied. Monkey C was a multiparous female when brought from the wild and had been in captivity for 15 years. In addition she was the only female who was postmenopausal (monkey #75026; see Chapter 16, this volume). Thus she was at least 20 y.o., and probably more than 25 y.o. and the oldest animal in the group.

Nevertheless, longitudinal study of a number of monkeys is necessary to determine whether the kind of deviant behavior observed in monkey C was likely due to age or other factors idiosyncratic to the individual monkey. Ideally, such observations should be done on animals maintained in social groups so as to determine when the behavior change occurs, and whether the change leads to loss of rank or follows it. One could determine whether inappropriate social behavior typically occurs first as an increase in submissive responses and whether the onset of such behavior is first seen in interactions with kin or with members of other genealogies. Finally, one could evaluate the effects of aging behavioral change on the maintenance of various role functions, *e.g.*, leader, aunt, or territorial defender.

An apparent constriction in the range of appropriate social behavior has been reported in elderly people (20) in terms of a decrease in the amount and variety of social behavior (8). Cumming and Henry (9) have described social disengagement in elderly people as a mutual, cooperative withdrawal between society and the individual, and Neugarten (27) reported intrapsychic changes occurring in middle age leading to introversion well before overt behavior revealed any indication of social disengagement. In rhesus monkeys, Boer and Davis (6) reported that animals housed in pairs showed a marked decline in social interaction with the pairmate over a 14-year span, but the global rating measure used did not allow one to determine the details of the relationship, or the effect of time on the range of behavioral interactions. In other human studies, Atchley (2) concluded that decreases in social interaction were not voluntary but resulted from societal rejection. Havighurst *et al.* (16) have also reported that older people who were most satisfied with their lives were ones who resisted disengagement. In one of the few studies in this area using nonhuman primates, S. Fitts (personal communication) analyzed differences in self-directed and object investigation behavior, and amount and variety of social behavior when old animals were paired together, or paired with younger animals. No differences were found between young and old animals in self-directed vs. object-directed behaviors that might be taken as indicators of "turning inward." Both old and young monkeys showed more social interaction with peers than with monkeys older or younger than themselves, but there were no differences in the range of interaction between old and young monkeys for either age-mate. Thus, the data did not support the hypothesis of social disengagement in old monkeys. Fitts also sought to determine whether the behavior of old monkeys was more temporally stereotyped than that of younger monkeys. She found that older monkeys showed greater predictability than younger ones in the temporal sequence of their own behaviors irrespective of the age of their pairmate. Younger monkeys showed more predictable sequential interactions when paired with younger monkeys than with older ones. The results supported the hypothesis that behavioral sequences of the older monkeys were more stereotypically organized than those of younger monkeys. While such increased predictability supported the concept of behavioral rigidity in older animals, lack of information on normative behavior between adult animals in the social setting precluded judgment as to appropriateness of such behavioral sequences. Results of the present study indicate that the social responses of an older individual can be outside the range of normal for the species.

Of the animals commonly available for study of social problems related to man, only nonhuman primates exhibit the kinds and variety of social organizations necessary to serve as models of the interactions between status, role, and social competence of the aging individual. Detailed longitudinal study of aging nonhuman primates living in such social structures should yield valuable information relating social factors to the human aging process.

ACKNOWLEDGMENTS

This research was supported in part by National Institutes of Health grants RR00166, RR52177 and AG62145, and by a Research Associate Award from the Veterans Administration.

REFERENCES

1. Angst, W. (1975): Basic data and concepts on the social organization of *Macaca fascicularis*. *Primate Behav.*, 4: 325–388.
2. Atchley, R. C. (1972): Societal disengagement. In: *The Social Forces in Later Life*, edited by R. C. Atchley. Belmont, California. Wadsworth Printing Company.
3. Bernstein, I. S. (1972): Daily activity cycles and weather influences on a pigtail monkey group. *Folia Primat.*, 18: 390–415.
4. Bernstein, I. S. (1975): Activity patterns in a gelada monkey group. *Folia Primat.*, 23: 50–71.
5. Blaffer-Hrdy, S. (1978): Matriarchs and "Altruists": the behavior of senescent females in macaque and langur sisterhoods. In: *Other Ways of Growing Old*, edited by P. T. Amoss and S. Harrell. In press. Stanford, CA, Stanford University Press.
6. Boer, A. P. and Davis, R. T. (1968): Age changes in the behaviors of monkeys induced by ionizing radiation. *J. Gerontol.*, 23: 331–342.
7. Carpenter, C. R. (1964): *Naturalistic Behavior of Non-human Primates*. University Park; Penn State University Press.

8. Cumming, E., Dean, L. R., Newell, D. S., and McCaffrey, I. (1960): Disengagement: a tentative theory of aging. *Sociometry*, **23**: 23-35.

9. Cumming, E., and Henry, W. E. (1961): *Growing Old: The Process of Disengagement*. New York; Besie Books.

10. Cutler, H. (1976): Evolution of longevity in Primates. *J. Human Evol.*, **5**: 169-202.

11. Dittus, W. P. (1975): Population dynamics of the toque monkey. In: *Socioecology and Psychology of Primates*, edited by R. H. Tuttle, pp. 124-151, Paris; Mouton.

12. Dunbar, R., and Dunbar, P. (1975): Social dynamics of gelada baboons. *Contrib. Primat.*, **6**:1-154.

13. Eisenburg, J. R., Muckenhirn, N. A., and Rudan, R. (1972): The relation between ecology and social structure in primates. *Science*, **176**: 863-874.

14. Gartlan, J. S. (1968): Structure and function in primate society. *Folia Primat.*, **8**: 89-120.

15. Gartlan, J. S. (1973): Influence of phylogeny and ecology on variations in the group organization of primates. *Symp. 4th Int. Cong. Primat.*, 88-101.

16. Havighurst, R. J., Neugarten, B. L., and Tobin, S. (1968): Disengagement and patterns of aging. In: *Middle Age and Aging*, edited by B. L. Neugarten. Chicago; University of Chicago Press.

17. Imanishi, K. (1960): Social organization of subhuman primates in their natural habitat. *Current Anthrop.*, **1**: 393-407.

18. Itani, J., and Nishimura A. (1973): The study of infrahuman culture in Japan: a review. *Symp. 4th Int. Cong. Primat.*, 26-50.

19. Jay, P. (1963): The social behavior of the langur monkey. Ph.D. thesis, University of Chicago, Chicago.

20. Kimmel, D. C. (1974): *Adult Development and Aging*. New York; John Wiley.

21. Kummer, H. (1957): Soziales Verhalten einer Mantelpavian-Gruppe. *Beiheft Schweiz. Z. Psychol.*, **33**: 1-91.

22. Kummer, H. (1971): *Primate Societies: Group Techniques of Ecological Adaptation*. Chicago; Aldine.

23. Loy, J. (1975): The descent of dominance in *Macaca:* Insights into the structure of human societies. In: *Socioecology and Psychology of Primates*, edited by R. H. Tuttle, pp. 153-180. Paris; Mouton.

24. Maxim, P. E. (1976): An interval scale for studying and quantifying social relations in pairs of rhesus monkeys. *J. Exp. Psychol.*, *Gen.*, **105**:123-147.

25. Maxim, P. E. (1978): Quantification of social behavior in pigtail monkeys. *J. Exp. Psychol.*, *Anim. Behav. Proc.*, **4**: 50-67.

26. Missakian, E. A. (1972): Genealogical and cross-genealogical dominance relations in a group of free ranging rhesus monkeys (*Macaca mulatta*) on Cayo Santiago. *Primates*, **13**: 169-180.

27. Neugarten, B. L. (1972): Personality and the aging process. *Gerontologist*, **12**: 9-15.

28. Sade, D. S. (1971): A longitudinal study of social behavior of rhesus monkeys. In: *The Functional and Evolutionary Biology of Primates*, edited by R. H. Tuttle, pp. 378-398. Chicago; Aldine-Atherton.

29. Schaller, G. (1964): *The Year of the Gorilla*. Chicago; University of Chicago Press.

30. Sugiyama, Y. (1966): An artificial social change in a hanuman langur troop. *Primates*, **7**: 41-72.

31. Van Lawick-Goodall, J. (1973): The behavior of chimpanzees in their natural habitat. *Amer. J. Psychiat.*, **130**: 1-12.

32. Yamada, M. (1971): Five natural troops of Japanese monkeys on Shodoshima Island. II. A comparison of social structure. *Primates*, **12**: 125-150.

6

Gene Expression in Brain

Margaret N. Farquhar, Kathleen J. Kosky and Gilbert S. Omenn
Division of Medical Genetics, University of Washington
Seattle, Washington

INTRODUCTION

Gene expression in mammalian brain is higher than in other complex tissues. DNA-RNA hybridization studies with adult mouse, rabbit, and human brain RNA have shown that 25 to 40% of single copy DNA (ScDNA) is expressed as RNA in brain compared with 10 to 12% in liver, kidney or spleen (1, 2, 10, 11). Much of the transcribed RNA is degraded in the nucleus (heterogenous nuclear RNA, HnRNA); however, about 20% of the various sequences are transported to the cytoplasm for use in protein synthesis (1). The high level of transcription in brain represents a capacity for expression of thousands of different DNA sequences.

Studies of gene expression at different stages of normal and abnormal development suggest that brain development is associated with large changes in gene expression. Comparisons of RNA diversity in fetal and adult mice (2, 10), rabbits (2), and humans (11) show that twice as many sequences are expressed in the adult as in the fetal brain. Whether this difference reflects increased transcription in all cells or increased differentiation such that there is more cellular diversity in the adult is not known. Studies of gene expression in rat brain have demonstrated differences based on environmental rearing conditions. For example, brain RNA from rats raised in impoverished environments shows less sequence diversity than that from littermates raised under enriched conditions (12). Our studies on HnRNA in rat brain have shown differences in amounts of HnRNA present under conditions affecting growth. Maternal hypoglycemia during pregnancy and weaning results in offspring with reduced brain and body weights compared with offspring of controls. Although the affected animals show few if any behavioral abnormalities, the concentration of the complex class of HnRNA sequences in brain is reduced by about 40%.

Many current theories of aging suggest that alterations in gene expression during senescence might be responsible for differences in cell function observed in aging. Theories based on error catastrophe in macromolecular synthesis (16), somatic mutation (5), and failures of regulatory mechanisms (13) all rely to some extent on changes in gene expression during aging. Generally, these mechanisms propose random changes that lead to various deficiencies in function. In contrast, Finch (9) has suggested that nonrandom changes in patterns of gene expression occur in aging as part of an ongoing process first seen in early development. Most studies of proteins in young and old mammals have shown no substantial differences, either in enzyme activities (9) or in electrophoretic patterns of proteins (3, 23). Those differences that do seem to correlate with aging suggest differences in regulation of the amount of specific proteins produced, rather than changes in structural genes or amino acid sequences in many proteins (9).

Although the regulation of protein synthesis is not fully understood, it has recently been proposed that some HnRNA sequences may function in control of expression of various genes (7). Since a large proportion of HnRNA contains sequences that do not code for protein, Davidson et al. (7) proposed a class of regulatory transcripts that could modulate the expression of structural genes during development. If this were the case, then hybridization studies with HnRNA would reflect primarily the transcription of genes that do not code for proteins and probably function in regulation. Thus, changes in regulation of gene expression could be reflected in the amount and types of sequences found in HnRNA. If these regulatory sequences change as a function of age, we might expect to see differences in transcription during aging similar to those observed during development.

Approximately 95% of ScDNA sequences are homologous between chimpanzee and human and 85% are homologous between macaque and human (14), whereas less than 5% are homologous between rodent and human (4). In addition to phylogenetic relationships, several other factors make the macaque a desirable model for studying age-related differences in gene expression. Because cellular RNA is rapidly degraded after death, it is necessary to obtain tissues within minutes of death and to use purification procedures that minimize RNA degradation, which virtually excludes the use of human material. Moreover, the experiments require a large amount of tissue. In studies with rodents, this necessitates pooling samples from many small animals, whereas 20 to 30 g of brain tissue is readily obtainable from a single macaque, thus facilitating comparisons of individual animals. We therefore developed techniques for studying gene expression in these animals so that we could determine whether there are age differences in gene expression similar to those previously observed early in normal development or later in abnormal development.

To determine whether there are changes in gene expression in aging, we have measured the extent of transcription in brain of 4-, 10- and 20-y.o. pigtail macaques (*Macaca nemestrina*). Tritiated (^{3}H) ScDNA was hybridized to a vast excess of HnRNA. This fraction of cellular RNA contains all transcripts including ribosomal RNA, transfer RNA, and messenger RNA (mRNA) sequences which are used in protein synthesis, as well as other sequences which are degraded in the nucleus and are not directly involved in cytoplasmic protein synthesis. The extent of the reaction, i.e., the amount of ^{3}H ScDNA hybridized, is determined by the number of different RNA sequences present, commonly termed RNA complexity or diversity (7). The rate of the hybridization reaction is determined by the concentration of the various RNA sequences. Thus, differences in the extent of reaction reflect the amount of DNA that is transcribed, and the reaction rate is influenced by the number of copies of the RNA transcripts present in the cell.

MATERIAL AND METHODS

Brain tissue (left hemicortex, approximately 25 g) was excised within 4 min of cardiorespiratory arrest and frozen on dry ice (Table 6-1). To compare the age

Table 6-1. Yield HnRNA Percent DNA Hybridized from *M. nemestrina* Hemicortex.

Age (Years)	Subspecies	Yield HnRNA (mg/g tissue)	Percent DNA Hybridized (Mean ± SEM)	Average Percent DNA Hybridized (Mean ± SEM)
4	*M. nemestrina leonina*	0.55	12.1 ± 0.6	
4	*M. nemestrina leonina*	0.48	13.3 ± 0.5	13.5 ± 0.5
4	*M. nemestrina nemestrina*	0.52	15.0 ± 0.5	
10	*M. nemestrina leonina*	0.45	11.8 ± 0.7	
10	*M. nemestrina leonina*	0.51	12.7 ± 0.3	12.8 ± 0.4
10	*M. nemestrina nemestrina*	0.42	14.0 ± 0.2	
20	*M. nemestrina leonina*	0.45	12.3 ± 0.5	
20	*M. nemestrina leonina*	0.49	11.3 ± 0.5	12.7 ± 0.5
20	*M. nemestrina nemestrina*	0.45	14.5 ± 0.6	

groups under similar experimental conditions, three sets of specimens, each including samples taken from one 4-, one 10- and one 20-y.o. female *M. nemestrina*, matched for subspecies and body weight, were identified by animal number and used in a single experiment. The ages of individual animals were not obtained until all experiments were completed.

The unlabeled DNA used in these experiments was isolated from liver or spleen. Radioactive DNA was prepared from *M. mulatta* cell cultures. Previous studies have shown DNA from *M. mulatta* to be indistinguishable from that of *M. nemestrina* in hybridization properties. ^{3}H ScDNA was isolated from the radioactive DNA by renaturation to $C_0 t = 500$ (mol 1^{-1} sec) followed by hydroxyapatite chromatography (11). Fragment sizes of DNA sequences measured by sedimentation in alkaline sucrose (21) showed unlabeled sheared DNA $\simeq 500$ nucleotides and ^{3}H DNA $\simeq 300$ nucleotides.

Crude nuclear pellets were obtained by centrifugation of tissue homogenates in 0.25 M sucrose, 10 mM $MgCl_2$, and 10 mM Tris, pH 7.6 at 1000 X g for 10 min. Nuclei were washed once in the same buffer containing 0.1% NP40 (Shell Oil Co.). Two procedures were used to extract HnRNA from the nuclear pellets: (a) conventional phenol extraction as described by Edmonds and Caramela (8), followed by two treatments with DNase I (10 μg/ml in 10 mM $MgCl_2$, 10^{-4} M $CaCl_2$, 10 mM Tris, pH 7.4 at 37°C for 20 min); and (b) treatment with proteinase K (Sigma) at 0.25 mg/g tissue in 5 volumes of buffer containing 1% SDS, 5 mM EDTA, 10 mM Tris, pH 7.5 for 1 h at 40°C, followed by phenol extraction as described above. All HnRNA preparations were passed over Sephadex G-50 to remove salt and small fragments and screened for possible contaminating DNA by a modification of a fluorimetric assay using diaminobenzoic acid (22).

RNA-DNA hybridization reactions were carried out with ^{3}H ScDNA (2-3 μg/ml) and brain HnRNA (20 mg/ml) in 1.2 M NaCl, 1 mM EDTA, 0.05% SDS, 10 mM Tris, pH 7.6 in sealed capillary tubes heated to 100°C for 5 min and then incubated at 67°C for various times up to 5 days. The extent of hybrid formation was determined by treatment of half the sample with purified *Aspergillus oryzae* S_1 nuclease in 0.03 M Na acetate, pH 4.6, 0.3 M NaCl, 3 mM $ZnSO_4$, and 10 μg/ml calf thymus CDNA (24). DNA-DNA duplex formation was determined by treatment with RNase A (20 μg/ml and RNase T_1 (5 μg/ml) in 0.05 NaCl at 37°C for 16 h before S_1 nuclease digestion.

RESULTS

Initially, HnRNA was prepared from brain samples by conventional phenol extraction procedures (8). In this preliminary study of specimens from animals not in the matched samples, phenol-extracted HnRNA from hemicortex of 2 10-y.o. and 2 20-y.o. animals showed considerable variability in yield (0.18 to

0.54 mg RNA/g tissue) and size. Because the extent of hybridization is dependent on the number of different sequences present (sequence diversity) and the rate of reaction varies with the size of the hybridizable sequences, these factors must be controlled when comparing hybridization of different RNA preparations. The variability in size and yield was substantially reduced by incubation of nuclei in the presence of proteinase K and SDS before phenol extraction and this method was used to prepare all HnRNA samples for hybridization. Polyacrylamide gel electrophoresis (15) profiles of HnRNA samples described in Table 6-1 showed no differences in size with 9 samples used for hybridization.

The kinetics of hybridization of ^{3}H ScDNA and HnRNA from macaque left hemicortex are shown in Figure 6-1. Data are shown for one of the matched groups (*M. nemestrina nemestrina*) using HnRNA from a 4-, 10- and 20-y.o. animal. Reaction kinetics and the extent of reaction are the same for all animals. Apparent saturation of the ^{3}H ScDNA sequences occurs at R_0t values above 20,000 and these points have been averaged together in Table 6-1. Hybridization due to DNA-DNA duplex formation (3.6%) was subtracted, and the average values were corrected for reactivity of the ^{3}H ScDNA (90%) as determined by its renaturation with excess unlabeled DNA. Similar data were obtained for the

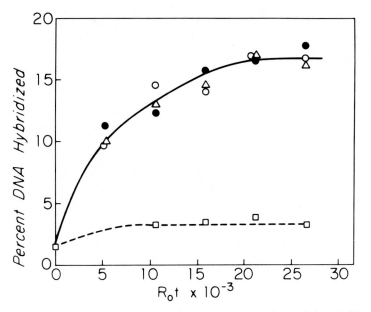

Fig. 6.1. Hybridization of macaque brain HnRNA from 4- (●), 10- (○), and 20-y.o. (△) *M. nemestrina nemestrina* to ^{3}H ScDNA. DNA-DNA duplex formation (□) was determined by resistance of hybrids to RNase.

other two matched groups (*M. nemestrina leonina*). Although no age differences were observed, hybridization values were consistently higher with HnRNA from *M. nemestrina nemestrina* than from *M. nemestrina leonina* (Table 6-1). When data from 4-, 10- and 20-y.o. animals from each matched group are averaged together, the average percent ^{3}H ScDNA hybridized is 12.3 for the 6 *M. nemestrina leonina* and 14.5 for the 3 *M. nemestrina nemestrina*. Despite the small number of animals, this difference is highly significant (p < 0.005, two-tailed *t*-test).

Corrected saturation values (Table 6-1) indicate that approximately 13% of the ^{3}H ScDNA sequences are represented in the HnRNA transcripts. Assuming that only one strand of the DNA is transcribed (and thus only half of the ^{3}H ScDNA is potentially hybridizable to HnRNA), this indicates that at least 26% of ScDNA is expressed in left hemicortex.

Comparison of the yield of HnRNA by age group (Table 6-1) shows a higher yield from brain of 4-y.o. animals than from 10- and 20-y.o. animals. However, when these data are analyzed as a function of postmortem interval (Table 6-2), the delay between cardiorespiratory arrest and the time the tissue is obtained seems to account for some of the differences in yield. Based on data from all ages, the mean yield is reduced from 0.52 mg/g tissue for tissue obtained before cardiovascular arrest to 0.42 mg/g tissue for that obtained 4 min later.

Postmortem intervals of 0 to 4 min did not seem to influence the hybridization results. This is consistent with the expectation that limited random degradation of HnRNA sequences would not influence the extent of hybridization. The samples are all brought to the same concentration for hybridization and the reaction is carried out under conditions of vast RNA excess. Thus, only extensive degradation or loss of particular subsets of sequences would be expected to reduce the hybridization results.

Table 6-2. Yield HnRNA and Percent DNA Hybridized as Function of Delay Between Cardiorespiratory Arrest and Cortical Excision.

Minutes	Yield RNA (mg/g tissue) Age Group (Years)				Percent DNA Hybridized Age Group (Years)			
	4	10	20	Mean	4	10	20	Mean
0 or less	0.55 0.52		0.49	0.53	12.1 15.0		11.3	12.8
+1	0.48		0.45	0.47	13.3		12.3	12.8
+2		0.45 0.51	0.45	0.47		11.8 12.7	14.5	13.0
+4		0.42		0.42		14.0		14.0

In other experiments with brain HnRNA from chimpanzee or human autopsy samples, we have observed significantly decreased HnRNA yield, size and hybridization values with postmortem intervals of 30 min or more. Thus, degradation of HnRNA occurs rapidly, and tissues probably should be obtained within 5 min after death. HnRNA yield and size variation can also be reduced, even in samples obtained rapidly, by the addition of SDS, which prevents nucleic acid-protein interactions, and proteinase K, which hydrolyzes nucleases and other proteins.

DISCUSSION

Our studies with HnRNA from left hemicortex of 4-, 10-, and 20-y.o. female macaques revealed no statistically significant differences in size, concentration, or sequence diversity of RNA transcripts. The similarities of HnRNA sequences in brains of macaques of various ages suggest that change in transcription of these sequences is not a major consequence of aging, compared with the large differences found during normal and abnormal development. RNA-DNA hybridization experiments, which in other systems have shown differences in sequence diversity as measured by the extent of reaction (12) or differences in concentration of various RNA sequences as determined by reaction kinetics (Farquhar, Johnson, Omenn, unpublished results), have not indicated differences in either of these parameters between young and old macaques. Although no direct studies have compared mRNA as a function of age, the lack of aberrant proteins in senescence (9, 23) suggests no major abnormalities in mRNA synthesis. Thus, our data suggest that transcription of noncoding sequences (major fraction of HnRNA) in macaques proceeds similarly to that of coding sequences (mRNA) in brain of other species.

Other RNA-DNA hybridization studies (6) have shown reduced transcription of single copy DNA sequences in old mice. However, measurements of template activity of chromatin from young and old dogs showed no age-related differences in transcription (20). The difficulty of defining senescence in species with quite different lifespans may account for some of the apparent inconsistencies in the results. The macaques in the present study were probably just entering senescence, so we cannot rule out the possibility that alterations in gene expression occur in very old animals.

Although major changes in gene expression do not seem to occur during aging in macaques, small changes in gene activation or synthesis and degradation rates of specific RNA sequences cannot be ruled out. Generally, hybridization methods are sensitive enough to detect differences of ±1% expression of ScDNA. Since transcription of 1% of ScDNA can specify 4000–5000 HnRNA sequences of average size, differences of expression of lesser number of sequences would not be detectable. Just as detailed studies of specific enzymes have revealed differences not seen in protein synthesis in general (9), experiments with limited types of DNA and RNA sequences might reveal restricted classes of molecules that differ in young and old animals. Recent advances in isolation and characterization of tissue-specific mRNA (19) have shown that there are large differences in the abundance of various sequences in a particular cell type and that perturbations such as viral transformation (18) or hormone treatment (17) can change the relative concentrations of cellular RNA molecules. Further studies with classes of abundant or rare sequences or with sequences found in limited regions of the brain might show differences attributable to aging that are not otherwise detectable. This study has shown that high molecular weight nucleic acids suitable for hybridization experiments can be obtained from macaques by the procedures described, making further studies with specific sequences feasible.

ACKNOWLEDGMENTS

We thank Ronald Lee for technical assistance and G. S. McKnight for suggesting SDS-proteinase K extraction procedures. This research was supported by grants RR00166, RR52177, AG62145 from the National Institutes of Health. Dr. Omenn was an investigator of the Howard Hughes Medical Institute.

REFERENCES

1. Bantle, J. A. and Hahn, W. E. (1976): Complexity and characterization of polyadenylated RNA in the mouse brain. *Cell*, 8: 139–150.
2. Brown, I. R., and Church, R. B. (1972): Transcription of nonrepeated DNA during mouse and rabbit development. *Devel. Biol.*, 29: 73–84.
3. Caplan, R., Cheung, S. and Omenn, G. S. (1974): Electrophoretic profiles of proteins of human cerebral cortex: Population and developmental characteristics. *J. Neurochem.*, 22: 517–520.
4. Coon, H. G., Horak, I. David, I. B. (1973): Propagation of both parental mitochondrial DNAs in rat-human mouse-human hybrid cells. *J. Mol. Biol.*, 81: 285–298.
5. Curtis, H. J. (1966): *Biological Mechanisms of Aging.* Springfield, Ill.; Thomas.
6. Cutler, R. G. (1975): Transcription of unique and reiterated DNA sequences in mouse liver and brain tissues as a function of age. *Exp. Geront.*, 10: 37–60.
7. Davidson, E. H., Klein, W. H. and Britten, R. J. (1977): Sequence organization in animal DNA and a speculation on HnRNA as a coordinate regulatory transcript. *Dev. Biol.*, 55: 69–84.
8. Edmonds, M. and Caramela, M. G. (1969): The isolation and characterization of adenosine monophosphate-rich polynucleotides synthesized by Ehrlich ascites cells. *J. Biol. Chem.*, 244: 1314–1324.
9. Finch, C. E. (1972): Enzyme activities, gene function and aging in mammals. *Exp. Geront.*, 7: 53–67.

10. Grouse, L., Chilton, M. D., and McCarthy, B. J. (1972): Hybridization of ribonucleic acid with unique sequences of mouse deoxyribonucleic acid. *Biochemistry*, **11:** 798–805.

11. Grouse, L., Omenn, G. S. and McCarthy, B. J. (1973): Studies by DNA-RNA hybridization of transcriptional diversity in human brain. *J. Neurochem.*, **20:** 1063–1073.

12. Grouse, L. D., Schrier, B. K., Bennett, E. L., Rosenweig, M. R. and Nelson, P. G. (1978): Effect of environmental complexity on rat brain total RNA diversity. *J. Neurochem.* **30:** 191–203.

13. Hahn, H. P. von. (1970): Structural and functional changes in nucleoprotein during the aging of the cell. *Gerontologia*, **16:** 116–128.

14. Kohne, D. E. (1970): Evolution of higher-organism DNA. *Quarterly Rev. Biophys.*, **3:** 327–375.

15. Loening, U. E. (1967): The fractionation of high molecular weight ribonucleic acid by polyacrylamide gel electrophoresis. *Biochem. J.*, **102:** 251–257.

16. Orgel, L. E. (1963): The maintenance of the accuracy of protein synthesis and its relevance to aging. *Proc. Nat. Acad. Sci. USA*, **49:** 517–521.

17. Parker, M. G. and Mainwaring, W. P. (1977): Effects of androgens on the complexity of poly (A) RNA from rat prostate. *Cell*, **12:** 401–407.

18. Rolton, H. A., Birnie, G. D., and Paul, J. (1977): The diversity and specificity of nuclear and polysomal poly A+ RNA populations in normal and MSV transformed cells. *Cell Diff.*, **6:** 25–39.

19. Ryffel, G. U. and McCarthy, B. J. (1975): Complexity of cytoplasmic RNA in different mouse tissues measured by hybridization of polyadenylated RNA to complementary DNA. *Biochemistry*, **14:** 1379–1385.

20. Shirey, T. and Sobel, H. (1972): Compositional and transcriptional properties of chromatins isolated from cardiac of young-mature and old dogs. *Exp. Geront.*, **7:** 15–29.

21. Studier, F. W. (1965): Sedimentation studies of the size and shape of DNA. *J. Mol. Biol.*, **11:** 373–390.

22. Thomas, P. S. and Farquhar, M. N. (1978): Specific measurement of DNA in nuclei and nucleic acids using diaminobenzoic acid. *Analytical Biochemistry*, **89:** 35–44.

23. Vaughn, W. J. (1977): Electrophoretic analysis of brain proteins from young adult and aged mice. *Gerontology*, **23:** 110–126.

24. Vogt, V. M. (1973): Purification and further properties of single-strand-specific nuclease from *Aspergillus oryzae*. *Eur. J. Biochem*, **33:** 192–200.

7

Monoamine and Neurophysin Systems

John R. Sladek, Jr., Thomas H. McNeill, Patricia Walker, and Celia D. Sladek

Departments of Anatomy and Neurology,
University of Rochester School of Medicine,
Rochester, New York

INTRODUCTION

Histofluorescence analysis of the mammalian brain indicates a widespread distribution of monoamines (MA) throughout the central nervous system (14, 15, 23). Numerous functional correlates have been determined for these dopaminergic (DA), noradrenergic (NE), and serotonergic (5-HT) neuronal systems. That DA is involved in the control of basal ganglion motor activity and its dysfunctional state in Parkinsonism is well appreciated (19). NE and 5-HT both seem to affect the conscious state (27) and play a role in thermal regulation (29). Endocrine mechanisms are affected significantly by the tubero-infundibular DA system and the reticulo-infundibular NE system. Extensive neuroendocrine studies indicate a MA influence in the control of various hypothalamic releasing hormones (13, 24, 31) and vasopressin (28).

Aging is accompanied by a variety of changes in the morphology (5, 33), physiology and neurochemistry of the brain. Among the latter are changes in MA synthetic enzymes demonstrated in various mammals, including man (10, 25). Accordingly, certain functions influenced by MAs undergo age-related alterations (7, 11).

A previous study examined some histofluorescence correlates of aging in human brain (30). Perikaryal MA groups including the locus ceruleus (LC), substantia nigra (SN) and hypothalamic arcuate nucleus contained a modest number of weak to medium fluorescent perikarya. Their number and intensity were higher in brain slices incubated with alpha-methylnorepinephrine. These important findings, however, are difficult to correlate solely with age-related causes, owing to technical problems in applying the histofluorescence technique to human brain, and to heterogeneity of the sample population. A more uniform population can be achieved by the use of nonhuman primates as reported here.

METHODS

The subjects were 9 female pigtail macaques (*Macaca nemestrina*), 3 each of 3 different ages (4, 10 and 20 y.o.). Their brains were removed within 17 to 27 min after death, and the brain stem and hypothalamus were prepared for fluorescence histochemistry as previously described (18). The 9 macaques were grouped into 3 sets (each containing a 4-, 10- and 20-y.o.) for comparisons and each set was freeze-dried as a unit for 8 weeks, following which the brains were vapor-treated with paraformaldehyde for 2 hr (65% relative humidity at 80°C). Each set was embedded into a single paraffin block and serially sectioned at 10 μM as a single specimen.

Quantitative analysis was performed on a modified Leitz MPV-2 microspectrofluorometer. Instrument settings were standardized during all spectral scans. The LC, SN and nucleus raphe dorsalis (Rd) were chosen as three representative loci for NE, DA and 5-HT neurons, respectively. Spectral scans were made on randomly chosen cells on 3-9 neuroanatomical sections from each nucleus of each animal and at least 10 neuronal perikarya were analyzed in each section.

The measuring diaphragm was fixed at a 10 μM diameter for all scans. This allowed us to measure fluorescence of the perinuclear cytoplasm of each neuron without surrounding neuropil fluorescence. The mean and standard deviation of all measures were calculated and plotted.

Qualitative analysis was performed with narrow-band excitation filters and K460 barrier filters. This enabled a positive distinction between the blue fluorescence of catecholamines (CA), i.e., NE and DA vs. the yellow fluorescence of 5-HT.

Immunocytochemistry of neurophysin was performed on alternate sections to those examined for histofluorescence using bovine neurophysin antiserum (BNP) (26, 36). Neurophysin-containing cell bodies were analyzed for relative numbers and neurophysin content. Sections for cross-comparisons of BNP patterns in young and old animals were stained simultaneously to prevent variations due to the technical procedure.

All analyses were made on coded sections so that the observer was unaware of the animals' ages.

RESULTS

Perikaryal Groups

MA histofluorescence was observed within neuronal perikarya of brain stem loci in all animals. The positions of CA-containing perikarya corresponded to those reported for other primate species, viz., within the lateral reticular formation, LC, subceruleus, and ventral tegmental area. Subjective observation of the aged animals indicated that CA fluorescence of the LC was more intense than that of the SN or 5-HT fluorescence of the Rd, although in the 4-y.o. the fluorescence intensity values of these groups seemed comparable. While the position of MA cell groups did not vary with age, the intensity of MA histofluorescence of individual neurons within specific groups displayed qualitative and quantitative variations between different ages.

Old macaques displayed considerably less 5-HT and a marked accumulation of lipofuscin. This made it hard to discern 5-HT because the fluorescence of lipofuscin and 5-HT was often similar in color. However, the physical form of the fluorescence was different for each substance: 5-HT appeared as nongranular, diffuse cytoplasmic fluorescence, whereas lipofuscin appeared in the form of intense, punctate granules. Furthermore, spectral analysis revealed a distinct difference between the wave lengths of these fluorophors and yielded positive 5-HT spectra in all ages. 5-HT fluorescence had to be examined carefully because 0.5- to 3-min exposure to blue light could produce a fading of the 5-HT fluorophor, but not the lipofuscin fluorophor. Thus, if large areas were exposed to blue light fluorescence for extended periods, the 5-HT fluorophor could be overlooked. To avoid this problem, we used tungsten, dark-field illumination for locating raphe nuclei before fluorescence analysis.

All known brain stem CA cell groups in macaque were examined for intraneuronal CA and lipofuscin content. Individual perikarya were graded visually for histofluorescence intensity. Table 7-1 summarizes the findings for each brain stem CA cell group in 4- and 20-y.o. macaques. Quantitative spectral data are described below.

Perikarya containing 5-HT fluoresced with a strong intensity in the young adult, but occurred in fewer numbers and were less intense in the aged adults. The distribution of 5-HT cell groups in *M. nemestrina* corresponded to patterns reported for *M. arctoides* (35). In general, 5-HT perikarya were distributed throughout the raphe nuclei and extended laterally into the adjacent reticular formation with some extension of 5-HT perikarya, for example, into the LC as reported in *M. arctoides* (37).

CA-containing perikarya were not seen routinely in diencephalic groups in young animals, but were seen occasionally in 20-y.o. specimens. While CA cell groups A-11 to A-14 (3) have not been definitively mapped in the macaque

Table 7-1. Relative Intensity (visually graded) of CA
Fluorescence in Brain Stem of 4- and 20-y.o. *M. nemestrina.*

Cell Group[1]	CA Intensity	
	4 Yr.	20 Yr.
M1	B	D
M2	B	B
M4	B	B
M5	B	B
M6	B	B
Msc	B	B
M7	B	B
M8	D	D
M9	D	VD
M10	D	D
Mcg	B	B
Mdr	B	B
Area Postrema	B	B

[1]Nomenclature for MA cell groups from Garver and Sladek (15); M
prefix for macaque substituted for A prefix used in rat by Dahlström and Fuxe to accommodate interspecies differences. Fluorescent perikarya were graded: B, bright; D, dull; VD, very dull.
Three animals were examined in each age group.

diencephalon, comparable groups do exist.   Those corresponding roughly to
A-11 and A-12 (arcuate nucleus) of the rat were particularly evident in the older
monkeys.   They appeared as small, intensely fluorescent perikarya which were
difficult at times to differentiate from the intense CA varicosity fluorescence of
the arcuate nucleus. CA perikarya of the hypothalamus were generally devoid of
lipofuscin although pigment granules occasionally were observed within them.

Varicosity Patterns

CA-containing varicosities were seen throughout the brain stem and hypothalamus in unevenly dense patterns.   Certain areas did not seem to have a reduction
in varicosity density distribution with age.   These included the brain stem reticular
formation, particularly at mesencephalic levels, nuclei of the hypothalamus, and
the various raphe nuclei.   However, certain other nuclei, such as the hypoglossal
nuclei, demonstrated a reduction in CA density with age (Figure 7-1).   The young
macaques displayed a 2+ (low) density of CA varicosities, some often in contact
with the large multipolar neurons of the hypoglossal nucleus.   However, 10- and
20-y.o. macaques displayed few, if any, varicosities within this nucleus.
Many varicosities, although present in routine numbers, were unusually large

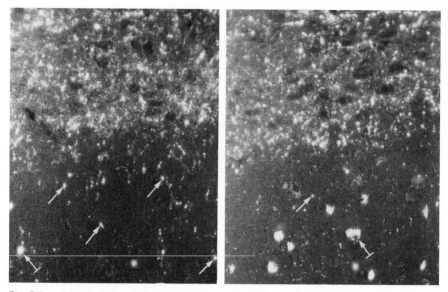

Fig. 7-1. Hypoglossal and dorsal motor vagal (DMX) nuclei in *M. nemestrina*. Left: in 4-y.o. animal, hypoglossal nucleus (→) has low density of CA varicosities and some lipofuscin (↦), while DMX (upper third) has medium density of CA varicosities. Right: in 20-y.o. animal, hypoglossal nucleus has fewer CA varicosities and increased lipofuscin, while DMX pattern remains constant. ✕ 145.

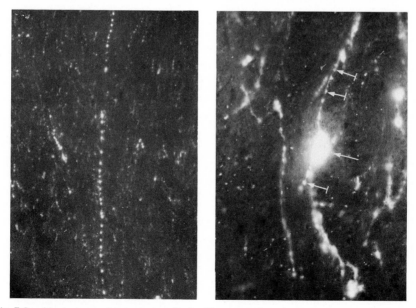

Fig. 7-2. Ventral noradrenergic bundle in *M. nemestrina*. Left: Typical linear profile of fine-sized varicosities in hypothalamus of a 4-y.o. animal. ✕ 95. Right: Linear profile of fine-sized varicosities (↦) showing unusually large swelling (→) in 20-y.o. animal. ✕ 300.

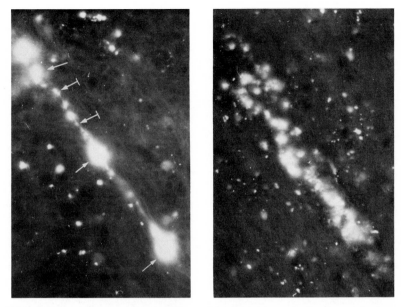

Fig. 7-3. Patterns of varicosities in 20-y.o. *M. nemestrina.*   Left: Unusually large CA varicosities (→) in linear profile with normal varicosities (↦) in pontine reticular formation. ×600. Right: Aggregate of medium-large varicosities (common in older macaques) in dorsal hypothalamus. ×450.

in the older animals (Figures 7-2, 7-3). Often a linear profile of uniform, fine-sized varicosities was interrupted by 1 to 4 varicosities of 5 to 10 times greater size. Such varicosities were abundant in 10- and 20-y.o. macaques and uncommon in 4-y.o. animals. Such aberrant varicosities were heterogeneously distributed, and were sparse or nonexistent in the superior and inferior colliculi, dorsal motor vagal nucleus, periaqueductal grey of the mesencephalon, and reticular formation (Fig. 7-2).

Table 7-2. CA Varicosity Distribution in Hypothalamic Nuclei of 4- and 20-y.o. *M. nemestrina.* [1]

Nucleus or Region	4-Year Old	20-Year Old
Arcuate	3–4+	4–5+
Dorsomedial	4–5+	4–5+
Median eminence	5+	5+
Paraventricular	4–5+	4–5+
Suprachiasmatic	2+	2+
Supraoptic	4–5+	4–5+
Ventromedial	1+	1+

[1] Varicosity density is graded on a standard 1+ (very low) to 5+ (very high) scale (12).

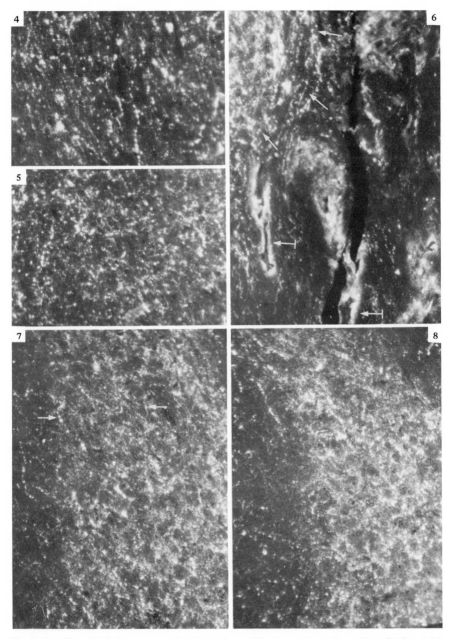

Fig. 7-4. (Top left) Arcuate nucleus in a 4-y.o. *M. nemestrina.* A medium (3+) to high density (4+) of CA varicosities characterizes this nucleus in the young adult. ×100.

Fig. 7-5. Arcuate nucleus in a 20-y.o. *M. nemestrina.* The density of CA varicosities appears slightly higher than that of the 4-y.o. animal (Fig. 4). ×100.

Scattered throughout the brain stem and hypothalamus were groupings, or aggregates, of varicosities (Figure 7-3). In many instances, these aggregates were composed of numerous tightly packed varicosities of different sizes; they were not observed in the 4-y.o. animal.

CA varicosity patterns were seen in high densities within the hypothalamus of young and old animals (Table 7-2). Very few differences were noted in terminal distribution patterns, although a slight shift toward higher density was observed in the arcuate nucleus of older specimens (Figures 7-4, 7-5). The median eminence contained a maximum density (5+) of varicosities in the contact zone, especially around the portal vessels (Figure 7-6).

Numerous varicosities appeared in juxtaposition to nonfluorescent neuronal perikarya in many nuclei including the arcuate nucleus, dorsomedial nucleus and the magnocellular components of the paraventricular nucleus (PVN) (Figures 7-7, 7-8) and to a lesser extent, supraoptic nucleus (SON). Apparent axosomatic juxtaposition was verified in part by optically dissecting neurons by fine-focus adjustment through successive focal planes in a single tissue section. This allowed us to view the perimeter of a single perikaryon with its adjacent CA varicosities. CA varicosities often surrounded the proximal portion of dendrites.

Ascending Pathways

CA fluorescence was seen in the dorsal NE pathway in all ages. The bundle seemed to originate from neurons of the LC and ascended toward the cerebellum and cerebrum as dense collections of intensely fluorescent, nonvaricose linear strands. A short distance rostral to their origin, some fibers became more varicose and the entire bundle appeared as a mixture of varicose and nonvaricose fibers (Figure 7-9). This ascending pathway was somewhat reduced in size and intensity in the 10- and 20-y.o. animals.

The ventral NE pathway also was visible in all ages. It seemed to arise from medullary and pontine cell groups (i.e., M_1, M_2, M_5, Msc) as described previously (16). In the pons this collection of fibers passed through the nucleus subceruleus from which it appeared to gain fibers. Perikarya gave rise to intense linear profiles of fine to often large, interconnected varicosities which extended rostrally

---

Fig. 7-6. (Top right) Arcuate nucleus, median eminence in a 20-y.o. *M. nemestrina* showing a high density of CA varicostities (→). Intense, CA fluorescence (⊢→) surrounds portal vessels of the median eminence. ×160.

Fig. 7-7. (Bottom left) Paraventricular nucleus of the hypothalamus in a 4-y.o. *M. nemestrina*. This magnocellular, neurosecretory nucleus is characterized by a high density of CA varicosities, many of which appear in a pericellular position (→). ×120.

Fig. 7-8. (Bottom right) Paraventricular nucleus in a 20-y.o. *M. nemestrina* showing density and cellular position of CA varicosities similar to those in 4-y.o. animal (Fig. 7). ×120.

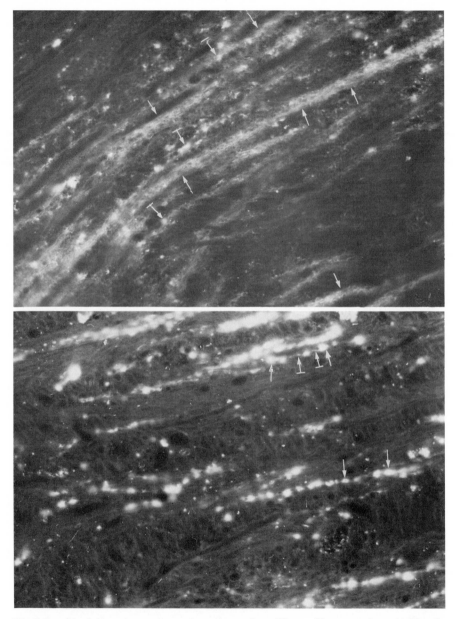

Fig. 7-9. (Top) Dorsal noradrenergic pathway in a 20-y.o. *M. nemestrina.* Unlike the ventral pathway, the dorsal pathway appeared as a combination of varicose (⊢→) and non-varicose (→) fluorescence. Nonvaricose fluorescence predominated in the proximal portion of bundle (illustrated) near the LC and gave rise to varicose profiles distally in the mesencephalon and diencephalon. ×320.

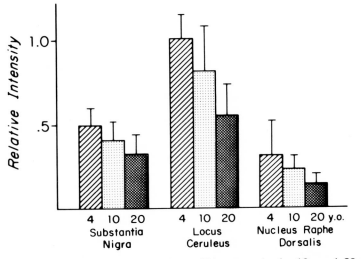

Fig. 7-11. Mean relative intensity of different MA groups in 4-, 10-, and 20-y.o. *M. nemestrina.* Relative intensity is plotted as a function of age. Mean ± S.D.

through the diencephalon (Figure 7-10). Qualitative differences were not noted in the appearance of the ventral NE pathway in different aged specimens.

Lipofuscin Fluorescence

Lipofuscin autofluorescence also appeared within the cytoplasm of MA neurons, although never to the extent as within non-MA neurons. For example, the inferior olivary complex and the red nucleus, which are not sites of MA perikarya, demonstrated extensive accumulations of lipofuscin fluorescence in older animals. Similar accumulations were seen in older animals within nuclei of the reticular formation and the basilar pons, geniculate bodies, superior and inferior colliculi, efferent nuclei of the cranial nerves, and the hypothalamus.

Lipofuscin within non-MA perikarya was a fairly uniform finding, but MA neurons had more variable amounts of this pigment. For example, the LC displayed many perikarya that were devoid of lipofuscin together with other perikarya that contained it. Furthermore, the number of perikarya per MA group that contained lipofuscin and the amount of lipofuscin per perikaryon increased with age. For example, the percentage of lipofuscin-bearing perikarya in the LC rose from 20% in the 4-y.o.'s to 50% in the 20-y.o. animals. Similar increases

---

Fig. 7-10. (Bottom) Ventral noradrenergic pathway in a 20-y.o. *M. nemestrina.* Linear profiles of varicosities (→) often interconnected by nonvaricose segments of the axon (↦) distinguished this pathway in all ages examined. ×350.

were noted in most other MA groups of the pons and medulla, although even in 20-y.o. animals the amount of lipofuscin contained in MA perikarya was considerably less than that seen in non-MA perikarya. Mesencephalic and hypothalamic MA groups were relatively free of lipofuscin in all ages examined.

Quantitative Microspectrofluorometry

Relative intensities (RI) of neuronal perikarya of the SN, LC and Rd of the 4-, 10- and 20-y.o. macaques are shown in Fig. 7-11. Since these brains were processed simultaneously, embedded in a single block of paraffin and sectioned as a single specimen, it is possible to compare relative mean intensity values of the

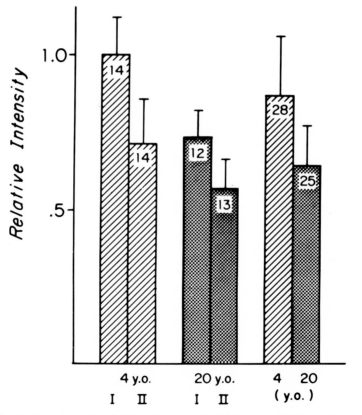

Fig. 7-12.   Relative intensity of NE perikarya of the LC in 4- and 20-y.o. *M. nemestrina.* Group I neurons did not contain lipofuscin, group II neurons did. Bars at far right represent mean RI of all cells scanned in the 4-y.o. vs. 20-y.o. animals. Mean ± S.D. Number of cells analyzed in each group appears in each bar.

3 nuclei. Fluorescence intensity was determined for 10 cells on 7, 9, and 3 sections respectively in the SN, LC and Rd. Perikarya of the 20-y.o. animal had significantly less fluorescence intensity than those of the 4- and 10-y.o. animals in all 3 nuclear groups (p $<$ 0.001, Student's t-test). While the mean intensity was lower in the 10-y.o. than in the 4-y.o. animals, this difference was not statistically significant. However, differences between 10- and 20-y.o. animals were statistically significant. The data also indicate that mean intensity of ceruleal perikarya exceeded that of the SN, which exceeded Rd perikarya.

   Figure 7-12 illustrates the RI of NE-containing LC perikarya from a pair of 4- and 20-y.o. animals. In each brain, NE perikarya were grouped according to

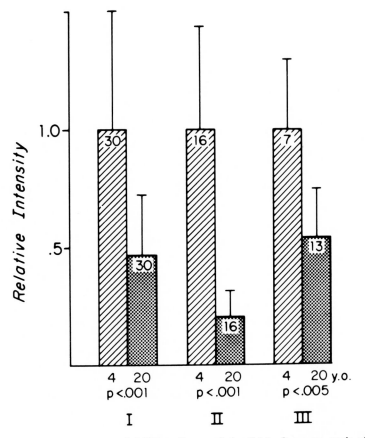

Fig. 7-13. Relative intensity of 5-HT perikarya of the Rd in 3 groups, each of which included one 4- and one 20-y.o. *M. nemestrina.* Mean ± S.D. Numbers of calls analyzed in each animal appear in each bar.

the presence (Group II) or absence (Group I) of autofluorescent lipofuscin granules. In both animals the mean NE fluorescence intensity was significantly less in perikarya with lipofuscin than without it ($p < 0.001$). The mean intensity of the lipofuscin-free neurons was significantly less in the 20-y.o. than in the 4-y.o. animal ($p < 0.001$). The mean NE intensity of lipofuscin-positive neurons also was significantly lower in the 20-y.o. animals than in the 4-y.o. ($p < 0.001$). The mean intensity of the pooled groups is significantly lower in the 20-y.o. brain than in the 4-y.o. brain ($p < 0.001$) and the difference between the means is similar to that observed in LC neurons of the animals presented in Figure 7-11.

RIs of 5-HT containing neurons of the raphe were analyzed in 3 pairs of 4-y.o. and 20-y.o. macaques (Figure 7-13). In each pair the mean RI was significantly lower in perikarya from the older animal (Student's t-test). RI values were normalized to the mean intensity of the 4-y.o. animal in each group. It was not possible to analyze 5-HT content independent of lipofuscin in 20-y.o. animals owing to the predominance of this pigment in raphe perikarya.

Neurophysin Localization

Brown reaction precipitate representative of the magnocellular peptide neurophysin was found primarily in the perikarya of the SON and PVN and in their axonal processes. The staining intensity of these magnocellular perikarya in the 4-y.o. animals seemed similar to that seen in Bouin's fixed tissue prepared for routine immunocytochemistry (40), suggesting that the antigenicity of the peptide remained strong following the freeze-drying process (26). Semiquantitative comparisons of hormonal content and neuronal cell number within the SON and PVN were made between the 4-, 10-, and 20-y.o. monkeys. A decrease in the intensity and total number of cells stained with BNP was seen in the PVN in the 20-y.o. compared with the 4-y.o. animal (Figures 7-14, 7-15). Randomized cell counts (21) of stained cells within the nucleus showed a 50% decrease in the number of cells heavily stained for BNP in the 20-y.o. animals. Not all cells that stained in the PVN presented a homogeneous staining intensity. Most cells in the 20-y.o. seemed to stain much lighter than in the 4-y.o. animals while some seemed to stain with the same intensity as in the younger animals. There was a decrease in the number and hormone content of the axonal fibers of the hypothalamo-neurohypophyseal tract in the 20-y.o. animals (Figures 7-16, 7-17). Some of the Herring bodies measured as large as 100 μM in diameter. Observations in the SON were similar, but not totally congruent with those of the PVN. There was a prominent increase in the number and size of Herring bodies and a significant decrease in the number and staining intensity in the fibers leaving the SON in the 20-y.o. monkey. The medial portion of the SON showed no significant difference in the staining intensity or number of cells stained in the 20-y.o. animals. However, in the most rostral portion of the more lateral regions of the SON there was about a 50% decrease in the number of dark-staining cells. Unlike

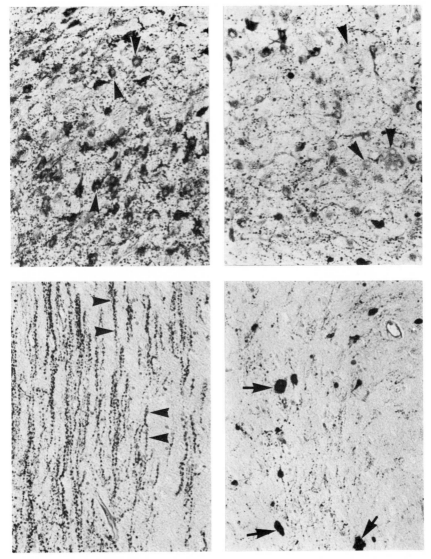

Fig. 7-14. (Top left) Paraventricular nucleus in a 4-y.o. *M. nemestrina.* Immunocyto-chemical staining for bovine neurophysin depicts immunoreactive perikarya (▶) and a dense reticulum of positive staining beaded fibers. ×90.

Fig. 7-15. (Top right) Paraventricular nucleus in a 20-y.o. *M. nemestrina* showing a de-crease in the number of cells stained and in the staining intensity of some of the cells (▶) compared with that in the younger macaque (Fig. 14). ×90.

Fig. 7-16. (Bottom left) Hypothalamo-neurohypophyseal tract in a 4-y.o. *M. nemestrina* showing numerous beaded fibers (▶) on a course to the neural lobe. ×100.

Fig. 7-17. (Bottom right) Hypothalamo-neurohypophyseal tract in a 20-y.o. *M. nemestrina* showing a decrease in number of fibers. The presence of large Herring bodies (→) is a prominent feature of the old macaque. ×100.

the cells in the PVN, the remaining cells stained with the same intensity as in the younger animal.

DISCUSSION

Spectral quantitation revealed significant differences in intraneuronal MA content within the LC, SN and Rd in young and aged macaques. The relation of reduced neuronal neurotransmitter content to neural activity in these neurons is unknown. The tuberoinfundibular DA system has been investigated extensively in this regard and the proposal is that DA neurons of that system demonstrate greater fluorescence intensity in active states than in inactive states (13, 22). From this perspective, one might interpret the decreased fluorescence of MA neurons with age to reflect a decrease in neuronal traffic. On the other hand, it could represent constant or increased activity with inadequate synthesis to maintain transmitter stores.

The LC demonstrated the highest relative, intraneuronal content of MA of any of the nuclear groups examined. Fluorescence of the dorsal NE pathway appeared less prominent in old versus young specimens, consistent with the decreased amount of NE seen within the LC, the bed nucleus of this pathway. Brody (6) found that in the human, the LC was one of few brain stem nuclei examined that underwent a decrease in neuronal number with age. Cell counts have not been completed in the present study; however, coupled with Brody's observation, the finding of reduced NE in the LC and dorsal NE pathway of nonhuman primates suggests that cerebral function of the aged primate may suffer both a downward shift in neuronal numbers and a decreased biosynthetic capability in the cells that remain.

The SN also demonstrated a progressive decrease in the level of neuronal fluorescence with increased age. Reduced nigrostriatal DA in humans is associated with Parkinson's disease, a relatively common syndrome in the elderly. Although Parkinsonian symptoms were not observed in the 20-y.o. monkeys, the lowered intraneuronal DA levels could indicate a pre-Parkinsonian state, which might not result in extrapyramidal motor deficit until a more advanced age resulted in a further reduction in DA content.

A common feature of aged macaque brain stem and hypothalamus was the presence of unusually large varicosities, often seen in continuity with strings of normal-sized varicosities. This observation supports a similar finding in aged human brain stem (30). It was a prominent feature of the ascending fibers of the ventral noradrenergic bundle in the macaque, and was also seen elsewhere in brain stem and hypothalamus. These structures are somewhat reminiscent of the fluorescent droplets described in the rat hypophysis and median eminence (1, 2). Björklund *et al.* (1) indicated that these droplets might represent dilated stumps of degenerating axons, especially since they contained lamellated membrane structures associated with disintegrated vesicles. If that interpretation is true, the present findings might represent degeneration of CA terminal systems in the aged animal. They also occurred in the younger adult to a lesser extent. They have not been seen in the ascending noradrenergic systems of neonatal macaques (16).

Lipofuscin was a common feature of all animals examined. Consistent with a previous report (4), the highest intraneuronal content of lipofuscin was seen in the oldest animal. The MA cell groups appeared more resistant to the accumulation of lipofuscin than the non-MA cell groups, with considerably less lipofuscin within the LC than within the hypoglossal nucleus or inferior olivary complex. Analysis of the relation of lipofuscin accumulation to intraneuronal NE content revealed that neurons that contained lipofuscin in a given age group had relatively less NE than neurons free of lipofuscin. However, factors other than lipofuscin accumulation must also be responsible for the reduced MA content in neurons of the aged animal, because NE content of lipofuscin-free neurons of the 20-y.o. animal was significantly lower than that of lipofuscin-free neurons of the young adult as well.

The visualization of both the ventral and dorsal ascending noradrenergic bundles in older animals extends our earlier observation in which we found the ventral bundle in both neonates and young adults, but observed the dorsal bundle only in neonates (16). The dorsal bundle, although reduced in intensity and harder to see in the older animals, was probably discovered because we used a more refined optical system in the present investigation. Ploem illumination, oil immersion objectives and narrow band excitation all lend themselves to the optimal visualization of low level fluorescence, even within preterminal axonal systems. These bundles do not normally fluoresce in adult rat (39) or cat (34). Why they remain a constant feature in the macaque but not in rat or cat is unknown at present. One can speculate that the systems either are more active in the phylogenetically more advanced brain or that, at least in the ventral system, they possess a series of terminal collaterals, through the ascending portions of the bundle within the reticular formation and diencephalon, which may integrate ventral noradrenergic activity with lower centers.

The present data concerning age-related changes in the number and hormone content of magnocellular neurosecretory neurons of the PVN and SON as well as histologic changes in the hypothalamo-neurohypophyseal tract suggest a decreased availability of neurohypophyseal hormones in the 20-y.o. macaque. Since the perikaryon is not a storage site for newly synthesized hormone, this decrease in staining may reflect a decrease in hormone synthesis accompanying old age. That most cells of the PVN and only some cells of the SON show these changes suggests that this is not a generalized phenomenon but a specific alteration in individual perikarya. However, whether this potential disruption in synthetic machinery is due to an alteration in afferent stimuli, receptor activity or *in situ* alteration in protein synthesis is uncertain. Since BNP cross reacts with both neurophysins in the monkey (41), a more detailed evaluation of age-related changes specific to either oxytocin-containing or vasopressin-containing cells cannot be made from the present data. Experiments using antisera generated against human estrogen-stimulated neurophysin specific for oxytocin and human nicotine-stimulated neurophysin specific for vasopressin are currently underway on these animals in an attempt to answer such questions.

The decreased staining intensity in the hypothalamo-neurohypophyseal tract as well as the increased size and number of Herring bodies confirm previous observations in the aged rat (32). The occurrence and morphologic structure of Herring bodies in normal neurosecretory neurons are similar to those seen in degenerating processes; however, autophagy does occur in Herring bodies in younger tissues, so the presence of these structures does not necessarily represent a degenerative process (9). It is generally accepted that the formation of Herring bodies represents an accumulation of granular vesicles in a cell process due to a slow-down or disturbance in axoplasmic flow (38). Experimental findings in fish (20) have shown that the formation of degenerating cells and large Herring bodies after sustained starvation may be attributed to a decrease in axoplasmic flow. Geinisman *et al.* (17) recently reported a decrease in axoplasmic transport of glycoproteins in the septal hippocampal pathway in senescent rats. The decrease in apparent hormone content in the hypothalamo-neurohypophyseal tract and the increase in the number of Herring bodies may suggest a decrease in axoplasmic flow accompanying old age in the neurosecretory pathway as well.

The present investigation has examined certain histofluorescence and immunocytochemical correlates of aging in the nonhuman primate brain. Significant decreases were seen in MA content of identified neuronal perikarya of the LC, SN and Rd, and in BNP content of the PVN. If reduced transmitter content is equated with functional deficit as in the case of Parkinson's disease, these data may indicate an alteration in the activity of MA and neuropeptide systems. These changes might be manifested in MA-influenced activities, such as temperature regulation, arousal, sleep and neuroendocrine balance, all of which can show functional alterations in the elderly.

ACKNOWLEDGMENTS

This research was supported by National Institutes of Health grants AG00847, AM19761 and NS00259 to the University of Rochester, and RR00166, RR52177 and AG62145 to the University of Washington, and by a Rochester Plan Summer Fellowship. We thank Dr. Earl A. Zimmerman for providing the bovine neurophysin antiserum used in this study.

REFERENCES

1. Björklund, A., Enemar, A., and Falck, B. (1968): Monoamines in the hypothalamo-hypophyseal system of the mouse with special reference to the ontogenetic aspects. *Z. Zellforsch.*, **89**: 590–607.
2. Björklund, A., Falck, B., Nobin, A., and Stenevi, U. (1974): Organization of the dopamine and noradrenaline innervation of the median eminence-pituitary region in the rat. In: *Neurosecretion–The Final Neuroendocrine Pathway*, edited by F. Knowles and L. Vollrath, pp. 209–222. Berlin; Springer-Verlag.
3. Björklund, A., Moore, R. Y., Nobin, A., and Stenevi, U. (1973): The organization of tubero-hypophyseal and reticulo-infundibular catecholamine neuron systems in the rat brain. *Brain Res.*, **51**: 171–191.
4. Brizzee, K. R., Ordy, J. M., and Kaack, B. (1974): Early appearance and regional differences in intraneuronal and extraneuronal lipofuscin accumulation with age in the brain of a non-human primate (*Macaca mulatta*). *J. Gerontol.*, **29**: 366–381.
5. Brody, H. (1955): Organization of the cerebral cortex. III. A study of aging in the human cerebral cortex. *J. Comp. Neurol.*, **102**: 511–556.
6. Brody, H. (1976): An examination of cerebral cortex and brainstem aging. In: *Neurobiology of Aging*, edited by R. D. Terry and S. Gershon. New York; Raven Press.
7. Clemens, J. A. and Meites, J. (1971): Neuroendocrine status of old constant-estrous rats. *Neuroendocrinology*, **7**: 249–256.
8. Dahlström, A., and Fuxe, K. (1965): Evidence for the existence of monoamine neurons in the central nervous system. I. Demonstration of monoamines in cell bodies of brainstem neurons. *Acta. Physiol. Scand.*, **62**: 1–55. Suppl. 232.
9. Dellman, H. D. (1973): Degeneration and regeneration of neurosecretory systems. *Int. Rev. Cytol.*, **36**: 215–315.
10. Finch, C. E. (1973): Catecholamine metabolism in the brains of aging male mice. *Brain Res.*, **52**: 261–276.
11. Finch, C. E. (1976): The regulation of physiological changes during mammalian aging. *Quart. Rev. Biol.*, **51**: 49–83.
12. Fuxe, K. (1965): Evidence for the existence of monoamine neurons in the central nervous system. III. The monoamine nerve terminal. *Z. Zellforsch.*, **65**: 573–596.
13. Fuxe, K., and Hökfelt, T. (1969): Catecholamines in the hypothalamus and the pituitary gland. In: *Frontiers in Neuroendocrinology*, edited by W. Ganong and L. Martini, pp. 47–96. New York; Oxford University Press.
14. Fuxe, K., Hökfelt, T., and Ungerstedt, U. (1969): Distribution of monoamines in the mammalian central nervous system by histochemical studies. In: *Metabolism of Amines in the Brain*, edited by G. Hooper. London; Macmillan.
15. Garver, D. L., and Sladek, J. R., Jr. (1975): Monoamine distribution in primate brain. I. Catecholamine-containing perikarya in the brain stem of *Macaca speciosa*. *J. Comp. Neurol.*, **159**: 289–304.
16. Garver, D. L. and Sladek, J. R., Jr. (1976): Monoamine distribution in primate brain. II. Brainstem catecholaminergic pathways in *Macaca speciosa* (*arctoides*). *Brain Res.*, **103**: 176–182.
17. Geinisman, Y., Bondareff, W., and Telser, A. (1977): Transport of (^{3}H) fucose labeled glycoproteins in the septohippocampal pathway of young adult and senescent rats. *Brain Res.*, **125**: 182–186.
18. Hoffman, D. L., and Sladek, J. R., Jr. (1973): The distribution of catecholamines within the inferior olivary complex of the gerbil and rabbit. *J. Comp. Neurol.*, **151**: 101–112.
19. Hornykiewicz, O. (1966): Dopamine (3-hydroxytryptamine) and brain function. *Pharmacol. Rev.*, **18**: 925–964.

20. Jasinski, A. (1968): Modifications in the neurosecretory system of the fish, *Misgurnus fossilis*, induced by lasting inanition. *Z. Zellforsch.*, 88: 537–548.
21. Konigsmark, B. W. (1970): Methods for the counting of neurons. In: *Contemporary Research Methods in Neuroanatomy*, edited by W. J. H. Nauta and S. O. E. Egbessor, pp. 315–340. New York; Springer Verlag.
22. Lichtensteiger, W. (1971): Effect of electrical stimulation on the fluorescence intensity of catecholamine-containing tuberal nerve cells. *J. Physiol.*, 218: 63–84.
23. Lindvall, O., and Björklund, A. (1974): The organization of the ascending catecholamine neuron systems in the rat brain as revealed by the glyoxylic acid fluorescence method. *Acta Physiol. Scand.*, **Suppl.** 412: 1–48.
24. McCann, S. M., Kalra, P. S., Kalra, S. P., Donoso, A. O., Bishop, W., Schneider, H. P. G., Fawcett, C. P., and Krulich, L. (1972): The role of monoamines in the control of gonadotropin and prolactin secretion. In: *Gonadotropins*, edited by B. Saxena, C. Beling, and H. Gandy, pp. 49–60. New York; John Wiley.
25. McGeer, E. G., and McGeer, P. L. (1975): Age changes in the human for some enzymes associated with metabolism of catecholamines, GABA, and acetylcholine. In: *Neurobiology of Aging*, edited by J. M. Ordy and K. R. Brizzee, pp. 287–305. New York; Plenum Press.
26. McNeill, T. H., and Sladek, J. R., Jr. (1978): Fluorescence-immunocytochemistry: Simultaneous localization of catecholamines and gonadotropin releasing hormone. *Science*, 200: 72–74.
27. Morgane, P. J., and Stern, W. C. (1974): Chemical anatomy of brain circuits in relation to sleep and wakefulness. In: *Advances in Sleep Research*, edited by E. Weitzman, pp. 1–131. New York; Spectrum.
28. Moses, A. M. (1964): Inhibition of vasopressin release in rats by chlorpromazine and reserpine. *Endocrinology*, 74: 889–893.
29. Myers, R. D., and Yaksh, T. L. (1969): Control of body temperature in the unanesthetized monkey by cholinergic and aminergic systems in the hypothalamus. *J. Physiol. (Lond.)*, 202: 483–500.
30. Olson, L., Nyström, B., and Seiger, A. (1973): Monoamine fluorescence histochemistry of human post mortem brain. *Brain Res.*, 63: 231–247.
31. Porter, J. C., Kamberi, I. A., and Ondo, J. G. (1972): Role of biogenic amines and cerebrospinal fluid in the neurovascular transmittal of hypophysiotrophic substances. In: *Brain-Endocrine Interaction: Median Eminence: Structure and Function.*, edited by K. M. Knigge, D. E. Scott, and A. Weindle, pp. 245–253. Karger, Basel.
32. Rodeck, H. K., Lederis, K., and Heller, H. (1960): The hypothalamoneurohypophysial system in old rats. *J. Endocrinol.*, 21: 225.
33. Scheibel, M. E., Lindsay, R. D., Tomiyasu, U., and Scheibel, A. (1975): Progressive dendritic changes in aging human cortex. *Exp. Neurol.*, 47: 392–403.
43. Sladek, J. R., Jr. (1973): Age-dependent differences in catecholamine distribution within cat reticular formation. *Exp. Neurol.*, 38: 520–524.
35. Sladek, J. R., Jr., and Garver, D. (1976): Serotonergic perikarya and pathways in *Macaca arctoides*. *Soc. Neurosci. Proc.*, 2: 475.
36. Sladek, J. R., Jr., Sladek, C. D., McNeill, T. H. and Wood, J. G. (1978): New sites of monoamine localization in the endocrine hypothalamus as revealed by new methodological approaches. In: *Neural Hormones and Reproduction Brain Endocrine Interaction III*, edited by D. E. Scott, G. P. Kozlowski, and A. Weindl, pp. 154–171. Basel; Karger.
37. Sladek, J. R., Jr., and Walker, P. (1977): Serotonin-containing neuronal perikarya in the primate locus coeruleus and subcoeruleus. *Brain Res.*, 134: 359–366.

38. Sloper, J. C. (1966): The experimental and cytopathological investigation of neuro-secretion in the hypothalamus and pituitary. In: *The Pituitary Gland*, edited by G. W. Harris and B. T. Donovan, pp. 131–239. Berkely, California; University of California Press.

39. Ungerstedt, U. (1971): Stereotaxic mapping of monoamine pathways in the rat brain. *Acta Physiol. Scand.*, Suppl. **367**: 1–48.

40. Zimmerman, E. A., and Antunes, J. L. (1976): Organization of the hypothalamic-pituitary system: Current concepts from immunohistochemical studies. *J. Histochem. Cytochem.*, **24**: 807–815.

41. Zimmerman, E. A., Defendini, R., Sokol, H. W., and Robinson, A. G. (1975): The distribution of neurophysin-secreting pathways in the mammalian brain: Light microscopic studies using the immunoperoxidase technique. *Ann. N.Y. Acad. Sci.*, **248**: 92–112.

8

Serotonin Uptake by Platelets and Brain Synaptosomes

Gilbert S. Omenn, Lynne T. Smith, and Daniel R. Hanson

Division of Medical Genetics,
University of Washington,
Seattle, Washington

INTRODUCTION

A number of the behavioral and emotional problems of old age are presumed to be due to age-related changes in the central nervous system. Understanding and treatment of such disorders depends on accurate assessment of basic neuro-chemical processes in the brain. However, obtaining direct measurements of such cerebral processes for diagnostic purposes is impossible in the living patient. Our laboratory is engaged in a series of experiments to identify peripheral bio-chemical measures that may serve as accurate indices of central nervous system processes, including evaluation of platelet serotonin uptake as an index of the neurotransmitter reuptake by serotonergic neurons in the brain.

Reuptake into the presynaptic neuron of released neurotransmitters is the most important step in controlling the intrasynaptic concentration and neural effects of monoamine neurotransmitters (1, 3). In addition, neuronal reuptake is a major functional site of action for tricyclic antidepressants, amphetamines, and antihistaminic drugs. There is considerable evidence that platelets may serve as model systems for uptake, binding, and release of neurotransmitter monoa-mines, at least for serotonin, in the brain (6, 8). Human platelets actively take up serotonin (5-hydroxytryptamine, 5HT), store it in electron-dense granules as molecular aggregates with ATP and calcium and release 5HT together with adenine nucleotides and other platelet factors in the primary phase of platelet aggregation (9). Serotonin is one of the many substances capable of stimulating the primary aggregation process, indicating that platelets must have receptors for 5HT. The high-affinity uptake system for 5HT has kinetic parameters similar to those reported for animal brain synaptosome preparations, and tricyclic dibenzazepine antidepressants and amphetamines, which inhibit neuronal reuptake of 5HT and catecholamines, also inhibit 5HT uptake into platelets. The impossibility of obtaining brain tissue sufficiently fresh to compare properties of 5HT uptake in the two tissues in the human has made it desirable to evaluate these processes in the macaque.

The present work had three objectives: (a) to determine whether platelet serotonin uptake varies with age in a nonhuman primate, *M. nemestrina*; (b) to compare the properties of the platelet uptake system with the properties of uptake into brain synaptosomes prepared from the same animals and tested at the same time; and (c) to compare results of the macaque study with previous findings in mice and man.

METHODS

Venous blood specimens (10–20 ml) were obtained before or at the time of sacrifice from 3 4-y.o., 10 10-y.o. and 5 20-y.o. *M. nemestrina* (Table 8-1). Blood for platelets was taken with the animal under ketamine anesthesia just before sacrifice. Brain tissue from the left caudate adequate for fresh synaptosome preparations was obtained within 3 min of cardiorespiratory arrest from the 4-y.o. macaques. All platelet specimens were kept at room temperature and analyses were begun within 1 hr of sampling.

Whole venous blood collected with K_3-EDTA as anticoagulant was centrifuged at 200 Xg for 10 min at room temperature. An aliquot of the platelet-rich plasma (PRP) was counted in a Coulter Counter, model Z_{B1}; the platelet counts ranged from 143,800 to 1,432,000/μl PRP. All samples were diluted to a concentration of 200,000 platelets/μl with Krebs-bicarbonate buffer, pH 7.4 (143 mM Na^+), equilibrated with 95% O_2–5% CO_2. Mg^{++} and Ca^{++} were omitted from the buffer. Synaptosomes were prepared according to a modification of Cahill's method (2).

Uptake experiments were performed in 400-μl Beckman plastic microfuge tubes with a total reaction mixture volume of 250 μl, as previously described (5). Imipramine was used to characterize the susceptibility of the uptake system to inhibition (5). The apparent Km, V_{max}, and inhibition constant K_i were calculated by standard methods (5).

Table 8-1. Uptake of Serotonin by Macaque Platelets.

Age (Years)	Platelet Count (thousands/μl PRP)	K_m Serotonin ($\times 10^{-7}$ M)	V_{max} (pmol/10^7 plts/5 min)	K_i Imipramine ($\times 10^{-8}$ M)
4	995	2.2	8.4	—
4	892	2.5	10.4	—
4	558	4.3	12.5	—
Mean ± SEM	815 ± 132	3.0 ± 0.6	10.5 ± 1.2	
10	643	3.7	6.6	—
10	1030	2.3	7.0	0.5
10	1049	3.4	13.7	1.1
10	381	2.8	11.0	—
10	1159	5.6	6.8	1.1
10	1102	5.5	3.0	—
10	837	3.0	15.9	—
10	962	2.7	13.1	—
10	962	1.9	1.8	0.9
10	1432	3.8	4.0	1.3
Mean ± SEM	957 ± 91	3.5 ± 0.4	8.3 ± 1.5	1.0 ± 0.1
20	663	4.9	6.9	0.2
20	1004	4.2	9.5	1.1
20	480	3.7	8.5	—
20	522	3.8	8.4	—
20	144	5.4	5.0	—
Mean ± SEM	562 ± 252	4.4 ± 0.3	7.1 ± 0.9	0.6
Normal Human Subjects				
N = 54, Age 28 ± 2	542 ± 23	4.0 ± 0.2	10.2 ± 1.0	1.2 ± 0.2
One human subject (11 occasions)	609 ± 16	3.4 ± 0.2	8.1 ± 0.8	1.0 ± 0.1

Human data from Reference 5.

RESULTS AND DISCUSSION

The results from PRP samples are summarized in Table 8-1. The range of K_m values for serotonin uptake was narrow, from 1.9 to 5.6 $\times 10^{-7}$ M. Values were slightly higher with age: the results of a regression analysis were marginally significant at p = 0.07. The range of values for V_{max} was 1.8 to 15.9 picomoles/ 10^7 platelets/5 min: the values were slightly lower with age, but the results of analysis were not significant. In both analyses, *t*-test comparison of 4-y.o. vs. 20-y.o. animals gave 0.10 > p > 0.05. For the 7 animals on whose platelets the inhibitory potency of imipramine was tested, the range of K_i values was 0.2 to 1.3×10^{-8} M.

The variability of platelet counts, especially in the oldest group of macaques, was striking. However, there was no definite difference by age. Preparation of a standard concentration of platelets in the buffered and diluted PRP provided comparability. The determination of kinetic properties of the uptake mechanism was not dependent on the original platelet count, assuming that the platelets were normal. The V_{max} of individual samples was not correlated with the original platelet counts. There are many sources of potential variation due to morphological and biochemical heterogeneity of platelets, but the narrow ranges of results obtained indicate that those sources were not influential in this test system.

Direct comparison of the platelet system and brain synaptosomes in the same experiments from the same animals is essential to validation of the platelet model, but previously lacking in the literature. Table 8-2 presents the results for the 3 4-y.o. macaques as well as analogous pooled results for several strains of mice. As shown in Figure 8-1, synaptosomes have a 2-component high-affinity uptake system, while platelets have only a single-component system. In the mouse, we have shown that the higher-affinity component can be abolished reversibly by incubating synaptosomes with platelet-free plasma (7). The two apparent K_m's for macaque synaptosomes were 1.4 and 7.7×10^{-7} M. We do not know whether these two uptake components are altogether independent, so we cannot apply a correction for two independent, simultaneous uptake processes (4). Such corrections would have the effect of increasing the spread between the two K_m values,

Table 8-2. Comparison of Serotonin Uptake by Platelets and by Synaptosomes.

| | | | Synaptosomes | | | |
| | Platelets | | (1) | | (2) | |
	K_m	V_{max}	K_m	V_{max}	K_m	V_{max}
4-y.o. macaques						
A	2.2	8.4	1.6	8.6	9.2	32.2
B	2.5	10.4	1.5	6.6	8.0	21.3
C	4.3	12.5	1.1	4.6	5.8	13.2
Mean ± SEM:	3.0 ± 0.6	10.5 ± 1.2	1.4 ± 0.2	6.6 ± 1.2	7.7 ± 1.0	22.2 ± 5.5
Units	$\times 10^{-7}$ M	Picomoles/ 10^7 platelets per 5 min	$\times 10^{-7}$ M	Picomoles/ 80 mg per 2 min		
Inbred Strains of Mice (AKR, DBA, BALB/C, C57Bl, Swiss)						
(N = 27 experiments)	1.5 ± 0.2		0.55 ± 0.02		6.1 ± 0.6	

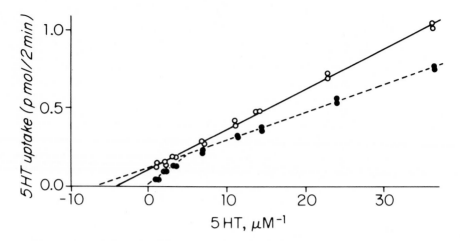

Fig. 8-1.   Lineweaver-Burk plots (1/v versus 1/S) to estimate −1/Km from x-intercept and 1/Vmax from y-intercept. 5HT, the concentration of serotonin, is corrected for amount of uptake and entrapped volume. The two sets of data represent serotonin uptake by caudate region synaptosomes (●−−−●) and by platelets (○——○) from monkey A.

making them even further from the apparent K_m for macaque platelets (3.7 × 10^{-7} M for 18 subjects).

There was not enough individual variation in either brain results or platelet results to answer the important question of whether deviation from mean values is congruent in the two tissues in the same individuals. Similarly, there was not sufficient variation in these parameters in our results for five strains of mice (7) to permit the necessary genetic analysis of identity or nonidentity of platelet and synaptosome uptake systems.

The K_m and V_{max} values for serotonin uptake into macaque platelets and the K_i for inhibition by imipramine were very similar to those obtained with human platelets (Table 8-1). Comparable data on human synaptosomes are not available, because sufficiently fresh specimens cannot be obtained from human subjects. Nevertheless, the macaque systems seem to provide a very useful and closely related analogue to the human system. The fact that *in vitro* differences in the kinetics of serotonin uptake into platelets (one component) and into synaptosomes (two components) is true of macaques as well as of mice strengthens the supposition that findings based on mice in this area are relevant to the human. Whether serotonin uptake processes in the platelets and synaptosomes are different or are under identical genetic control still awaits the finding of individuals or strains with sufficient differences in uptake parameters to permit a test of the congruence of the variation.

ACKNOWLEDGMENTS

This research was supported by grants RR00166, RR52177 and AG62145 from the National Institutes of Health. Dr. Omenn was an investigator of the Howard Hughes Medical Institute.

REFERENCES

1. Axelrod, J. (1965): The metabolism, storage, and release of catecholamines. *Rec. Prog. Hormone Res.*, **21**: 597–619.
2. Cahill, A. L. and Medzihradsky, F. (1976): Interaction of central nervous system drugs with synaptosomal transport processes. *Biochem. Pharmacol.*, **25**: 2257–2264.
3. Iversen, L. L. (1967): *The Uptake and Storage of Noradrenaline in Sympathetic Nerves.* New York; Cambridge University Press.
4. Neal, J. L. (1971): Analysis of Michaelis kinetics for two independent, saturable membrane transport functions. *J. Theor. Biol.*, **35**: 113–118.
5. Omenn, G. S. and Smith, L. T. (1978): Pharmacogenetic investigations of platelet uptake of serotonin. II. Platelet uptake of serotonin and dopamine in Huntington disease. *Neurology*, **28**: 300–303.
6. Omenn, G. S., and Smith, L. T. (1978): A common uptake system for serotonin and dopamine in human platelets. *J. Clin. Invest.*, **52**: 235–240.
7. Smith, L. T., Hanson, D. R., and Omenn, G. S. (1978): Comparisons of serotonin uptake by blood platelets and brain synaptosomes. *Brain Res.*, **146**: 400–403.
8. Sneddon, J. M. (1973): Blood platelets as a model for monoamine-containing neurones. *Prog. Neurobiol.*, **1**: 151–198.
9. Weiss, H. J. (1975): Platelet physiology and abnormalities of platelet function. *New Engl. J. Med.*, **293**: 531–541.

9

Pineal Taurine Content

John Claude Krusz, Zebulon V. Kendrick, and Steven I. Baskin
Department of Pharmacology,
The Medical College of Pennsylvania,
Philadelphia, Pennsylvania

INTRODUCTION

Taurine (2-aminoethane sulfonic acid) is an ubiquitous amino acid that is present in considerable amounts throughout the brain and in peripheral excitable tissues (8). Numerous neuroendocrine and physiologic roles have been postulated for taurine in the central nervous system (CNS) (1, 3, 15). It is the most abundant amino acid in the rabbit brain at birth, then decreases some 6 mo later (4). It is also the most abundant acidic substance in human pineal gland (17), and very high concentrations of taurine have been reported in the pineals of other species (5, 6). Taurine levels in tissue from developing human and rhesus monkey were 3 to 4 times greater than those observed up to 3 mo postnatally (16). Fetal, postnatal, and adult levels of taurine have been determined in various areas of the CNS, but they have not been evaluated in the senescent animal. This investigation was undertaken to assess taurine levels in the pineal gland of the young, mature and aging pigtail macaque (*Macaca nemestrina*).

MATERIALS AND METHODS

Pineal glands were removed at sacrifice (between 8:00 and 10:30 a.m.) from 4-, 10-, and 20-y.o. monkeys, placed on blue ice and shipped to our laboratory (see Chapter 3). Upon receipt, 24 to 48 hr after removal, tissue samples were immediately frozen at $-20°$. The frozen tissues were weighed and homogenized in 50 μl of cold saturated picric acid using 1 ml glass-walled tubes with Teflon pestles. Then 35 μl of the homogenized tissue were placed in microhematocrit

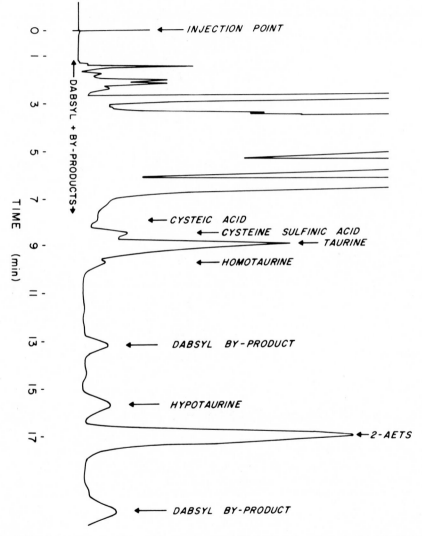

Fig. 9-1. Representative chromatogram showing HPLC taurine assay from monkey pineal. Peaks for taurine, taurine precursors, a taurine homolog, and the internal standard (2-AETS) are labeled.

capillary tubes (nonsiliconized) and centrifuged for 15 min in an IEC-MB micro-hematocrit centrifuge to separate tissue proteins and cell fragments. Ten μl of the clear supernate were reacted with 4-dimethylamino-azobenzene-4'-sulfonyl chloride (dabsyl chloride; Polysciences, Warrington, Pa.) in acetone as described previously (11). The reaction mixture consisted of: 10 μl picric acid extract of pineal; 5 μl (50 nmoles) 2-aminoethyl thiosulfuric acid (2-AETS) (Yoshitomi Ltd., Osaka, Japan), as an internal standard; 285 μl $NaCO_3$–$NaHCO_3$ buffer, pH 8.9; and 500 μl dabsyl chloride. The reaction was allowed to proceed at $70°C$ for 6 min with constant shaking in a Dubnoff metabolic shaker, and was terminated by brief immersion in ice. The dabsylated taurine product is stable at room temperature for up to 8 months.

A series of internal standard taurine concentrations in picric acid (2.5-100 nmole) was assayed concurrently with the monkey tissue samples. A linear standard curve was prepared from these internal standards, plotted as the ratio of the height of the taurine peak to that of the 2-AETS peak, against the taurine concentration (14). The taurine concentration in the monkey tissue sample was determined from the standard curve.

A Waters high-pressure liquid chromatograph (Model U6K injector, model 440 Absorbance detector, model 6000A solvent delivery system) was used for the taurine assay. The solvent system and operating conditions have been recently described in similar studies of aging rat pineals (9). Distilled deionized water was used and all solvents were filtered through millipore filters and de-gassed before use. At a flow rate of 2 ml/min, the assay times were 8.5 min for taurine and 16 min for 2-AETS (Figure 9-1).

Analysis of variance and regression analysis (significant at $p < 0.05$) were used for testing differences of pineal taurine concentration among the 3 age groups.

RESULTS

Taurine levels in pineals of monkeys from all 3 age groups are shown in Table 9-1. Although none of the age groups differed significantly from one another in their pineal taurine contents, the trend was for the 10- and 20-y.o. animals to exhibit slightly lower mean levels of taurine than the 4-y.o. animals. However, all 3 age groups showed consistently high taurine concentrations in the pineal gland.

In rats pineal taurine fluctuates with a diurnal rhythm (12). In this study, 2 animals were sacrificed on a given day—1 about 8:00 a.m., and 1 about 10:30 a.m. The data in Table 9-1 were re-evaluated by comparing animals sacrificed at the earlier hour with those taken later. Statistical analysis did not reveal any differences within any of the age groups based on hour of sacrifice. Animals from all 3 age groups were also matched for sex and again, no age-related differences were found.

Table 9-1. Relation of Pineal Taurine Concentration to Age Group.

4 Year			10 Year			20 Year		
Species	Sex	Taurine Concentration	Species	Sex	Taurine Concentration	Species	Sex	Taurine Concentration
Mn	F	72.6	Mn	F	23.5	Mn	F	76.6
Mn	F	59.6	Mn	F	69.6	Mn	F	30.3
Mn	F	53.9	Mn	F	35.4	Mn	F	41.6
			Mn	F	60.5	Mn	F	61.4
			Mn	F	42.1	Mn	M	46.7
			Mn	F	25.4	Mf	M	77.4
			Mn	F	93.8			
			Mn	F	66.7			
			Mn	M	85.3			
			Mf	M	36.2			
x̄ ± s.d.		62.0 ± 9.6	x̄ ± s.d.		53.8 ± 24.9	x̄ ± s.d.		55.7 ± 19.3

Mn, *M. nemestrina*; Mf, *M. fascicularis*; F = female, M = male; x̄ = mean; s.d. = standard deviation. Taurine concentration expressed as μmoles/gm tissue.

The assay method for taurine also demonstrates that the precursors for taurine are present in the pineal (Figure 9-1). For instance, cysteine sulfinic acid, cysteic acid, hypotaurine and homotaurine (a taurine homolog) were detected in all tissues studied. Although the precise pathway for taurine biosynthesis in the pineal is not known, most of these compounds have been implicated as precursors of taurine in other tissues (8). The presence of taurine precursors suggests that biosynthesis of taurine occurs in the pineal; the presence of homotaurine may be a novel finding, subject to further substantiation.

DISCUSSION

Taurine has been proposed to be an endogenous neuromodulator in the brain as well as in peripheral tissue (1). Nonuniform distribution of taurine in the CNS has given rise to speculation about its physiologic role(s) in normal and abnormal brain function. It has been postulated to be an inhibitory amino acid neurotransmitter (13). This postulate is based, in part, on taurine's ability to interact with calcium and other intracellular ions (1, 7) and on its depressant effect on the spontaneous firing of neurons in the CNS. In these respects, it resembles other known inhibitory substances such as gamma-aminobutyric acid and glycine.

Our taurine assay, using high-pressure liquid chromatography (HPLC), allows one to analyze very small quantities of tissue rapidly, sensitively and reproducibly for this biogenic amine and its precursors. This assay system routinely detects picogram amounts of the substances within 20 min. Other methods, such as ion-exchange columns, require considerably more time, and are far less sensitive and specific. Studies in our laboratory indicate that the ability of the rat pineal to take up exogenous ^{14}C-taurine is not diminished by bilateral superior cervical ganglionectomy. Indeed, uptake of taurine is increased in the ganglionectomized female but not in the male (10). This suggests that the major store of taurine resides in the pinealocytes and/or in the glial elements rather than in the sympathetic nerves within the pineal gland.

The results of the present study in pigtail macaques corroborate previous findings of high taurine levels in the pineal gland in the rat, cat, human, and other primates. Furthermore, they indicate that the variation among individuals within age groups, particularly in the 10- and 20-y.o. groups, is considerably greater than mean differences among age groups. The lack of a decline in pineal taurine content in monkeys up to 20 y.o. is noteworthy, considering the finding by Sladek *et al.* (Chapter 7, this volume) that the neuronal content of the monoaminergic neurotransmitters norepinephrine, dopamine and serotonin in the brainstem of these animals was markedly lower in older age groups than in the younger groups. Thus, if there is a decline in pineal taurine with age, its onset must occur considerably later than the onset of decline in brainstem monoamines. This interpretation is consistent with our finding of high concentrations (40 to 60 μmoles/gm) of taurine in pineal glands of the Fischer 344 rat throughout most of its lifespan. In that species, a significant decrement occurred only in very old (28 mo) animals, compared with adults 6 to 24 mo old (9). The mortality rate for the 28-mo-old rat is approximately 50%, which probably makes the 28-mo-old animal biologically older than the 20-y.o. monkeys used in the present study. Thus, the results of this and the previous study in rodents suggest a virtually life-long role for this biogenic amine in the pineal gland of mammals.

ACKNOWLEDGMENTS

We thank Mrs. Helen E. Flaherty for her secretarial assistance. This work was supported by National Institutes of Health grants AG00003, CA22170 and RR005418 to the Medical College of Pennsylvania and RR00166, RR52177 and AG62145 to the University of Washington, and by a grant from the PMA Foundation.

REFERENCES

1. Barbeau, A., Inoue, N., Tsukada, Y., and Butterworth, R. F. (1975): The neuropharmacology of taurine. *Life Sci.*, **17**: 669–677.

2. Baskin, S. I., and Dagirmanjian, R. (1973): The effect of taurine on the pigmentation of the bullfrog tadpole. *Comp. Biochem. Physiol.*, **44A**: 297–302.

3. Baskin, S. I., Leibman, A. S., and Cohn, E. M. (1976): Possible functions of taurine in the central nervous system. *Adv. Biochem. Psychopharm.*, **15**: 153–164.

4. Chanda, R., and Himwich, W. A. (1970): Taurine levels in developing rabbit brain and other organs. *Dev. Psychobiol.*, **3**: 191–196.

5. Crabai, F., Sitzia, A., and Pepeu, G. (1974): Taurine concentrations in the neurohypophysis of different animal species. *J. Neurochem.*, **23**: 1091–1092.

6. Green, J. P., Day, M., and Robinson, J. D. (1962): Some acidic substances in neoplastic mast cells and in the pineal body. *Biochem. Pharmacol.*, **11**: 957–960.

7. Huxtable, R., and Bressler, R. (1974): Taurine concentration in congestive heart failure. *Science*, **184**: 1187–1188.

8. Jacobsen, J. G., and Smith, L. H. (1968): Biochemistry and physiology of taurine and taurine derivatives. *Physiol. Rev.*, **48**: 424–511.

9. Krusz, J. C., Baskin, S. I., and Kendrick, Z. V. (1978): Age-related changes in pineal taurine content in the aging rat and monkey. *Gerontologist*, in press.

10. Krusz, J. C., Dix, R. K., and Baskin, S. I. (1978): Factors that affect uptake and endogenous content of taurine in the pineal. *Fed. Proc.*, **37**: 907.

11. Lin, J. K., and Chang, J. Y. (1975): Chromophoric labeling of amino acids with 4-dimethylaminoazobenzene-r′-sulfonyl chloride. *Anal. Chem.*, **47**: 1634–1638.

12. Nir, I., Briel, G., Dames, W., and Neuhoff, V. (1973): Rate pineal free amino acids diurnal rhythm and effect of light. *Arch. Int. Physiol. Biochem.*, **81**: 617–627.

13. Oja, S. S., and Lahdesmaki, P. (1974): Is taurine an inhibitory neurotransmitter? *Med. Biol.*, **52**: 138–143.

14. Peat, M. A., and Jennison, T. A. (1977): Analysis of theophylline in serum and whole blood samples by high-pressure liquid chromatography. *J. Anal. Toxicol.*, **1**: 204–207.

15. Reiter, R. J., and Fraschini, F. (1969); Endocrine aspects of the mammalian pineal gland: a review. *Neuroendocrinology*, **5**: 219–255.

16. Sturman, J. A., and Gaull, G. E. (1976): Taurine in the brain and liver of the developing human and rhesus monkey. In: *Taurine*, edited by R. Huxtable and A. Barbeau, pp. 73–84. New York; Raven Press.

17. Vellan, E. J., Gjessing, L. R., and Stalsberg, H. (1970): Free amino acids in the pineal and pituitary glands of human brain. *J. Neurochem.*, **17**: 699–701.

10

Autoimmune Antibodies and Other Immunological Characteristics

W. H. Stone and K. Nandy

Laboratory of Genetics and the Wisconsin Regional Primate Research Center,
University of Wisconsin, Madison, Wisconsin;
Geriatric Research, Education and Clinical Center,
Veterans Administration Hospital, Bedford, Massachusetts;
and Department of Anatomy and Neurology,
Boston University Medical School,
Boston, Massachusetts

INTRODUCTION

Loss of physiologic adaptability is a hallmark of old age. Because the immune system is intimately involved with adaptation, it is understandable that immunologists and gerontologists have begun to coordinate their efforts to investigate aging (13, 31, 32). Thomsen and Kettel (27) were first to present evidence that seemed to demonstrate a dramatic decrease in the naturally occurring blood group antibodies with age in man. These studies have since been extended and the results show that anti-A and anti-B levels in older humans decrease markedly (9). However, these data were obtained on hospitalized patients and were not analyzed statistically. Our own data (unpublished) on a population of normal old people do not support the contention that the level of naturally occurring blood group antibodies decreases markedly with age.

Several studies in man indicate that immunoglobulin (Ig) levels vary with age but the results are contradictory. The most definitive study sampled more than 70 persons 95 years old and found a small but consistent increase in IgA and IgG (sub-class IgG1 and IgG3) levels, whereas the level of IgM remained relatively constant (22). The finding that IgM did not vary is interesting in light of the reported decrease in naturally occurring blood group antibodies which are supposedly IgM. It is also pertinent that cell mediated immunity (T cell function) seems to be affected far more by age than antibody mediated immunity (B cell function). In any case, it seems quite clear that aging is accompanied by impaired lymphocyte function (12, 13).

Variation with age in naturally occurring antierythrocyte antibodies in non-human primates has not been reported, but a few reports have appeared on Ig levels in primates. Voormolen-Kalova *et al.* (29) studied 60 chimpanzees ranging in age from 1 to 12 y.o. and found that the levels of Ig varied widely for all age groups. However, some trends were apparent: the IgG levels of chimpanzees older than 1 year remained constant, while IgM levels remained at about 50% of the young adult values until 7 y.o., and then gradually increased to the adult level. The IgA levels reached about 70% of the adult level by 1 year of age and then showed a gradual increase. The IgD levels did not change with age.

The development of the major Ig classes from infancy to adulthood in rhesus monkeys is well documented but practically nothing is known about their levels in old age. The IgA and IgM levels increase gradually from birth until 2 or 3 y.o., when they reach about 80% of the adult level; by 5 y.o. they reach the adult values (30). The IgG levels rise more gradually, but also reach adult levels by about 6 or 7 y.o. (7).

The most notable manifestation of immunosenescence is the appearance of autoantibodies and autoimmune diseases (4), which increase dramatically with age (8, 31). In humans, autoimmune antibodies have been detected against nucleic acids of the cell nucleus (as in systemic lupus erythematosus), smooth muscles (as in biliary cirrhosis), striated muscle (as in myasthenia gravis), parietal cells (as in pernicious anemia), thyroid epithelial cells (as in autoimmune thyroid diseases), and adrenal cortical cells (as in Addison's disease). Presumably the brain reactive antibodies reported by Nandy are also autoimmune (14-21).

There is a growing literature on autoimmune diseases in nonhuman primates, but these studies have not delineated the possible correlations with age. Furthermore, very few of these autoimmune diseases represent spontaneous models; most are induced experimentally, and are neither etiologically nor pathologically identical to the spontaneous models.

Autoantibodies against neural tissue have been demonstrated in sera of old rodents and implicated as a possible etiological factor in the neuronal degeneration of aging (14, 15, 17, 18, 21, 28). Although these antibodies have been detected in the sera of rodents and humans, they have not yet been reported in nonhuman primates.

The present study was designed to determine if any of the following immunologic parameters varied with age in pigtail macaques (*Macaca nemestrina*): (a) naturally occurring antibodies reactive with rhesus and pigtail macaque or human erythrocytes, (b) major immunoglobulin classes (IgG, IgM and IgA), and (c) autoantibodies against various tissues, especially brain. The overall goal was to ascertain the extent to which the macaque can be used as a model of human aging with respect to these parameters.

METHODS

Serum samples were obtained before sacrifice from 18 pigtail macaques, 3 4-y.o., 10 10-y.o., and 5 20-y.o. including 16 females and 2 males. They were frozen, shipped on dry ice, and thawed just before testing. All the samples were coded for testing and whenever possible all the tests for a given parameter were performed on all the samples at the same time. Usually the tests were set up in duplicate and read blind by two different persons.

Fluorescent Antibody Assays for Autoimmune Antibodies.

We assayed for various "autoantibodies" using cryostat sections of rat or monkey stomach (for parietal cells, mitochondrial, nuclear and smooth muscle antibodies) and thyroid (for cytoplasmic and thyroglobulin antibodies) (1). We used the indirect, double-layer test. Briefly, varying dilutions of test sera were layered over the above tissues and incubated at room temperature $(22 \pm 2°C)$ in a moist chamber for 30 min. After washing, fluorescent conjugated goat anti-monkey Ig was added as a second layer. Tissues were examined by a Zeiss microscope equipped with vertical illumination to determine if specific staining had occurred.

Controls for nonspecificity included: (a) demonstration of nonstaining using fluorescent labeled antiserum alone; (b) loss of staining using fluorescent labeled antiserum previously absorbed with monkey IgG; (c) failure of staining with fluorescent conjugated antifibrinogen; (d) blocking of staining by prior incubation with unconjugated antimonkey Ig followed by the fluorescent reagent. Fluorescein conjugation (33) was done using a molar F:P ratio of approximately 2.

The relative levels of the brain-reactive antibodies (BRA) were measured by Nandy using the indirect immunofluorescence method (14). Rabbit antimonkey IgG (Cappel Laboratories) was conjugated with fluorescein isothiocyanate (FITC) by the dialysis method (28). Since a preliminary study revealed reaction of the monkey sera with mouse brain sections, cryostat sections (10 μm) of mouse brain were used to demonstrate BRA in monkey sera. Frozen mouse brain sections were pretreated with serum from individual monkeys before incubation with FITC-labeled antimonkey IgG (14).

Alternate serial sections of cerebrum were also stained with thionin and the total number of cells per unit area was counted using an ocular grid in a microscope. Using the same method, the number of cells in the cerebral cortex showing specific fluorescence per unit was counted for sera from monkeys of different ages. The percentage of cells showing specific fluorescence in 10 sections of cerebrum, and the averages, were calculated for each serum. The control tests for the nonspecific fluorescent staining of the antimonkey IgG were done by absorption of antimonkey IgG with normal monkey serum before incubation, and by treatment of mouse brain sections with FITC-labeled normal rabbit globulin. The specificity of the BRA was tested by absorption of the positive sera by brain homogenates.

Assay for Naturally Occurring Anti-Red Blood Cell (RBC) Agglutinating Antibodies.

Each serum sample was titrated in a tube test in serial dilutions against a panel of RBC from human volunteers of known ABO blood type. At least two donors of each type were used. Each sample was also tested for naturally occurring antibodies against the RBC from each of 8 pigtail and 10 rhesus macaques (*M. mulatta*). Two drops of appropriately diluted serum were used with one drop of a 3% suspension of thrice-washed RBC. The tests were incubated for 30 min at 37°C, centrifuged at 1000 RPM for 30 sec, and read. The titers were transformed into scores using $\log_2$ of the highest dilution of serum giving 50% or greater agglutination as the end point.

Assay for Levels of Major Ig Classes

To quantify the levels of the major Ig classes, the serum samples were tested by single radial diffusion—a gel precipitation technic that we have used extensively (24). We closely followed the procedure of Voormolen-Kalova *et al.* (29, 30). Antisera specific for the human Ig classes (IgG, IgM and IgA) were prepared by the method of Radl *et al.* (23). These antisera cross-reacted strongly with the serum Ig of the pigtail macaques and were considered satisfactory to measure the relative concentrations of the three major Ig classes. Furthermore, there is good evidence that the major Ig classes are nearly homologous among the various primates (6, 11). The radial immune assays were set up on plastic petri dishes to which a standard amount of the appropriate antiserum was added in 0.7% agarose. Separate plates were set up to assay for each Ig class. Three standard samples of human serum, each containing varying amounts of IgG, IgM and IgA, were pipetted into 3 wells in each plate. The serum samples from the pigtail macaques were appropriately diluted and pipetted into the remaining wells. The tests were incubated at room temperature in a moist chamber for 20 to 96 hr until the diameters of the rings of precipitation stabilized. They were read at 18- to 24-hr intervals under constant light using a magnification lens equipped with a ruled scale in mm. A standard curve was drawn using the diameters squared (D^2) of the 3 known samples for each Ig class. The amount of the specific Ig in each serum sample was calculated from the standard curve. In general, the standard curve gave a very clear-cut straight line and the unknown samples tested out as expected when various dilutions were run in the same test. In other words, a $\frac{1}{10}$ dilution of a serum gave reactions that calculated out to about $\frac{1}{10}$ the number of mg/100 ml of serum found with the undiluted serum.

RESULTS

Assay for BRA in monkey sera consistently resulted in a bright greenish fluorescence in the cells of the mouse cerebral cortex, indicative of antigen-antibody reactions. Negative results were indicated by a dark field without any fluorescence except in cases of orange-yellow fluorescence in the lipofuscin pigment in the cytoplasm of the neurons of old mice. The percentage of the total cells showing specific fluorescence was calculated and tabulated for each monkey. The reactions were mostly weak or moderate; in general, sera from older animals gave stronger reactions. Although the percentage of reacting cells varied widely in all age groups (with considerable overlap), there was a gradual and significant increase in the percentage of reacting cells with the sera from older monkeys (Figure 10-1). The difference was more significant between the 10- and 20-y.o. groups ($p = 0.001$) than between 4- and 10-y.o. groups ($p = 0.05$) (Table 10-1).

The incidence of autoantibodies against nuclear DNA, smooth muscle, parietal cells and mitochondria, detectable by fluorescent screening technics, was exceedingly low (Table 10-2). We observed no reactors at all among our sample of 20 sera. However, 2 monkeys (70371 and 76220) showed very weak (1:25) antithyroid antibodies. Normal adult human levels of antithyroid may reach titers of 1:250. Here again, the low titers may have been due to the antihuman antibodies used to develop the reactions. Taken together, there was no evidence that autoantibodies against these tissues showed any age effect.

As shown in Table 10-2, naturally occurring antierythrocyte antibodies reactive with pigtail cells (intraspecific antibodies) were found in only one sample, from monkey 76201, a 20-y.o. female. The antibodies were weak (4 units) and reacted with all 8 pigtail test samples, indicating that the antibodies were either nonspecific or were reacting with a high frequency (public) blood factor. In contrast, 5 of the samples showed naturally occurring interspecific antibodies for rhesus (*M. mulatta*) erythrocytes. However, these were also weak (2–4 units). Unlike the intraspecific antibodies of monkey 76201, these antibodies detected individual differences among the panel of rhesus cells. In fact, 3 of the sera behaved like monospecific blood typing reagents (26). Three of the 5 samples came from 20-y.o. monkeys, 1 from a 10-y.o. (although this monkey, 72399, may be wrongly classified and is perhaps a 20-y.o.; see page 39); and 1 from a 4-y.o. monkey. It would appear that the incidence of these interspecific antibodies tends to be higher in the 20-y.o. animals, suggesting an age correlation

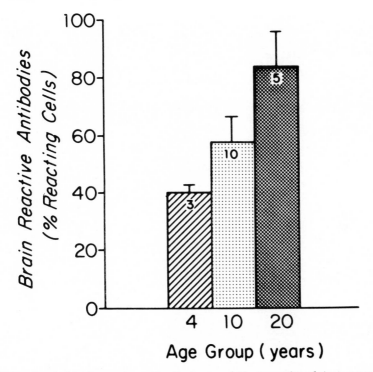

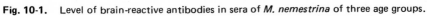

Fig. 10-1. Level of brain-reactive antibodies in sera of *M. nemestrina* of three age groups.

Table 10-1. Percentage of Reacting Cells in the Brain Tissue Using Sera from Female *M. nemestrina* of Different Ages.

	Age Group	
4 y.o.	10 y.o.	20 y.o.
38.4	50.4	67.8
36.4	52.5	64.4
37.2	58.9	85.1
	40.0	88.5
	45.5	89.7
	49.5	
	56.2	
	50.8	
	70.2	
	57.6	
37.3 ± 1.0	53.1 ± 8.1	79.1 ± 12.0
Significance level (t-test)	(p = 0.05)	(p = 0.001)

Table 10-2. Naturally Occurring Erythrocyte Agglutinins,[1] Immunoglobulin Levels, and Autoantibodies in the Sera of *M. nemestrina*.

Age (years)	Anti-RBC		Antihuman RBC			Immunoglobulin Levels[2]			Autoantibodies	
	nemestrina	mulatta	A	B	O	IgG	IgA	IgM	Screen[3]	Antithyroid[4]
20	0	0	7	9	7	2292	19.0	9.3	0	0
20	0	3	12	8	7	893	8.5	5.0	0	0
20	0	4	12	3	0	2292	11.0	7.5	0	0
20	4	2	11	8	7	1706	8.0	5.0	0	0
20	0	0	12	13	9	1917	16.0	6.0	0	0
10	0	0	11	12	9	1706	8.0	6.0	0	0
10	0	0	10	6	6	2042	10.0	9.3	0	0
10	0	3	11	8	6	1917	10.0	6.5	0	0
10	0	0	10	0	0	1792	10.0	6.5	0	0
10	0	0	11	9	6	1917	14.2	10.8	0	1
10	0	0	8	5	5	1583	11.0	9.0	0	0
10	0	0	10	6	6	1917	6.8	7.4	0	0
10	0	0	11	8	3	2167	...	5.0	0	0
10	0	0	9	7	6	2167	13.0	6.0	0	0
10	0	0	10	9	3	2417	11.0	6.0	0	0
4	0	0	9	9	7	1792	14.2	5.4	0	0
4	0	2	12	12	8	1706	11.0	7.5	0	0
4	0	0	12	6	7	1270	8.0	6.0	0	0

[1]Log$_2$ of highest dilution giving 50% or greater agglutination; [2]mg/100 ml of serum; [3]fluorescent Ab screen (see text); [4]anti-thyroglobulin

(R = 0.406). Curiously, all 3 of the reactors belonged to the subspecies *M. nemestrina leonina*. It is clear from these data that while the frequency of these naturally occurring antibodies may correlate with age, the strengths do not.

Table 10-2 also shows that all of the pigtail sera contained strongly reactive interspecific antibodies for one or more types of human erythrocytes. What is more, at least half of the sera possessed anti-A titers significantly greater than anti-B or anti-O titers. This result might have been anticipated since all rhesus sera possess naturally occurring antihuman A antibodies (26). There is no evidence for an age effect on any of these 3 parameters.

The relative levels of IgG, IgA, and IgM also showed no age effect (Table 10-2). The range of IgG levels (893–2419 mg/100 ml) was somewhat higher than the range found in normal adult humans (800–1840 mg/100 ml). In contrast, the ranges for IgA (6–19 mg/100 ml) and for IgM (3–11 mg/100 ml) were considerably lower than those found in normal humans (IgA, 90–370 mg/100 ml; IgM, 50–255 mg/100 ml).

DISCUSSION

One of the conspicuous changes in the brain of aging mammals is the progressive loss of nerve cells (3). Brizzee *et al.* (2) demonstrated a significant decrease in mean neuron packing density in the submolecular cerebral cortical laminae in aged rhesus monkeys compared with young adult ones. It is pertinent to ask if this loss of nerve cells is a result of an autoimmune disease involving BRA.

Previous studies have demonstrated BRA in sera of old mice but not of young, and BRA levels seemed to increase progressively as a function of age. Different protein fractions of the serum of old mice (albumin, β-globulin and γ-globulin) were used in place of sera and only the γ-globulin fraction gave the positive reaction with the neurons (28). Using sera from mice of different ages, we noted that the onset of BRA in sera occurred at 6 to 12 months of age and thereafter increased progressively as a function of age (14). The nature of the antigen was investigated using sera from young and old germ-free mice and control mice of the same age. No significant difference was noted in the number of mice having positive sera in germ-free and control groups of the same age. Therefore, the development of BRA in the sera of these mice is probably due to the stimulation of the animals' immune systems by an autogenous antigen (15).

Burnet's (5) "Forbidden Clone Theory" postulates that clones of mutant lymphocytes lacking antigen can proliferate and ultimately attack the host's own tissues. Another theory that may explain some autoantibodies proposes that certain tissues are never exposed to the reticulo-endothelial system during embryonic development so that auto- or self-tolerance does not develop (31). If later in life the sequestered antigens become exposed (through trauma, infection, lack of surveillance, or any degenerative process of aging) to the lymphoreticular system, an immune (autoimmune) reaction could result, such as antisperm antibodies in vasectomized men and monkeys.

There has been considerable speculation on the underlying pathophysiology of neuronal degeneration in the brain of aging mammals. Antibodies specific against brain tissue may play a significant role in the age-related loss of nerve cells (16–19, 21). An increase in the age-related frequency of the gammaglobulin fraction of human sera that binds with neurons in brain sections has also been noted (10). This fraction, presumably a humoral antibody, binds to cytoplasmic constituents of neurons with increased frequency and intensity with advancing age. Human sera also demonstrate an age-related increase in levels of BRA (20). Although the antibodies against brain tissue have been detected in rodents as well as in man, the presence of such antibodies in nonhuman primates has not yet been studied. This study extends the earlier studies in rodents and humans by showing that BRA are present in sera of the pigtail macaque and that the levels increase as a function of age. The precise significance of such antibodies in the loss of neurons in the brain or in the decline in cognitive functions will require further investigation.

Other than the BRA, we did not observe any significant autoantibodies in our sample of 20 monkeys. As with the Ig assays, this could be due to the test system, which was designed to assay for human antibodies. However, it is more likely that the incidence of such antibodies is simply too low in normal individuals to pick them up in such a small sample of aged individuals (25). The occurrence of agglutinating antibodies reactive against the erythrocytes of either *M. nemestrina* or *M. mulatta*, or both, is not surprising since transplacental immunization due to incompatible blood types between mother and fetus has been described in several nonhuman primate species including rhesus macaque (26). It would appear that the frequency of such antibodies (5/18 females showed antirhesus) is higher than expected. However, 2 of these 5 females were previously on an immunogenetics project and were very likely immunized with either pigtail or rhesus blood cells. This helps explain why these sera show specificities of well-known rhesus blood groups (26).

While it was no surprise to find high-titered antihuman A antibodies in the sera of the pigtail macaques, the presence of strong antihuman B in 3 of the sera samples is unexplained. Clearly, the low levels of antihuman 0 represent species-specific rather than type-specific antibodies.

The levels of IgG are considerably higher than those found in normal adult humans. In contrast, the levels of IgM and IgA are considerably lower and show a much narrower range than those shown in humans. This could be due to our assay system which used reagents specific for human immunoglobulins, so that we were measuring cross-reactions and not homologous ones. If this were so, it is even more difficult to explain the high IgG levels.

ACKNOWLEDGMENTS

We gratefully acknowledge Ms. Gwen Wallace, Ms. Barbara De Boer, Ms. Sylvia Oemichen and Ms. Nancy Roy, who provided much of the technical help for these studies. We also thank Dr. R. Hong, Department of Pediatrics, University of Wisconsin at Madison, for his collaboration.

This research was supported in part by National Institutes of Health grants RR00167, RR00166, RR52177, AG62145, HD07385 and NS12964, and by a grant from the Veterans Administration. This is paper No. 2245, Laboratory of Genetics, and No. 18-044 Primate Research Center, University of Wisconsin, Madison.

REFERENCES

1. Bignazzi, P. E., and Rose, N. (1976): Tests for antibodies to tissue-specific antigens. In: *Manual of Clinical Immunology*, edited by N. R. Rose and H. Friedman, p. 682. Washington, D.C.; American Society for Microbiology.
2. Brizzee, K. R., Ordy, J. M., Hanschi, J., and Kaack, B. (1976): Quantitative assessment of changes in neuron and glia cell packing density and lipofuscin accumulation with age in the cerebral cortex of a nonhuman primate (*Macaca mulatta*). In: *Neurobiology of Aging*, edited by R. Terry and S. Gershon, pp. 229-244. New York; Raven Press.
3. Brody, H. (1955): Organization of the cerebral cortex. III. A study of aging in the human cerebral cortex. *J. Comp. Neurol.*, 102: 511–556.
4. Burnet, F. M. (1974): Autoimmunity and aging. *Progr. Immun.*, 5: 27.
5. Burnet, F. M. (1974): *Intrinsic Mutagenesis, a Genetic Approach to Aging*, p. 244. Philadelphia; Wiley & Sons.
6. Carbonera, A. O. (1971): In: *Comparative Genetics in Monkeys, Apes and Man*, edited by A. B. Chiarelli, pp. 257–271. New York; Academic Press.
7. Eitzman, D. V. (1970): Immunoglobulin levels in the *Macaca mulatta*. *Folia Primat.*, 12: 313–316.
8. Good, R. A., and Yunis, E. J. (1974): Association of autoimmunity, immuno-deficiency and aging in man, rabbits, and mice. *Fed. Proc.*, 33: 2040-2050.
9. Grundbacher, F. J. (1976): Genetics of anti-A and anti-B levels. *Transfusion*, 16: 48.
10. Ingram, C. R., Phegan, K. J., and Blumethal, H. T. (1974): Significance of an aging-linked neuron binding gamma-globulin fraction of human sera. *J. Geront.*, 29: 20-27.
11. Lakin, J. D., Patterson, R., and Pruzansky, J. J. (1967): Immunoglobulins of the rhesus monkey (*Macaca mulatta*). *J. Immunol.*, 98: 745–756.
12. Makinodan, T. (1976): Immunobiology of aging. *J. Amer. Geriat. Soc.*, 24: 249–252.
13. Makinodan, T., and Yunis, E., editors (1977): *Immunology and Aging*. New York; Plenum Medical Book Co.
14. Nandy, K. (1972): Brain-reactive antibodies in mouse serum as a function of age. *J. Geront.*, 27: 173-177.
15. Nandy, K. (1972): Neuronal degeneration in aging and after experimental injury. *Exp. Geront.*, 7: 303-311.
16. Nandy, K. (1972): Brain-reactive antibodies in serum of germ-free mice. *Mech. Age Dev.*, 1: 133–138.
17. Nandy, K. (1973): Neuronal degeneration in aging. In: *Development and Aging in the Neurons System*, edited by M. Rockstein, pp. 43–61. New York; Academic Press.

18. Nandy, K. (1975): Significance of brain-reactive antibodies in serum of aged mice. *J. Geront.*, **30**: 412–416.
19. Nandy, K. (1977): Immune reactions in aging brain and senile dementia. In: *The Aging Brain and Senile Dementia*, edited by K. Nandy and I. Sherwin, pp. 181–196. New York; Plenum Press.
20. Nandy, K. (1978): Brain-reactive antibodies in aging and senile dementia. In: *Alzheimer's Disease–Senile Dementia and Related Disorders*, edited by R. Terry, R. Katzman and K. Bick. New York; Raven Press.
21. Nandy, K., Fritz, R. B., and Threatt, J. (1975): Specificity of brain-reactive antibodies in serum of old mice. *J. Geront.*, **30**: 269–274.
22. Rádl, J., Sepers, J. M., Skvaril, F., Morell, A., and Hijmans, W. (1975): Immunoglobulin patterns in humans over 95 years of age. *Clin. Exp. Immunol.*, **22**: 84–90.
23. Rádl, J., van den Berg, P., Voormolen, M., Hendriks, W. D. H., and Shaefer, U. W. (1974): Homogeneous immunoglobulins in sera of rhesus monkeys after lethal irradiation and bone marrow transplantation. *Clin. Exp. Immunol.*, **16**: 259–265.
24. Rapacz, J., Korda, N., and Stone, W. H. (1974): Serum antigens of cattle. IV. Immunogenetics of a soluble antigenic determinant derived from lysed erythrocytes. *Genetics*, **80**: 323–329.
25. Sharp, G. C., Irvin, W. S., La Roque, R. L., Velez, C., Daly, V., Kaiser, A. D., and Holman, H. R. (1971): Association of autoantibodies to different nuclear antigens with clinical patterns of rheumatic disease and responsiveness to therapy. *J. Clin. Invest.*, **50**: 350–359.
26. Stone, W. H. (1975): Immunogenetic studies of rhesus. In: *The Rhesus Monkey*, Vol. II, edited by G. H. Bourne, p. 436. New York; Academic Press.
27. Thomsen, O., and Kettel, K. (1929): Die Stärke der menschlichen Isoagglutinine und entsprechenden Blutkörperchenrezeptoren in verschiedenen Lebensaltern. *Z. Immunitätsforschung*, **63**: 67–93.
28. Threatt, J., Nandy, K., and Fritz, R. (1971): Brain-reactive antibodies in serum of old mice demonstrated by immunofluorescence. *J. Geront.*, **26**: 316–323.
29. Voormolen-Kalova, M., van den Berg, P., and Rádl, J. (1974): Immunoglobulin levels as related to age in nonhuman primates in captivity. I. Chimpanzees. *J. Med. Primat.*, **3**: 335–342.
30. Voormolen-Kalova, M., van den Berg, P., and Rádl, J. (1974): Immunoglobulin levels as related to age in nonhuman primates in captivity. II. Rhesus monkeys. *J. Med. Primat.*, **3**: 343–350.
31. Walford, R. L. (1969): *The Immunologic Theory of Aging*, p. 248. Copenhagen; Munksgaard.
32. Walford, R. L. (1974): Immunologic theory of aging: current status. *Fed. Proc.*, **33**: 2020–2027.
33. Wood, B. T., Thompson, S. H., and Goldstein, G. (1965): Fluorescent antibody staining. III. Preparation of fluorescein-isothiocyanate-labeled antibodies. *J. Immunol.*, **95**: 225–229.

11

Cerebral Microcirculation

Elizabeth M. Burns, Thomas W. Kruckeberg, and Lynn E. Comerford
College of Nursing,
University of Illinois Medical Center,
Chicago, Illinois

INTRODUCTION

Several theories regarding decline in cerebral functioning in senescence have been based on observed or hypothetical changes in the cerebrovascular system (4, 18). The adult brain represents approximately 2% of human body weight, but accounts for 20 to 25% of the total oxygen consumption and glucose utilization. Cerebral blood flow constitutes a comparably disproportionate fraction of total cardiac output. Compared with other organs of the body, the brain, unable to obtain sufficient energy from anaerobic glycolysis, is critically vulnerable to interruption in the supply of these metabolic substrates. Thus, any age-related changes in the cerebral microvasculature that compromise blood flow might be expected to impair brain function.

In addition to its great reliance on the cardiovascular system to meet its fuel requirements, the brain is uniquely dependent on the blood brain barrier (BBB), a restrictive, selectively permeable interface that regulates entry and egress of substances between the blood and the parenchyma of the central nervous system (14). The BBB exists from an early age and its maturation varies with species (6, 7). It maintains an optimal microenvironment for cells in the brain permitting normal neuronal activity in sensory, cognitive and motor functions. Alterations of the BBB with increasing age may also be a major cause of declining mental function during senescence (20).

The cerebral capillaries, which constitute a major portion of the BBB, are the primary focus of this study. Electron microscopic studies following injections of horseradish peroxidase and microperoxidase intravenously and interventricularly have clearly identified the endothelium of brain capillaries and their tight junctions as the anatomical substrate of the multifaceted regulatory mechanism known as the BBB (2, 3, 8, 15). In addition to its function as a physical barrier, the BBB plays an active role in the maintenance of an optimal ionic composition of extracellular fluid in the brain (5). Cerebral capillaries contain a significantly greater volume of endothelial mitochondria than do capillaries from other tissues (11, 12) indicating that they have a larger work capability than capillaries elsewhere in the body. The contribution of the cerebral capillaries to the function of active transport remains uncertain, however, because of the technical difficulty of distinguishing between the roles of the choroid plexus and cerebral capillaries in maintaining differences between ionic concentrations in extracellular fluid and plasma (14).

The paucity of studies on the effects of aging on cerebral microvasculature is surprising. Schwink and Wetzstein (17) reported capillary endothelial attenuation with increasing age in rats. In this study we investigated age-related ultrastructural alterations of the cerebral capillaries from three age groups of pigtail macaque (*Macaca nemestrina*), young, mature and old adults. The characteristics under study were the thickness of the capillary wall and its components, and the numbers of mitochondria in the endothelial cells lining capillaries in the frontal and occipital cortex.

METHODS

Tissues were taken from 18 *M. nemestrina* (3 4-y.o., 10 10-y.o. and 5 20-y.o. animals, all females except 1 male each in the 10- and 20-y.o. groups). Full-depth sections of cerebral cortex, 1–3 mm thick, were removed from the frontal and occipital poles of the cerebrum within 3 min after respiration ceased. All samples were immediately immersed in McDowell's fixative (Chapter 3) and shipped via air at ambient temperature. Small sections (0.5–1.0 mm thick) were removed from the lateral surface of all samples, post-fixed in OsO_4, stained *en bloc* with uranyl acetate (9) and dehydrated in ethyl alcohol and propylene oxide. They were embedded in epone and cured at 60°C for 72–96 hours. Ultrathin sections were made perpendicularly to the cortical pial surface. Sections were further stained on the grid with uranyl acetate and Reynold's lead. Photomicrographs were made using an Elmiskop I or a Philips 300 electron microscope. At least 10 capillary profiles were photographed from each cortical sample. Capillaries sectioned lengthwise or tangentially were excluded from analysis.

Evaluation of age-related changes in cerebral capillaries (Figures 11-1, 11-2)

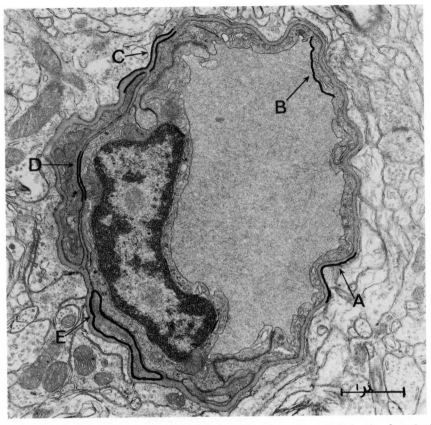

Fig. 11-1. A cross-sectional area of an entire capillary from the occipital pole of cerebral cortex of a 10-y.o. male *M. nemestrina*. A, external boundary of capillary profile delineating the outer edge of the outer basal lamina (BL_o); B. endothelial membrane representing boundary of the lumen; C, BL_o, inner and outer edges, outlined; D, portion of the inner basal lamina (BL_i) between endothelium to the right and pericyte to the left; E, small portion of a pericyte, cross-sectional view. 21,000X.

was based on (a) cross-sectional area of the entire capillary; (b) cross-sectional area of the capillary lumen; (c) thickness of the outer basal lamina which completely surrounds the capillary (BL_o); (d) cross-sectional area of pericytes; (e) cross-sectional area of the inner basal lamina, i.e., basal lamina between endothelial cell and pericyte (BL_i); and (f) endothelial mitochondria per capillary profile.

Measurements (a) and (b) were made with an Optomax, a modular image analyzer consisting of a central processor, television scanner and video monitor.

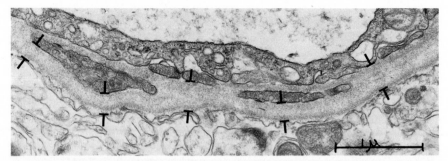

Fig. 11-2. Segment of capillary wall, in cross-section, from the frontal pole of cerebral cortex of a 20-y.o. female *M. nemestrina*. Pairs of T-bars indicate 30-mm intervals along the BL_O at which 2-point measurements were made with the Grafacon stylus. 29,200X.

The Optomax senses the optical density of the image, scans the image, divides it into picture elements, and gives the total number of picture elements for that image. Picture elements were calibrated daily.

To measure cross-sectional areas of capillary profiles from photomicrographs, the Optomax scanner was linked with a macro lens which was focused first on the outline of the outer edge of BL_o (Figure 11-1, A), thus measuring the area of the entire capillary profile, and second on the outline of the luminal endothelial membrane (Figure 11-1, B), similarly measuring the area of the capillary lumen. After scanning the selected optical image, the Optomax logic summed the total number of picture elements visualized. This number was multiplied by a calibration factor that took into account the optical magnification, thus giving the area of the image under examination. Raw data were corrected for photographic magnification and areas were expressed in square microns.

Measurements c–e were made with a Grafacon planimeter (Model #1010A, Bolt Beranek and Newman, Inc.) attached to a PDP-8 computer. Points at which the width of the BL_o was to be measured were determined by placing each photomicrograph on the tablet of the Grafacon planimeter. The stylus was traced along the BL_o (Figures 11-1, C). When the stylus had traversed 3 cm, the computer rang a bell and the location of the stylus tip was marked (Figure 11-2). After the BL_o was marked at 3-cm intervals in all photomicrographs, two-point measurements of the BL_o width were made perpendicularly to the limiting membranes of the BL_o. Each marked site was measured by touching the tip of the Grafacon stylus to the plasma membrane of the endothelium or pericyte adjacent to the BL_o and again at the junction of the BL_o with the plasma membrane of the astrocytic endfeet (Figure 11-2, T-bars). The BL_o measurements thus included both the lamina densa and lamina lucida of the BL_o. The cross-sectional areas of the BL_i (Figure 11-1, D) and pericytes (Figure 11-1, E) were measured for at least four representative profiles from each sample by tracing their respective outlines with the Grafacon stylus.

The number of endothelial mitochondria per cerebral capillary profile was estimated from the same electron photomicrographs. The criterion used in counting mitochondria was visualization of a bilaminar membranous structure containing cristae.

Measurements and counts included in this study were made without knowing the age of the animal. After measurements were completed, all data were arranged according to animal number, area of cerebral cortex, and age group. Statistical analyses included means, standard deviations, standard errors of the mean, Student's t-tests and linear regressions.

RESULTS

All measurements and statistical analyses are summarized in Table 11-1. The cross-sectional areas of capillary walls in the frontal and occipital cortices are presented in Row C. These areas were estimated by subtracting the area of the lumen (Row B) from the area of the entire capillary (Row A). The capillary walls were significantly thinner in the older groups than the younger groups (Figure 11-3). The regression coefficients were equal for the frontal and occipital areas. Combining data from the two areas, the difference in means between the 4-y.o. and 20-y.o. groups was 40%. The pericytes, one component of the capillary wall, showed no significant difference in cross-sectional area with age (Table 11-1, Row D). The cross-sectional area of the remaining components, the endothelial cells and basal laminae (Row E), were smaller in older than younger age groups. Their size was calculated by subtracting the pericyte area (Row D) from the capillary wall area (Row C). Again, the difference was significant in both.

No significant change occurred with age in the thickness of the BL_o (Table 11-1, Row F) of capillaries; the regression coefficients for the two cortical areas were equivalent, and the magnitude of the difference between the 4-y.o. and 20-y.o. groups was 36%. However, this structure was significantly thicker in the frontal cortex than in the occipital at all ages (in each case $p = 0.001$). The BL_i of the frontal cortex tended to decrease with age (Row G).

Loss and replacement of endothelial cells in the capillaries of peripheral organs is reported to result in increased thickness of the perivascular basal laminae (21). If the same is true of cerebral capillaries, our finding that the BL_o was not thickened in older animals suggests that the replacement of cerebral capillaries beyond early postnatal development is rare.

The number of endothelial mitochondria per capillary profile declined significantly with age in the frontal cortex, but not in the occipital cortex (Row H): in

Table 11-1. Morphological Characteristics of the Cortical Microvasculature in Three Groups of *Macaca Nemestrina*.

Characteristic	Site	N	4 y.o. mean s.d.	10 y.o. mean s.d.	20 y.o. mean s.d.	R	P
A. Entire Capillary Cross-sectional Area, μ^2	frontal	10–18	31.6 ± 8.1	29.3 ± 9.9	22.8 ± 2.2	-0.39	NS
	occipital	11–24	36.6 ± 10.4	28.0 ± 6.2	20.7 ± 3.5	-0.64	<0.01
B. Capillary Lumen Cross-sectional Area, μ^2	frontal	10–18	7.3 ± 2.7	10.1 ± 6.1	6.7 ± 3.3	-0.15	NS
	occipital	11–24	10.4 ± 2.5	9.4 ± 4.5	6.1 ± 2.1	-0.42	NS
C. Capillary Wall Cross-sectional Area, calculated as A–B, μ^2	frontal	10–18	24.4 ± 5.5	19.2 ± 4.2	15.9 ± 3.2	-0.55	0.02
	occipital	11–24	26.3 ± 11.8	19.4 ± 4.6	14.6 ± 2.2	-0.55	0.02
D. Pericytes, Cross-sectional Area, μ^2	frontal	12–34	1.5 ± 0.2	0.9 ± 0.7	0.9 ± 0.2	-0.21	NS
	occipital	14–25	1.3 ± 1.2	0.6 ± 0.3	0.4 ± 0.2	-0.43	NS
E. Endothelial Cells and Basal Laminae Cross-sectional Area, calculated as C–D, μ^2	frontal	10–34	22.9 ± 5.3	18.3 ± 4.5	15.0 ± 3.0	-0.53	0.03
	occipital	11–25	25.0 ± 5.3	18.3 ± 4.5	15.0 ± 3.0	-0.55	0.02
F. Outer Basal Lamina (BL_O), Thickness, μ	frontal	159–354	0.13 ± 0.02	0.20 ± 0.05	0.19 ± 0.08	0.28	NS
	occipital	165–376	0.11 ± 0.01	0.14 ± 0.03	0.13 ± 0.03	0.14	NS
G. Inner Basal Lamina (BL_I), Cross-sectional Area, μ^2	frontal	12–34	0.23 ± 0.13	0.11 ± 0.06	0.10 ± 0.03	-0.47	0.05
	occipital	14–25	0.12 ± 0.05	0.09 ± 0.03	-.09 ± 0.01	-0.39	NS
H. Endothelial Microchondria per Capillary Profile	frontal	10–18	3.5 ± 1.0	3.3 ± 0.9	2.3 ± 0.5	-0.50	0.04
	occipital	11–24	3.8 ± 1.5	2.5 ± 0.7	2.8 ± 0.3	-0.21	NS

Means are based upon measurements from 3 4-y.o., 10 10-y.o., and 5 20-y.o. animals. N = range of numbers of capillary profiles sampled per animal. R = regression coefficient. Significance estimates (p) are based on linear regression analyses of measurements vs. age group. NS indicates p > .10.

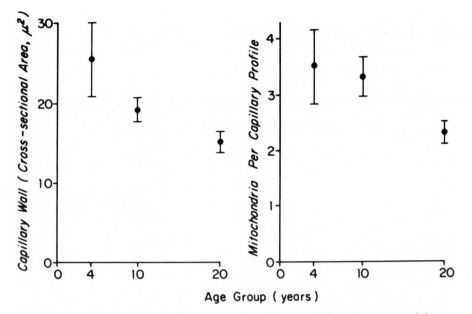

Fig. 11-3. Left: mean cross-sectional areas of capillary walls from the cortex of 3 age groups of *M. nemestrina* (combined data from frontal and occipital poles). Right: numbers of mitochondria in endothelial cells of capillaries from the frontal cortex. Circles represent means; vertical bars represent standard errors of the means.

the frontal cortex, the difference appeared to be much greater between the 20-y.o. and 10-y.o. groups than between the 10-y.o. and 4-y.o. groups (Figure 11-3).

DISCUSSION

The walls of capillaries in the cerebral cortex of *M. nemestrina* are thinner in animals over 20 y.o. than in younger animals. Such thinning may increase the vulnerability of cerebral vessels to mechanical damage, exposing the surrounding parenchyma to substances in the blood from which it is ordinarily protected. Nandy (10) has proposed that breaks in the BBB, exposing cerebral antigens to the immune system, may account for the development of brain-reactive antibodies seen in old mice and in the old macaques of this study (see Chapter 10, this volume).

   To the extent that cerebral capillaries become thinner and lose their structural integrity with age, one might also expect to find impairment of parenchymal function due to chronic local ischemia. Healthy aging humans show no significant decline in cerebral blood flow, oxygen consumption, or venous oxygen tension at rest (18, 19). However, little is known about the capacity of the cerebral microvasculature in aged organisms to respond to conditions that require increased blood flow to the brain. Further research is needed to determine whether the thinning of capillaries in the brain leads to decreased numbers of capillaries per unit volume and to functional impairment. Aside from the possible destructive consequences, the 40% decline in cross-sectional area of the cerebral capillary walls seen in both cortical areas and the 50% decline in thickness of the BL_i seen in the frontal cortex could also influence permeability characteristics of the capillaries. Chronic changes in BBB permeability could have long-term effects on surrounding parenchymal cells and could account for some of the changes in potency and neurotoxicity of psychotropic drugs observed in the elderly. Such changes have usually been attributed to decreased neuronal mass, reduced metabolic functioning of brain cells (16) or to changes in plasma proteins that influence the amounts of free and protein-bound drugs in the circulation (1) of the elderly.

Of course, the interendothelial tight junctions are believed to be the most important sites preventing the entry of inappropriate substances into brain parenchyma. Whether the efficacy of tight junctions declines with increasing age has not been reported for any species. Further ultra-structural studies in aging animals are needed to answer this question.

The findings that the decline in wall thickness was due primarily to thinning of the endothelial cells, and that in frontal cortex the number of mitochondria per endothelial cell was reduced, may indicate a decline in the active transport capacity of the cerebral component of the BBB with age. Numerous transport systems for metabolic substrates (21) have been identified in the BBB, including those for glucose, amino acids, nucleic acids and choline. These substances are transported via carrier mediated mechanisms which may be passive or active (13, 19). While the question of active transport across the cerebral capillaries as opposed to capillaries in the choroid plexus has not been answered definitively, the fact that cerebral capillaries contain greater numbers of mitochondria than capillaries in other organs (12) makes it reasonable to propose the existence of metabolic pumping mechanisms in their endothelial lining. Impairment of active transport mechanisms in the BBB in older primates could have serious consequences for endothelial function and indirectly for neuronal functioning.

It is clear that morphologic changes occur in the cerebral capillaries of the aging primate. This work should be repeated in shorter lived animals to identify species that share these characteristics of aging in order that functional studies requiring larger numbers of subjects can be performed.

ACKNOWLEDGMENTS

Micro Measurements, Inc., Burlington, MA kindly provided access to the Optomax for this study. This work was supported in part by grants PHS NU 1548-03,

8T063078 and PHS NU 500-3, and by grants RR00166, RR52177, and AG62145 from the National Institutes of Health. We thank Ms. Karen Hashimoto and Ms. Sally Swedine for technical assistance and Drs. Daniel Parrish and Rudolph Vracko for their generosity in providing access to the graphics computer facility of the General Medical Research Program, Veterans Administration Hospital, Seattle, Washington.

REFERENCES

1. Bressler, R., and Palmer J. (1973): Drug interactions in the aged. In: *Drug Issues in Geropsychiatry*, edited by W. E. Fann and G. L. Maddox, pp. 49–57. Baltimore: Williams & Wilkins.

2. Brightman, M. W. (1965a): The distribution within the brain of ferritin injected into cerebrospinal fluid compartments. II. Parenchymal distribution. *J. Cell Biol.*, **26**: 99–123.

3. Brightman, M. W. (1967): Intracerebral movement of proteins injected into blood and cerebrospinal fluid. *Anat. Rec.*, **157**: 219.

4. Brizzee, K. R., Klara, P., and Johnson, J. E. (1975): Changes in microanatomy, neurocytology and fine structure with aging. In: *Neurobiology of Aging*, edited by J. M. Ordy and K. R. Brizzee, pp. 425–462. New York: Plenum Press.

5. Davson, H. (1976): The blood-brain barrier. *J. Physiol.*, **255**: 1–28.

6. Donahue, S. (1964): A relationship between fine structure and function of blood vessels in the central nervous system of rabbit fetuses. *Am. J. Anat.*, **115**: 17–26.

7. Donahue, S., and Pappas, G. D. (1961): The fine structure of capillaries in the cerebral cortex of the rat at various stages of development. *Am. J. Anat.*, **108**: 331–347.

8. Feder, N. (1971): Microperoxidase: An ultrastructural tracer of low molecular weight. *J. Cell Biol.*, **51**: 339–343.

9. Graham, R. C., and Karnovsky, M. J. (1966): The early stages of absorption of injected horseradish peroxidase in the proximal tabules of mouse kidney: Ultrastructural cytochemistry by a new technique. *J. Histochem. Cytochem.*, **14**: 291–302.

10. Nandy, K. (1973): Brain reactive antibodies in serum of aged mice. In: *Progress in Brain Research Vol. 40*, edited by D. H. Ford, pp. 437–454. Elsevier Scientific Publishing Co., Amsterdam.

11. Oldendorf, W. H., and Brown, W. J. (1975): Greater number of capillary endothelial cell mitochondria in brain than in muscle (38889). *Proc. Soc. Exp. Biol. Med.*, **149**: 736–738.

12. Oldendorf, W. H., Cornford, M. E., and Brown, W. J. (1977): The large apparent work capability of the blood-brain barrier: A study of the mitochondrial content of capillary endothelial cells in brain and other tissues of the rat. *Ann. Neurol.*, **1**: 409–417.

13. Pardridge, W. M. (1977): Regulation of amino acid availability to the brain. In: *Nutrition and the Brain, Vol. 1*, edited by R. J. Wurtman and J. J. Wurtman, pp. 141–204. New York: Raven Press.

14. Rapoport, S. I. (1976): *Blood Brain Barrier in Physiology and Medicine.* New York: Raven Press.

15. Reese, T. S., and Karnovsky, M. J. (1967): Fine structural localization of a blood-brain barrier to exogenous peroxidase. *J. Cell Biol.*, **34**: 207–217.

16. Salzman, C., Shader, R. U., and Harmatz, J. S. (1975): Response of the elderly to psychotropic drugs: predictable or idiosyncratic? In: *Aging, Vol. 2, Genesis and Treat-

ment of Psychologic Disorders in the Elderly, edited by S. Gershon and A. Raskin, pp. 259–272. New York: Raven Press.

17. Schwink, A., and Wetzstein, R.   (1966): Die Kapillaren in Subcommissuralorgan der Ratte. *Z. Zellforsch.*, **73**: 56–88.

18. Sokoloff, L.   (1976): Circulation and energy metabolism of the brain. In: *Basic Neurochemistry*, 2nd Edition, edited by G. J. Siegel, R. W. Albers, R. Katzman and B. W. Agranoff, pp. 388–413. Boston: Little, Brown and Co.

19. Sokoloff, L., Fitzgerald, G. G., and Kaufman, E. E.   (1977): Cerebral nutrition and energy metabolism. In: *Nutrition and the Brain, Vol. 1, Determinants of the Availability of Nutrients to the Brain*, edited by R. J. Wurtman and J. J. Wurtman, pp. 87–140. New York: Raven Press.

20. Thompson, L. W.   (1976): Cerebral blood flow, EEG, and behavior in aging. In: *Neurobiology of Aging*, edited by R. D. Terry and S. Gershon, pp. 103–120. New York: Raven Press.

21. Vracko, R.   (1974): Basal lamina scaffold—anatomy and significance for maintenance of orderly tissue structure. *Am. J. Pathol.*, **77**: 314–338.

12

Cerebellar Cell Populations, Lipofuscin Pigment, and Acetylcholinesterase Activity

Kalidas Nandy and Vijaya K. Vijayan

Geriatric Research, Education and Clinical Center,
Veterans Administration Hospital, Bedford, Massachusetts;
Department of Anatomy and Neurology, Boston University Medical School,
Boston, Massachusetts; and Department of Human Anatomy,
University of California School of Medicine,
Davis, California

INTRODUCTION

During the postmaturity period of life, the mammalian cerebellum undergoes structural and neurochemical alterations that may contribute to the progressive functional decrements characteristic of senescence. These changes include a decline in energy use (25), substantial acquisition of lipofuscin by neuronal and glial cells of the cerebellar cortex and the deep nuclei (8, 31), loss of spines, decreased aborizations (45), and vacuolation and thickening (1) of the Purkinje-cell (P-cell) dendrites. Quantitative morphometric comparisons of the cerebella of young and old animals should yield more concrete and precise data on age differences in the cerebellar circuitry. The cerebellum, owing to its heterogenous neuronal populations and cytoarchitectural features, has not been a popular target for cell counting. The granule cells constitute one of the most densely aggregated neurons in the brain (23); the difficulties of accurately identifying and enumerating the various neuronal and glial cell populations in routine paraffin sections have been discussed (12, 34). In contrast, the P-cells are a unique category of neurons distributed in a monocellular array at the junction of the molecular and the granule cell layers. They have distinct, deeply staining nucleoli and can be easily counted in sections, tangential or perpendicular to the cell sheet (2). Since the axons of the P-cells project to the deep nuclei and indirectly convey to them the afferent inputs reaching the cerebellar cortex, a substantial reduction in their total number may be assumed to undermine the efficiency of the cerebellum as a motor apparatus.

The available information on the fate of the P-cell population in aging mammals has been recently reviewed (17, 18). While there is no common trend in experimental animals, a curvilinear reduction in the total number of P-cells was demonstrated in the human, starting in the sixth decade and progressing at the rate of 2.5% per decade (14, 15, 17). To date, there have been no parallel studies on lifespan changes in P-cell numbers in nonhuman primates.

Another consistent change in mammalian aging is deposition of lipofuscin pigment in neuronal cytoplasm (30, 31, 35, 39, 42, 43, 47). This pigment has also been studied in the neurons of the cerebral cortex in rodents (6, 7, 30, 31, 35) and in squirrel monkey (*Saimiri sciureus*) (4), and in the P-cells and dentate nucleus cells of the rhesus macaque (*Macaca mulatta*) (8). However, no study has been reported on lipofuscin in the P-cells of the pigtail macaque, *M. nemestrina*.

To ascertain the suitability of *M. nemestrina* as a model of human aging, we studied the population of P-cells and their lipofuscin content in the cerebellum of adolescent, young adult and mature adult animals. We also measured the activity of the cholinergic neurotransmitter enzyme, acetylcholinesterase (AChE), in the cerebellum of young and old *M. nemestrina*.

METHODS

Within 20 min of cardiorespiratory arrest, the cerebellum was excised and bisected in the midline. The left hemisphere was cut parasagittally into 5-mm thick blocks, frozen by placing on a glass slide on dry ice, and shipped on dry ice to one investigator (K. N.) for P-cell and granule cell density and lipofuscin pigment in P-cells. The right hemisphere was cut into three blocks by parasagittal cuts, 5 mm from the midline and 3 mm from the lateral border. The medial and lateral blocks were placed in McDowell's fixative (26) (see also Chapter 3, this volume) and shipped at ambient temperature to the other investigator (V. K. V.) for P-cell counts. The central block was frozen and shipped on dry ice for AChE determinations.

All of the subjects were pigtail macaques (*M. nemestrina*). Because of shipping problems, the number of subjects contributing data on different measures varied with the laboratory and the vulnerability of specimens to ambient conditions during shipment. Lipofuscin determinations (Table 12-1) were made on

13 subjects (12 females; 1 male, 20 y. o.); cell counts in the cerebellar hemisphere (Table 12-2) were done in 11 females; cell counts in the vermis (Table 12-3) were done in 20 subjects including 3 males (1 10-y. o., 2 20-y. o.); and AChE determinations (Table 12-4) were made in 18 subjects including the same 3 males.

The left cerebellar hemispheres were cut into small pieces (10 mm × 10 mm) and 10-μm frozen serial sections were cut in a cryostat. Ten sections, using every third section from five separate pieces, were briefly fixed in 10% neutral buffered formalin solution. Lipofuscin pigment was studied in formalin-fixed unstained sections in a fluorescence microscope and the pigment was identified by its characteristic autofluorescence. Semiquantitative measurements were done by counting the number of intersections overlying pigment particles in P-cells in ten consecutive fields using an ocular grid in a fluorescence microscope (31).

Frozen sections fixed with formalin were also stained with toluidine blue and hematoxylene and eosin (H & E). Only nucleated P-cells and granule cells in ten consecutive fields in ten sections cut from each of five pieces were counted. The number of P-cells and granule cells per unit area was calculated by averaging the numbers for all fields in all sections for each animal.

The vermis specimens in McDowell's fixative were embedded in paraplast, and serial sagittal sections (6 μm thick) were cut. The sections in each series were stained with both H & E and cresyl violet. The stained sections were placed in a photographic enlarger and photographed at ×6. These photographs were used for identifying lobules and for orienting the slides during the remainder of the procedure. The measurements and cell counts were done on adjacent sections stained by different methods and the results were compared.

In each section, the P-cells were enumerated at the magnification of ×312 (×25 objective, ×1.25 optovar, ×10 eyepiece of a Zeiss photo-microscope) and the counts were recorded for the total number of cells (T) as well as for nucleolated cells (N) only. For each lobule the ratio of N to T (N:T ratio) was calculated. From the number of P-cells and the length of the P-cell line (PCL), P-cells/mm PCL were calculated.

For AChE determinations, the frozen blocks of the cerebellar hemisphere were allowed to thaw slightly and from each block sample slices were taken and combined. The samples were homogenized (1:10, w/v) in 0.5% Triton-X-100 in Tris-EDTA buffer, pH 8.6. The homogenate was used for AChE assay by Ellman's (16) procedure as described previously (46). Total protein was determined by the method of Lowry et al. (24). AChE activity was expressed as μmole substrate hydrolyzed/min/g wet weight and as μmole substrate hydrolyzed/min/mg protein.

Age differences were tested for in all measures by *t*-test for differences among the 3 age groups in all possible pairs.

RESULTS

Upon activation at a wave length of 3650 Å, lipofuscin pigment was visualized by its yellow-orange autofluorescence with an emission spectrum of 2800 to 4000 Å. Lipofuscin was consistently demonstrated in the cytoplasm of the P-cells in all animals from all age groups studied. The distribution of the pigment varied from fine granules to perinuclear aggregation to polar clumps, and the amount increased with age. There was a considerable overlapping in the number of intersections overlying pigment particles, especially in the 4-y. o. and 10-y. o. groups, and the difference was not statistically significant. On the other hand, the amount of pigment in the P-cells of the 20-y. o. group was significantly higher than in the younger age groups (Table 12-1).

The P-cells and granular cells in left cerebellar hemisphere were counted using fresh frozen sections stained by toluidine blue and H & E stains. The number of P-cells per unit area was uniformly low in all age groups, and seemed to decline gradually with increasing age. Although the differences between the adjacent groups were not significant, there seemed to be a significant loss of these cells between 4 and 20 years of age. The granule cells, on the other hand, showed a much higher number per unit area and no significant difference was noted between the age groups (Table 12-2).

In the right vermis, the length of the highly folded line along which the P-cells occurred was measured separately for lobules V and VI. Lobule V had an average PCL of 4.68 cm, and lobule VI had an average PCL of 4.21 cm per animal. Repeated measurements of the line using the curvimeter gave very close values.

Table 12-1. Lipofuscin Pigment in P-cells of the Left Cerebellar Cortex of *M. nemestrina* (Mean Number of Grid Intersections Overlying Lipofuscin Granules in 10 Consecutive Fields).

Age (n)	4 y. o. (3)	10 y. o. (5)	20 y. o. (5)
	10.6	15.2	19.9
Lipofuscin	9.4	10.6	18.2
Content	11.6	14.8	20.6
		12.2	18.4
		9.2	22.4
Mean ± S.D.	10.5 ± 1.1	12.2 ± 1.7	19.9 ± 1.7
Significance level by t-test		(p = 0.5)	(p = 0.001)

Table 12-2. Cell Counts per Unit Area in Cortex of the Left Cerebellar Hemisphere of Female *M. nemestrina*.

	Purkinje Cells per Unit Area			Granule Cells per Unit Area		
	4 Years	10 Years	20 Years	4 Years	10 Years	20 Years
	2.6	2.0	1.3	6.4	5.0	4.8
	2.6	1.8	1.5	5.6	6.5	5.4
	2.4	2.2	1.3	5.9	6.7	6.1
		1.7			6.4	
		1.9			8.7	
Mean ± S.D.	2.5 ± 0.1	1.9 ± 0.2	1.4 ± 0.1	6.0 ± 0.4	6.7 ± 1.3	5.4 ± 0.7

Significance levels

$p = 0.4$ $p = 0.1$ $p = 0.71$ $p = 0.71$

$p = 0.001$ $p = 0.71$

The total number of cells counted for any lobule or its subdivision in a cresyl violet-stained section of the vermis closely matched the number obtained for the corresponding area in the immediately adjacent section of the series. Of 15,583 P-cells counted in all sections combined, 8,357 were in lobule V and 7,226 in lobule VI. When nucleolated cells alone were included in the count, the total number was 6,875, of which 3,662 were in lobule V and 3,213 in lobule VI. On an average, 146 nucleolated P-cells were enumerated in lobule V, and 129 in lobule VI. The mean N:T ratio for all samples was $0.438 ± 0.163$ (S.E.M.) for lobule V and $0.447 ± 0.014$ (S.E.M.) for lobule VI. In other words, nucleolated cells accounted for 43.8% of the total cells counted in lobule V and 44.6% of those in lobule VI. There was no significant difference in the mean N:T ratio with age, for either lobule V or VI or for their combined mean.

The mean number of P-cells/mm PCL in the right cerebellar vermis at 4, 10

Table 12-3. Total (T) and Nucleolated (N) P-cells/mm PCL in the Cerebellar Vermis of the *M. nemestrina* (Mean ± S.D., n = number of animals).

Age (n)	Lobule V		Lobule VI		Lobules V & VI Combined	
	T	N	T	N	T	N
20 (8)	6.90 ± 0.90	3.01 ± 0.65	7.09 ± 1.05	3.15 ± 0.79	7.04 ± 0.76	3.09 ± 0.71
10 (9)	7.06 ± 0.60	2.92 ± 0.54	6.71 ± 0.66	2.87 ± 0.60	6.88 ± 0.54	2.90 ± 0.57
4 (3)	7.38 ± 1.21	2.67 ± 0.59	7.50 ± 1.18	3.52 ± 0.17	7.41 ± 1.19	3.02 ± 0.21

Table 12-4. AChE Activity and Protein Content in the Cerebellum.

Age (n)	AChE Activity μmole/g wet weight/min	Protein Content mg/g wet weight	AChE Activity μmole/mg protein/h
4 (3)	7.35 ± 1.18	115.5 ± 9.64	3.82 ± 0.57
10 (10)	7.69 ± 2.37	128.0 ± 26.26	3.55 ± 1.11
20 (5)	7.11 ± 1.05	134.83 ± 10.7	3.20 ± 0.56

Each value is Mean ± S.D.
n = number of animals

and 20 years of age is given in Table 12-3. No age group differences were found in the cell counts/unit length PCL for lobules V and VI separately or combined (no t-test between the age-group means presented in Table 12-3 reached a significance of p ≤ 0.05). Similarly, no significant sex difference in the density of P-cell distribution was apparent at any age. Protein and AChE activities in the right cerebellar hemispheres (Table 12-4) did not show any significant age-related differences.

DISCUSSION

Two consistent age differences in the mammalian brain are the loss of neurons and intracytoplasmic deposition of lipofuscin pigment. The increase of lipofuscin with age has been reported in various rodents and in humans and certain nonhuman primates (3, 4, 11, 21, 28-33, 35, 37, 38, 41-44, 47). The early origin and the age-related increase of the pigment has been demonstrated in the dentate nucleus and P-cells of the cerebellum as well as in the neurons of other parts of the CNS in rhesus monkeys (5, 8, 10). Age-associated increase in lipofuscin deposition has been found in the hypothalamus (13), lateral geniculate body (19, 20), cerebral cortex, hippocampus, and mammillary bodies of the macaque. However, the pigment has not been thoroughly investigated in the cerebellar P-cells of these animals. The present study indicates that P-cells in these animals, like the neurons in other areas of the brain, also exhibit the progressive accumulation of pigment with age.

The number of P-cells per unit area in cerebellar hemisphere consistently decreased with age, but no such change was demonstrated in the vermis. The reason for this difference is not clear. The methods of preservation and preparation of the specimens for cell counting were quite different and may have masked age differences in the vermis. There is, however, ample evidence for differential rates of cell loss in different brain structures, and it is possible that P-cell loss in the cerebellar hemispheres occurs at a greater rate than in the vermis. Furthermore, P-cells of the hemisphere which are functionally or metabolically different than those of the vermis might be more prone to age-related degeneration. The granule cells, on the other hand, do not seem to change in number with age. Although every effort was made to distinguish these cells from the neuroglial cells, some mistake in distinguishing the two might be possible. Since the neurogilial cells have been reported to increase with age in mammalian brain (9), any confusion between granular and glial cells might also account for the lack of any difference in the number of granule cells in the 3 age groups.

The lack of alteration in cerebellar AChE activity with age was comparable to findings in man (27), and in mouse (46). Himwich (22) reported a tentative reduction in AChE activity of cortical areas, spinal cord, cerebellum and thalamus of 15- to 16-y. o. rhesus macaques. Only a limited number of animals was used in this preliminary study and any possible brain pathology was not excluded. Samorajski and Rolsten (40), on the other hand, failed to find a significant loss in cerebellar AChE activity in rhesus macaques between 3 and 18 y. o. While it seems likely that fluctuations in AChE levels may not be indicative of the aging process in general, quantitation of AChE content in specific layers of the cerebellum, as has been accomplished for the adult rhesus macaque (36), would be invaluable in permanently excluding discrete and layer-specific alterations in the level of this enzyme during aging.

In summary, the present study indicates that there is an age-related decline in the number of P-cells in the cerebellum of pigtail macaques, while the granule cells remain unchanged. Lipofuscin pigment was demonstrated in the P-cells in all age groups and the pigment deposition increased as a function of age. These observations seem to correlate with studies in other animals including human and other nonhuman primates.

ACKNOWLEDGMENTS

This study was supported by National Institutes of Health grants NS12964, RR00166, RR52177 and AG62145, and by a grant from the Veterans Administration. The technical assistance of Ms. Nancy Roy is gratefully acknowledged.

REFERENCES

1. Andrew, W. (1938): Purkinje cell in man from birth to senility. *Z. Zellforsch.*, **28**: 292–304.
2. Armstrong, D. M., and Schild, R. F. (1970): A quantitative study of the Purkinje cells in the cerebellum of the albino rat. *J. Comp. Neurol.*, **139**: 449–456.

3. Bondareff, W. (1957): Genesis of intracellular pigment in the spinal ganglia of senile rats. An electron microscopic study. *J. Geront.*, **12**: 364–369.
4. Bourne, G. H. (1973): Lipofuscin. *Progr. Brain Res.*, **40**: 187–201.
5. Brizzee, K. R. (1973): Quantitative histological studies on aging changes in cerebral cortex of rhesus monkeys and albino rats with notes on effects of prolonged low-dose ionizing irradiation in the rat. *Progr. Brain Res.*, **40**: 141–160.
6. Brizzee, K. R., Cancilla, P. A., Sherwood, N., and Timiras, P. S. (1969): The amount and distribution of pigments in neurons and glia of the cerebral cortex. *J. Geront.*, **24**: 127–135.
7. Brizzee, K. R. and Johnson, F. A. (1970): Depth distribution of lipofuscin pigment in cerebral cortex of albino rat. *Acta Neuropath.*, **16**: 205–219.
8. Brizzee, K. R. Kaack, B., and Klara, P. (1975): Lipofuscin: intra- and extraneuronal accumulation and regional distribution. In: *Neurobiology of Aging*, edited by J. M. Ordy and K. R. Brizzee, pp. 463–484. New York; Plenum Press.
9. Brizzee, K. R., Ordy, J. M., Hansche, J., and Kaack, B. (1976): Quantitative assessment of changes in neuron and glia cell packing density and lipofuscin accumulation with age in the cerebral cortex of a non-human primate (*Macaca mulatta*). *Aging*, **3**: 229–244.
10. Brizzee, K. R., Ordy, J. M., and Kaack, B. (1974): Early appearance and regional differences in intraneuronal and extraneuronal lipofuscin accumulation with age in the non-human primate (*Macaca mulatta*). *J. Geront.*, **29**: 366–381.
11. Brody, H. (1955): Organization of cerebral cortex. III. A study of aging in the human cerebral cortex. *J. Comp. Neurol.*, **102**: 511–556.
12. Clos, J., and Legrand, J. (1973): Effects of thyroid deficiency on the different cell populations of the cerebellum in the young rat. *Brain Res.*, **63**: 450–455.
13. El-Shazzawi, E., and Malaty, H. A. (1975): Electron microscopic observations on extraneuronal lipofuscin in the monkey brain. *Cell Tiss. Res.*, **161**: 555–565.
14. Ellis, R. S. (1919): A preliminary quantitative study of the Purkinje cells in normal, subnormal and senescent human cerebella, with some notes of functional localization. *J. Comp. Neurol.*, **30**: 229–252.
15. Ellis, R. S. (1920): Norms for some structural changes in the human cerebellum from birth to old age. *J. Comp. Neurol.*, **32**: 1–32.
16. Ellman, G. L., Courtney, K. D., Andres, V., Jr. and Featherstone, R. M. (1961): A new and rapid colorimetric determination of acetylcholinesterase activity. *Biochem. Pharmacol.*, **7**: 88–95.
17. Hall, T. C., Miller, A. K. H., and Corsellis, J. A. N. (1975): Variations in the human Purkinje cell population according to age and sex. *Neuropath. Appl. Neurobiol.*, **1**: 267–292.
18. Hanley, T. (1974): "Neuronal fall-out" in the aging brain: a critical review of the quantitative data. *Age and Aging*, **3**: 133–151.
19. Hasan, M., and Glees, P. (1972): Electron microscopic appearance of neuronal lipofuscin using different preparation techniques including freeze-etching. *Exp. Geront.*, **7**: 345–351.
20. Hasan, M., and Glees, P. (1973): Ultrastructural age changes in hippocampal neurons, synapses and neuroglia. *Exp. Geront.*, **8**: 75–83.
21. Hasan, M., Glees, P., and Spoerri, P. E. (1974): Dissolution and removal of neuronal lipofuscin following dimethylaminoethyl p-chlorophenoxyacetate administration to guinea pigs. *Cell Tiss. Res.*, **150**: 369.

22. Himwich, W. A. (1973): Neurochemical patterns in the developing and aging brain. In: *Development and Aging in the Nervous System*, edited by M. Rockstein, pp. 151–170. New York; Academic Press.

23. Lange, W. (1975): Cell number and cell density in the cerebellar cortex of man and other mammals. *Cell Tiss. Res.*, **157**: 115–124.

24. Lowry, O. H., Rosebrough, N. J., Farr, A. L., and Randall, R. J. (1951): Protein measurement with the Folin phenol reagent. *J. Biol. Chem.*, **193**: 265–275.

25. Maker, H. S., Lehrer, G. M., Silides, D. J., and Weiss, C. (1973): Regional energy metabolism during maturation and aging of mouse cerebellum. *Progr. Brain Res.*, **40**: 493–308.

26. McDowell, E. M., and Trump, B. F. (1976): Histologic fixatives suitable for diagnostic light and electron microscopy. *Arch. Pathol. Vet. Med.*, **100**: 405–414.

27. McGeer, E., and McGeer, P. L. (1976): Neurotransmitter metabolism in the aging brain. *Aging*, **3**: 389–403.

28. Meier, C., and Glees, P. (1971): Effect of centrophenoxine on the old age pigment in satellite cells and neurons of senile rat spinal ganglia. *Acta Neuropath.*, **17**: 310.

29. Nanda, B. S., and Getty, R. (1974): Lipofuscin pigment in the nervous system of aging pig. *Aging Pigment*, *Current Research*, **1**: 11–18.

30. Nandy, K. (1968): Further studies on the effects of centrophenoxine on the lipofuscin pigment in the neurons of senile guinea pigs. *J. Geront.*, **23**: 82–92.

31. Nandy, K. (1971): Properties of neuronal lipofuscin pigment in mice. *Acta Neuropath. (Berlin)*, **19**: 25–32.

32. Nandy, K. (1978): Morphological changes in the aging brain. In: *Senile Dementia*: *A Biomedical Approach*, edited by K. Nandy, pp. 19–32. Amsterdam; Elsevier/North-Holland.

33. Nandy, K., and Lal, H. (1978): Neuronal lipofuscin and learning deficit in aging mammals. In: *Proceedings of 10th Collegium Internationale Neuropsychopharmacologicum Congress*. New York; Pergamon Press.

34. Palkovits, M., Magyar, P., and Szentagothai, J. (1971): Quantitative histological analysis of the cerebellar cortex in the cat. III. Structural organization of the molecular layer. *Brain Res.*, **34**: 1–18.

35. Reichel, W., Hollander, J., Clark, J. H., and Strehler, B. L. (1968): Lipofuscin pigment accumulation as function of age and distribution in rodent brain. *J. Geront.*, **23**: 17–78.

36. Robins, E., and Smith, D. E. (1952): A quantitative histochemical study of eight enzymes of the cerebellar cortex and subjacent white matter in the monkey. *Res. Publ. Ass. Res. Nerv. Ment. Dis.*, **32**: 305–327.

37. Samorajski, T., Keefe, J. R., and Ordy, J. M. (1964): Intracellular localization of lipofuscin age pigments in the nervous system. *J. Geront.*, **19**: 262–276.

38. Samorajski, T., Ordy, J. M., and Keefe, J. R. (1965): The fine structure of lipofuscin age pigment in the nervous system of aged mice. *J. Cell Biol.*, **26**: 779–795.

39. Samorajski, T., Ordy, J. M., and Rady-Reimer, P. (1968): Lipofuscin pigment accumulation in the nervous system of aging mice. *Anat. Rec.*, **160**: 555–574.

40. Samorajski, T., and Rolsten, C. (1973): Age and regional differences in the chemical composition of brains of mice, monkeys and humans. *Progr. Brain Res.*, **40**: 253–265.

41. Sekhon, S. S., and Maxwell, D. S. (1974): Ultrastructural changes in neurons of the spinal anterior horn of aging mice with particular references to the accumulation of lipofuscin pigment. *J. Neurocytol.*, **3**: 59–72.

42. Sulkin, N. M. (1953): Histochemical studies of the pigment in human autonomic ganglion cells. *J. Geront.*, 8: 435–448.
43. Sulkin, N. M. (1955): The properties and distribution of PAS-positive material in the nervous system of the senile dog. *J. Geront.*, 10: 135–144.
44. Sulkin, N. M., and Sirvanji, P. (1960): The experimental production of senile pigments in nerve cells of young rats. *J. Geront.*, 15: 2–9.
45. Terry, R. D., and Wiśniewski, H. M. (1975): Structural and chemical changes of the aged human brain. *Aging*, 2: 127–141.
46. Vijayan, V. K. (1977): Cholinergic enzymes in the cerebellum and the hippocampus of the senescent mouse. *Exp. Geront.*, 12: 7–11.
47. Whiteford, R., and Getty, R. (1966): Distribution of lipofuscin in the canine and porcine brain as related to aging. *J. Geront.*, 21: 31–44.

13

Survey of Changes
in the Eye

Elise Torczynski

Ophthalmic Pathology Laboratory, Department of Ophthalmology,
College of Medicine, University of South Florida,
Tampa, Florida

INTRODUCTION

To obtain meaningful laboratory data on age-related ocular differences, the animal eye chosen as the model for investigation should closely resemble the human globe in important aspects. For studies on a particular, acutely induced process, eyes of nonprimates are used as the disease produced is comparable to that in man, e.g., herpetic keratitis in rabbits, phacoanaphylactic endophthalmitis in rats. However, anatomical and functional variations in the eyes of nonprimates preclude their usefulness as models of certain chronic physiologic or pathologic processes in the human eye. Classic signs of aging in the human eye include lenticular enlargement, fibrosis of the ciliary body and degenerations of the peripheral retina and ora serrata (2, 11). To evaluate these, eyes of nonprimates are unsuitable. The lens in the infant rat virtually fills the globe, making assessment of enlargement with age of doubtful value. Senescent decline in accommodation may be linked to ciliary fibrosis but accommodation is lacking in rats, rabbits, dogs and cats. The junction of peripheral retina and ciliary epithelium has no oral bays in dogs and cats and is termed the ora lineata, to distinguish it from the ora serrata in man. Further, the retina in rabbits is not vascularized; retinal vessels in dogs and cats arise from the ciliary vessels; foveas and maculas are poorly differentiated in nonprimates (1). Eyes of nonhuman primates, however, are structurally almost identical to the human eye, and hence, most useful in studying aging processes.

While a few nonhuman primate studies are available regarding age related differences in specific ocular tissues (3, 6, 10), a broad survey encompassing all the ocular structures in macaques has not been reported. Hyalinization in the trabecular meshwork when sectioned tangentially, which has been noted in humans (70 to 90 y.o.), occurs to a lesser extent in *Macaca mulatta* (18 y.o.) (10). Hara et al. (3) noted an increase in mitochondria and a decrease in the rough endoplasmic reticulum in the nonpigmented ciliary epithelium in a *M. fascicularis* (18 y.o.) and a human (55 y.o.). They also reported thickening of the anterior basal membranes, more fenestrations in the capillary endothelium and many lipid inclusions in the ciliary epithelium of the older specimens.

This study was undertaken to determine to what extent the eyes of nonhuman primates, in particular *M. nemestrina*, are an appropriate model for aging changes in the human. Particular attention was given to deviations believed to be the consequence of increasing age, rather than to other factors such as diet, specific diseases, and activity level. Changes most frequently noted in the aging human eye include enlargement of the lens, nuclear sclerosis, Hassal-Henle warts in Descement's membrane peripherally, a decrease in the number of endothelial cells of the cornea, subepithelial fibrosis and intra-muscular fibrosis in the ciliary body, peripheral cystic degeneration of the retina, paving-stone degeneration of the retina, vitreous degeneration, and thinning and sclerosis of the blood vessels. All told, the macaque eyes were examined for more than 25 characteristics that have been related to aging in the human eye (2, 4, 11).

MATERIAL AND METHODS

The left eyes of 23 macaques, 21 *M. nemestrina* and 2 *M. fascicularis*, were studied. The sample included 19 females and 4 males. Nine animals including 1 male *M. Fascicularis* were 20 y.o.; 11 including 1 male *M. fascicularis*, 10 y.o.; and 3, 4 y.o. With the animal under anesthesia, the left eye was injected with 0.1 to 0.3 ml of McDowell's fixative (see Chapter 3, this volume) from a tuberculin syringe several minutes before cardiorespiratory arrest. The eyes were removed within 40 min of death and placed immediately in McDowell's fixative except for one which was removed after the animal, a 20-y.o. female, died of natural causes. Each globe was measured, transilluminated and examined externally and internally under a dissecting microscope. Twenty-one globes were opened horizontally. Two were sectioned vertically to include pathological changes noted on the gross examination. The central segment including the pupil and optic nerve (PO) was embedded in paraffin and processed routinely for light microscopy. Sections of the calottes were taken when indicated. Representative PO sections and cross-sections of the optic nerve were stained with hematoxylin and eosin, periodic acid Schiff's, Bodian's stain, Masson's trichrome, Alcian blue, Kinyoun's acid fast stain and cresyl violet.

Specimens of the central cornea within the pupillary border were taken in 6 monkeys (2 each from 4-, 10-, and 20-y.o. monkeys). A seventh specimen was taken from one monkey listed as 10-y.o., as other studies in this project indicated that this animal may have been older. A flat preparation of the endothelium, 1.0 X 2.0 mm often with remnants of Descemet's membrane and stroma attached, was stained with hematoxylin and eosin. Representative specimens of pigment epithelium in the parafoveal region from the same 7 monkeys were processed for electron microscopy (EM) to evaluate the presence of lipofuscin as the results with the Kinyoun's acid fast stain were not conclusive.

RESULTS

Three eyes were not included in the summary results because of injury in 2 and corneal edema in 1. They are described separately. Results from the remaining 20 eyes are listed in Table 13-1 and detailed findings of selected parameters are presented in Table 13-2. Many of the globes were partially collapsed, probably as a result of the premortem puncture, but the measurements did not indicate any change in size as the monkeys aged. The sclera in the monkey's eye thins markedly posterior to the insertion of the ocular muscles and collapses more easily than in the human eye.

The *M. nemestrina* globes, except when collapsed artifactually, ranged in size from 20.5 to 22.0 mm in the anteroposterior, horizontal and vertical diameters (average 21.0 mm). There was no size difference between males and females. The *M. fascicularis* globes were smaller, averaging 18.0 mm in all diameters.

Conjunctiva

A trace of subepithelial elastotic degeneration was seen in 1 10-y.o. and 1 20-y.o. monkey. Nests of lymphocytes were seen in two globes (1 10-y.o. and 1 20-y.o.), the significance of which is unknown.

Cornea

All of the corneas were clear. Their sizes were proportional to the size of the globe and did not vary with age. Regardless of age, Descemet's membrane adjacent to the trabecular meshwork was often discontinuous over short distances, the fragments were not thickened and the final, tapering segment extended onto the trabecular processes. Nodular excrescences of Descemet's membrane pe-

Table 13-1: Characteristics of Aging in the Human Eye and Their Prevalence in 18 *M. nemestrina* and 2 *M. fascicularis* Ranging from 4 y.o. to Over 20 y.o.

Ocular Structure	Changes Reported In Aging Human Eye	Prevalence of Changes In Aging Macaques
Conjunctiva	Subepithelial elastotic degeneration	+
Cornea	Arcus senilis	0
	Hassal-Henle Warts	0
	Fewer endothelial cells	+++
Iris	Atrophy, sclerosis	0
Trabeculum	Sclerosis, flattening	0
Lens	Increase in size	+++
	Nuclear sclerosis	++
Ciliary Body	Subepithelial fibrosis	+
	Intramuscular fibrosis	+
	Epithelial cysts	+++
Vitreous	Liquefaction	+++
	Condensation	++
	Posterior detachment	0
Retina	Paving-stone degeneration	++
	Iwanoff Blessig Cysts	+
Retinal Pigment Epithelium	Pigmentation irregularities	0
	Lipofuscin	+
Bruch's Membrane	Calcification	0
	Drusen	0
Optic Nerve	Pial thickening	0
	Corpora arenacea	0
	Corpora amylacea	0
Choroid	Narrowing of lumina choriocapillaris	0
	Flattening of choriocapillaris	0
	Sclerosis of vessels	0
Blood Vessels	Sclerosis	0
Sclera	Plaques	0

0, not observed; +, mild changes in some animals; ++, moderate changes in older animals; +++, usually observed in the oldest specimens.

ripherally (Hassal-Henle warts) were not noted in any globe, but in one globe from a 20-y.o. animal, minimal thickening of the final segment of Descemet's membrane was noted. The corneal endothelium, as seen in flat preparation, showed a modest decrease in the number of endothelial cells with advancing years (Figure 13-1). The preparation on 1 4-y.o. monkey was folded and could not be used. The number of endothelial cell nuclei in 10 nonoverlapping fields,

Table 13-2. Parameters Showing Detectable Variation in the Aging M. nemestrina.

Subject Age Group (Years)	Sex	Lens	Ciliary Body			Vitreous	Retina	
			Subepithelial Fibrosis	Muscular Sclerosis	Epithelium		Peripheral Cystic Degeneration	Number Of Paving Stone Areas
4*	F	0	0	0	0	G	+	0
4*	F	0	0	0	0	G	+	0
10	F	H, CF, PSC+	+	0	0	L	+	0
10	F	H+	+	0	+	L	+	0
10*	F	H+, CF+	+	0	+	L	+	0
10*	F	H+	+	++	0	L	0	0
10	F	H+	+	+	P+	L	0	1
10	F	0	+	+	C+	L	++	0
10	F	H+	+	+	C+	L	++	2
10	M	0	+	+	0	L	0	0
10	M	0	+	+	0	G	++	0
20	F	0	+	+	C+	L	0	0
20	F	D	+	+	C+	L	++	>9
20	F	H+, CF+	0	0	0	L	0	0
20	F	H++, PSC+, CF+	++	+	P+++	L	+++	>9
20	F	H++	+	0	C+	L	++	2
20	F	H+++	++	+	C+	L	0	0
20	F	H+++	+++	+	C+	L	+++	0
20*	M	H+++, CF+	++	++	0	L	0	0
20*	M	H++	0	+	C+	L	0	>9

*Animal from which flat preparations of corneal endothelium and EM of retinal pigment epithelium were made.

0, none or normal; +, trace; ++, mild; +++, moderate; C, cysts of ciliary epithelium; CF, cortical fragmentation and degeneration, lens fibers; D, lens disrupted artifactitiously with sectioning; F, female; G, gelatinous vitreous; H, homogeneity of nuclear fibers of lens as seen microscopically; L, liquefied vitreous; M, male; P, proliferation of ciliary epithelium; PSC, posterior subcapsular cataract.

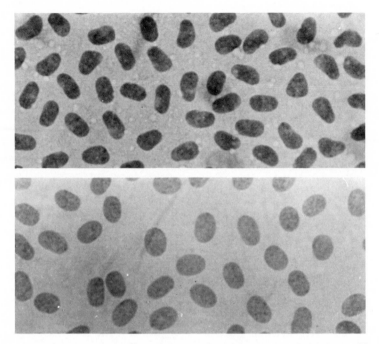

Fig. 13-1. *Upper:* Flat preparation, central corneal endothelium from 4-y.o. *M. nemestrina* (#73166). Nuclei are regularly spaced. Hematoxylin and eosin; ×500. *Lower:* Flat preparation, central cornea of 20-y.o. *M. nemestrina* (#75026). Nuclei are fewer in number and larger in size with aging. Hematoxylin and eosin; ×500.

viewed at a magnification of 1,000 were counted. In the 4-y.o. macaque, the number of nuclei averaged 105/high power field (hpf); in 10-y.o. monkeys, 78/hpf; and in 20-y.o. animals, 73/hpf.

Lens

The lenses increased in size with age; the anteroposterior and equatorial diameters measured 3.0 × 8.0 mm in the 4-y.o. monkeys, 3.5 to 4 × 8.5 to 9 mm in 10-y.o. monkeys and 4.0 to 5 × 9.5 to 10 mm in 20-y.o. monkeys. All lenses were yellow, probably as a result of fixation. Opacification of the nucleus was noted in the 20-y.o. monkeys. Cortical clefts were seen in lenses from a few of the oldest animals. Outlines of lens fibers and small interfibrillar clefts were present in the center of the lenticular nucleus in the 4-y.o. monkey (Figure 13-2, upper), in 3 10-y.o. monkeys, and in 1 20-y.o. monkey. Cataractous changes including moderate homogeneity of the lenticular nucleus (Figure 13-2, lower),

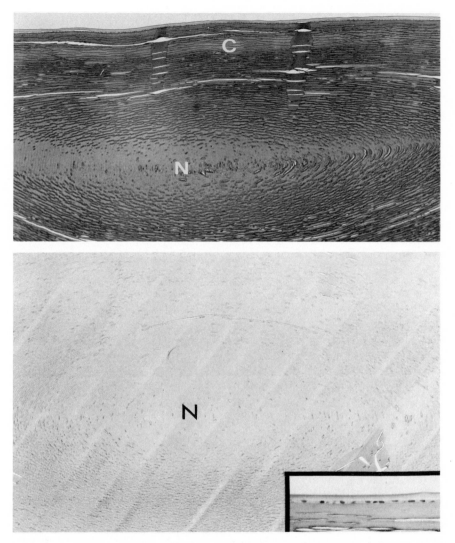

Fig. 13-2. *Upper:* Fibers are easily distinguished in lenticular nucleus (N) and cortex (C) of 10-y.o. female *M. nemestrina* (#76220). Hematoxylin and eosin; ×31. *Lower:* Lens enlarged, nucleus mildly homogeneous in 20-y.o. female *M. nemestrina* (#76200). Hematoxylin and eosin; ×31. *Inset:* Fading and loss of a few epithelial nuclei from anterior lens of 20-y.o. female *M. nemestrina* (#76201). Hematoxylin and eosin; ×125.

decrease in clefting, Morgagnian globules in the cortex, bladder cells, and degenerating fibers were seen in some of the 20-y.o. animals (Table 13-2).

Ciliary body

Subepithelial fibrosis and hyalinization of the ciliary muscle were not seen in 4-y.o. macaques. A trace of subepithelial fibrosis was present in the 10-y.o. monkeys and was usually, but not always, found in 20-y.o. monkeys (Figure 13-3). A small amount of muscular sclerosis was present in 1 20-y.o. animal and at most a trace occurred in the other 10- and 20-y.o. animals. Cysts or proliferation of the ciliary epithelium were present in 5 10-y.o. and 6 20-y.o. animals (Table 13-2).

Vitreous

The vitreous was gelatinous in the 2 youngest monkeys, and in 1 10-y.o. monkey. Liquefaction and collapse of the vitreous were found in the eyes of 8 10-y.o. and 9 20-y.o. monkeys.

Retina

The retina was attached in all eyes. Peripheral cystic degeneration was not a conspicuous feature on gross inspection of the globes at any age, but was observed microscopically. A single vacuole or cyst in the retina at the ora, usually temporally, was noted in 2 4-y.o. and 7 10-y.o. monkeys (Figure 13-4). Four of the 20-y.o. monkeys had more than 1 cyst and 5 had none. Microscopically, the peripheral retina was thin on the temporal side and the nuclei were scant and irregular; nasally the retina was better preserved. In eyes without cysts, the capillaries in the inner retinal layers reached almost to the ora.

The retinal pigment epithelium anterior to the equator was heavily and regularly pigmented. Diffuse depigmentation, often seen in human globes, was not observed in any specimen. Paving-stone changes, also called cobblestone degeneration, which are flat pale areas 0.25 to 1.5 mm in diameter that are sharply demarcated from the adjacent tissues by a faint rim of pigmentation (Figure 13-5), were not seen in the 4-y.o. monkeys; one or two patches were seen in 2 10-y.o. animals, and one to many areas in 4 20-y.o. animals. Microscopically, sections of areas with paving-stone changes demonstrated marked atrophy of the retina, clumping or absence of pigment epithelial cells, migration of heavily pigmented macrophages into the retina, focal atrophy of the choroid, and chorioretinal adherence.

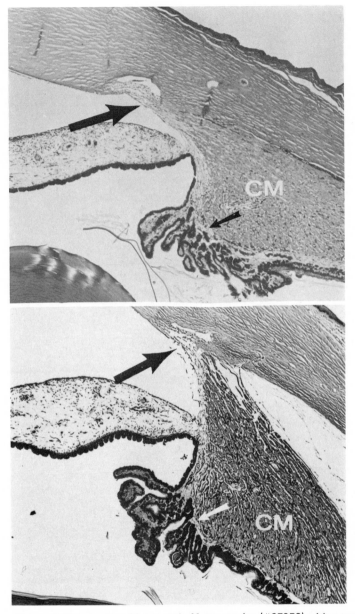

Fig. 13-3. *Upper:* Ciliary body in 20-y.o. male *M. nemestrina* (#67350) with a trace of intramuscular fibrosis and mild subepithelial fibrosis (small black arrow). The trabecular meshwork (large arrow, both figures) is thin or normal. Melanocytes in moderate numbers are intermixed with ciliary muscle (CM). Hematoxylin and eosin; ×31. *Lower:* Ciliary body in 20-y.o. female *M. nemestrina* (#76200) with little, if any, subendothelial fibrosis (white arrow) and no muscular fibrosis. Hematoxylin and eosin; ×31.

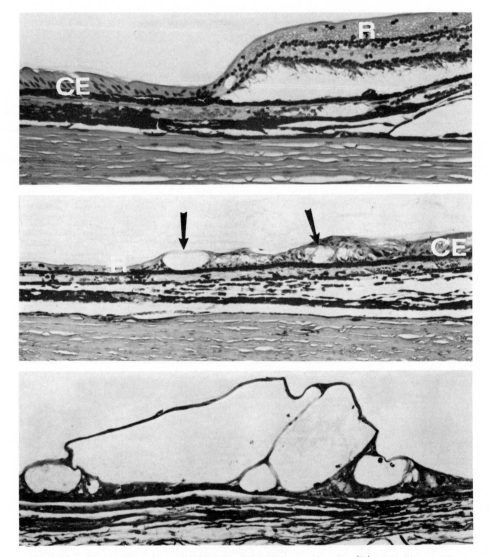

Fig. 13-4. *Upper:* Vacuole marks junction of orderly, nasal retina (R) with ciliary epithelium (CE) in 10-y.o. female *M. nemestrina* (#76318).   Hematoxylin and eosin; ×125. *Middle:* Trace of cystic degeneration (↓) temporally; retina (R) is thin and depleted of nuclei.   Fine strands of collapsed vitreous above, bridging ora.   Ciliary epithelium (CE) in 10-y.o. female *M. nemestrina* (#71336). Hematoxylin and eosin; ×79. *Lower:* Moderate cystic degeneration of peripheral retina in 20-y.o. female *M. nemestrina* (#76199). Hematoxylin and eosin; ×79.

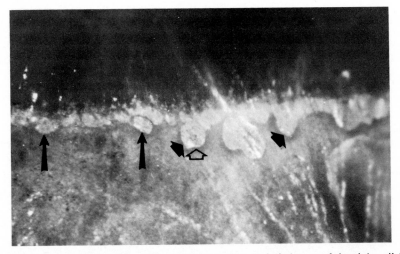

Fig. 13-5. Paving stone degeneration of the kind that encircled most of the globe, slightly anterior to similar changes in human retina. Irregular, flat areas (↑), sometimes confluent (◆), at ora, sharply demarcated from normal retina, occasionally rimmed by pigment (⬠) in 20-y.o. male *M. fascicularis* (#77005); ×10.

Other tissues

Basophilic stippling of Bowman's membrane peripherally was not noted. The trabecular meshwork in all eyes showed thin, flat plates separated by well defined spaces. Cysts of the iris pigment epithelium were seen in 1 20-y.o. monkey; the iridic stroma and musculature were otherwise unremarkable. The following were not found in any specimen: drusen, basophilia of Bruch's membrane, thickening of the pia of the optic nerve, corpora amylacea in the retina and optic nerve, corpora arenacea in the nerve, sclerosis of the choriocapillaris, choroidal, or other ocular vessels, or degenerative changes in the sclera.

ELECTRON MICROSCOPY

In the retinal pigment epithelial cells surveyed by EM, a few lipofuscin granules were seen in 4-y.o. animals. The number of lipofuscin granules appeared to increase with age in the sections studied, but the sample was too small for quantitative comparison (Figure 13-6).

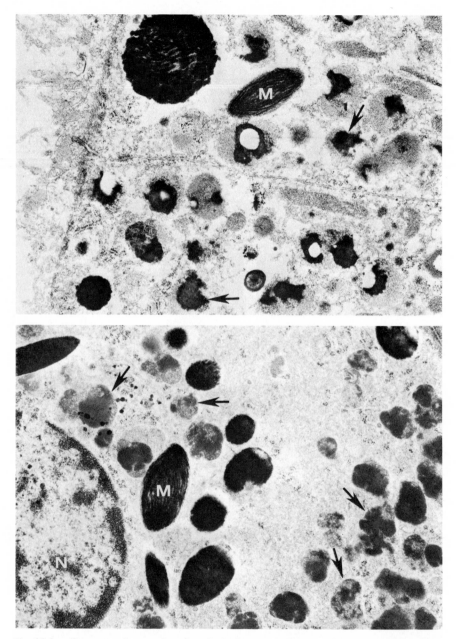

Fig. 13-6.   Electron micrographs of retinal pigment epithelium from parafoveal region. *Upper:* Densely melaninized round and ovoid pigment granules (M) are interspersed with some accumulations of lipofuscin (↑) in 4-y.o. female *M. nemestrina* (#73166); ×26,390. *Lower:* Many lipofuscin granules (↑) near nucleus (N) and lower right in 20-y.o. male *M. fascicularis* (#77005); ×26,390.

SPECIAL CASES

Monkey 75282 (4 y.o.)

The globe contained a 3- to 4-mm thorn or splinter encased in a dense fibrotic scar posterior to the equator of the lens superiorly. A defect in the ciliary epithelium, a white band (proliferating ciliary epithelium and old blood), vitreous liquefaction and a large amount of peripheral cystic degeneration as well as one patch of paving-stone degeneration were noted. The remainder of the retina and the optic nerve were unremarkable.

Monkey 70371 (10 y.o.)

A defect in the iris of the right eye had been first noted seven years before sacrifice. Grossly, the pupil was large and irregular, outlined by remnants of atrophic iris superiorly. The iris was absent inferiorly. Inferonasal and inferotemporal colobomas of the ciliary body were seen. The lens was cataractous and flattened inferiorly. A perforation of the sclera inferiorly was filled with degenerating uvea and dense scar tissue. There was moderate peripheral cystic degeneration and paving-stone degeneration of the retina (see p. 39).

Monkey 72399 (10 y.o.)

The cornea, near the limbus, was hazy. Microscopically, focal corneal edema, thinning of the iris stroma, and a basophilic subconjuctival degenerative plaque (calcific) were noted. The endothelium, on flat preparations, averaged 99 cells/ hpf, a higher number than expected for an animal of this age.

DISCUSSION

In terms of proportional lifespan, the 20-y.o. macaque is roughly comparable to a 50- to 65-y.o. human; the macaque's maximum lifespan is 30 to 35 years and the human's about 100 years.

The eyes of aging macaques showed a number of changes similar to those observed in humans. The number of corneal endothelial cells decreased with age and the nuclei of the remaining cells were spaced further apart and were irregular and mildly pleomorphic, as in the human (5). The lens increased in size between 4 and 20 years of age. Mild nuclear sclerotic changes were found in some 20-y.o. macaques. Sclerosis of the human lens occurs slowly and mild changes are often noted at age 50. Subendothelial fibrosis of the ciliary body in man is evident at age 20 and continues to increase throughout life. A well-defined layer of subendothelial connective tissue along the pars plana and pars ciliaris was present in the 20-y.o. monkeys but hyalinization of the ciliary processes and intramuscular fibrosis were scanty and less than might be expected if the age of 20 years in macaques is equivalent to 50 years in man. Cysts were found in 24% of human eyes at 40 and the number increased to 34% by age 70 (8). Cysts and proliferation of the ciliary epithelium were also a prominent feature in the oldest macaques. Paving stone degeneration occurs in 20% (9) to 31% (7) of 40-y.o. humans and was found in a proportionate number of 20-y.o. macaques.

Vitreous liquefaction in man is common by the age of 60 and appeared at an earlier age in these monkeys, as the vitreous was liquefied in all but one of the macaques in the 10-y.o. group.

Peripheral cystic degeneration in macaques, present in most humans by age 20, was less than expected. Of interest is the case of the 4-y.o. animal (#75282) with a large foreign body behind the lens. This eye contained abundant peripheral cystic degeneration and an area of paving stone, suggesting that trauma may initiate or accelerate aging processes. Lipofuscin was found in the retinal pigment epithelium at all ages and seemed more abundant as the animals aged, but the data are limited.

Surprisingly, some alterations associated with human aging were not observed in the eyes of macaques in this study. Hassal-Henle warts, found occasionally in man at age 20 and almost universally by age 60, were not found in any of the animals. While Rohen and Leutjen-Drecoll (10) found subtle fibrosis by EM in the trabecular meshwork in both older monkeys and humans, in the present study the trabecular meshwork in all eyes as examined by light microscopy was remarkably free of fibrosis. The trabecular plates were thin and the spaces ample. Other parameters not found included atrophy of the iris, mild thickening of the pial columns, drusen on Bruch's membrane, thinning of the peripheral choroid and diffuse depigmentation of the retinal pigment epithelium and choroid anterior to the equator. Arcus senilis was not noticed, which is consistant with the low fat diet and absence of atherosclerosis in these animals (see Chapter 20, this volume).

A final word should be said about atrophy and hyalinization, two processes often equated with uncomplicated aging in tissues—the "wear and tear" theory. Atrophy implies the slow but irreversible loss of component cells of a tissue; and hyalinization, the infiltration of structures, usually blood vessels or connective tissues, by eosinophilic material, usually collagen. Pathologists familiar with the human eye often judge age by the amount of hyalinization in the ciliary body, yet in the 20-y.o. monkeys examined here, intramuscular sclerosis of the ciliary body was scanty. Similarly, the septal columns in the choriocapillaris may appear flatter (atrophic) or more eosinophilic (sclerotic) in the periphery of the human eye although occasionally one finds an octagenarian whose eyes are relatively free of atrophy and sclerosis. We found neither atrophy nor sclerosis of the peripheral choriocapillaris in these macaques.

Differences in the human eye that are seen frequently in the elderly and thought to result almost exclusively from physiologic aging may be the result of other, less well defined and controlled factors, e.g., level of activity, genetic makeup, diet and systemic illnesses, rather than the sole consequence of the "wear and tear" of aging, a vague concept at best. For example, cataracts are found in some people in their fifties and not in others until their seventies or eighties. It would seem that this phenomenon of ocular aging can be accelerated or retarded by other influences.

The data derived in this study indicate that the eye of the macaque is a reasonable model for age-related changes in man, exhibiting some but not all of the ocular differences associated with human aging at proportional ages.

ACKNOWLEDGMENTS

I thank Ms. Sandra Livingston for preparing the histological sections. This research was supported in part by grants RR00166, RR52177 and AG62145 from the National Institutes of Health.

REFERENCES

1. Duke-Elder, S. (ed.) (1958): *System of Ophthalmology*. Vol. I. *The Eye in Evolution*. St. Louis; C. V. Mosby.
2. Duke-Elder, S. (ed.) (1962): *System of Ophthalmology*. Vol. VII. *The Foundations of Ophthalmology*, pp. 182–184. St. Louis; C. V. Mosby.
3. Hara, K., Luetjen-Drecoll, E., Prestele, H. and Rohen, J. (1977): Structural differences between regions of the ciliary body in primates. *Invest. Ophthalmol.*, 16: 912–924.
4. Hogan, M. and Zimmerman, L. (1964): *Ophthalmic Pathology*. Philadelphia; W. B. Saunders Co.
5. Kaufman, H., Capella, J., and Robbins, J. (1966): The human corneal endothelium. *Amer. J. Ophthalmol.*, 61: 835–841.
6. Kuwabara, T. (1975): The maturation of the lens cell. *Exp. Eye Res.*, 20: 427–443.
7. Okun, E. (1960): Gross and microscopic pathology in autopsy eyes. II. Peripheral chorioretinal atrophy. *Amer. J. Ophthalmol.*, 50: 574–583.
8. Okun, E. (1961): Gross and microscopic pathology in autopsy eyes. IV. Pars plana cysts. *Amer. J. Ophthalmol.*, 51: 1221–1230.
9. O'Malley, P., Allen, R. and Straatsma, B. (1965): Paving-stone degeneration of the retina. *Arch. Ophthalmol.*, 73: 169–182.
10. Rohen, J. and Leutjen-Drecoll, E. (1971): Age changes of the trabecular meshwork in human and monkey eyes. *Altern U. Entwicklung*, 1: 1–36.
11. Rones, B. (1938): Senile changes and degeneration of the human eye. *Amer. J. Ophthalmol.*, 21: 239–255.

14

Peripheral Tactile Innervation

Joan Witkin

Department of Anthropology, Columbia University, New York, N.Y.

INTRODUCTION

Nerve endings in the skin of humans have been extensively studied for their anatomical properties (3-5, 7, 10). Some studies of nerve endings in nonhuman primates have also been made (see refs. 13 and 19 for reviews). Tactile corpuscles (Meissner's corpuscles as defined by Winkelman (20)) are of particular interest as they occur exclusively in ridged skin on highly sensitive areas such as hands and feet of primates and the under surface of the prehensile tail in New World monkeys. They are found only in some marsupials among nonprimate mammals (13).

Studies of age changes in human peripheral innervation have shown that the density of tactile corpuscles drops with age (2, 6, 8, 11, 15, 16). No studies have been reported of changes with aging in the peripheral innervation of nonhuman primates.

This study focuses on age-related differences in the density and morphology of tactile corpuscles in digital skin of the index finger, thumb and great toe of the pigtail macaque. Some attention is given to sex and subspecific differences as well.

METHODS

The material for this study was volar skin from the distal phalanges of the right index fingers, thumbs and great toes of 16 female and 2 male pigtail macaques

(*Macaca nemestrina*). The female sample included 3 age groups, 4-y.o. (n = 3), 10-y.o. (n = 9), and 20-y.o. (n = 4). Two subspecies, *M. n. nemestrina* (Mnn) and *M. n. leonina* (Mnl) were represented in the 10- and 20-y.o. groups of females. The 4-y.o. animals were all Mnn. The male sample included 1 10-y.o. and 1 20-y.o. animal, both Mnn.

Each digit was excised within 1 hr of cardiorespiratory arrest. The nail was split to enhance penetration of the fixative and the sample was fixed in McDowell's fixative (Chapter 3), then shipped at ambient temperature. Upon receipt, the tissues were placed in 10% neutral formalin. Portions of volar skin from the medial side of the index finger and thumb and the lateral side of the great toe were excised and embedded in paraffin. Sections were cut at 7 μm parallel to the long axis of the digits, perpendicular to the surface of the skin (Figure 14-1), and affixed to slides coated with a gelatin and chrome alum solution. Five serial sections were placed on each slide and at least 9 slides were made from each specimen. At least 2 and usually 3 or more slides from each specimen were impregnated with silver (17). Other slides were stained with hematoxylin and eosin or with orcein.

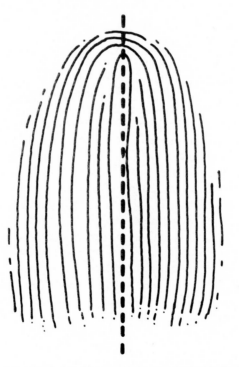

Fig. 14-1. Drawing of thumbprint of *M. nemestrina*; dashed line indicates plane of section.

Tactile corpuscles were counted and, to establish comparable counts from different specimens and from apical and proximal areas of the same specimen, an index, tactile corpuscle density per dermal papilla, was used. The arrangement of external, papillary ridges (Figure 14-1) produced cross sections of ridges in apical portions of the digits and longitudinal sections in proximal portions. On a slide containing 5 sections at 7 μm, about 4 dermal papillae were found in each external ridge at the apex of the digit, 2 on each side of the intermediate ridge containing the sweat duct. Therefore, the number of external ridges was multiplied by 4 in calculating tactile corpuscle density in apical regions. In proximal areas, where ridges were cut longitudinally, the total counts of dermal papillae were used. All counts were made blindly, i.e., the ages of the animals were not obtained until the observations had been recorded. The data were analyzed using means, standard deviations, analyses of variance, correlation coefficients and t-tests.

For studying the morphology of tactile corpuscles and other components of innervation, thick (50 μm) frozen sections were made and treated with silver impregnation (ref. 20 as modified by Roman at Oregon Regional Primate Research Center). Pigment deposition in cells of the basal layer of the epidermis was studied in sections stained by the Sevier-Munger (17) silver method.

RESULTS

Tactile corpuscles in the digital skin of the pigtail macaques (Figure 14-2) were similar to those of humans except that they were less complex. They were found in the apices of the dermal papillae, in close apposition to the epidermal border. Each corpuscle was innervated by 2 or 3 myelinated fibers. One or 2 nonmyelinated fibers with endings in the dermal/epidermal junction of the skin often accompanied the nerves innervating the corpuscle. The tactile corpuscles contained winding nerve fibers interleaved by flattened lamellar cells. Only occasionally did nerves in the corpuscles have expanded endings, and those were smaller than those in humans. In a sample of 66 tactile corpuscles in the thumbs, the size varied from about 42 to 96 μm long (mean 66 μm) and 12 to 48 μm wide (mean 22 μm). A few corpuscles in the index finger and great toe were measured, and fell within the range of sizes for the thumb sample.

Age changes in the morphology of tactile corpuscles were studied in the thumb. The only difference noted was that no lobulated corpuscles were seen in the 4-y.o. animals while a few were seen in those of the 10- and 20-y.o.'s. The size of the corpuscles did not change consistently with age: the means were 61 μm by 22 μm in the 4-y.o.'s, 66 μm by 29 μm in the 10-y.o.'s and 62 μm by 26 μm in the 20-y.o. animals. The corpuscles did not seem to move away from the epidermal border with age. The number of tactile corpuscles per papilla in

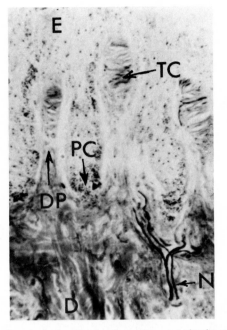

Fig. 14-2. Vertical section through skin of volar surface, proximal portion of distal phalanx of index finger from a 10-y.o. female pigtail macaque showing the dermal epidermal junction where tactile corpuscles (TC) and pigmented cells (PC) are located. Dermal papillae (DP) project from the dermis (D) into the epidermis (E). Tactile corpuscles in the dermal papillae are innervated by nerves (N) exiting into the deeper dermis. Sevier-Munger silver stain. Original magnification 480×.

the thumb and index finger greatly exceeded that in the great toe (Table 14-1). In the thumb and index finger the proximal portions had more tactile corpuscles than apical portions.

Comparisons of tactile corpuscle densities among the 3 age groups showed the densest distributions to be in the proximal region of the thumb in the 4-y.o. group. Mean densities for the 4-y.o. group were consistently higher than for the 10-y.o. group, and those of the 10-y.o.'s were higher than those of the 20-y.o.'s in all digits. Scatterplots of the total means, i.e., densities combining data from the apical and proximal portions of each digit, are given in Figure 14-3.

The coefficients of correlation for the index finger and thumb densities with age were highly significant, except for the apical index finger (Table 14-2). The great toe correlations were not significant. To determine whether the absolute size of the animal was related to the density of tactile corpuscles, the correlation coefficient was calculated between the weights of the animals at sacrifice and

Table 14-1. Mean Number of Meissner's Corpuscles per Papilla in Different Digits of Pigtail Macaques in Three Age Groups. s.d. = standard deviation

Age Group (Years)	Number of Animals		Index Finger			Thumb			Great Toe		
			Apical	Proximal	Total	Apical	Proximal	Total	Apical	Proximal	Total
4	3	mean	.147	.250	.200	.170	.370	.270	.080	.043	.060
		s.d.	.038	.030	.036	.036	.069	.052	.017	.040	.035
10	10	mean	.093	.210	.153	.111	.243	.177	.030	.043	.037
		s.d.	.047	.061	.064	.050	.089	.056	.038	.027	.020
20	5	mean	.080	.100	.090	.054	.168	.112	.028	.032	.030
		s.d.	.027	.053	.034	.029	.126	.064	.026	.029	.022
All	18	mean	.098	.186	.143	.105	.243	.174	.038	.040	.039
		s.d.	.047	.079	.058	.054	.115	.077	.034	.034	.029

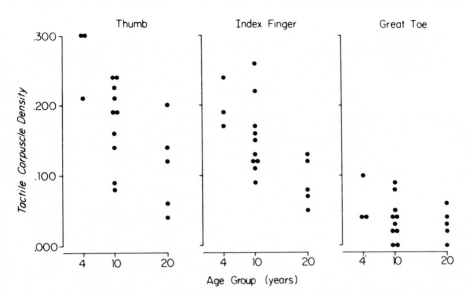

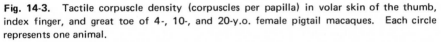

Fig. 14-3. Tactile corpuscle density (corpuscles per papilla) in volar skin of the thumb, index finger, and great toe of 4-, 10-, and 20-y.o. female pigtail macaques. Each circle represents one animal.

their combined (apical and proximal) tactile corpuscle density for each of the three digits. No significant correlation was found.

Comparing subgroups on the basis of sex and subspecies differences, some further observations were possible. Of the 2 males, the 10-y.o. (#70546) weighed 14.4 kg and a 20-y.o. (#67350), who had weighed more than 12.0 kg in his prime, weighed only 8.7 kg. Unlike those of the females, the densities for

Table 14-2. Relation to Age of Meissner's Corpuscle Indices from Apical and Proximal Portions of the Thumb, Index Finger, and Great Toe of 18 Pigtail Macaques. r = Pearson's Correlation Coefficient, p = Significance Level. Correlation Coefficients Are Omitted for Samples in Which p > 0.10.

	Thumb		Index Finger		Great Toe	
	r	p	r	p	r	p
Apical	−.72	<.01	−	.11	−	.12
Proximal	−.54	.02	−.71	<.01	−	.59
Combined	−.65	<.01	−.66	<.01	−	.24

the 20-y.o. were 30 to 50% higher than those for the 10-y.o. animal. Because of this discrepancy and the fact that both males were of the same subspecies, the males were omitted from analyses of the 2 subspecies independently or in comparison with one another. Because there were no 4-y.o. Mnl that age group was omitted, leaving a sample of 13 females (7 Mnn and 6 Mnl). In both the 10- and 20-y.o. age groups, the mean density of corpuscles was 30 to 60% greater in the Mnl subspecies than in the Mnn subspecies (Table 14-3). Despite the small number of subjects, this difference was significant for the index finger of the 10-y.o. groups (p = 0.01 by two-tailed t-test). The decline in the tactile corpuscle density with age was further substantiated by the observation that, within subspecies, there was no overlap between the 2 age groups with regard to corpuscle density in either the thumb or the index finger.

The distribution of pigment in cells of the basal layer of the epidermis was different in the 3 age groups (Figure 14-4). In the 4-y.o. animals they were highly dendritic with the pigment relatively dispersed. In the 10-y.o. animals, fewer pigmented dendrites were seen, and the pigment was more concentrated. In the 20-y.o.'s, the pigment was quite concentrated, especially in cells at the base of the epidermal intermediate ridge. These results were consistent with findings reported by Snell and Bischitz (18) who reported age-related differences in melanocytes of abdominal skin of man.

Table 14-3. Relation of Density of Meissner's Corpuscles to Age in Two Subspecies of Pigtail Macaque. Mnn = *Macaca nemestrina nemestrina*, Mnl = *Macaca nemestrina leonina*, $\bar{x}$ = mean, s.d. = standard deviation.

Age Group (Years)		Thumb		Index Finger	
		Mnn	Mnl	Mnn	Mnl
10		.16	.24	.13	.16
10		.19	.21	.12	.26
10		.14	.23	.17	.22
10		.08	−	.11	−
10		.24	−	.15	−
10		.19	−	.12	−
	$\bar{x} \pm$ s.d.	.17 ± .05	.23 ± .05	.13 ± .02	.21 ± .05
20		.04	.12	.05	.07
20		−	.20	−	.08
20		−	.06	−	.13
	$\bar{x} \pm$ s.d.	.04	.13 ± .07	.05	.09 ± .03

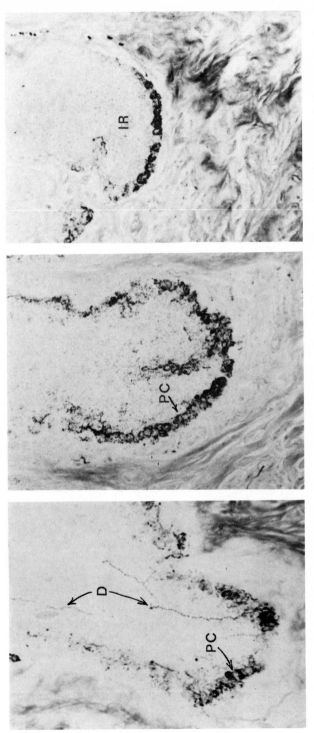

Fig. 14-4. Distribution of pigment in cells (PC) of the basal epidermal layer of skin from the index finger of pigtail macaques in 3 age groups: 4-y.o. (left), 10-y.o. (middle), 20-y.o. (right). Pigment is seen in long, dendritic processes (D) of pigment cells in 4-y.o. In 20-y.o. most pigment is concentrated in cells at base of intermediate ridge (IR). Sevier-Munger silver stain. Original magnification 320×.

DISCUSSION

Meissner's corpuscles in humans are cylindrical structures found in or near dermal papillae of the glabrous skin. They are composed of a mass of non-myelinated nerve fibers rolled upon themselves. Flattened laminar cells are interspersed among the fibers. Several myelinated type "A" fibers innervate each corpuscle. Branches of one nerve in the dermal plexus often serve more than one corpuscle. Elastic fibers invest the surface of the corpuscle forming a capsule (4, 5). Tonofibrils of the epithelial cells in the epidermis may be continuous with collagen fibers of the dermis, some of which enter the Meissner's corpuscles (1). This arrangement might be the anatomical substrate for the corpuscle to act as a rapidly adapting mechanoreceptor responding to high frequency mechanical vibration (14). Patients with diseases in which the density of Meissner's corpuscles is reduced show decreased appreciation of the stimuli of touch, pain and temperature as well as of two-point, vibration, and joint position sense (9).

The fact that densities of Meissner's corpuscles differ greatly from one area to another and that areas of greater sensitivity have higher densities is further support for the role of the corpuscle in acute tactile reception. In humans the greatest densities occur in the index finger. Furthermore, in each digit the distal phalanx has the highest density and the proximal phalanx, the least. The thenar and hypothenar eminences and the middle phalanx have intermediate densities (11). The density in the little finger is at least double that in the great toe (2). In the present study of distal phalanges in the pigtail macaque, indices were also much higher in the thumb and index finger than in the great toe. Furthermore, proximal regions of the distal phalanges had more tactile corpuscles than did the apical portions.

Differences between tactile corpuscles in humans and in nonhuman primates were first reported by Meissner (12). He noted that these "Tastkörperchen" were smaller and less elaborate in other primates than in humans. In the present study, macaque tactile corpuscles were also smaller, about 65 by 20 μm compared with about 80 by 30 μm in humans (2). They were innervated by only 2 or 3 myelinated nerves. As in humans, some nonmyelinated nerve fibers accompanied the nerves entering the corpuscle, branching off within the dermal papilla and ending at the epidermal border. Within the tactile corpuscle the myelin sheath was lost. The nerves coiled around among the flattened laminar cells and ended among them. Nerve endings generally were not expanded as they are in humans, or were expanded only slightly.

Cauna (6) concluded that it is possible to determine the approximate age of an individual by a careful study of the Meissner's corpuscles, as they elongate and coil on themselves with advancing age. In a 91-y.o. man he found corpuscles

240 μm long. The other major change with age was the gradual retreat of the corpuscles from their original close apposition to the epidermal border. Such was not the case in the pigtail macaques of this study. This may be a species difference or due to the fact that our macaque sample represented a younger group relative to maximal lifespan than was investigated in the human study. Meissner (12) reported (for an unspecified number of corpuscles) that corpuscles in the volar skin of the hand of adult humans were 56 to 83 μm long and 20 to 25 μm wide. Those of a 6-y.o. child were 20 to 33 μm long by 10 to 20 μm wide. In a 14-month-old infant they were 11 to 12.5 μm long by 10 to 12.5 μm wide. He made no mention of other morphological changes accompanying age.

The ideal method of counting tactile corpuscles depends upon the use of whole mounts of fresh frozen tissue. It is possible to obtain punch biopsy (3 mm) specimens of skin (2). These specimens are mounted flat and treated for specific and nonspecific cholinesterase. Counts per surface area can then be made directly. Another method, which eliminates differences caused by relative sizes is to calculate counts per sweat duct. Counts in the present study were standardized by comparison with the number of papillae. Although this method of counting is not identical to that employed in previous studies on humans, the tactile corpuscle densities that were calculated indicate the relative concentrations of this nerve ending. This method confers a notable advantage. The dermatoglyphic pattern is established prenatally and although the skin dimensions alter as the animal grows, the total number of ridges is fixed. Therefore, densities in different age groups are fairly comparable. Inconsistencies due to tissue shrinkage and/or differences in surface area resulting from growth of the animal or weight loss are minimized. In the present study there was no correlation between weight and corpuscle density. Had the densities of tactile corpuscles been determined on a surface area basis, this independence from the weight of the animal may not have existed. The major problem in using densities for counts in the present study is that it is more difficult to compare with results with studies on humans in which surface area was the standard.

In early postnatal infants the full complement of Meissner's corpuscles is developed (5). As the body grows and its surface expands, the density of corpuscles falls. As the body ages, there is a further decrease in the concentration of the corpuscles, due to attrition and loss. Ronge (16) found a reduction of 80% in the density of Meissner's corpuscles in the distal phalanx of the index finger in males between 1 and 80 years. Cauna (6) reported a decrease of about 90% in the palmar aspect of the distal phalanx between a 3 year old and an 83 year old.

There were no infant or juvenile animals in this study. Female macaques may become reproductively active by as early as $3\frac{1}{2}$ years and probably have a maximal lifespan of about 30 years (Chapter 3, this volume). It is probably reasonable to equate 4-y.o. macaques to adolescent and young adult humans (11 to 20 years); 10-y.o. macaques to adult humans (20 to 45 years) and 20-y.o. macaques to 45- to 60-y.o. humans.   To compare macaques with humans, findings extracted from earlier studies were used to calculate percentage decreases across age ranges presumed to be roughly equivalent to those of the animals of the present study (Table 14-4).   Humans undergo a reduction of 41 to 62% in mean density of Meissner's corpuscles in the fingers from early adulthood to late middle age.   The decreases seen in pigtail macaques range from 50 to 58%, depending upon the digit sampled.   It should be noted that all of the human studies cited in Table 4 reported corpuscle concentrations per millimeter of surface area.   Pérez (15) found that the decreases in corpuscles per surface area were greater than those per papilla.   Hence, it is possible that the decreases found in the present study would be greater had the densities been measured per surface area.

Densities of tactile corpuscles in the great toes in the present study were more variable than in other digits and although there was a 50% reduction in the means of the densities between 4 and 20 years, the standard deviations within the age groups were so high that this figure cannot be trusted.   Pérez (15) found greater decreases in corpuscles in the second phalanx than in the distal phalanx of the index finger and Bolton et al. (2) reported greater decreases for the great toe than for the index finger (Table 14-4).   It would be worthwhile to study corpuscle densities and tactile sensibility as a function of age in various regions to see whether greater losses are indeed encountered more often in areas that are less critical for tactile input.

The paradoxical finding in this study of greater tactile corpuscle density in the 20-y.o. than in the 10-y.o. male probably does not reflect sex differences, but a size difference.   In humans the fact that the density is higher in females

Table 14-4. Decline in Tactile Corpuscle Density with Age in Humans and Pigtail Macaques.

Species	Age Range (years)	Digit	Percent Decrease
Human (Ronge '43)	16 to 53	Index finger	55%
Human (Cauna '65)	11–18 to 47–64	Index finger	47%
Human (Bolton et al., '66)	11–30 to 51–70	Fifth finger	53%
Human (Bolton et al., '66)	11–30 to 51–70	Great toe	62%
Human (Pérez '31)	8–14 to adult	–	41%
Pigtail macaque	4 to 20	Thumb	58%
Pigtail macaque	4 to 20	Index finger	55%
Pigtail macaque	4 to 20	Great toe	50%

than males of a given age (6) has been attributed to the smaller size of the females. The weight of the younger male in this study was 66% greater than that of the older one, suggesting that the same factor might be at work. Counts from a 10- and a 20-y.o. male of a different macaque species, the longtail macaque (*M. fascicularis*), who weighed 4.2 kg and 4.6 kg respectively, showed differences in density counts in all 3 digits of 40 to 60%, comparable to those seen in the female pigtail macaques. Subspecific differences were found between Mnn and Mnl. Densities were significantly higher in the index finger in Mnl. One would like to know whether there are functional differences related to this.

The tactile corpuscle density in the great toe was more variable and showed less age dependence than that in either the index finger or thumb. However, densities from less heterogeneous groups of animals were more likely to be age dependent. When males were dropped from the sample, the apical great toe density showed predictable age decreases and when the female sample was limited to 1 subspecies, both the apical and total great toe indices were age dependent. Further study of age changes in peripheral innervation should be designed using animals of 1 sex and 1 subspecies.

ACKNOWLEDGMENTS

This study was supported in part by National Institutes of Health grants RR00166, RR52177, AG62145, and NS12436, and National Science Foundation grant DNS 74-20149.

REFERENCES

1. Andres, K. H., and von Düring, M. (1973): Morphology of cutaneous receptors. In: *Handbook of Sensory Physiology*, Vol. II, edited by A. Iggo, pp. 3–28. New York; Springer-Verlag.
2. Bolton, C. F., Winkelmann, R. K., and Dyck, P. J. (1966): A quantitative study of Meissner's corpuscles in man. *Neurology (Minneap.)*, 16: 1–10.
3. Breathnach, A. (1977): Electron microscopy of cutaneous nerves and receptors. *J. Invest. Dermatol.*, 69: 8–26.
4. Cauna, N. (1956a): Nerve supply and nerve endings in Meissner's corpuscles. *Am. J. Anat.*, 99: 315–350.
5. Cauna, N. (1956b): Structure and origin of the capsule of Meissner's corpuscle. *Anat. Rec.* 124: 77–94.
6. Cauna, N. (1965): The effects of aging on the receptor organs of the human dermis. In: *Advances in Biology of the Skin*, Vol. 6, edited by W. Montagna, pp. 63–96. Oxford; Pergamon Press.
7. Cauna, N., and L. L. Ross (1960): The fine structure of Meissner's touch corpuscles of human fingers. *J. Biophys. Biochem. Cytol.*, 8: 467–482.
8. Dickens, W. N., Winkelmann, R. K., and Mulder, D. W. (1963): Cholinesterase demon-

stration of dermal nerve endings in patients with impaired sensation: a clinical and pathological study of 41 patients and 37 control subjects. *Neurology (Minneap.)*, **13:** 91–100.

9. Dyck, P. J., Winkelmann, R. K., and Bolton, C. F. (1966): Quantitation of Meissner's corpuscles in hereditary neurologic disorders: Charcot-Marie-Tooth disease, Roussy-Levy syndrome, Dejerine-Sottas disease, hereditary sensory neuropathy, spinocerebellar degenerations and hereditary spastic paraplegia. *Neurology (Minneap.)*, **16:** 10–17.

10. Hashimoto, K. (1973): Fine structure of the Meissner corpuscle of human palmar skin. *J. Invest. Dermatol.*, **60:** 20–28.

11. Hermann, H. (1953): Über die nervösen Endkörperchen in der Haut der menschlichen Hand. *Handb. Zb. Haut-u. Geschl.-Kr.*, **14:** 277–279.

12. Meissner, G. (1853): *Beitraege zur Anatomie und Physiologie der Haut.* Leipzig; Leopold Voss.

13. Montagna, W. (1972): The skin of nonhuman primates. *Am. Zool.*, **12:** 109–124.

14. Munger, B. L. (1971): Patterns of organization of peripheral sensory receptors. In: *Handbook of Sensory Physiology*, Vol. 1, edited by W. R. Lowenstein, pp. 523–526. New York; Springer-Verlag.

15. Pérez, R. M. (1931): Contribution a l'étude des terminaisons nerveuses dans la peau de la main. *Trav. Lab. Rech. Biol. Univ. Madrid*, **27:** 187–226.

16. Ronge, H. (1943): Altersveränderungen der Meissnerschen Körperchen in der Fingerhaut. *Z. Mikr.-Anat. Forsch.*, **54:** 167–177.

17. Sevier, A. C., and Munger, B. L. (1965): A silver method for paraffin sections of neural tissues. *J. Neuropath. Exp. Neurol.*, **24:** 130–135.

18. Snell, R. S., and Bischitz, P. G. (1963): The melanocytes and melanin in human abdominal wall skin. *J. Anat.*, **97:** 361–376.

19. Winkelmann, R. K. (1963): Nerve endings in the skin of primates. In: *Evolutionary and Genetic Biology of Primates*, edited by J. Buettner-Janusch, pp. 229–259. New York; Academic Press.

20. Winkelmann, R. K. (1965): Nerve changes in aging skin. In: *Advances in Biology of the Skin*, Vol. 6, edited by W. Montagna, pp. 51–61. Oxford; Pergamon Press.

21. Winkelmann, R. K., and Schmitt, R. W. (1957): A simple silver method for nerve axoplasm. *Proc. Mayo Clinic*, **37:** 217–222.

15

Ultrastructure of the Adenohypophysis

John E. Aschenbrenner

Department of Basic Health Sciences, Division of Anatomy,
North Texas State University Health Science Center,
Texas College of Osteopathic Medicine, Fort Worth, Texas

INTRODUCTION

Microscopic observations of the adenohypophysis of the rhesus monkey (*Macaca mulatta*) date back to the early work of Dawson (6). With the advent of electron microscopy such studies should have continued, but in fact, few electron microscopic studies have been reported on the fine structure of this gland in the nonhuman primate. They are limited to descriptive studies of the cells of the adenohypophysis in the longtail macaque (*M. fascicularis*) (17) and baboon (*Papio hamadryas*) (1). Only recently have serious attempts been made to classify anterior pituitary cells functionally using immunofluorescence methods (7) to record experimentally induced changes in the cellular architecture (5, 14, 15), or to observe changes that normally occur in different physiological states (12).

The effects of aging on the histology and cytology of the adenohypophysis have been documented by light microscopy in mouse (16), rat (9, 11, 13), and man (4). The present electron microscopic study was conducted to assess aging changes in the adenohypophyseal cells of nonhuman primates.

MATERIAL AND METHODS

Hypophyseal tissue was obtained from 19 pigtail macaques (*M. nemestrina*; 17 females, 2 males) and 2 longtail macaques (*M. fascicularis*; males). With the animals under ketamine and nembutal anesthesia, the tissue was obtained within 30 min of cardiorespiratory arrest. Each pituitary was removed, coded, and sectioned in the midsagittal plane. The right half was fixed in McDowell's fixative (Chapter 3, this volume) and forwarded to our laboratory at ambient temperature.

The adenohypophysis was separated from the neurohypophysis by careful dissection of the hemisected specimens while in McDowell's fixative. Tissue blocks were cut from the most anterior region of the gland and extended 1–2 mm posteriorly and laterally from the hemisected surface. These aliquots were divided into 6 to 8 smaller cubes measuring less than 0.5 mm per cut surface area. The cubes were washed twice with cold 0.2 M sodium cacodylate buffer, followed with postfixation in 1.5% aqueous osmium tetroxide prepared with 0.2 M sodium cacodylate buffer. They were osmified for 45 min, then dehydrated through an ascending series of ethyl alcohols, treated with propylene oxide, and embedded in Epon 812. Ultrathin silver sections were cut by a Porter-Blum MT-2 ultramicrotome with a DuPont diamond knife. The sections were mounted on 200-mesh copper grids, stained with a saturated solution of uranyl acetate in 50% ethyl alcohol, and with 1.0% aqueous lead citrate to enhance contrast.

Several specimens and at least 6 grids per monkey were examined by both visual and photographic recording of random and selected tissue employing either an RCA-3G or an AEI Cornith 500 electron microscope.

The parenchymal cells of the adenohypophysis were classified according to Yamashita's (17) nomenclature based on granule size. Differentiation was in terms of four cell types: somatotrophs, gonadotrophs, corticotrophs, and thyrotrophs, characterized by successively smaller granules in that order. All observations were made before ages were known, and then correlations were established between data and age.

RESULTS

The cytoarchitecture of tissue from the anteromedial portion of the adenohypophysis in 4-y.o. macaques is illustrated in Figure 15-1. Three adenohypophyseal cells, two somatotrophs and a gonadotroph appear adjacent to a hypophyseal sinusoid. The most prevalent cells in this part of the adenohypophysis are somatotrophs, rotund cells possessing secretory granules with an average diameter of 425 nm. The somatotrophs shown in Figure 15-1 contain a normal complement of secretory granules. The gonadotrophic cells are generally angular in contour with secretory granules averaging 250 nm in diameter. The gonadotroph in Figure 15-1 seems to be only partially granulated, since the organelle structures are readily discernible. The cellular contours, nuclear morphology and other organelle features seem normal. The basal laminae associated with both the endothelial and parenchymal cells appear as thin homogeneous gray lines. No

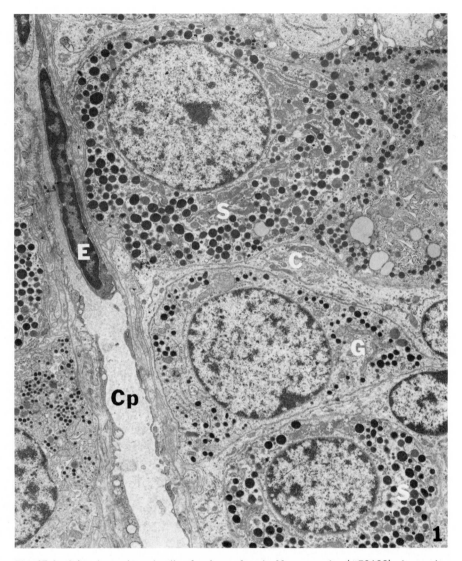

Fig. 15-1. Adenohypophyseal cells of a 4-y.o. female *M. nemestrina* (#73166). A gonado-troph (G) is situated between two somatotrophic cells (S). The elongate cell processes of two agranular cells (C) demarcate the boundaries of the gonadotroph. Note the capillary space (Cp) and the endothelial cell (E) comprising its wall. 7,700×

thickening of the basal laminae in either case is apparent, and the pericapillary spaces show no augmented collagen deposition.

Analysis of the cytologic characteristics that might be observed to increase in frequency in monkeys of increasing age focused on two general areas, viz., secretory granules within the pituitary cells, and alterations of organelle morphology. A normal complement of granules was assumed if 50% or more of the cells in the electron micrographs satisfied the established criteria for granularity (17). A state of granular depletion was assumed if less than 50% of the cells satisfied those criteria. Cells undergoing degenerative changes usually exhibited one or more of the following characteristics: irregular cell and nuclear configurations, displacement of the nucleus to an eccentric position within the cell, mitochondrial aggregation within the cytoplasm, hypertrophy and dilatation of the cisternal space of the endoplasmic reticulum, and cellular vacuolization.

Figures 15-2 to -6 reflect the electron microscopic imagery of tissues from older animals. Figure 15-2 shows a typical pattern for adenohypophyseal tissue in the 10-y.o. group. Many cells have angular and pleomorphic contours, while the nuclei are shrunken instead of rounded and are eccentrically positioned within the cell; the chromatin appears heterogeneous and moderately electron dense. Many cells are vacuolated. The gonadotrophic cell has an aggregation of mitochondria in the perinuclear cytoplasm. Dilatation of the cisternal spaces of the endoplasmic reticulum occurs in several cell types, especially the gonadotrophic cells. The secretory granules are generally not dispersed throughout the cells, but aggregate subjacent to the cell membrane. The basal lamina associated with the lobules of the parenchymal tissue seems thickened, and there appears to be an increase of collagen deposited in the pericapillary space. However, the latter observation was not consistently detected in 10-y.o. animals. The somatotroph depicted at the bottom of the micrograph demonstrates similar ultrastructural change and so may be experiencing an alteration in its functional state as well.

A moderate derangement of intracellular structures and a reduction in cell granularity often occurred in gonadotrophic cells of 10- and 20-y.o. animals. Figure 15-3 illustrates a gonadotroph from a 20-y.o. female, showing severe cisternal dilatation and reduction in cell granularity. The eccentric position of the nucleus within the cell and the aggregation of mitochondria in the perinuclear cytoplasm suggest regressive changes that result in ultrastructural deformation. This case may be particularly significant because the animal (#75026), a 20-y.o. female, was the only clearly postmenopausal macaque in this study. She had no menses in 5 months preceeding sacrifice, consistently high luteinizing hormone (LH) levels, very low estradiol levels, and a senile vaginal epithelium (Chapter 16, this volume). Figure 15-4 illustrates the fine structural detail within a gonadotroph from a 10-y.o. female macaque. Although this animal (#69256) was not postmenopausal, a number of signs indicative of reproductive decline were present;

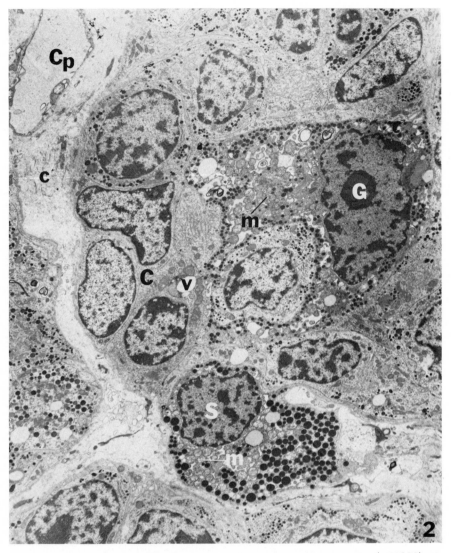

Fig. 15-2. Adenohypophyseal tissue from a 10-y.o. female *M. nemestrina* (#71336). A gonadotroph (G) demonstrates altered morphology.   To the left of the gonadotroph are 3 agranular cells (C); one is vacuolated (v). A somatotroph (S) (bottom) has granules situated atypically within the cytoplasm. The mitochondria (m) in both the gonadotroph and somatotroph are aggregated in the perinuclear zone.   The capillary (Cp) and the relatively enlarged pericapillary space contain abundant deposits of collagen (c). 4,700X

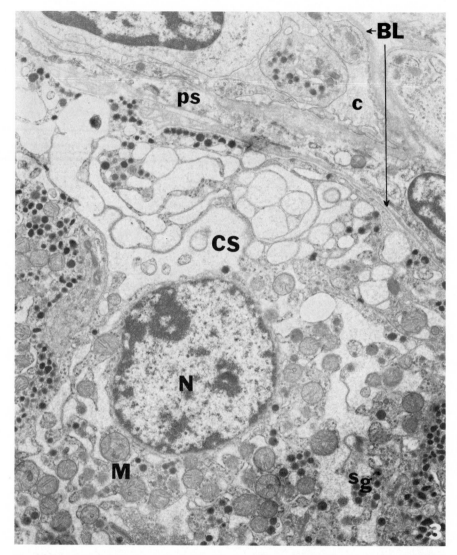

Fig. 15-3.   A gonadotrophic cell obtained from a 20-y.o. female *M. nemestrina* (#75026) showing depletion of secretory granules (Sg).   The cisternal spaces of the endoplasmic reticulum (CS) are irregular in contour and appear filled with an electron lucent, fine granular material.   Mitochondria (M) are positioned in the apical cytoplasm of this cell, while the cell base is in apposition with the basal lamina (BL) bordering the pericapillar space (ps).   The capillary (c) contains portions of white blood cell elements.   The basal lamina associated with both the endothelial surface of the capillary and the parenchymal tissue appears slightly thickened.   Nuclear morphology is not severely distorted in this cell. 9,000×

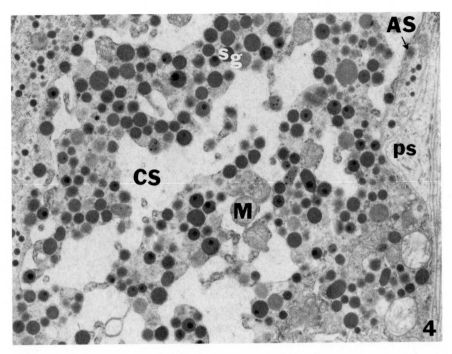

Fig. 15-4.   Cytoplasm of a gonadotroph undergoing degenerative change in a 10-y.o. female *M. nemestrina* (#69256).   Note the secretory granules (Sg) and enlargement of the cisternal space (CS) of the endoplasmic reticulum.   Mitochondria (M) appear among packets of granules.   Active emission of the secretory granules (AS) apparently continues despite the severe derangement of cell structure.   The pericapillary space (ps) between the parenchymal cell and the capillary sinusoid receives the secretory product.   14,000×

these included advanced ovarian atrophy, and the highest level of LH of any animal in the study (Chapter 16).   The cisterna of the endoplasmic reticulum is considerably distended, dense core secretory granules are organized into discrete packets, and some granules are apparently being released into the pericapillary space.

Figure 15-5 illustrates partial degranulation in a gonadotroph from a 20-y.o. female. The cell contour appears normal; however, the organelles are not obscured by secretory granules.   Note the multivesiculated structure in the perinuclear cytoplasm of the gonadotroph.   Similar structures were further examined by electron microscopy (Figure 15-6).   They do not appear to be membrane bound, and are composed of vacuolated opaque lamellar crystalline substance in a granular matrix.   Many gonadotrophic cells and a few somatotrophic cells from 10- and 20-y.o. macaques contained these structures with their typical form of vacuolization.

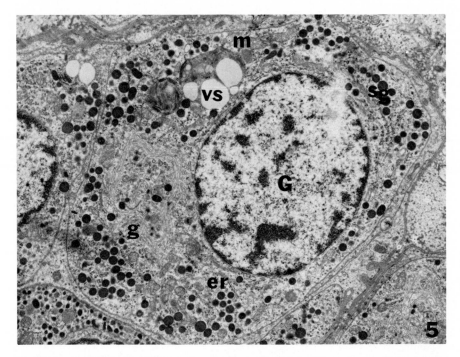

Fig. 15-5.   Gonadotroph (G) from the adenohypophysis of a 20-y.o. female *M. nemestrina* (#76201). Partial degranulation is evident in that other organelles such as the Golgi complex (g), mitochondria (m), and endoplasmic reticulum (er) are not obscured by the secretory granules (Sg).   A peculiar multivesiculated structure (vs) appears in the cytoplasm as well. 9,000×

The numbers of animals showing degeneration and degranulation of gonadotrophic cells in different age groups are presented in Table 15-1. The degenerative changes were differentially distributed across the three age groups, i.e., the probability of obtaining the distribution presented in Table 15-1, assuming no relation to age, is less than 0.05.   Older animals showed more degenerative changes.

Though degranulation of the gonadotrophs occured only in the 10- and 20-y.o. age groups, its relation to age within those groups was not as clear. Attempts to relate the degree of granulation to serum levels of a number of hormones, however, produced some notable findings. Gonadotrophic cells in both of the animals with persistently high LH levels (#75026 and #69256) were degranulated. Furthermore, the ratio of triiodothyronine (T_3) to thyroxine (T_4) in the animals with degranulated gonadotrophs was significantly higher than in those with normal granulation.   There was no overlap in the two distributions (Figure

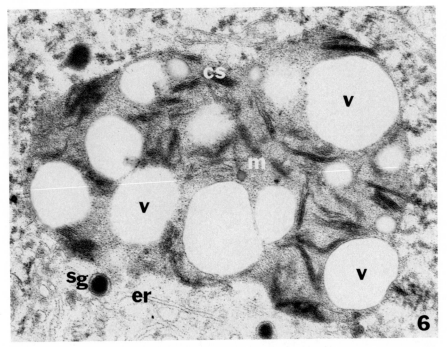

Fig. 15-6. High resolution electron micrograph of a multivesiculated structure observed in many gonadotrophic cells of monkeys 10 and 20 y.o. The matrix of the structure (m) contains a filamentous crystalline substance (cs) and vesiculated areas (v). The endoplasmic reticulum (er) and a membrane bound secretion granule (Sg) are present in the cytoplasm. 49,000×

Table 15-1. Relation of Age to Incidence of Degeneration and Degranulation in Gonadotrophic Cells of Macaque Adenohypophysis.

		Age Group (years)			
Cell Condition		4	10	20	p
Degeneration	present	1	7	7	0.05
	absent	2	4	0	
Degranulation	present	0	4	5	0.16
	absent	3	7	2	

p = probability as calculated by Fisher's exact test (2).

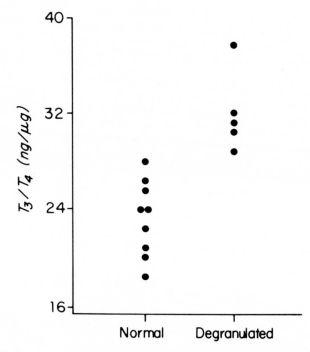

Fig. 15-7. Ratio of serum triiodothyronine to thyroxine ($T_3 : T_4$) in animals with normal vs degranulated hypophyseal gonadotrophs. Each circle represents 1 animal.

15-7; $p < 0.001$ by two-tailed t-test). The difference was related primarily to elevated T_3, less to reduced T_4 levels in the animals with degranulated gonadotrophs. No significant differences were found between the two groups with regard to circulating prolactin, estrogens, progesterone, or androgens (see Chapter 16, this volume).

DISCUSSION

The major age-related finding in the adenohypophyses of pigtail and longtail macaques was an increase in degenerative changes in the ultrastructure of the gonadotrophic cells. Particularly in the 20-y.o. animals the gonadotrophs were hypertrophic with loss of cellular contour, pleomorphic nuclei, cytoplasmic vacuolization, and enlarged, dilated endoplasmic reticulum. Such changes are characteristic of castrated animals (5) and are also reported to occur in the gonadotrophic cells of senescent humans (11).

The basophils that produce the gonadotrophins, follicle stimulating hormone and luteinizing hormone, become more prominent with age and are often vacuolated (3, 13). In the human female, aging is associated with reduced ovarian estrogen production to such an extent that augmented secretion of gonado-trophin occurs (10). Female rhesus macaques in the third decade of life similarly have episodes of abnormally high gonadotrophin secretion during the interval immediately preceding ovulation (8). The two animals in this study with con-sistently high serum LH levels both showed marked degeneration of gonado-trophic cells. Thus, the degenerative changes noted in the older animals of this study may reflect episodic or continuously increased secretion of gonadotrophic hormones in response to declining target organ function.

Multivesiculated structures containing crystalline inclusions were also fre-quently observed in the gonadotrophic cells of the older animals. Identical in-clusions have recently been observed in the pituitary gonadotrophs of spayed young rhesus monkeys primed with estrogen (14, 15). They occur most fre-quently in animals with low levels of circulating estrogen and are postulated to be related to the dynamics of increased gonadotrophin secretion by the pituitary.

The finding that 2 animals with degranulated gonadotrophs had persistently elevated serum LH levels is consistent with the view that sustained secretion of gonadotrophic homones can deplete the cells of granules. The significance of the relationship between degranulation of gonadotrophic cells in the adenohy-pophysis and the $T_3 : T_4$ ratio is unclear and merits further investigation.

All of the findings of this study must be considered in light of the fact that only one portion of the adenohypophysis was sampled, namely, the 3 to 4 mm^3 in the anteromedial region of the gland. Most of the results, however, corroborate observations obtained from other species, including the human. Taken in the context of the menopausal pattern characteristic of the higher primates, they lend support to the concept that the macaque is a suitable animal model for the study of aging in gonadotrophic functions of the human hypophysis.

ACKNOWLEDGMENTS

I thank Dr. John E. Milmore of the American Health Foundation, Valhalla, New York for the measurements of thyroid hormones, Dr. James E. Carnes for tech-nical advice, Mrs. Janice Sissom for photographic assistance, and Ms. Diana Rudolph for typing the manuscript.

This project was supported in part by Faculty Research Grant No. 13140 of the Texas College of Osteopathic Medicine, Fort Worth, Texas, by the Multi-disciplinary Center Grant 90-A-10501 from the Administration on Aging, and by National Institutes of Health grants RR00166, RR52177 and AG62145 to the University of Washington, Seattle, Washington.

REFERENCES

1. Azzali, di G. (1961): Studio citochimico ed al microscopio elettronico sulle cellule adenoipofisarie dei Primati (*Comopithecus hamadryas*). *Biochim. Biol. Sper.*, 1: 67-91.

2. Bradley, J. V. (1968): *Distribution Free Statistical Tests*. Englewood Cliffs, N.J.; Prentice-Hall.

3. Brizzee, K. R., Klara, P., and Johnson, J. E. (1975): Changes in microanatomy, neurocytology and fine structure with aging. In: *Neurobiology of Aging: An Interdisciplinary Life-Span Approach*, edited by J. M. Ordy and K. R. Brizzee, pp. 452-453. New York; Plenum Press.

4. Charipper, H. A., and Pearlstein, A. (1961): Aging changes in the thyroid and pituitary glands. In: *Structural Aspects of Aging*, edited by G. H. Bourne and E. M. H. Wilson, pp. 267-275. New York; Hafner Publishing Co.

5. Costoff, A. (1977): Ultrastructure of the pituitary gland. In: *The Pituitary: A Current Review*, edited by M. B. Allen, Jr., and V. B. Mahesh, pp. 59-76. New York; Academic Press.

6. Dawson, A. B. (1954): The regional localization of five distinct morphological types of cells in the anterior pituitary of the rhesus monkey. *Anat. Rec.*, 120: 810.

7. Herbert, D. C. (1976): Immunocytochemical evidence that luteinizing hormone (LH) and follicle stimulating hormone (FSH) are present in the same cell type in the rhesus monkey pituitary gland. *Endocrinology*, 99: 1554-1557.

8. Hodgen, G. D., Goodman, A. L., O'Conner, A., and Johnson, D. K. (1977): Menopause in rhesus monkeys: model for study of disorders in the human climacteric. *Amer. J. Obstet. Gynecol.*, 127: 581-584.

9. Lansing, W., and Wolfe, J. M. (1942): Changes in the fibrillar tissue of the anterior pituitary of the rat associated with advancing age. *Anat. Rec.*, 83: 355-366.

10. Lazarus, L., and Eastman, C. (1976): Assessment of hypothalamic-pituitary function in old age. In: *Hypothalamus Pituitary and Aging*, edited by A. V. Everitt and J. A. Burgess, pp. 108-109. Springfield, Ill.; Charles C Thomas.

11. Lockett, M. F. (1976): Aging of the adenohypophysis in relation to renal aging. In: *Hypothalamus Pituitary and Aging*, edited by A. V. Everitt and J. A. Burgess, pp. 283. Springfield, Ill.; Charles C Thomas.

12. Pasteels, J. L., Gausset, P., Danguy, A., Ectors, F., Nicoll, C. S., and Varavudhi, P. (1972): Morphology of the lactotrophs and somatotrophs of man and rhesus monkeys. *J. Clin. Endocrin. Metab.*, 34: 595-967.

13. Solomon, D. H., and Shock, N. W. (1972): Studies of adrenal cortical and anterior pituitary function in elderly men. In: *Endocrines and Aging*, pp. 121-122. New York; MSS Information Corporation.

14. Tseng, M. T., and Kittinger, G. W. (1974): Crystalline inclusions in the pituitary gonadotrophs of estrogen-primed spayed rhesus monkeys (*Macaca mulatta*). *Tiss. and Cell*, 6: 551-556.

15. Tseng, M. T., Kittinger, G. W., and Spies, H. G. (1974): An ultrastructural study of the gonadotroph in oophorectomized rhesus (*Macaca mulatta*) adults treated with estrogen. *Proc. Soc. Exp. Biol. Med.*, 147: 412-417.

16. Weiss, J., and Lansing, A. I. (1953): Age changes in the fine structure of anterior pituitary of the mouse. *Proc. Soc. Exp. Biol.*, 82: 460.

17. Yamashita, K. (1967): Electron microscopic observations on the anterior pituitary of the crab-eating monkey (*Macaca irus*). *Okajimas Fol. Anat. Jap.*, 43: 229-323.

16

Reproductive Senescence in Female Nonhuman Primates

Charles E. Graham*, O. Ray Kling, and Robert A. Steiner
Yerkes Regional Primate Research Center,
Emory University, Atlanta, Georgia;
Department of Gynecology and Obstetrics,
University of Oklahoma College of Medicine,
Oklahoma City, Oklahoma;
Departments of Physiology & Biophysics and Obstetrics & Gynecology,
and Regional Primate Research Center,
University of Washington, Seattle, Washington

INTRODUCTION

The gradual decline of reproductive function in women is characterized by increased variation in intermenstrual interval and decreased average duration of menstrual periods owing to irregular maturation of residual follicles or to incomplete, or failed, luteal maturation. Periods of amenorrhea become more common (20, 22), culminating in the menopause at about age 45-50. Cessation of menses is accompanied by a number of morphological, physiological and hormonal changes which have been well described (3, 5, 9, 14, 20, 22, 26).

The ovaries of postmenopausal women contain few primary follicles but frequently have larger follicles with cystic enlargement, thecal hypertrophy, or intrafollicular hemorrhage (4). Thecal interstitial gland tissue is frequently plentiful and well differentiated. Other characteristics include general cellular atrophy, decrease in volume of the cortex and consequent wrinkling of the ovarian surface (ovarium gyratum), cortical stromal hyperplasia, accumulation of intra- and extracellular pigments (lipofuscin and hemosiderin), calcification of

*Present address: International Center for Environmental Safety, Albany Medical College, P.O. Box 1027, Holloman A.F.B., New Mexico 88330.

medial coats of arteries, and thickening and hyalinization of arterial walls (3, 14, 26). Numerous hyalinized areas derived from atretic follicles or degenerated corpora lutea replace much of the cortex. Accumulation of ceroid (a lipochrome pigment) occurs to a moderate extent (18, 19).

The corpus uteri of aged women often involutes. The myometrial fibers become greatly attenuated and interstitial fibrosis develops in varying degrees. The myometrial blood vessels are frequently thickened and prominent owing to obliterative subintimal sclerosis, often with calcification of the media. The postmenopausal endometrium is often atrophic, characterized by a flattened epithelium and reduced glands (3, 14, 26). Glandular cystic or adenomatous uterine hyperplasia is not infrequent in women and may be associated with persistent estrogen secretion (3, 26). In one study, only 22% of postmenopausal human endometria were totally inactive (3).

The human cervix uteri does not regress in size to the extent that the corpus does, so that during the menopause the mass of the cervix may be twice that of the corpus. The tall columnar glands slowly involute and secretion becomes reduced. Stratified epithelium characteristically spreads cranially in the endocervical canal, sometimes cutting off glands and forming Nabothian follicles (6, 14, 16). Stenosis of the cervical canal may occur. The stratified epithelium of the ectocervix becomes atrophic, reflecting a similar change in the vagina. Changes in the vagina are related to loss of estrogen stimulation which results in decreased thickness of the vaginal epithelium. This leads to increased susceptibility to inflammation and infection, often resulting in senile vaginitis (14).

The hormonal pattern characteristic of human menopause consists of high levels of the gonadotrophins, luteinizing hormone (LH) and follicle stimulating hormone (FSH) and low serum levels of estradiol and progesterone (20) due to ovarian failure. The ratio of estrone to estradiol increases because the production of estradiol in the ovary ceases, whereas a significant amount of estrone continues to originate from peripheral aromatization of circulating androstenedione secreted by the adrenal gland or ovarian stroma (9). Thus, the relative (though not the absolute) amount of circulating estrone increases.

While few studies have been reported of reproductive senescence in nonhuman primates, it is clear that the efficiency of reproductive function declines midway in the second decade of life in several baboon and macaque species (Chapter 2, this volume). In the pigtail macaque (*Macaca nemestrina*), the proportion of pregnancies ending in stillbirth increases from less than 1% to more than 50% in females over 15 y.o. (G. P. Sackett and R. A. Holm, personal communication). Recent information indicates that in the latter half of the third decade of life, female rhesus macaques (*M. mulatta*) enter a state of menopause that is closely similar to that of the human (10). Vaginal bleeding declines progressively and eventually ceases, and patterns of circulating steroid and gonadotropic hormones change similarly to those in the human female, i.e., blood levels of ovarian steroids decline, while gonadotropin levels increase. Amenorrhea, follicular depletion, absence of corpora lutea, and cortical fibrosis of the ovaries have been reported in 2 rhesus monkeys over 23 y.o. (25), but no systematic histopathological study of the genital tract has been done in aged macaques.

In this study we examined the reproductive history, histology of the female reproductive tract, and gonadotropin and ovarian steroid levels in pigtail macaques of several age groups in order to evaluate the extent and nature of senescent changes in this species.

MATERIALS AND METHODS

The subjects were 17 female pigtail macaques in 3 age groups: 4 y.o. (n = 3), 10 y.o. (n = 9), and 20 y.o. (n = 5). As indicated in Chapter 3, the 20-y.o. group probably included some animals much older than 20.

Blood for hormone assays was obtained before sacrifice. For menstruating animals, samples were obtained on 2 days in the first 3 days after onset of menstruation. For animals that were not cycling, several samples were taken over the course of a month. All samples were taken between 8:30 a.m. and 12:00 noon with the animal under ketamine anesthesia. Four samples were taken at 20-min intervals. The first was used for determination of estrogens, androgens, and progesterone (investigator O.R.K.) using chromatography and radioimmunoassay systems (12). Antibodies were purchased from G. E. Abraham, University of California, and were titrated to yield 30% binding of added tracer steroid. A portion of the first and all of the succeeding 3 samples from each blood drawing session were analyzed for serum LH concentration (investigator R.A.S.). Serum LH was measured by a double antibody method (21) with LER-1056-C2 as the reference standard, and antiovine LH antibody (No. 15, a gift of Dr. Gordon Niswender). The limit of sensitivity of the assay was equivalent to 0.3 ng/ml LER-1056-C2.

At sacrifice (Chapter 3) the genital tract was excised within 20 min of cardiorespiratory arrest in most animals, and within 90 min in all. The ovaries were sectioned into blocks 3 to 4 mm thick, the uterus and vagina incised longitudinally, and all specimens fixed in Bouin's fluid. After 3 days, they were transferred to 70% ethanol and shipped at ambient temperature for gross and histological examination (investigator C.E.G.). The vagina, uterus and ovaries were washed, separated and weighed individually. Cervix, uterine corpus and oviducts were separated. Half of each ovary was reserved for future study; the other half, a transverse sample of uterine corpus, representative transverse samples of oviducts and vagina, and a sagittal slice from the cervix, were embedded in paraffin and sectioned (6 μm). Ovaries were sectioned serially and every 50th section was mounted. Sections were stained with hematoxylin and eosin (H & E) and duplicate sections from the original uterine corpus were subjected to diastase digestion, stained with periodic acid-Schiff, and counter-stained with aniline blue and hematoxylin (Allochrome method). The vagina and cervix were cut longitudinally and the other organs, transversely. Selected sections were stained by special methods according to Pearse (17).

Only specimens from the 10- and 20-y.o. groups were studied morphologically. Examination of all specimens was done without knowing the ages of the animals. The frequency or abundance of histological features was rated either on a 2-point scale as present or absent or on a 4-point scale (0-3). Nonparametric statistical analyses were applied to test for relations between such features as age and hormonal indices.

RESULTS

There was little difference between 10- and 20-y.o. animals in mean weight of the reproductive organs (Table 16-1). The total recovered ovarian weights of the 10-y.o.'s ranged from 0.11 to 0.62 g and those for the 20 y.o.'s from 0.14 to 0.26 g, but while mean ovarian weight was somewhat less for the older group the difference was not statistically significant. The weight of the uterine corpus varied considerably within the 2 groups. In 1 10-y.o. the uterine corpus was quite involuted (<2.0 g) and 2 20-y.o.'s had atrophic uterine corpora (the smaller weighed 0.78 g). Regression of uterine cervix weight in these individuals was relatively less than that of the corpus (ratio <0.5). Mean uterine weight did not statistically differ between the 2 age groups.

Table 16-1. Reproductive Organ Weights (g) in *M. nemestrina*.

	10 y.o. (n = 9) Mean ± s.d.	20 y.o. (n = 5) Mean ± s.d.
Ovaries		
Combined Weight	0.34 ± 0.17*	0.22 ± 0.07**
% of Body Weight × 100	0.64 ± 0.33*	0.57 ± 0.26**
Uterine Corpus		
Weight	4.21 ± 1.40	3.28 ± 1.03
% of Body Weight × 100	7.86 ± 3.95	7.23 ± 4.21
Uterine Cervix		
Weight	4.82 ± 1.61	3.63 ± 0.57
% of Body Weight × 100	9.07 ± 2.06	8.52 ± 2.26
Corpus/Cervix Ratio	0.86 ± 0.32	0.82 ± 0.40

* n = 8
**n = 3

Table 16-2. Histologic Characteristics of the Ovary in Relation to Age, Evaluated on a Scale of 0–3, Showing Number of Animals in Each Category.

Organ and Characteristics	Frequency or Abundance								P
	10 years (n = 9)				20 years (n = 5)				
	0	1	2	3	0	1	2	3	
Ovary									
Regression or Fibrosis	5	2	2	0	0	3	1	1	0.16
Normal Follicles									
Primary	0	2	4	3	1	2	2	0	0.40
Secondary	1	3	5	0	2	2	1	0	0.41
Tertiary	3	1	3	2	3	2	0	0	0.32
Atretic Follicles									
Primary	2	4	3	0	2	3	0	0	0.48
Secondary	7	2	0	0	4	1	0	0	0.49
Tertiary	2	1	5	1	3	2	0	0	0.16
Corpus Luteum									
Functional*	7	2	–	–	3	2	–	–	0.58
Regressed*	2	7	–	–	3	2	–	–	0.27
Auxiliary*	5	4	–	–	3	2	–	–	0.42
Ceroid cells	1	3	4	1	1	0	1	3	0.23
Interstitial Tissue	5	3	0	1	1	2	1	1	0.43
Rete Tubules	6	3	0	0	4	1	0	0	0.42
Large Thick-Walled Vessels	1	4	4	0	1	0	4	0	0.07
Small Convoluted Vessels	0	8	1	0	1	1	2	1	0.02

p = probability as calculated by Fisher's exact test.
*Assessed as present or absent and scored as 0 or 1, respectively.

The salient histologic findings are summarized in Tables 16-2 and 16-3. Ovaries of several animals in the 10-y.o. group showed a limited amount of cortical fibrosis (Figure 16-1). Marked cortical atrophy (Figure 16-2) was seen in 1 20-y.o. animal (#75026), and some fibrosis was seen in all 20-y.o. animals.

Follicles in all stages of development (Figure 16-1) were abundant in most of the 10-y.o. animals, though follicular depletion was noted in 2 animals (#72399 and #76274). A relatively high frequency of atretic follicles was seen in 3 of the 10-y.o.'s.   None of the 20-y.o.'s showed an abundance of follicles, and in 1 (#75026) no follicles were found.

No corpus luteum was found in 2 10-y.o. animals. Since one had menstruated recently, a corpus luteum was probably present in one of the hemiovaries not examined; the other was amenorrheic. Evidence of a recently regressed corpus

Table 16-3. Histologic Characteristics of Secondary Sex Organs in Relation to Age, Evaluated on a Scale of 0–3, Showing Number of Animals in Each Abundance Category.

Organ and Characteristic	Frequency or Abundance								
	10 Years (n = 9)				20 Years (n = 5)				
	0	1	2	3	0	1	2	3	P
Uterine Corpus									
Endometrium*	8	1	–	–	3	2	–	–	0.51
Pigment granules	7	1	1	0	4	1	0	0	1.00
Myometrium*	8	1	–	–	3	2	–	–	0.51
Adenomyosis	5	3	1	0	0	4	1	0	0.13
Uterine Cervix									
Development of glands	0	4	4	1	0	3	2	0	1.00
Amount of secretion	4	4	0	1	2	3	0	0	1.00
Ectocervical epithelial development	0	3	3	2	0	4	0	1	0.46
Nabothian cysts	8	0	1	0	1	2	0	0	0.50
Epidermization of glands	3	3	1	2	3	0	0	0	0.50
Erosions	7	2	0	0	3	0	0	0	0.99
Vagina									
Development of epithelium	1	1	3	4	0	1	1	2	1.00
Subepithelial leukocytic infiltration	5	4	0	0	0	2	1	1	0.09

p = probability as calculated by Fisher's exact test.
*Note: endometrium and myometrium are rated on a 2-point scale where 0 = active and 1 = atrophic.

luteum was found in all of the 20-y.o.'s except #75026; however, 3 subjects lacked evidence of recent menses.

Several large aggregations of yellowish-pigmented cells with foamy, vacuolated cytoplasm were seen in the ovaries of most animals in both age groups (Figure 16-3). These cells exhibited positive reactions to the following tests (17): periodic acid-Schiff after diastase digestion, McManus Sudan black B, hematoxylin lake, Lillie's Nile blue, and Long Ziehl-Nielson. Schmorl's reaction and the Turnbull blue method were negative. Thus the material in these cells was judged to be a lipofuscin pigment in an early stage of oxidation. Its histochemical characteristics most closely approximated the ceroid type, and the cells were regarded as ceroid cells. Corpora lutea in advanced stages of degeneration also contained vacuolated cells with traces of Schiff-positive material. This material was not tested further, but the large aggregations of ceroid cells were

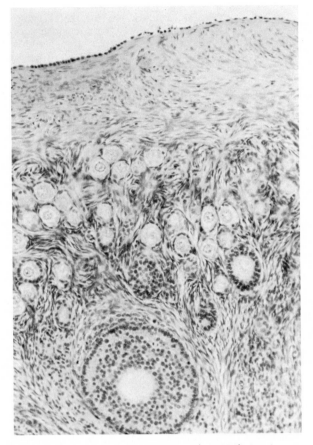

Fig. 16-1.   Ovarian cortex of 10-y.o. *M. nemestrina* (#70371) showing some fibrosis, but abundant primary and secondary follicles. HE, ×200.

probably of luteal origin. Although comparison of the amount of ceroid in the 2 age groups did not yield statistically significant results, 3 20-y.o. animals had very large amounts of the pigment, whereas only 1 10-y.o. did. Extracellular pigment deposition was not observed.

Interstitial tissue was scanty in the ovaries of both age groups, except for the 10-y.o. animal that had a large number of atretic follicles. The rete ovarii was abundant in 10-y.o. animals (Figure 16-4), but considerably less in the 20-y.o. group. Large, thick-walled vessels and small, coiled arterioles (Figure 16-5) were

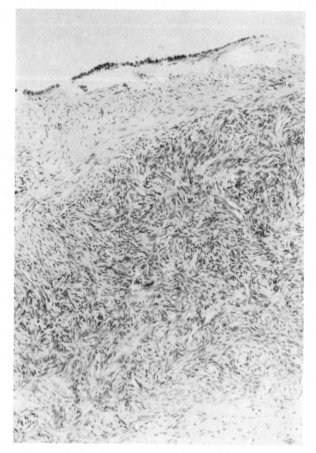

Fig. 16-2. Atrophic ovarian cortex of 20-y.o. *M. nemestrina* (#75026) showing area depleted of follicles. HE, ×200.

significantly more common and well developed in the 20-y.o. than the 10-y.o. animals.

The data on the accessory genital organs are summarized in Table 16-3. An inactive endometrium was found in 1 10-y.o. animal. An atrophic uterine corpus with greatly reduced endometrial tissue and small, inactive glands were seen in 2 20-y.o.'s (Figure 16-6). In these 2 animals the myometrium was characterized by closely packed nuclei (Figure 16-7), indicating that myometrial regression resulted from loss of cytoplasm. Frequent and sometimes extensive areas of

Fig. 16-3.   Ceroid-containing cells among dense collagen in ovarian cortex of 20-y.o. *M. nemestrina* (#76199).   Hematoxylin, aniline blue and periodic acid Schiff after diastase digestion, ×640.

hyaline degeneration occurred in both age groups, usually associated with the walls of small blood vessels. The extent of this change was not related to age. Aggregates of pigment (probably hemosiderin, although diagnostic tests were not performed), were noted in 2 10-y.o. and 1 20-y.o. animal. The 20-y.o. animal also had large aggregations of ceroid cells in the myometrium which resembled those seen in the ovary. Adenomyosis (Figure 16-7) was present in all of the older animals and in half of the younger group.

A solid, uncapsulated, spherical tumor 0.9 mm dia. (Figure 16-8) was found in the myometrium of a 10-y.o. animal (#72399). It was composed of closely packed polygonal cells (Figure 16-9) in most areas, with occasional areas of more loosely packed, oval cells and some areas of focal necrosis. The cells contained large clefted nuclei and a variable number of nucleoli, surrounded by a sparse matrix of PAS-positive material with no reticulin present. Blood vessels ramified through this material. Occasional cells possessed an enlarged nucleus or multiple nuclei; paired nuclei were frequent. The cytoplasm was usually eosinophilic, though nests of less eosinophilic cells with dumbbell-

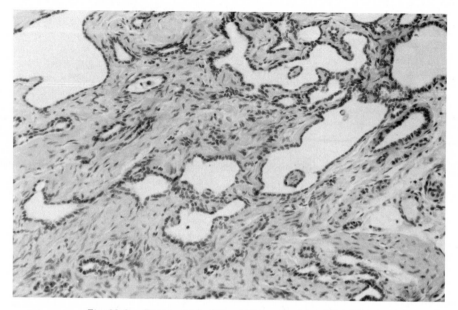

Fig. 16-4.   Rete ovarii in 10-y.o. *M. nemestrina*. HE, ×200.

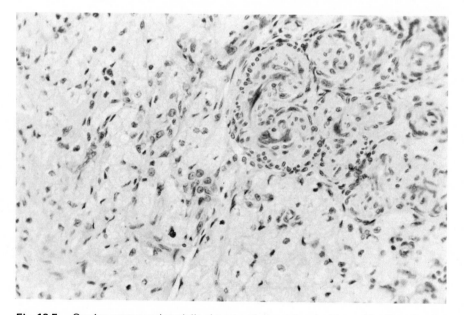

Fig. 16-5.   Ovarian cortex and medulla almost entirely replaced with ceroid cells and coiled vessels in 20-y.o. *M. nemestrina* (#75026). HE, ×400.

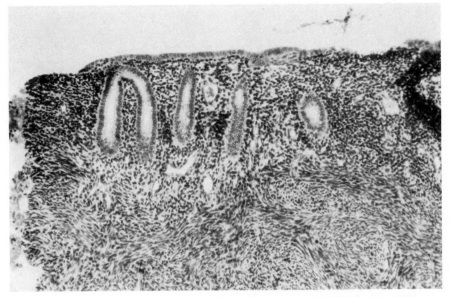

Fig. 16-6.   Atrophic endometrium in 20-y.o. *M. nemestrina* (#75026). HE, ×200.

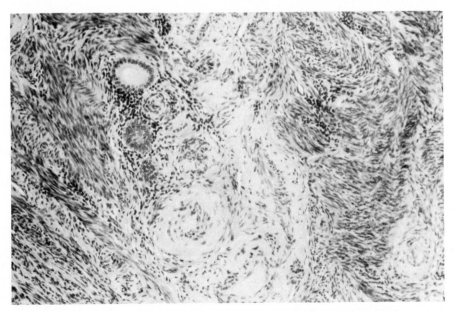

Fig. 16-7.   Myometrium of 20-y.o. *M. nemestrina* (#75026), showing closely packed nuclei and hypotrophic cytoplasm of smooth muscle. Center shows an area of hyalinization associated with blood vessels, and adenomyosis. HE, ×200.

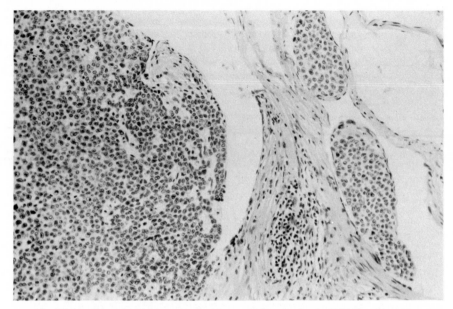

Fig. 16-8.   Edge of uterine tumor in 10-y.o. *M. nemestrina* (#72399). HE, ×200.

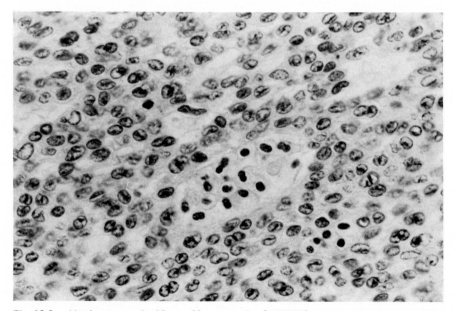

Fig. 16-9.   Uterine tumor in 10-y.o. *M. nemestrina* (#72399), showing focus of pale cells with dumbbell shaped nuclei, surrounded by numerous cells with deeply-clefted or double nuclei. HE, ×640.

shaped or fragmented nuclei were prominent. The margins of the tumor infiltrated the surrounding stroma (Figure 16-8) and some peripheral nodules of tumor cells seemed to be located within lymphatics. The tumor was similar to endolymphatic stromal myosis (15, 17), an extremely rare tumor of uterine stromal origin in humans and to our knowledge not previously reported in non-human primates. Other sources have identified the tumor as a leiomyoblastoma (Armed Forces Institute of Pathology: accession #1622173 A-REG). No other areas of tumor were noted at necropsy or during histopathological analysis. No tumors were found in the 20-y.o. animals.

A unilateral adhesion of the oviduct, ovary and uterine corpus was noted in

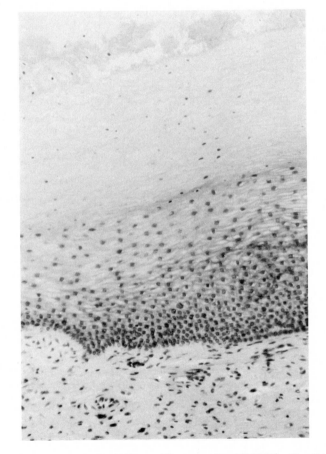

Fig. 16-10. Vaginal epithelium of 10-y.o. *M. nemestrina* (#69256). The thick cornified epithelium is characteristic of the functional phase of the menstrual cycle. HE, ×200.

a 10-y.o. animal (#76273). Histologic sections showed foci of endometriosis within this mass. This animal did not have a history of pelvic surgery.

In the uterine cervix, somewhat greater epithelial hypertrophy and glandular activity were seen in the younger than in the older age group. There was no increase in distribution of squamous epithelium in the endocervical canal of aged monkeys, in contrast to the usual condition in women; consequently, Nabothian cysts were rare. Erosions of the ectocervical epithelium due to everted columnar epithelium were absent, although in 2 10-y.o. animals small erosions of the ectocervix due to denudation of squamous epithelium were present.

There was also little difference in vaginal morphology between the 2 age groups. The degree of vaginal development was related to other evidence of ovarian activity (Figure 16-10). The incidence of leucocytic infiltration was

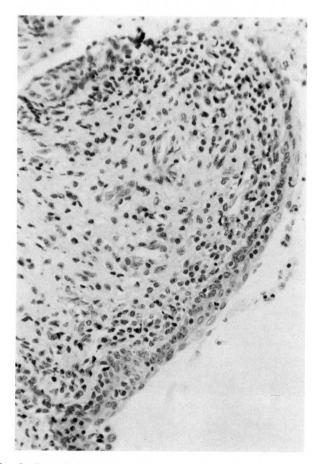

Fig. 16-11.   Senile vaginal epithelium of 20-y.o. *M. nemestrina* (#75026). HE, ×400.

Table 16-4. Serum hormone levels in relation to age.

Hormone	4 Years (n = 3)		10 Years (n = 9)		20 Years (n = 4)	
	$\bar{x}$	RANGE	$\bar{x}$	RANGE	$\bar{x}$	RANGE
Testosterone (pg/ml)	121	59–225	388	121–825	328	197–534
Dihydrotestosterone (pg/ml)	442	203–682	1178	681–2183	777	422–1658
Androstenedione (pg/ml)	468	204–943	1033	810–1398	1104	629–1525
Dehydroepiandrosterone (ng/ml)	24	12–47	123	80–211	60	24–114
Estrone (pg/ml)	36	27–51	46	27–77	51	42–60
Estradiol (pg/ml)	30	20–39	67	25–113	66	17–112
Progesterone (pg/ml)	131	74–176	184	65–398	185	80–281
Luteinizing Hormone (ng/ml)	1.6	1.0–2.2	2.8	0.6–11.5	2.1	1.1–3.9

similar for the 2 groups. Only 1 animal (#75026) had a truly senile vaginal epithelium; it was composed entirely of basal and parabasal epithelial cells and the epithelium was extensively infiltrated by leucocytes (Figure 16-11).

The mean hormonal levels of animals in the 3 age groups are given in Table 16-4. Most hormonal variables were within the expected range for non-menopausal pigtail macaques (21). Regression against age approached significance only for Δ^4-androstenedione (Δ^4-A: p $<$ 0.06), a trend caused by 2 4-y.o.'s whose values were low. Testosterone (T) and dihydrotestosterone (DHT) were also considerably depressed in 2 4-y.o. animals. Androgen levels were relatively elevated in 3 10-y.o.'s (T, 539-825 pg/ml; DHT, 681-2183 pg/ml; Δ^4-A, 1190-1398 pg/ml), and in 1 20-y.o. (#76202) (T, 533 pg/ml; DHT, 1657 pg/ml; Δ^4-A, 1130 pg/ml). No significant difference in LH levels was found among the 3 age groups. Elevated, fluctuating LH levels occurred in 1 10-y.o. (#69256) over a 3-week period during which 4 blood samples were drawn at 20-min intervals on 4 separate occasions (range 4.89-14.32 ng/ml; group mean 2.8 ng/ml); no normal menstrual cycle was seen in this animal. Elevated serum LH values were also found in 1 20-y.o. animal (#75026) ($\bar{X}$ = 3.9 ng/ml; group mean 2.1 ng/ml). Serial plasma samples drawn over a period of 1 hr in this subject showed moderate fluctuation, varying between 3.37 and 4.56 ng/ml. The concentrations of estrone in this subject were within the normal range, but those of estradiol-17β ($\bar{X}$ = 17 pg/ml) were the lowest observed in the study.

DISCUSSION

One 20-y.o. pigtail macaque in this study (#75026) showed all the functional, hormonal and morphologic characteristics of human menopause. She was amenorrheic. The luteinizing hormone level was elevated and gonadotrophs in the anterior pituitary were hypertrophied in a manner characteristic of castrate and senescent humans (Chapter 15, this volume). The estrone/estradiol ratio was low due to a low estradiol-17β level. There were marked changes in the ovary, including low weight, complete follicular depletion, absence of luteal tissue and replacement of most of the cortex and medulla by ceroid cells, coiled vessels, and fibrosis. The uterus and vagina were atrophic. These findings confirm in a second macaque species the menopausal syndrome reported by Hodgen *et al.* (10) to occur in the rhesus macaque. Unfortunately, this animal entered captivity as an adult, making it impossible to obtain an accurate estimate of her age.

The 4 remaining 20-y.o. animals showed evidence of recent ovarian cyclicity. Although statistical trends in histomorphological characteristics of the genital tract were not generally demonstrable, changes characteristic of aging were present in some nonmenopausal 20-y.o.'s. Monkey #76200 had the most marked aging changes, including advanced follicular depletion, fibrotic cortex, thick-walled and convoluted vessels, involutional uterus, and atrophic cervix. Two other 20-y.o.'s also showed a moderate number of convoluted and thick-walled ovarian vessels; they and monkey #76200 had considerable accumulation of ceroid cells, and degranulation of pituitary gonadotrophs (Chapter 15). Degranulation of gonadotrophs was noted in 5 of 7 20-y.o. animals examined. Of these, only #75026 showed elevated LH levels. Thus, while both animals with elevated LH levels had degranulated gonadotrophs, one subject being a 10-y.o. and the other, a 20-y.o., there was no correlation between the degree of degranulation of gonadotrophs and increased LH levels in the subjects as a group.

Like the nonmenopausal females in the 20-y.o. group, individual animals in the 10-y.o. group showed a variety of morphological changes in the reproductive tract generally associated with aging in the human female. A considerable amount of ceroid was found in the ovaries. Moderate atresia of primary follicles, hypertrophic interstitial tissue, distention of lymphatics, and sustained LH elevation were noted in animal #69256. Follicular depletion with a high proportion of atretic follicles were found in animal #72399, but the LH level was not elevated and testosterone was low. Three 10-y.o.'s had somewhat elevated androgen levels, but this change was not correlated with any other variable. Other findings scattered among females of both age groups that were similar to findings in the aging human female included atrophy of endometrium and myometrium, extracellular pigment deposition in the endometrium, hyalinization and vascular changes in the myometrium, reduced epithelial activity in the cervix, and regressed and leucocytic infiltration of the vaginal epithelium.

Ovarian changes reported in the human female, but not seen in the present study, included folding of the ovarian surface, extracellular pigmentation, calcification of medial coats of arteries, and thickening and hyalinization of arterial walls. Certain changes in the human uterus associated with senescence were not seen in the present study, such as glandular cystic, or adenomatous hyperplasia associated with persistent estrogen secretion and often associated with abundant interstitial tissue in the ovary. The human senescent endocervical canal is characterized by spread of stratified squamous epithelium, extending upwards from the portio, blocking the endocervical glands, and resulting in the formation of endocervical cysts, called Nabothian follicles. The absence of these changes in the pigtail macaque may reflect species differences. Alternatively, they could reflect the small and varied age of the sample studied or lack of exposure of captive macaques to dietary and other factors to which the modern human female is ordinarily exposed. The same factors may relate to the absence of tumors in the aged group.

Studies of reproductive senescence in other nonhuman primates have been few. A study of aged chimpanzees has shown that this species can survive as long as 48 years in captivity (7). Such animals showed increased amenorrhea, altered mean cycle length compared with that of the same subjects when aged 15–25 years, and considerably reduced frequency of conception. As in some aging women, follicular depletion was evident in some subjects, as well as arteriosclerosis of ovarian vessels, extracellular pigment deposition and folding of the ovarian surface. A high incidence of tumors, especially fibrothecomas, was noted. No evidence of menopause was detected in these chimpanzees: all had at least one menstrual cycle in the last year of life, and most were menstruating regularly.

A comprehensive survey of reproductive senescence in nonprimate mammals will not be attempted here. It is known that fertility decreases with age in some mammals (2, 5, 13). For instance, under laboratory conditions mice may experience irregular cycles with age that merge into a final anestrous condition, or continued intermittent estrogen activity (24). Some strains of mice show oocyte depletion comparable to that of the human female (13). However, there are no data to indicate that the endocrinological changes characteristic of perimenstrual women are paralleled in nonprimates.

In the rat, increased hypothalamic responsivity to estrogen has been noted, resulting in altered control of gonadotropin secretion with age. This change is reflected in increased frequency of constant estrus and of pseudopregnancy (1). In this species the ovary is probably not responsible for senile sterility, which clearly precedes depletion of the oocyte stock (11). By contrast in women, menopause is closely associated with oocyte depletion, although a causal relationship cannot yet be proven (4).

A number of histological differences between senescent ovaries of the mouse and human have been summarized (23). Mice do not have the accumulation of residual structures, namely, corpora albicantra, corpora fibrotica and hyalinized vessel walls, that characterizes aged human and monkey ovaries. Mouse ovaries do not develop papillary projections of the germinal epithelium, although they develop much more extensive ingrowth and cystic structures derived from the germinal epithelium than are seen in human ovaries; neither of these changes was seen in the pigtail macaque. Whereas in humans and macaques the germinal epithelium frequently presents a columnar appearance (sometimes mucus secreting in women), in mice transitions to the granulosa cell type predominate. Both mouse and human rete tubules are said to undergo proliferative changes during senescence. Rete tubules were poorly developed in the aged pigtail macaque, although they were extensive in the 10-y.o.'s. There is also a tendency for proliferation or accumulation of interstitial cells in the ovary of aged mice; a similar change (thecomatosis) has been reported in a proportion of postmenopausal human ovaries (3, 26) and in young and old chimpanzees (6, 8), but was not evident in aged macaques of this study.

Ceroid, a lipochrome pigment, was extensively distributed in the ovaries of some of the 10- and 20-y.o. macaques; therefore, it cannot be said to be characteristic solely of old age in these animals. However, the aged animals had greater amounts of this material. The ceroid was associated with regressing luteal bodies in the ovaries. Costoff and Mahesh (4) have reported an increase in the related pigment, lipofuscin, in corpora lutea of postmenopausal women, and deposition of ceroid has been reported in association with local parenchymal involution (18, 19). Ceroid is a typical residue of involution in aging rat and mouse ovaries, where it appears in involuting interstitial cells and granulosa cells, and is eventually taken up by phagocytes (23). Additional study will be required to determine whether the pigtail macaque resembles the rodent more than the human in the degree of ceroid degeneration in the aged ovary.

In summary, a menopausal condition such as occurs in women has not been described in other mammals with the exception of the macaques. Although the sample of aged pigtail macaques studied here is insufficiently large for us to generalize about the characteristics of reproductive senescence, the trends suggest many similarities with the human female. These conclusions are of great interest because chimpanzees, although phylogenetically closer to man, continue to experience reproductive cyclicity until death, even when it is delayed until the fifth decade. Pending study of older chimpanzees, should they become available, it appears from the present study that macaques such as *M. mulatta* and *M. nemestrina* will be the preferred primate models for the study of some aspects of human reproductive senescence.

ACKNOWLEDGMENTS

This study was supported in part by National Institutes of Health grants RR00166, RR52177 and AG62145 to the University of Washington, and RR00165 to the Yerkes Primate Center.

REFERENCES

1. Aschheim, P. (1976): Aging in the hypothalamic-hypophyseal ovarian axis in the rat. In: *Hypothalamus, Pituitary and Aging*, edited by A. V. Everitt and J. A. Burgess, pp. 376-418. Springfield, Ill.; Thomas.
2. Bader, R. (1937): Alterserscheinungen an Menschen und Makakenovarien. *Zool. Anz.*, **120**: 33-39.
3. Bigelow, B. (1958): Comparison of ovarian and endometrial morphology spanning menopause. *Obstet. Gynec.*, **11**: 487-513.
4. Costoff, A., and Mahesh, V. B. (1975): Primordial follicles with normal oocytes in the ovaries of postmenopausal women. *J. Am. Geriat. Soc.*, **23**: 193-196.
5. Engle, E. T. (1944): Menopause—introduction. *J. Clin. Endocr.*, **4**: 567-570.
6. Graham, C. E. (1973): Functional microanatomy of the primate uterine cervix. In: *Handbook of Physiology*, Section 1, Vol. II, Part 2, edited by R. O. Greep and E. B. Astwood, pp. 1-24. Washington, D.C.; American Physiological Society.
7. Graham, C. E. (n.d.): Reproductive function in aged female chimpanzees. *Am. J. Phys. Anthrop.*, **50**: 291-300.
8. Graham, C. E., and McClure, H. M. (1977): Ovarian tumors and related lesions in aged chimpanzees. *Vet. Pathol.*, **14**: 380-386.
9. Grodin, J. M., Siiteri, P. K., and McDonald, P. C. (1971): Extraglandular estrogens in the postmenopause. In: *Menopause and Aging*, edited by K. J. Ryan and D. C. Gibson, pp. 15-35. Washington, D.C.; U.S. Dept. of Health, Education and Welfare, publication #(NIH)73-319.
10. Hodgen, G. D., Goodman, A. C., O'Connor, A., and Johnson, D. K. (1977): Menopause in rhesus monkeys: model for study of disorders in the human climacteric. *Am. J. Obstet. Gynec.*, **127**: 581-584.
11. Jones, E. C. (1970): The aging ovary and its influence on reproductive capacity. *J. Reprod. Fertil.*, Suppl. **12**, 17-30.
12. Kling, O. R., and Westfahl, P. K. (1978): Steroid changes during the menstrual cycle of the baboon *Papio cyanocephalus* and human. *Biol. Reprod.*, **18**: 392-400.
13. Krohn, P. L. (1955): Tissue transplantation techniques applied to the problem of the aging of the organs of reproduction. In: *Ciba Foundation Colloquia on Aging*, Vol. 1, pp. 141-161. London; Churchill.
14. Lang, W. R., and Aponte, G. E. (1967): Gross and microscopic anatomy of the aged female reproductive organs. *Clin. Obstet. Gynec.*, **10**: 454-465.
15. Norris, H. J., and Taylor, H. B. (1966): Mesenchymal tumors of the uterus. I. A clinical and pathological study of 53 endometrial stromal tumors. *Cancer*, **19**: 755-766.
16. Ober, K. G., Schneppenheim, P., Hamperl, H., and Kaufmann, C. (1958): Die Epithelgrenzen im Bereiche des Isthmus Uteri. *Arch. Gynaekol.*, **190**: 346-383.
17. Pearse, A. G. E. (1960): *Histochemistry, Theoretical and Applied*, 2nd edition. Boston; Little, Brown.
18. Reagan, J. W. (1950): Ceroid pigment in human ovary. *Am. J. Obstet. Gynec.*, **59**: 433-436.
19. Rockenshaub, A. (1950): Theca- und Stroma-Luteinzelien des Elerstockes als fluoreszierende Körnchenzellen ("Fluorozyten"). *Geburtsh. u. Frauenheilk.*, **10**: 829-834.
20. Sherman, B. M., West, J. H., and Korenman, S. G. (1976): The menopausal transition: Analysis of LH, FSH, estradiol and progesterone concentrations during menstrual cycles of older women. *J. Clin. Endocr.*, **42**: 629-636.
21. Steiner, R. A., Schiller, H. S., Illner, P., Blandau, R., and Gale, C. C. (1977): Sex

hormones correlated with sex skin swelling and rectal temperature during the menstrual cycle of the pigtail macaque (*Macaca nemestrina*). *Lab. Anim. Sci.*, **27**: 217-221.

22. Treloar, A. E., Boynton, R. E., Behn, B. G., and Brown, B. W. (1967): Variation of the human menstrual cycle through reproductive life. *Int. J. Fertil.*, **12**: 77.

23. Thung, P. J. (1961): Aging changes in the ovary. In: *Structural Aspects of Aging*, edited by G. H. Bourne, pp. 111-142. London; Pitman.

24. Thung, P. J., Boot, L. M., and Mühlbock, O. (1956): Senile changes in oestrous cycle and in ovarian structure in some inbred strains of mice. *Acta Endocr. (Kbh.)*. **23**: 8-32.

25. Van Wagenen, G., and Simpson, M. E. (1965): *Embryology of the Ovary and Testis in Homo Sapiens and Macaca mulatta*. New Haven; Yale University Press.

26. Woll, E., Hertig, A. T., Smith, G. V. S., and Johnson, L. C. (1948): The ovary in endometrial carcinoma, with notes on the morphological history of the aging ovary. *Am. J. Obstet. Gynec.*, **56**: 617-633.

17

Mammary Gland Responsivity to Prolactin Stimulation

David L. Kleinberg, Jean Todd, and Philip Chin
Department of Medicine,
New York University School of Medicine, New York, NY; and
Medical Research Service,
New York Veterans Adminstration Hospital, New York, NY

INTRODUCTION

Although the effects of prolactin on the mammary gland during pregnancy and lactation have been studied extensively, little is known about the function of prolactin at other times of life. Studies in rodents indicate that prolactin is largely responsible for the production of milk proteins (e.g., casein and α-lactalbumin) during pregnancy and lactation (12, 14). We have recently developed a radioimmunoassay for human α-lactalbumin that can measure this milk protein in picogram concentrations (2, 4), a development which enables us to study the effects of prolactin on the breast at most stages of life. These studies indicate that prolactin does affect normal mammary tissue, even in the absence of a stimulus such as pregnancy or suckling. α-Lactalbumin is routinely found in mammary tissue of nonpregnant, nonlactating, virgin, nulliparous, and multiparous nonhuman primates, and further production of this milk protein continues or increases when mammary tissues are maintained in organ culture in the presence of prolactin (5).

Prolactin has an important role in the growth of breast cancer in rodents (13, 15) but its role in human breast malignancies has not been determined. Breast cancer is a disease of aging. As a preliminary to exploring the role of prolactin in this disease, we designed this study to examine the effects of prolactin on normal mammary tissue from nonhuman primates at different stages of life.

METHODS

Mammary tissues from 3 4-y.o., 7 10-y.o., and 4 20-y.o. pigtail macaques (*Macaca nemestrina*) were studied in an organ culture system which has been previously described (5). With the animal under ketamine and nembutal anesthesia (Chapter 3, this volume), the left chest was shaved. Under sterile operating procedure, the skin was cleaned and an incision made in an arc from the left acromion to midsternum, to the lower costal margin, to midaxilla, and back to the acromion. The mammary tissue and overlying skin were excised by blunt dissection. The entire specimen was placed in 15 ml of cold Hanks' balanced salt solution with antibiotic and shipped on ice by air.

Cultures were set up within 24 hr after surgery. Extraneous tissue was removed and the thin sheet of mammary tissue was cut into 2-mm cubes weighing about 2.3 mg each. Pieces of tissue were placed on lens paper on a metal grid overlying a well containing 1 ml of medium in a Falcon organ culture dish. Each dish contained 10 pieces of tissue. Medium 199 was supplemented with porcine insulin, hydrocortisone and antibiotics; pooled human female serum was added in concentrations of 20%. The blood was obtained from adult volunteers and was tested to ensure that it contained no measurable α-lactalbumin. The concentration of prolactin in this serum pool was about 9 ng/ml, or 1.8 ng/ml in each culture dish. Ovine prolactin (NIH–P–S–10) was added where indicated. Cultures were maintained for 9 days at $37°C$ in an atmosphere of 95% air and 5% CO_2. Medium was changed on days 3, 6 and 9 and kept at $-20°C$ until analyzed.

Macaque α-lactalbumin is similar to that of humans, and was measured by our human radioimmunoassay (2, 4). When the results were expressed for the 3-, 6- and 9-day periods, they represented accumulated α-lactalbumin in medium for that 3-day period in culture. When tissue was homogenized for analysis, all pieces from a dish were pooled.

Stock solutions of ovine prolactin at 200 μg/ml were sterilized with a Millipore filter. To determine losses of prolactin due to filtration, trace concentrations of ^{131}I-ovine prolactin were added to the unlabeled material and counts were taken before and after sterilization. Results indicated that 28 to 40% (mean 33%) of the prolactin was lost. Therefore, the effective concentrations of ovine prolactin at 100 and 1000 ng/ml were approximately 67 and 670 ng/ml respectively. When ovine prolactin was used, it was present in the medium throughout the culture period.

Amino acid incorporation into proteins was measured by a 24-hr incubation of 2 μCi of tritiated (^{3}H) lysine (specific activity 60 Ci/mM) per dish on days 2, 5 and 8. After the 24-hr incubation the medium was harvested for α-lactalbumin determinations and the tissue examined for both α-lactalbumin and ^{3}H-lysine incorporation. Tissues were homogenized in 2 ml of 0.05 M phosphate buffer with a Polytron homogenizer. An aliquot was treated twice with cold 10% trichloracetic acid (TCA), centrifuged and then washed twice with 95% ethanol. ^{3}H-lysine in the precipitated protein was counted in a liquid scintillation counter and protein was measured by the method of Lowry (8). Results were expressed as cpm/mg of protein.

Tissue viability was evaluated by histological examination of paraffin sections stained with hematoxylin and eosin. Central necrosis occurred infrequently, but surrounding tissue was usually well preserved for periods of 9 days or more.

RESULTS

Studies in 4-Year-Olds

Organ culture studies were done on mammary tissues from 3 4-y.o. macaques. Tissues incubated with ovine prolactin (1000 ng/ml) were compared with control tissues incubated without prolactin to assess the effects on accumulation of α-lactalbumin in medium, α-lactalbumin content in tissues, and incorporation of ^{3}H-lysine into TCA-precipitable tissue protein. These parameters were examined in the same cultures after 3, 6 and 9 days (Figure 17-1).

At 3 days, α-lactalbumin was released into the medium in control and test cultures with significantly greater release in the prolactin-containing cultures from 2 of the 3 animals. Mean α-lactalbumin increase at 100 ng/ml ovine prolactin (not shown in Figure 17-1) was 26% (range 0-51%) and at 1000 ng/ml, 76% (range 4-115%). At 6 and 9 days, α-lactalbumin in the control medium fell precipitously to a mean of 11.2% and 1.6% of the 3-day levels, whereas the stimulatory effect of prolactin remained pronounced. At 6 days, α-lactalbumin in prolactin-containing dishes was significantly higher at both 100 ng/ml ($p < 0.005$ vs control) and 1000 ng/ml, ($p < 0.001$ vs control), and at 9 days it was 11 times and 59 times higher at 100 and 1000 ng/ml than in controls.

Production of α-lactalbumin was also greater in homogenates of tissues exposed to prolactin. Prolactin-treated tissues had 10 times more α-lactalbumin than controls (range 6.5-15 times) at 3 days and also showed marked increases at 6 and 9 days. That prolactin-treated cultures contained much higher concentrations of α-lactalbumin than the control tissues at all time periods indicated that new protein production was probably taking place in response to the addition of prolactin.

[3]H-lysine studies showed that this amino acid was incorporated into TCA-precipitable protein at each time period (3, 6 and 9 days), but no significant increases in uptake of lysine expressed as cpm/mg protein were found when prolactin was added to the medium. These preliminary studies suggest that prolactin has no apparent effect on total protein synthesis in these nulliparous

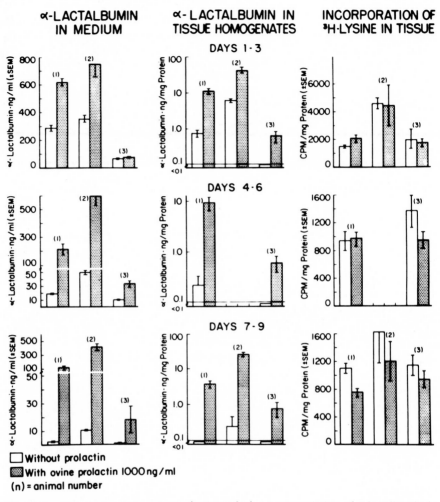

Fig. 17-1. Effect of ovine prolactin (1000 ng/ml) on accumulation of α-lactalbumin in medium bathing mammary tissue, the concentration of α-lactalbumin in the tissue homogenates, and incorporation of ³H-lysine into tissue at 3, 6, and 9 days in culture. Results from study of 3 4-y.o. female pigtail macaques.

animals and that its stimulatory effect on α-lactalbumin production is a specific one.

Comparison of the Effect of Prolactin on Mammary Tissue in Different Age Groups

α-Lactalbumin was detected in homogenates from freshly removed mammary tissue in all of the experimental animals tested. The amount varied from animal

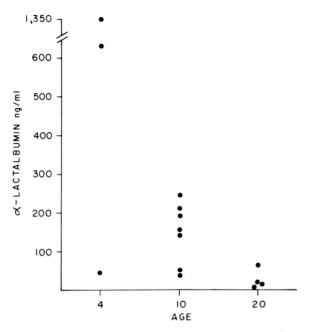

Fig. 17-2. Effect of prolactin on total α-lactalbumin production over 9 days in culture of mammary tissues from pigtail macaques representing 3 different age groups. Each dot represents the increase in α-lactalbumin production stimulated by 1000 ng/ml of ovine prolactin over controls.

to animal, and no significant differences were noted with age (t-test comparison of means by age group). Mean α-lactalbumin in the 3 4-y.o.'s was 307 ng/mg of protein (range 98-604), and in 9 others (10- and 20-y.o.'s) it was 172 ng/mg of protein (range 1.3-285).

To compare differences among the younger and older animals, total α-lactalbumin production for 9 days was calculated for control dishes and ovine prolactin-treated (1000 ng/ml) dishes and the mean difference between the two was determined. This difference, representing the stimulatory effect of prolactin, is shown in Figure 17-2. Means for the 4-, 10 and 20-y.o.'s were 675 ng/ml, 111 ng/ml, and 27 ng/ml, respectively. The differences were significant (p < 0.01 by t-test) when the 4-y.o.'s were compared with the 10- and 20-y.o.'s combined. The mean increase over controls was 194% for the 4-y.o.'s (range 54-324), 176% for the 10-y.o.'s (range 24-616), and 40% for the 20-y.o.'s (range 8-122).

DISCUSSION

Until recently, our knowledge of mammary physiology and the role played by prolactin has been limited to studies in rodents during mammary development and in pregnancy and lactation. Lyons et al. (9) first demonstrated that mammary development in rats was a complicated event requiring synergism of a number of hormones including estrogens, progesterone, glucocorticoids, growth hormone, and prolactin. The central role of prolactin in this process was emphasized by the fact that mammary development could not occur in its absence. During pregnancy, proliferation of lobuloalveolar elements takes place and if mammary tissues of midpregnant animals are maintained in organ culture, added prolactin stimulates milk protein production (12, 14) and lactation (1, 3). In pregnant animals, high concentrations of circulating estrogens have an inhibitory effect on lactation. Only after expulsion of the placenta with the resultant precipitous fall in estrogens and progesterone does active lactation begin (6, 9). Continued lactation is maintained by repeated suckling, during which pituitary prolactin secretion is episodically increased (11).

In nonhuman primates, mammary tissues from nonpregnant, nonlactating animals produce milk proteins (5, 6), although in lower concentrations than during pregnancy and lactation. The production of α-lactalbumin can be be maintained or increased in organ culture by addition of prolactin (5). The results of the present study indicate that the aging process itself does not prevent continued formation of α-lactalbumin by the mammary epithelium of these macaques. In fact, no significant differences were noted between the mean tissue concentration of α-lactalbumin in the 4-y.o. animals (none of which had ever lactated) and that in the older animals.

These studies do provide evidence, however, that mammary tissues from older animals may be less responsive to prolactin than those from younger ones. Although mean prolactin-stimulated increases in α-lactalbumin fell progressively with age (Figure 17-2), the differences were significant only when comparing the 4-y.o.'s with the 10- and 20-y.o.'s combined. It is tempting to speculate that greater significance might have been obtained if the number of animals, particularly those in the 4-y.o. and 20-y.o. groups, had been higher.

The cause of the decline in responsivity to prolactin with age is not clear. It is probably not closely related to the menopause. Only one of the animals (#75026) was postmenopausal (Chapter 16, this volume), and her α-lactalbumin response to prolactin stimulation was second highest of animals in the 20-y.o. group. The differences in responsivity between age groups occurred in the absence of any significant difference in mean estradiol levels. There was no correlation between responsivity to prolactin and the number of dysplasias noted in the contralateral breasts of the same animals (Chapter 18, this volume). The reduced responsivity in the older age groups may result from a reduced number of epithelial cells per unit weight of mammary tissue or from reduced capacity of individual cells in older animals to synthesize α-lactalbumin. Perhaps most intriguing is the fact that even breast tissue of the oldest female pigtail macaques, one of whom was clearly postmenopausal, was capable of responding to prolactin by production of α-lactalbumin, a function previously thought to be dormant or absent in the aged female.

ACKNOWLEDGMENTS

This study was supported in part by National Institutes of Health grants RR00166, RR52177 and AG62145 to the University of Washington.

REFERENCES

1. Elias, J. J. (1957): Cultivation of adult mouse mammary gland in hormone-enriched synthetic medium. *Science*, **126**: 842–844.
2. Kleinberg, D. L. (1975): Human α-lactalbumin: measurement in serum and in breast cancer organ cultures by radioimmunoassay. *Science*, **190**: 276–278.
3. Kleinberg, D. L., and Frantz, A. G. (1971): Human prolactin: measurement in plasma by *in vitro* bioassay. *J. Clin. Invest.*, **50**: 1557–1568.
4. Kleinberg, D. L., Todd, J., and Groves, M. L. (1977): Studies on human α-lactalbumin: radioimmunoassay measurements in normal human breast and breast cancer. *J. Clin. Endocr.*, **45**: 1238–1250.
5. Kleinberg, D. L., Todd, J., and Niemann, W. (1978): Prolactin stimulation of α-lactalbumin in normal primate mammary gland. *J. Clin. Endocr.*, **47**: 435–441.
6. Kleinberg, D. L., Todd, J., and Niemann, W. (1976): Effect of prolactin on α-lactalbumin in normal human and primate breast. *Clin. Res.*, **24**: 273A.
7. Kuhn, N. J. (1969): Progesterone withdrawal as the lactogenic trigger in the rat. *J. Endocr.*, **44**: 39–54.
8. Lowry, O. H., Rosenbrough, N. J., and Farr, A. L. (1951): Protein measurements with the folin phenol reagent. *J. Biol. Chem.*, **193**: 265–275.
9. Lyons, W. R., Li, C. H., and Johnson, R. E. (1958): The hormonal control of mammary growth and lactation. *Rec. Prog. Horm. Res.*, **14**: 219–254.
10. Meites, J., and Sgouris, J. T. (1954): Effects of altering the balance between prolactin and ovarian hormones on initiation of lactation in rabbits. *Endocrinology*, **55**: 530–534.
11. Noel, G. L., Suh, H. K., and Frantz, A. G. (1974): Prolactin release during nursing and breast stimulation in postpartum and nonpostpartum subjects. *J. Clin. Endocr.*, **38**: 413–423.
12. Palmiter, R. D. (1969): Hormonal induction and regulation of lactose synthetase in mouse mammary gland. *Biochem. J.*, **113**: 409–417.
13. Pearson, O. H., Llerena, O., Llerena, L., Molina, A., and Butler, T. (1969): Prolactin-dependent rat mammary cancer: a model for man? *Trans. Ass. Amer. Phys.*, **82**: 225–238.
14. Topper, Y. J. (1970): Multiple hormone interactions in the development of mammary gland *in vitro. Rec. Prog. Horm. Res.*, **26**: 287–308.
15. Welsch, C. W., Jenkins, T. W., and Meites, J. (1970): Increased incidence of mammary tumors in the female rat grafted with multiple pituitaries. *Cancer Res.*, **30**: 1024–1029.

18

Mammary Pathology

M. R. Warner

Meredith Mosle Laboratory for Cancer Research,
Department of Obstetrics and Gynecology, and
Department of Cell Biology, Baylor College of Medicine,
Houston, Texas

INTRODUCTION

As women age, their breasts tend to develop dysplasias in the late second and third decades, and tumors in the fourth and fifth decades of life. While rodents have been valuable in extending understanding of pathologic changes in mammary disease, models that more closely resemble the human are needed for experimental studies.

Normal development of mammary glands in nonhuman primates has been reviewed (4), but detailed descriptions exist only for the rhesus macaques (*Macaca mulatta*) (2, 8-10, 12-19, 26-31, 34, 35). Mammary dysplasias have been reported for rhesus macaques (5, 10, 23, 27), and tumors have been described in rhesus macaques, orangutans, mandrills, galagos and tree shrews (3, 18, 24). However, the effects of aging on the mammary glands of nonhuman primates have not been described. This study was designed to investigate the usefulness of the pigtail macaque (*M. nemestrina*) as an experimental model of normal and pathologic mammary development in the human.

MATERIALS AND METHODS

Subjects were 16 nonpregnant, nonlactating females and 4 male macaques ranging in age from 4 to more than 20 years. All of the females and 2 of the males were pigtail macaques; 2 males were longtail macaques (*M. fascicularis*).

The right mammary gland attached to the nipple and skin, with surrounding pectoral fascia, was obtained 10 to 20 min before cardiopulmonary arrest, fixed in 15% formalin, and shipped at ambient temperature. After 7 or more days in formalin, the skin was stretched and pinned to a cork board, post-fixed for 48 hrs in Tellyesnizky's fluid, then soaked in 70% ethyl alcohol for 24 hrs. Nipple dimensions were measured ±0.1 mm. Nipple volume was calculated by the formula $V = \pi r^2 1$, where V = volume, r = one half the maximum diameter, and 1 = the length.

Glands were dissected off the skin, which was trimmed close to the nipple. Dissected glands were defatted, stained with iron hematoxylin (1), and cleared, studied, and photographed in methysalicylate as a single piece. Tissues for histologic study were excised from processed wholemount preparations, dehydrated, embedded in paraffin, sectioned at 7 μm, and stained with a modification of Masson's trichrome stain or with Van Gieson's stain.

For weight determinations, blood vessels, nerves, fat, muscle, lymph nodes and subcutaneous connective tissue were removed from glands with the aid of a dissection microscope. Mammary tissues were blotted on Whatman #1 filter paper, then weighed on a top loading balance to ±0.01 g (Mettler PN 1200, Princeton, N.J.). The nipple with its skin was cut from the mammary gland and weighed similarly.

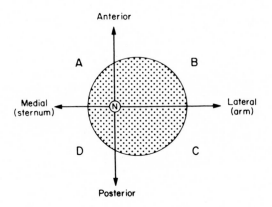

Fig. 18-1. Quadrants of the mammary gland of *M. nemestrina*. N, nipple.

Tissues were evaluated after examination of both wholemount preparations and histologic sections. Evaluations were done without knowing the age of the subjects.

Glands were divided into unequal quadrants (Figure 18-1), using the nipple as

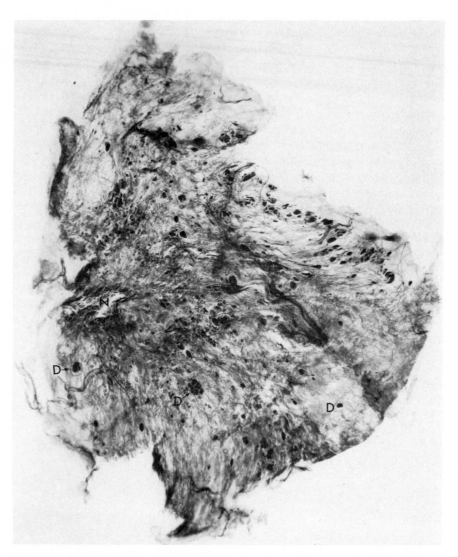

Fig. 18-2. Right mammary gland of a 20-y.o. female *M. nemestrina* containing numerous dysplasias, some of which are labeled (D). The nipple has been removed (N). Iron hematoxylin (IH), 1×.

an axis of orientation following the customary use in determining similar parameters in women (7).

Dysplasias were identified in stained wholemounts, magnified by a dissection microscope, as areas that differed in density or amount of secretion from the surrounding "normal" tissue. Wholemounts of entire glands were photographed by transmitted light (Figure 18-2). Dysplasias were identified on the photographs and then cut from the gland for serial histologic section. After diagnosis, the subgross and microscopic appearance of each dysplasia could be compared.

Correlations were examined between our data and those reported elsewhere in this volume, including steroid hormone values and luteinizing hormone (LH) (Chapter 16), cortisol (Chapter 19), prolactin, triiodothyronine and thyroxine, and immunoglobulins (Chapter 10).

Statistical analyses included the Mann Whitney U test (MWU) for differences between age groups and Spearman's rank coefficient (r_s) and Pearson's product moment coefficient (r_p) for correlations between dysplasia incidence and circulating hormones, lipids, and immunoglobulins.

RESULTS

Normal Morphology

The nipples, located toward the midline (Figure 18-1), contained 4 to 8 primary ducts (average 5.6). Some junctions of major ducts were seen (Figure 18-3). Nipple weight and width were not proportional to the number of primary ducts or to mammary lobularity. Half or more of the nipple volume was connective tissue. The central connective tissue investing the primary ducts was oriented concentrically and contained dense collagenous connective tissue with coarse elastic fibrils. In contrast, the outer, subepithelial connective tissue was composed of a network of looser collagenous fibers with numerous smooth muscle bundles and very fine elastic fibrils. It was highly vascular and had many sensory nerve endings. Circumference of the nipple and thickness of the outer connective tissue layer varied according to distance from the body wall. Investing connective tissue was thickest in the middle, and thinner at either end of the nipple. The hairless areola was small, and lacked adnexal glands, including Montgomery's glands. Although individual variation was great, the 4-y.o. animals had shorter nipples, with a significantly smaller volume than the 10-y.o. animals (Table 18-1; $p < 0.05$, MWU). Nipple weight and volume were proportional to body weight $(r_s = 0.87, p < 0.001; r_s = 0.79, p < 0.01$, respectively). Male nipples were considerably smaller (mean weight = 0.11 g) than those of females (mean weight = 3.65 g).

The mammary glands extended in a single plane of tissue, several millimeters thick, from the sternum to the anterior axillary line and from the clavicle to the

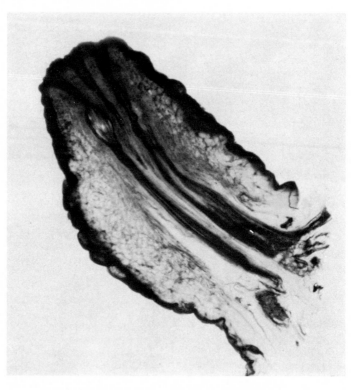

Fig. 18-3. Lobules of alveoli extend into the base of the nipple in a 10-y.o. female macaque. Note absence of lactiferous sinus. Longitudinal section. IH, 5×.

lower margin of the ribs. There was no axillary extension corresponding to the tail of Spence seen in women. The weights of quadrants A and D were similar, as were those of B and C. The glands of the 4-y.o. females were fully developed, so that the gland weight, ratio of gland weight to body weight, and index of mammary development (lobularity) did not vary with age (Table 18-1). The index of development was lower in the females who had not menstruated for 3 or more months than for those who were cycling regularly. The index of development did not vary consistently with sex, distance from the nipple, gland quadrant, or any of the relevant hormonal and morphological variables reported in other chapters of this volume.

Mammary development in males varied widely, from short, simple ducts through more complex branching structures, with moderate lobulo-alveolar development (Figure 18-4). The average weight of male glands was 0.29 g.

Table 18-1. Relationships of Age and Body Weight to Mammary Morphology in 16 Female Pigtail Macaques*.

	Age Group		
	4	**10**	**20**
Number of Animals	3	9	4
Body weight (kg)	4.33 ± 0.42	5.36 ± 0.29	4.36 ± 0.43
Right nipple			
Weight (g)	0.42 ± 0.13	0.49 ± 0.14	0.38 ± 0.20
Volume (mm^3)	296 ± 164	540 ± 309	318 ± 172
Right mammary gland			
Weight (g)	3.19 ± 1.25	3.84 ± 1.02	3.57 ± 1.43
Ratio to body weight × 10^4	7.37	7.16	8.19
Index of development*	4.00	3.13	3.75
Mammary dysplasias			
Number per gland	8.3 ± 12.7	188.7 ± 174.8	136 ± 177.9
Number per quadrant A	3.0 ± 5.2	28.0 ± 33.0	10.0 ± 6.2
B	2.7 ± 4.6	83.3 ± 84.0	53.3 ± 76.2
C	2.3 ± 2.5	55.1 ± 46.8	59.0 ± 87.4
D	0.3 ± 0.8	22.2 ± 21.0	14.0 ± 9.0
Cystic per gland	6.0 ± 8.7	12.6 ± 28.8	6.8 ± 5.0
Dense per gland	2.3 ± 4.0	176.0 ± 180.6	129.5 ± 182.5
Total per gland weight (#/g)	2.1 ± 2.7	49.7 ± 41.1	39.2 ± 43.3

*Index of mammary development: 0 = no alveoli; 1 = occasional alveoli; 2 = common alveoli and some small lobules with no secretion; 3 = common alveoli and medium lobules, sparse secretion; 4 = lobules common, some secretion. Findings represented by mean or mean ± standard deviation.

Pathology

The outstanding morphologic feature distinguishing mammae of the 10- and 20-y.o. females from those of the 4-y.o. animals was the much higher incidence of dysplasias in older animals. Eight types of abnormalities were distinguished microscopically. Like its normal counterpart, each dysplastic lobule was supplied by a central blood vessel, which often accompanied the interlobular duct. Secretion was sometimes present and varied widely in its staining characteristics and fat content. Cysts were seen in the form of fluid-filled spaces lined by a layer of flattened epithelium (Figure 18-5), and duct ectasias in the form of dilated ducts or ductules lined by more than 1 layer of epithelium, which was sometimes hyperplastic or metaplastic. Intraductal dysplasia, common in prelobular or intralobular terminal ducts, had 3 or more layers of epithelial cells (Figures 18-6, 18-7). The ducts were often dilated or contained papillomas and

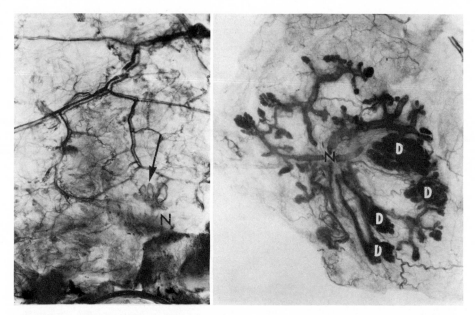

Fig. 18-4. Left: mammary gland of a 10-y.o. male macaque showing only a few simple ducts. N, nipple. IH, 2X. Right: discrete dysplasias (D) in an otherwise regressed gland in a 20-y.o. male macaque. IH, 4X.

hyperplasia of the investing connective tissue was common. Lobular dysplasia consisted of groups of ductules that were either larger or hypercellular compared with adjacent lobules. Hyperplastic lobules (Figures 18-8, 18-9) contained proliferating, highly branched ductules lined by hypertrophic cuboidal epithelium; basal nuclei and abundant eosinophilic cytoplasm were present, together with areas of epithelial or myoepithelial hyperplasia. Hypersecretory lobules looked like lactating tissue in an otherwise regressed mammary gland. Fine vacuoles, secretion in lumina, interstitial inflammatory cells and focal epithelial hyperplasia were seen (cysts and hypersecretory lobules looked similar in wholemounts). Sclerotic lobules were enlarged and contained an increased proportion of connective tissue, often hyalinized or sclerotic. Atypical lobules were enlarged, with layers of clusters of hypertrophic, hyperchromatic epithelial cells lining the ductules.

Presence of inflammatory cells varied among dysplasias of a single individual. A sample of 45 dysplasias was serially sectioned and examined. Leukocytes were present in 20% of lesions at 4 years, 50% at 10 years and none at 20 years. Concretions that stained like calcium were present in some dysplasias. Mucinous

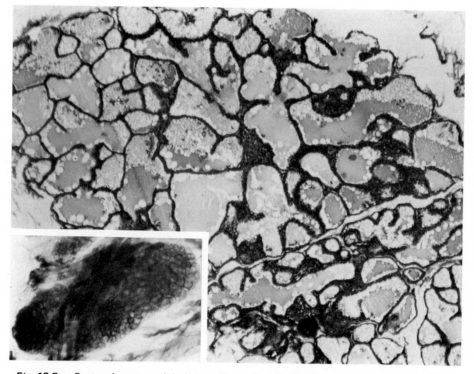

Fig. 18-5. Cyst and secretory lobule in a 20-y.o. female pigtail macaque. MT, 160X. Inset: same lesion viewed subgrossly; IH, 18X.

and apocrine metaplasia of epithelium and myoepithelial metaplasia of connective tissue were more frequent in the older animals.

The number of dysplasias per gland was highly variable, varying from none to over 500. The incidence was 15 to 20 times greater in the 10- and 20-y.o. groups than in the 4-y.o. group (differences significant at $P < 0.03$, MWU). The difference between the 10- and 20-y.o. groups was not significant. Within each of the older groups, the number of dysplasias was extremely variable, as reflected in the large standard deviations in Table 18-1. Total dysplasias were distributed similarly between quadrants of equivalent size (Table 18-2).

In contrast to the 10-y.o. females, neither of the 2 10-y.o. males had mammary dysplasias; the 2 20-y.o. males had 20 and 29 lesions per g of mammary tissue (Figure 18-4). (There was 1 pigtail and 1 longtail macaque in each age group.)

To explore possible relations between the incidence of mammary lesions and

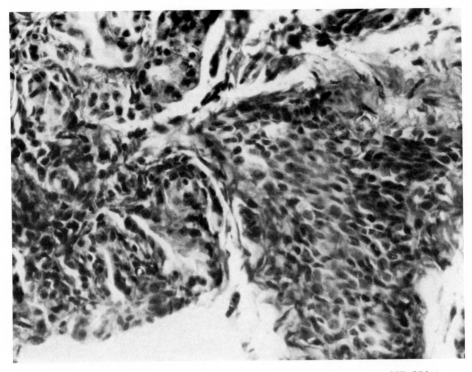

Fig. 18-6. Epithelial dysplasia of duct in a 4-y.o. female pigtail macaque. MT, 250×.

other characteristics of the animals, the lesions were classified subgrossly as cystic dysplasias or dense dysplasias using the dissection microscope. It was clear that the preponderance of difference between incidence of lesions in the 10- and 20-y.o. groups vs. the 4-y.o. group was attributable to larger numbers of dense dysplasias. Most of the dysplasias in the 4-y.o. females were cystic. Comparison of all dysplasias between quadrants of comparable size revealed no evidence that the distribution of cystic or dense dysplasias varied with quadrant of the mammary gland.

Because of the variability in gland size, the number of dysplasias per g of gland tissue (Table 18-1) was used in screening for correlations between mammary lesions and hormonal indices (Table 18-3). There were strong positive correlations between the number of dysplasias per g of gland tissue and the 3 serum androgens—testosterone, dihydrotestosterone, and delta-4-androstenedione. A positive correlation between triiodothyronine and incidence of dysplasias seemed to reflect a threshold effect in that, while none of the 6 animals with

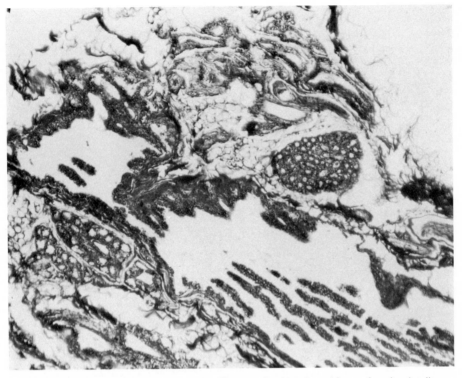

Fig. 18-7. Intraductal dysplasia and papillary projections in a 10-y.o. female pigtail macaque. MT, 160×.

triiodothyronine values below 165 mg/ml had more than 25 dysplasias/g, half of the animals with values above that level had 40 to 125 dysplasias/g. There was no correlation between serum levels of prolactin, the estrogens, cortisol, or immunoglobulins and the incidence of dysplasias. When coefficients of correlation were calculated separately for dense and cystic dysplasias, it was found that the positive correlations with the androgens and triiodothyronine were entirely attributable to the incidence of dense lesions ($p < 0.05$ in all cases). The incidence of cystic lesions did not correlate significantly with any parameter.

Other findings were that gland weight correlated positively with thyroxine ($r_p = 0.58$, $p < 0.02$) and estradiol ($r_p = 0.64$, $p < 0.01$). No relation was found between incidence of dysplasias and gland weight.

Five females in the 10-y.o. and 20-y.o. age groups had been maintained for most of their lives on daily isoniazide medication for prophylaxis against tuberculosis. The incidence of total lesions per g of tissue in these animals was no

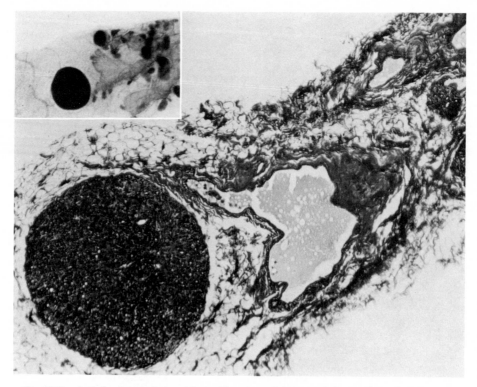

Fig. 18-8. Lobular hyperplasia with proliferation of ducts and changes in prelobular duct in 10-y.o. female pigtail macaque. MT, 160X. Inset: same lesion as seen in subgross specimen. IH, 18X.

different from that in the other 8 females by MWU test. The mean numbers of lesions per g mammary tissue were 45.7 and 43.9 in the treated and untreated groups, respectively.

For all ages, high body weight ($r_s = 0.49$) or high triglycerides ($r_s = 0.52$) (but not cholesterol) were correlated with increased numbers of total dysplasias ($p = 0.05$).

DISCUSSION

Human breast cancer is relatively common and its incidence is increasing. Its diagnosis is difficult, its prognosis is poor, and there is doubt as to the most effective therapy. The causes of breast cancer are not well understood, but the

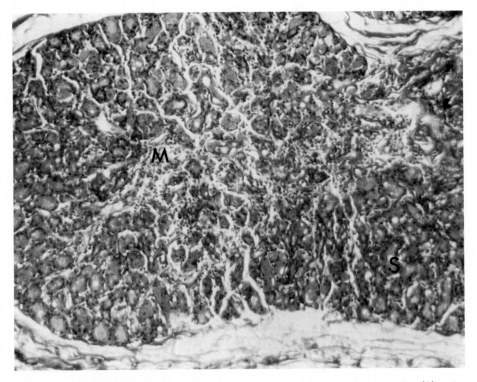

Fig. 18-9. Hyperplastic lobule in a 4-y.o. female pigtail macaque. Note secretion (S) and myoepithelial proliferation (M). MT, 160×.

Table 18-2. Mammary Distribution by Quadrant for Dysplasias in 16
M. nemestrina*.

Quadrant	Mean Total Cystic Dysplasias	Mean Total Dense Dysplasias
A	0.81 ± 0.49	18.0 ± 6.80
B	4.94 ± 2.97	55.75 ± 19.51
C	3.67 ± 2.29	42.50 ± 14.30
D	0.50 ± 0.26	15.56 ± 4.49

*Figures are ± standard error.

Table 18-3. Correlations Between the Number of Dysplasias Per Gram of Mammary Tissue and Levels of 13 Potentially Related Serum Parameters.

Data from the female *M. nemestrina* of all three age groups are included.

r_s = Spearman rank correlation coefficient; p = level of significance; NS = not significant, i.e., $p > 0.10$. Correlation coefficients are presented only for parameters yielding a p value less than 0.10.

Parameter	r_s	p
Prolactin	−	NS
Luteinizing hormone	−	NS
Estrone	−	NS
Estradiol	−	NS
Progesterone	+0.46	< .08
Testosterone	+0.59	< .02
Dihydrotestosterone	+0.70	< .01
Delta-4-androstenedione	+0.59	< .02
Triiodothyronine	+0.49	< .05
Thyroxine	−	NS
Cortisol	−	NS
Immunoglobulin-G	−	NS
Immunoglobulin-A	−	NS
Immunoglobulin-M	−	NS

influences of age, genetic background, hormones and other chemical agents, viruses, radiation and immunity, have been documented both for women (7, 11) and for rodent models (20, 21). A preneoplastic significance has been suspected for some dysplasias and a progression of changes from normal to neoplastic during the lifetime of the individual has been postulated, and experimentally verified in rodents, but not in women, in whom experimentation is unfeasible. The pigtail macaque may provide a useful natural model of the progressive changes from normal through dysplastic to neoplastic in mammary tissues.

Mammary characteristics in the human, dog, mouse and macaque are compared in Table 18-4. The morphology of the gland in pigtail macaques is similar to that described for rhesus macaques (30). It is similar to the human gland, in that it is exposed from puberty through menopause to the hormonal patterns characteristic of a species in which reproduction is described by a menstrual cycle rather than an estrus cycle, as in canines and rodents. Like the glands of rodents, however, the mammary glands of macaques have the experimental advantage that they consist of a single plane of tissue, making it possible to inspect for dysplasias without the serial sectioning necessary for canine and human glands. In addition, glands of the pigtail macaque lack the gradients of lobularity and heterogeneity of distribution of dysplasias with regard to location which have been reported for other species. Such homogeneity allows wider selection of tissues with uniform properties of growth and differentiative status for experimentation. The great variability in number of lesions among animals of a given age group enhances the value of the macaque model for identifying the determinants of lesion formation. At the same time, it places considerable responsibility on the investigator to examine control tissue carefully to ascertain that it is truly normal.

The kinds of dysplasia seen in the older pigtail macaques were similar to those observed in aging humans (7). Cysts, fibroadenomas, and hypersecretory lobules are common lesions in human glands. Cystic and hyperplastic lobular lesions have been reported in several monkey species (5, 23, 27). The ductal hyperplasias and dysplasias noted in this study have not been previously reported in nonhuman primates. The most marked increase in the number of such lesions occurred between the 4-y.o. and the 10-y.o. groups. These dense lesions of ductal epithelium may be morphologic precursors of mammary neoplasia, as they have been shown to be in rats and mice, and are suspected of being in women. The majority of mammary tumors reported in primates (3), including those experimentally induced (17, 26), have resembled human breast tumors in that they seemed to be derived from ductal epithelium. No frank tumors were seen in any of the animals in this study. This may be accounted for by the very small number of animals studied. It may also be related to the fact that menopause seems to occur later in the lifespan of the macaque than in that of the human female (10). To the extent that mammary tumorigenesis is related to a particular stage of reproductive life, its onset might be expected to occur later than age 20 years in the macaque. Finally, the failure of ductal lesions to proceed to a neoplastic stage in these animals may reflect the absence of dietary factors that predispose to breast cancer in the human female (22).

Although there was no significant difference in the total number of dysplasias per unit weight of gland tissue between the 10- and 20-y.o. groups, there was some difference in the kinds of lesions. Leukocytic infiltration and hyperplasia of periductal connective tissue were seen from the time of lesion onset in the 4-y.o. and particularly in 10-y.o. groups compared with the 20-y.o. group, where proliferative and metaplastic changes predominated. The failure to find larger numbers of lesions in the 20-y.o. groups may reflect the small sample size, selection by spontaneous death or colony culling procedures against the survival of less healthy animals in the 20-y.o. sample, or resorption of immunogenic lesions with age. The latter interpretation is consistent with the reduced incidence of leukocytic reactions seen in glands of the oldest age group.

The role of hormones in mammary development and neoplasia is unresolved (6). Although levels of circulating androgens have not previously been correlated with mammary dysplasia in animals, systemically administered testosterone is

Table 18-4. Comparison of Mammary Development Morphology, and Pathology in Human and Three Animal Models[A].

Parameter	Human	Dog	Mouse	Macaque[B]
Number of nipples	2	10	10	2
Ducts per nipple	15 to 25	7 to 15	1	4 to 8
Witch milk	yes	yes	no	no (30)
Prepubertal growth	isometric	minimal	isometric → allometric	isometric → allometric
Onset of duct growth	at birth; again at puberty	at first estrus	at birth; again at puberty	prepubertal, again at puberty
Gland contour	conical	conical or planar	planar	planar
Pattern of gland growth	duct and end bud or lobular expansion	duct and lobular expansion	duct and end bud	duct and end bud or lobular (1)
Connective tissue sheath around growing epithelium	yes	yes	yes	yes
Onset of lobule formations	first ovulation	first ovulation	first pregnancy or first functional corpus luteum	pre- or postpubertal (1, 30)
End of gland growth	30+ years, or after pregnancy	2–3 years	16 weeks (C_3H)	< 4 year
Change in epithelium during reproductive cycle	yes	yes	depends on luteal function	yes (29)
Growth inhibition present	possibly	possibly	yes	possibly
Gradient in lobularity from nipple to periphery	periphery denser	periphery denser in growing; nipple area in resting gland	center denser	no gradient (29)

Myoepithelium plays a role in galactopoesis	yes	yes	yes	—
Gland volume changes during reproductive cycle	yes	yes	—	yes (30)
Lobularity increases with number of reproductive cycles	yes	yes	yes, if corpus luteum functions	yes (1, 30)
Leukocytes in involuting glands	yes	yes	yes	yes
Onset of dysplasias	15–40 years	2–7 years	3–6 months	< 10 years
Dysplasias ovary-dependent	some	not all	no	no (27)
Dysplasia distribution heterogeneous	some (cysts)	yes	—	no
Onset of tumors	40–60 years	2–7 years	7 months	—
Tumors ovary-dependent	not all	usually not	usually not	—
Tumor distribution heterogeneous	yes	yes	—	—

A Unless otherwise credited, information is from Warner (33).
B Unless otherwise credited, information is from the present study.
— insufficient information

known to stimulate mammary growth and lobularity in rats (6), and in both male (30) and female (32) rhesus macaques. Testosterone, together with other hormones, such as progesterone and estrogens, also elicits lobular proliferation in the mammary gland of rats when applied directly to the tissue *in vivo* (6). Specific effects of dihydrotestosterone and androstenedione on the mammary glands have not been studied. Responsiveness of dysplasias to androgens, including androgens of adrenal origin, may account for the lack of response of dysplasias to ovariectomy in rhesus macaques reported by Speert (27). Data regarding serum androgens in women with breast dysplasia or neoplasia are sparse and conflicting (7, 11, 16).

The very strong correlations of the serum androgens testosterone, androstenedione, and dihydrotestosterone with breast dysplasia noted in the present study indicate that further examination of the role of these hormones in mammary neoplasia is warranted, both in animal models and in women.

The possible relationship of thyroid status to breast neoplasia has not been established (7, 11). Thus, the positive correlation between triiodothyronine and incidence of dysplasias, and the suggestion of a relationship to threshold levels of progesterone as well, merit experimental attention.

The failure of the present study to reveal any correlation between dysplasia incidence and other hormones, such as prolactin, luteinizing hormone, and the estrogens, could indicate that the kinds of dense lesions detected are not greatly influenced by these hormones. Most hormone levels were measured, however, in the early postmenstrual period, and it is possible that the values obtained at that stage of the reproductive cycle do not reflect the role of those hormones in the development of dysplasias.

ACKNOWLEDGMENTS

I am grateful to Dr. Ralph Giles for terminology used in classifying the dysplasias, Dr. John Milmore for prolactin and thyroid hormone values, Dr. R. Warner for computer time, Ms. Agnes Rogers for histology, and Ms. P. Arriaga, Ms. R. Branch and Ms. T. Brown for typing the manuscript. This work was supported in part by Public Health Service research grant CA18285, and by National Institutes of Health grants RR00166, RR52177 and AG62145 to the University of Washington.

REFERENCES

1. Aberle, S. D. B. (1934): Growth of mammary gland in the rhesus monkey. *Proc. Soc. Exp. Biol.*, **32**: 249–251.
2. Agate, F. J. (1952): The growth and secretory activity of the mammary glands of the pregnant rhesus monkey (*Macaca mulatta*) following hypophysectomy. *Amer. J. Anat.*, **90**: 257–283.

3. Appleby, E. C., Keymer, I. F., and Hime, J. M. (1974): Three cases of suspected mammary neoplasia in non-human primates. *J. Comp. Pathol.*, **84**: 351–364.
4. Buss, D. H. (1971): Mammary glands and lactation. In: *Comparative Reproduction of Nonhuman Primates*, edited by E. S. E. Hafez, pp. 315–333. Springfield, Ill.; Thomas.
5. Cameron, A. M., and Faulkin, L. J., Jr. (1974): Subgross evaluation of the nonhuman primate mammary gland: method and initial observations. *J. Med. Primatol.*, **3**: 298–310.
6. Cowie, A. T., and Tindal, J. S. (1971): *The Physiology of Lactation*. London; Edward Arnold.
7. Cutler, M. (1962): *Tumors of the Breast*. Philadelphia; Lippincott.
8. Folley, S. J., Guthkelch, A. N., and Zuckerman, S. (1939): The mammary gland of the rhesus monkey under normal and experimental conditions. *Proc. Roy. Soc. B*, **126**: 469–491.
9. Gardner, W. U., and VanWagenen, G. (1938): Experimental development of the mammary gland of the monkey. *Endocrinology*, **22**: 164-172.
10. Geschickter, C. F., and Hartman, C. G. (1959): Mammary response to prolonged estrogenic stimulation in the monkey. *Cancer*, **12**: 767–781.
11. Haagensen, C. D. (1971): *Diseases of the Breast*, 2nd Edition. Philadelphia; Saunders.
12. Hartman, C. G., and Speert, H. (1940): Cyclic changes in the mammary gland of the monkey. *Science*, **92**: 419.
13. Hartman, C. G., and Speert, H. (1941): Action of progesterone on the genital organs of the unprimed rhesus monkey. *Endocrinology*, **29**: 639–648.
14. Hill, W. C. O. (1951): The external genitalia of the female chimpanzee with observations on the mammary apparatus. *Proc. Zool. Soc. London*, **121**: 133–145.
15. Hodgen, G. D., Goodman, A. L., O'Connor, A., and Johnson, D. K. (1977): Menopause in rhesus monkeys: Model for study of disorders in the human climacteric. *Am. J. Obstet. Gynec.*, **127**: 581–584.
16. Jones, M. K., Ramsay, I. D., and Collins, W. P. (1977): Concentration of testosterone glucuronide in urine from women with breast tumors. *Brit. J. Cancer*, **35**: 885–887.
17. Kirschstein, R. L., and Rabson, A. S. (1972): Infiltrating duct carcinoma of the mammary gland of a rhesus monkey after administration of an oral contraceptive: A preliminary report. *J. Nat. Cancer Inst.*, **48**: 551–556.
18. Lapin, B. A. (1973): The importance of monkeys for the study of malignant tumors in man. In: *Nonhuman Primates and Medical Research*, edited by G. H. Bourne, pp. 213–224. New York; Academic Press.
19. Macpherson, E. E., and Montagna, W. (1974): The mammary glands of rhesus monkeys. *J. Invest. Dermatol.*, **63**: 17–18.
20. Medina, D. (1973): Preneoplastic lesions in mouse mammary tumorigenesis. *Methods Cancer Res.*, 7: 1–53.
21. Medina, D., and Warner, M. R. (1976): Mammary tumorigenesis in chemical carcinogen-treated mice. IV. Induction of mammary ductal hyperplasias. *J. Nat. Cancer Inst.*, **57**: 331–337.
22. Miller, A. B. (1977): Role of nutrition in the etiology of breast cancer. Cancer, **39**: 2704–2708.
23. Nelson, L. W., and Shott, L. D. (1973): Mammary nodular hyperplasia in intact rhesus monkeys. *Vet. Pathol.*, **10**: 130–134.
24. Pfeiffer, C. A., and Allen, E. (1948): Attempts to produce cancer in rhesus monkeys with carcinogenic hydrocarbons and estrogens. *Cancer Res.*, **8**: 97–109.
25. Smoilovskaia, E. Ia., Vadova, A. V., Podval'naia, M. Ta., Chachibaia, I. A. (1960): Carcinoma of the mammary glands arising in a monkey after hyperoestrinization and administration of radioactive silver (^{110}Ag). *Probl. Oncol.*, **6**: 666–675.

26. Speert, H. (1940): Gynecogenic action of desoxycorticosterone in the rhesus monkey. *Bull. Johns Hopkins Hosp.*, **67**: 189–195.

27. Speert, H. (1940): Hyperplastic mammary nodules in the castrate female rhesus monkey. *Bull. Johns Hopkins Hosp.*, **67**: 414–426.

28. Speert, H. (1940): Mode of action of estrogens on the mammary gland. *Science*, **92**: 461–462.

29. Speert, H. (1941): Cyclic changes in the mammary gland of the rhesus monkey. *Surg. Gynec. Obstet.*, **73**: 388–390.

30. Speert, H. (1948): The normal and experimental development of the mammary gland of the rhesus monkey with some pathological correlations. *Contrib. Embryol.*, **32**: 9–65.

31. Turner, C. W., and Allen, E. (1933): The normal and experimental development of the mammary gland of the monkey (Macacus rhesus). *Anat. Rec.*, **55**: 80.

32. vanWaagenen, G., and Folley, S. J. (1939): The effect of androgens on the mammary gland of the female rhesus monkey. *J. Endocrinol.*, **1**: 367–372.

33. Warner, M. R. (1972): Mammary gland morphology of female beagle dogs. Studies *in vivo* and *in vitro*. Ph.D. Thesis in Anatomy, University of California, Davis, California.

34. Zuckerman, S. (1931): The menstrual cycle of primates. Part IV. Observations on the lactation period. *Proc. Zool. Soc. Lond.*, 593–602.

35. Zuckerman, S., and Parkes, A. S. (1932): The menstrual cycle of the primate. V. The cycle of the baboon. *Prosectorium of the Zool. Soc.* 139–191.

19

Adrenocortical Structure and Function

Robert N. Moore, Harvey Schiller, and Douglas M. Bowden

Departments of Orthodontics and Anatomy,
West Virginia University Medical Center, Morgantown, West Virginia; and
Department of Laboratory Medicine and the Regional Primate Research Center
University of Washington, Seattle, Washington

INTRODUCTION

Senescence is commonly thought to involve increased vulnerability to stress (7, 9, 20). Because the adrenal cortex is stimulated to produce corticosteriods in many kinds of stress, some investigators have postulated that changes in the regulation of adrenocorticosteriod output may mediate certain aspects of biological aging. In the most general formulation of this concept, Finch (4) has included changes in the neural regulation of adrenocorticotropic hormone (ACTH) release among several cerebral events contributing to the "cascade of changing neural, endocrine, and target-tissue interactions" that culminates in death of the organism.

The basic mechanisms of adrenocorticosteroid control have been well studied. Physical and psychological stressors induce the transfer of corticotropic releasing factor (CRF) from the hypothalamus into the pituitary where it triggers the release of ACTH. The hormone passes in the general circulation to the adrenal glands and stimulates the synthesis and release of steroids from the adrenal cortex. While cells in the cortex are capable of synthesizing cholesterol, the common precursor of the various corticosteroid hormones, recent studies suggest that the cholesterol in serum lipoproteins contributes to steroid production in the adrenal gland (5). Cortisol and, to a lesser extent, corticosterone are the steroids produced in human and nonhuman primates under stress; rats produce only corticosterone (6).

Stressors such as exercise, cold, trauma, and threatening stimuli activate the hypothalamus-pituitary-adrenal system within minutes to increase the level of circulating corticosteroid (12). The corticosteroid acts on various target tissues to produce numerous physiological effects including the conversion of protein and fat to glucose, destruction of lymphocytes, suppression of inflammation and tissue repair, and impairment of auditory, gustatory, and olfactory perception. In addition, the hormone exerts a negative feedback effect on ACTH release, thereby contributing to the regulation of its own serum concentration (6). Thus, while knowledge of the functional significance of the many target organ responses is incomplete, activation of the hypothalamo-adrenal axis has for decades been regarded as one component of a general energy-mobilizing response to physical and psychological stressors.

Research on the relationship of aging to the hypothalamo-adrenal response has focused on resting serum corticosteroid levels, the magnitude of increase in serum levels in response to ACTH stimulation or various kinds of stressor, rates of corticosteroid turnover and elimination, and the effectiveness of the inhibitory feedback of circulating corticosteroid on ACTH release (18). These aging studies have been done in humans and rodents, but not in nonhuman primates. While there have been a few studies of morphologic changes in the adrenal cortex with age, no investigations have, to our knowledge, considered the ultrastructural or biochemical changes that may occur. The purpose of this chapter is to analyze certain key functional and structural parameters of the adrenal cortex in aging *Macaca nemestrina*. The parameters examined include resting levels of cortisol, elevation of serum cortisol in response to an acute stressor, adrenocortical content of cortisol precursors, and ultrastructural characteristics of the adrenal cortex.

METHODS

Subjects were 20 macaques (18 *M. nemestrina* and 2 *M. fascicularis*) ages 4 (n = 3), 10 (n = 9) and 20 (n = 4) y.o. All but 4 were females. One male of each species was 10 y.o. and the other, 20 y.o. Several weeks before sacrifice the resting serum cortisol level and response to restraint stress were determined. During this period the animals were housed in separate cages in one room. Entrance to the room was restricted to the investigators from late the preceding evening to 12 noon of the test day. Only one animal was tested on a given day, and at least one day intervened between test days. The blood draws were timed with a stop watch beginning at the time the investigators entered the room (8:30 a.m.). The animal was caught, strapped to a restraining table and up to 8 ml of blood were drawn from a leg or arm vein as rapidly as possible. This baseline drawing ended at 4 min regardless of the amount drawn. Successive drawings were made at 10 and 20 min from the time of entry. The animal was then returned to its cage. At 11:30 a.m. (160 min after termination of the stressor) a fourth blood sample was taken, again within 4 min of entering the room. The blood was spun down and the serum drawn off and frozen. Cortisol was determined by a competitive protein binding method (14).

On the day of sacrifice the animal was anesthetized with ketamine in its cage followed by nembutal at surgery (Chapter 3, this volume). Approximately 3 min before cardiopulmonary arrest, the left adrenal gland was removed and trimmed of all surrounding adipose tissue. Small portions of the gland, which included the zonae glomerulosa, fasciculata and reticularis, and the medulla, were immersed in ice-cold McDowell's buffered formaldehyde-glutaraldehyde fixative (Chapter 3). Other portions of the gland were weighed on an analytical balance and immersed in ice-cold methanol. The same procedure was done on the right adrenal gland 10 to 15 min after cardiopulmonary arrest. The specimens were packed in ice and shipped by air to Los Angeles the same day. Upon arrival at the laboratory, the specimens in formaldehyde-glutaraldehyde fixative were cut into pie-shaped, 1-mm thick wedges that included all zones. After the medulla was trimmed away, the specimens in methanol were homogenized and prepared for lipid fractionation. The methods for the electron microscopic and biochemical analyses have been previously described (13).

RESULTS

Serum Cortisol

The serum cortisol response to restraint stress was tested in 14 females. The resting cortisol levels of individual animals appear as the first points of the curves in Figure 19-1. The baseline value of 1 animal (#1 in Figure 19-1) was excluded from analysis because a fire alarm just before testing seems to have caused an elevated baseline level. Another animal (#3 in Figure 19-1) had a number of aberrant endocrinological indices and was omitted from the analyses for age effects.

Excluding those 2 animals, the mean resting levels for the 4-, 10-, and 20-y.o. groups were 37.7, 36.6, and 31.9 μg/dl. Though the trend was toward lower resting values for the 20-y.o. group, there was no significant regression against age, and the means were not significantly different. The serum cortisol levels recorded after 20 min of restraint showed even less evidence of correlation with age. Mean values for the 4-, 10- and 20-y.o. age groups were 52.9, 48.9, and 48.2 μg/dl. Comparison of the dynamics of cortisol response as reflected in

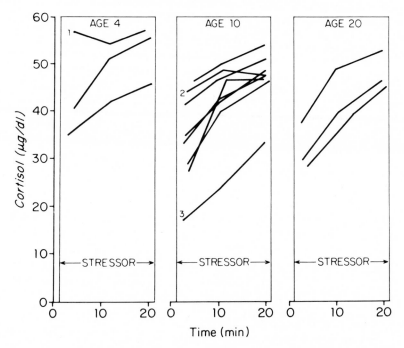

CORTISOL RESPONSE TO RESTRAINT

Fig. 19-1. Cortisol response to restraint in 14 female *M. nemestrina* of 3 different age groups. Time 0 represents entry of investigators into the animal room. Duration of the stressor represents the time from restraint of the animal to the end of the third blood draw. Curve 1 is from #74217, 2 from #76203, and 3 from #76272.

the shapes of the curves in Figure 19-1 gave no evidence that the rate of increase varied as a function of age. Evaluation of the return to resting levels following restraint stress was complicated by incomplete control over personnel entering the animal quarters. It is worth noting, however, that cortisol levels in the 20-y.o. animals, as in most of the younger ones, had returned to the resting level within 160 min.

Adrenocortical Biochemistry

Adrenal cortices from all 20 subjects were analyzed for cholesterol (C), cholesterol esters (CE), RNA, and DNA content (Table 19-1). While the males were low in number and heterogeneous of species, the trends in their data appeared sufficiently different from those of the females to warrant separate treatment.

The ratio of CE to DNA content in the 16 female *M. nemestrina* showed a

Table 19-1. Biochemical Values for 16 Female *M. nemestrina* Adrenal Glands (μg/ml wet adrenal weight).

	Age Group (years)		
	4	10	20
Number of animals	3	9	4
Cholesterol (C)	1.0 ± 0.4	1.0 ± 0.5	1.2 ± 0.7
Cholesterol esters (CE)	60.6 ± 28.1	52.7 ± 19.6	47.2 ± 24.9
RNA	8.7 ± 2.3	10.0 ± 1.7	10.8 ± 3.1
DNA	5.5 ± 1.8	6.8 ± 1.7	8.1 ± 2.0
C/DNA	0.17 ± 0.05	0.16 ± 0.1	0.16 ± 0.1
CE/DNA	13.1 ± 8.4	8.0 ± 3.7	5.8 ± 2.8

Values are mean ± standard deviation.

weak but significant regression against age ($r = 0.48$; $p = 0.04$) with animals in older groups showing lower values than in the younger groups (Figure 19-2). The differences between means for the different age groups failed to reach significance on this or any of the other biochemical variables (Table 19-1). The trend towards a decline in the CE/DNA ratio was seen only in the females. The

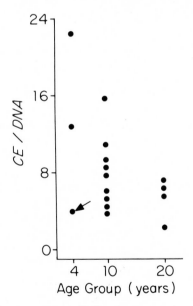

Fig. 19-2. CE/DNA ratio vs. age group. Each point represents one animal (*M. nemestrina*). Arrow indicates measure from monkey #75282, restrained for 10 min before anesthetization for sacrifice.

CE/DNA ratio in the 20-y.o. animal was 10 to 25% higher than in the 10-y.o. animal in both pairs of males (4.3 vs 3.4 for *M. nemestrina*, 3.7 vs 3.0 for *M. fascicularis*).

One 4-y.o. female, monkey #75282, received different treatment immediately before sacrifice than the other 15. Instead of being anesthetized in her home cage, she was caught and restrained 10 min for a final blood draw. This animal's CE/DNA ratio was considerably lower than those of the 2 other 4-y.o. females (Figure 19-2).

No relationship was found between any aspect of the cortisol response to restraint stress (resting level, peak level, or absolute increase) and any of the biochemical measures from the adrenal cortex. Several indices of serum cholesterol metabolism (Chapter 22), however, appeared to relate to the magnitude of the cortisol response. Figure 19-3 suggests that the absolute rise in serum cortisol observed during restraint correlated positively with serum levels of the enzyme lecithin:cholesterol acyltransferase (LCAT) and with cholesterol in the high density lipoprotein (HDL) fraction. It appeared to correlate negatively with the level of cholesterol in the very low-density lipoprotein fraction (VLDL). Note that the only highly aberrant point (arrow) in each of the scatterplots in Figure 19-3 represents data from the animal whose stress response curve is labeled #2 in Figure 19-1. This animal's response started from a high level, peaked within 10 min of the onset of the stressor, and was declining at 20 min. On the assumption that this animal may have been aroused before the investigators entered the room, her data were omitted and coefficients of correlation were calculated between the rise in cortisol and each of the three indices. The correlation coefficients and their significance (Kendall's rank test; ref. 8) were: LCAT ($n = 11$, $T = 0.48$, $p = 0.02$); HDL-cholesterol ($n = 9$, $T = 0.36$, $p = 0.06$); VLDL-cholesterol ($n = 9$, $T = -0.59$, $p = 0.01$). Scatterplots and correlation coefficients for rise in cortisol vs. cholesterol in the low density lipoprotein fraction and triglyceride levels in the various fractions revealed no further relationships.

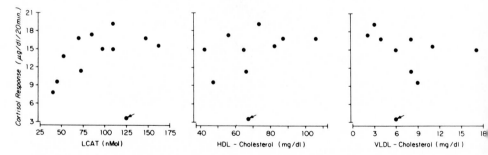

Fig. 19-3. Cortisol response to acute stress in relation to 3 indices of serum lipoprotein metabolism in 4-, 10- and 20-y.o. female *M. nemestrina*. Each point represents one animal. Arrows indicate measures from #76203.

Light Microscopy

Histologically, the adrenocortices from specimens in the 3 age groups were similar in their morphologic pattern. The gland was bounded by a dense, multilayered connective tissue capsule which penetrated between the nests of zona glomerulosa cells (Figure 19-4). The cells of this zone were defined by their compact focal architecture and relative lack of cytoplasmic lipid vacuoles. Although in some sections the transition between the zona glomerulosa and zona fasciculata was sharply demarcated, in the majority the boundary was ill defined.

The zona fasciculata (Figure 19-5) also exhibited a transitional morphology,

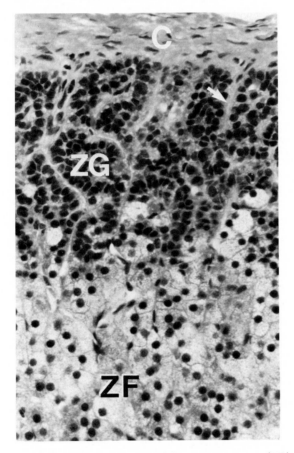

Fig. 19-4. Light micrograph of adrenal capsule (C), zona glomerulosa (ZG), and outer zona fasciculata (ZF) in 4-y.o. female *M. nemestrina* (#73166). The multilayered fibrous capsule extends into the zona glomerulosa (arrow). The transition to the outer zona fasciculata is distinct here due chiefly to the amount of cytoplasmic lipid. X150

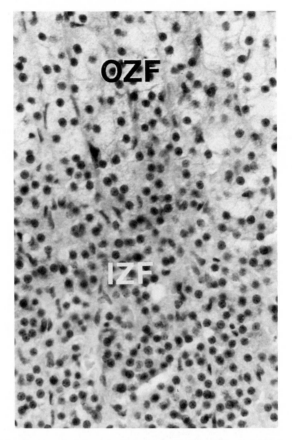

Fig. 19-5. Light micrograph of adrenal zona fasciculata showing the gradual transition from the heavily lipid-laden cells of the outer zona fasciculata (OZF) to the more compact cells of the inner zona fasciculata (IZF) in 10-y.o. *M. nemestrina* female #76273. ×150

with the cytoplasm of more peripheral cells being heavily laden with lipid while the more central cells were more compact. The traditionally described columnar arrangement of cells was very apparent in certain sections and absent in other areas of the same slide. It was not possible to conclude whether the variation was inherent in the architecture of the gland or was due to the plane of sectioning. The latter interpretation is quite plausible in view of the irregularly triangular gross morphology of the gland.

The zona reticularis (Figure 19-6) was composed of an irregular pattern of smaller cells with dense cytoplasm, minimal numbers of lipid vacuoles and prominent nuclei. The transition between these cells of the cortex and the

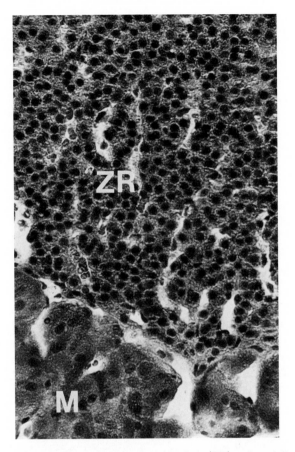

Fig. 19-6. Light micrograph of adrenal zona reticularis (ZR) and medulla (M) in 20-y.o. *M. nemestrina* female #75026. Notice the irregular, as opposed to net-like, pattern of the zona reticularis cells. ×150

medulla was very apparent. At the periphery of the medulla, focal islands of reticular cells were observed, suggesting an irregular junction between these 2 embryologically different portions of the gland.

Electron Microscopy

As with the histologic data, the various zones of the adrenal cortex were distinguishable by their organellar fine structure. The adrenal capsule was comprised of interlacing collagen fibers with varying numbers of fibroblasts and histiocytes.   The capsule was separated from the zona glomerulosa by a sub-endothelial space.   No microvillar projections of zona glomerulosa cells into this space were encountered.   In the zona glomerulosa (Figure 19-7) most nuclei were round, although some indented and lobular forms were seen.   In the cytoplasm mitochondria were either oval or round in profile and contained lamellar cristae.   These extensions of the inner mitochondrial membrane projected for varying lengths into the mitochrondrial matrix.   Many cristae were parallel to each other and perpendicular to the long axis of the mitochondrion.   Rough endoplasmic reticulum was frequently observed while smooth endoplasmic

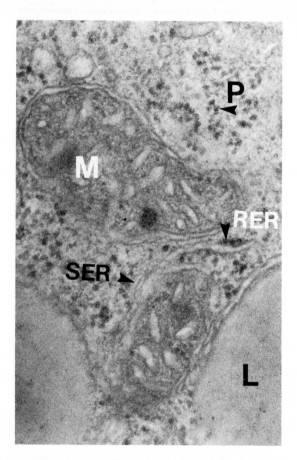

Fig. 19-7.   The cytoplasm in zona glomerulosa cells contained numerous polysomes (P) and mitochondria (M) with oval profiles and lamellar cristae. Rough endoplasmic reticulum (RER) was much more frequently observed than was smooth endoplasmic reticulum (SER). Lipid droplets (L) were occasionally encountered, especially in association with mitochondria. 20-y.o. *M. nemestrina* male #67350. ×67,200.

reticulum was less prominent. Numerous polysomes and occasional lysosomal dense bodies were evident throughout the cytoplasm. Lipid droplets were not prominent, but were occasionally encountered, usually in association with mitochondria.

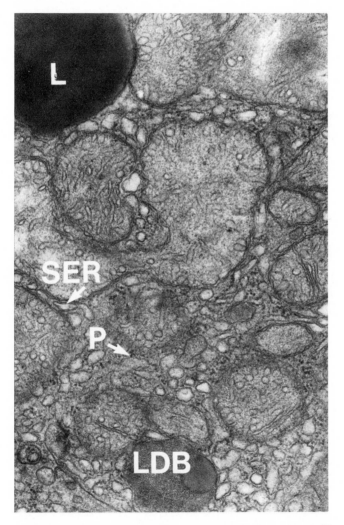

Fig. 19-8. Portions of cells of the inner zona fasciculata in 4-y.o. female *M. nemestrina* (#73166) illustrating the variation in mitochondrial shape and degree of inner membrane invagination. This zone contains numerous lipid droplets (L) and occasional lipofuscin dense bodies (LDB). Polysomes (P) are found throughout the cytoplasm, as is smooth endoplasmic reticulum (SER). ✕20,000

Cells of the zona fasciculata (Figure 19-8) generally had round to oval nuclear profiles. The organellar fine structure and composition differed from the zona glomerulosa in that the mitochondria had tubulovesicular cristae instead of the parallel, lamellar forms. In addition, the endoplasmic reticulum was predomi-

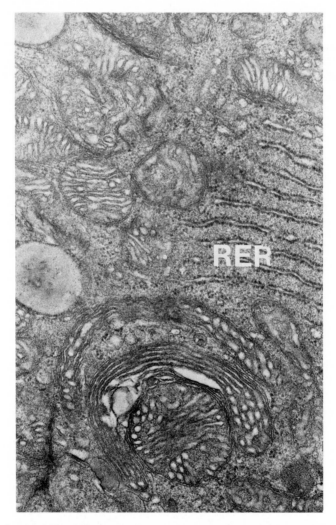

Fig. 19-9. Portion of another cell of the inner zona fasciculata in 10-y.o. female *M. nemestrina* (#70371). Notice the abundant rough endoplasmic reticulum (RER) and the collection of mitochondria into a multilayered membrane structure which may become a complex dense body. ✕ 22,800

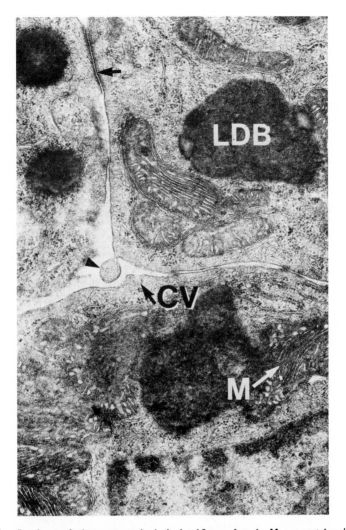

Fig. 19-10. Portions of the zona reticularis in 10-y.o. female *M. nemestrina* (#76274) showing bizarre-shaped mitochondria (M) with tubulovesicular and multilayered tubular cristae. Numerous lipofuscin-dense bodies (LDB) of varying sizes and compositions were found throughout the cytoplasm. The junctional complexes are of the zonula adherens type (arrow). Coated vesicles (CV) are observed as well as cytoplasmic fragments (arrow-head) which appear to be pinching off from the cellular membrane. ✕12,500

nantly smooth, although some rough profiles were present. The number of lipid droplets was greatly increased compared with those in the zona glomerulosa. The progressive diminution of cytoplasmic lipid in the zona fasciculata observed histologically was also evident on the fine structural level, but the cells did not seem to differ except in their lipid content. Similar distributions of polysomes

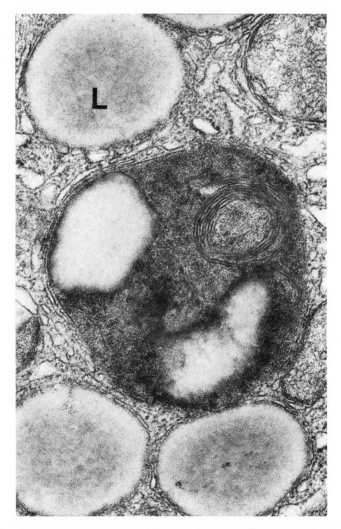

Fig. 19-11. Complex dense body in a cell from the zona reticularis showing membranous whorls as well as inclusions which resemble the adjacent lipid droplets (L); 4-y.o. *M. neme-strina* female #75282. ×26,500

and lysosomal dense bodies were observed throughout the cytoplasm while the Golgi apparatus appeared slightly more prominent than in cells of the zona glomerulosa.   Coated pits and vesicles were frequently encountered on the cellular membrane.

The gradual transition from zona fasciculata to zona reticularis indicated by light microscopy was confirmed by the observation of similar nuclear and cytoplasmic fine structure of cells in the two zones. An important exception, however, was the greater number of lipofuscin dense bodies which were encountered in the latter zone (Figure 19-9). These varied in both size and density and in their larger form have been termed complex dense bodies (1). The mitochondria in the zona reticularis had the same tubulovesicular structure as in the zona fasciculata, but they also contained multilayered lamellar profiles, generally in the long axis of the organelle (Figure 19-10). Lipid droplets were present, but not as numerous as in the more peripheral portions of the zona fasciculata. Other organelles appeared to be similarly distributed in the two zones.

No marked qualitative differences in the fine structure of nuclear or cytoplasmic organelles were noted in the older animals. Subtle changes such as bizarre shaped mitochondria, diminished mitochondrial tubulovesicular cristae and increased numbers of complex dense bodies (Figure 19-11) were apparent in many of the electron micrographs, but these structures varied between specimens and tissue blocks. Thus, any aging changes in the *M. nemestrina* adrenal cortex appeared to be quantitative in nature.

DISCUSSION

Data obtained in this study give an indication of the kinds of influence one may expect age to exert on adrenocortical structure and function in the nonhuman primate. The cholesterol ester content (CE/DNA ratio) of the adrenal cortex appears to decrease with age and there may be a declining trend in resting serum cortisol levels. The subtlety of the latter finding is consistent with the ambiguity of human studies showing either no change in resting serum levels, or declining levels beginning in the late fifth and sixth decades of life (7, 18). Age-related differences in the ultrastructure of the gland, if they exist, are not clearcut and most likely consist of changes in the volume fractions of cytoplasmic organelles as well as increased numbers of abnormal mitochondria and complex dense bodies. These findings, and the absence of others, must be regarded as tentative on several grounds. The animals in the youngest and oldest age group were small in number and heterogeneous with regard to sex, subspecies, and life history. Furthermore, if one assumes a three-decade lifespan for macaques, few if any of the subjects in this study could be considered senescent. Distortion or masking of results due to such factors can be eliminated only by studying larger groups of more homogeneous, older subjects.

Another important source of variability in the results was the fact that the adrenal cortex responds so promptly to acute stressors that the chemical composition and ultrastructure of the gland may be markedly altered simply by the process of taking the specimens (1). Although this process was controlled as well as scheduling constraints would allow, it probably accounted for some of the most divergent values in several aspects of the study. The pattern of results indicated two methodological challenges that must be addressed in future studies of this kind. First, resting levels of serum cortisol and the response to acute stress should be determined several times in every subject to minimize variability due to unanticipated or unidentified stressors acting before onset of the test. Second, the degree to which the anesthetics used at sacrifice influence adrenocortical activity must be assessed. The low adrenal cholesterol ester content and swollen endoplasmic reticulum seen in cells of the adenohypophysis of the 4-y.o. with the lowest CE/DNA ratio (#75282 in Figure 19-2; see Chapter 15, this volume) suggest that a 10-min period of restraint stress before anesthetization may markedly influence chemical and ultrastructural indices. By the same token, comparison of this animal's measures with those of the other subjects suggests that rapid administration of ketamine can largely abort activation of the hypothalamo-adrenal axis and allow one to obtain specimens at necropsy that are relatively representative of the adrenal in its resting state. These methodological issues demand further investigation.

This was, to our knowledge, the first coordinated application of physiological, biochemical, and ultrastructural analyses to the study of adrenocortical function in a nonhuman primate. Aside from its implications for biological aging and methodology, it resulted in some unanticipated and potentially valuable findings. Perhaps most intriguing were the correlations of the magnitude of the cortisol stress response with serum levels of LCAT and HDL-cholesterol. LCAT esterifies cholesterol in the blood stream, and recent studies suggest that the cholesterol in serum lipoproteins contributes to steroid production in the adrenal cortex (5). The fact that in this study the blood samples for the cortisol stress response, serum lipoprotein levels and LCAT activity were not drawn simultaneously but were separated by days or weeks suggests that the relationships implied in their correlations are stable over relatively long periods of time. The fact that HDL-cholesterol increases with age (Chapter 22) may explain why no decline was found in the cortisol stress response with age, despite an apparent decline in adrenocortical CE content. The elevated HDL-cholesterol and LCAT levels in older animals may in some way compensate for a lower CE content of the adrenal cortex in determining the amount of cortisol that can be synthesized in response to an acute stressor. Other mechanisms that may account for stability of response in the face of declining adrenocortical reserve include reduced rates of cortisol turnover (2, 19, 22) and decreased sensitivity of the feedback inhibition of ACTH release in the aging organism (3, 18).

Structurally, the adrenal cortex of *M. nemestrina* closely resembles that of adult male *M. mulatta* and *Saimiri sciureus* (1, 16). The adrenocortical morphology of the monkeys resembles that of the human (11) much more closely than that of rodents. The monkey differs from the rodent particularly in the amount of rough endoplasmic reticulum present and in the internal structure of mitochondria. Rough endoplasmic reticulum has not been observed in the normal rat adrenal (17); and perhaps its absence is related to the observation that the rat adrenal does not synthesize cortisol. Sheridan and Belt (21) have shown a considerable amount of rough endoplasmic reticulum in the guinea pig, a rodent whose adrenal produces cortisol (6), but not to the extent of the stacks observed in the macaque.

Classically, the cytoplasmic accumulation of lipofuscin and complex dense bodies (Figures 19-8, 19-10, 19-11) has been associated with aging. These structures are surrounded by a unit membrane and contain granules of several sizes, various membranous materials, and a granular background matrix. This is in distinction to the acid phosphatase-positive lysosomal dense bodies (15) which have a single limiting membrane and are formed in all zones of the cortex. Complex dense body formation has been examined in multiple organ systems including the adrenal (10) and has been shown to be intimately associated with the degeneration and removal of cells both in embryological development and adult tissues. This method of controlled cell deletion has been termed apoptosis. Structurally, changes appear to occur in two distinct stages. First, there is nuclear and cytoplasmic condensation presumably due to the loss of cellular water with subsequent breaking up of the cell into a number of membrane-bound, ultrastructurally well preserved fragments. These are then either shed from epithelially lined surfaces or are taken up as phagosomes by other epithelial cells or histiocytes. Thus, the complex dense bodies seen in the cytoplasm may have an auto- or heterophagic origin depending upon whether they are composed of organelles of the same or different cells.

Cell death and removal by apoptosis has been observed in the normal neonatal rat adrenal cortex and in the adrenal cortex of rats acutely deprived of ACTH either by prednisolone administration or, in the fetus, by intra-uterine hypophysectomy by decapitation (23). Most likely the apoptotic mechanism is present in the adult nonhuman primate adrenal cortex and is similarly influenced by changes in the hypothalamo-adrenal axis. Dense bodies similar to the one in Figure 19-8 have been shown in *S. sciureus* to have acid phosphatase activity and thus be of lysosomal origin (16). While the present study suggests that the lysosomal and complex dense bodies in the zona reticularis increase with age, a more definitive evaluation must await the stereologic evaluation of a larger and older sample.

ACKNOWLEDGMENTS

We appreciate the technical assistance of Ms. Cheryl Teets in testing of restraint stress and of Ms. Joyce Schumann and Dr. Sherry Faust in preparing the tissue sections. This study was supported in part by National Institutes of Health grants RR05304 to the University of California and RR00166, RR52177 and AG62145 to the University of Washington.

REFERENCES

1. Brenner, R. M. (1966): Fine structure of adrenocortical cells in adult male rhesus monkeys. *Am. J. Anat.*, **119**: 429–454.
2. Britton, G. W., Rotenberg, S., and Adelman, R. C. (1975): Impaired regulation of corticosterone levels during fasting in aging rats. *Biochem. Biophys. Res. Comm.*, **64**: 184–188.
3. Dilman, V. M. (1976): The hypothalamic control of aging and age associated pathology. In: *Hypothalamus, Pituitary and Aging*, edited by A. V. Everitt and J. A. Burgess, pp. 634–667. Springfield, Ill.; Thomas.
4. Finch, C. E. (1976): The regulation of physiological changes during mammalian aging. *Qtr. Rev. Biol.*, **51**: 49–83.
5. Glomset, J. A. (in press): Lecithin: cholesterol acyl-transferase, an exercise in comparative biology. In: *Progress in Biochemical Pharmacology, Lipoprotein Metabolism*, edited by S. Eisenberg and R. Paoletti. Basel; Karger.
6. Greep, R. O., Astwood, E. B., Blaschko, H., Sayers, G., Smith, A. D., and Geiger, S. R., eds. (1975): *Handbook of Physiology, VI.*, Sec. 7. Washington, D.C.; American Physiological Society.
7. Hochstädt, B. B., and Reichenbach, B. (1961): The process of aging and adrenocortical activity. *Geront. Clin. (Basel)*, **3**: 55–62.
8. Hollander, M., and Wolfe, D. A. (1973): *Nonparametric Statistical Methods*. New York; John Wiley.
9. Kaack, B., Ordy, J. M., and Trapp, B. (1975): Changes in limbic, neuroendocrine and autonomic systems, adaptation, homeostasis during aging. In: *Neurobiology of Aging*, edited by J. M. Ordy and K. R. Brizzee, pp. 209–231. New York; Plenum Press.
10. Kerr, J. F. R., Wyllie, A. H., and Currie, A. R. (1972): Apoptosis: A basic biological phenomenon with wide-ranging implications in tissue kinetics. *Br. J. Cancer*, **26**: 239–257.
11. Long, J. A., and Jones, A. L. (1967): Observations on the fine structure of the adrenal cortex of man. *Lab. Invest.*, **17**: 355–370.
12. Mason, J. W. (1975): Emotion as reflected in patterns of endocrine integrating. In: *Emotions, Their Parameters and Measurement*, edited by L. Levi, pp. 143–182. New York; Raven Press.
13. Moore, R. N., Penney, D. P., and Averill, K. (1978): Rat adrenocortical carcinoma 494: An integrated structural, stereological, and biochemical analysis. *Anat. Rec.*, **190**: 703–718.
14. Murphy, B. E. P. (1967): Some studies of the protein-bindings of steroids and their application to the routine micro and ultramicro measurement of various steroids in body fluids by competitive protein-binding radioassay. *J. Clin. Endocr.*, **27**: 973–990.

15. Penney, D. P., and Barrnett, R. J. (1965): The fine structural localization and selective inhibition of nucleosidephosphatases in the rat adrenal cortex. *Anat. Rec.*, **152**: 265–278.
16. Penney, D. P., and Brown, G. M. (1971): The fine structural morphology of adrenal cortices of normal and stressed squirrel monkeys. *J. Morph.*, **134**: 447–466.
17. Rhodin, J. A. G. (1971): The ultrastructure of the adrenal cortex of the rat under normal and experimental conditions. *J. Ultrastruct. Res.*, **34**: 23–71.
18. Riegle, G. D. (1976): Aging and adrenocortical function. **In:** *Hypothalamus, Pituitary and Aging*, edited by A. V. Everitt and J. A. Burgess, pp. 546–552. Springfield, Ill.; Thomas.
19. Romanoff, L. P., Baxter, M. N., Thomas, A. W., and Ferrechio, G. B. (1969): Effect of ACTH on the metabolism of pregnenolone-7a-H^3 and cortisol-4-C^{14} in young and elderly men. *J. Clin. Endocr.*, **28**: 819–830.
20. Selye, H., and Tuchweber, B. (1976): Stress in relation to aging and disease. In: *Hypothalamus, Pituitary and Aging*, edited by A. V. Everitt and J. A. Burgess, pp. 553–569. Springfield, Ill.; Thomas.
21. Sheridan, M. N., and Belt, W. D. (1964): Fine structure of the guinea pig adrenal cortex. *Anat. Rec.*, **149**: 73–98.
22. West, C. D., Brown, H., Simons, E. L., Carter, D. B., Kumagai, L. I., and Englert, E., Jr. (1961): Adrenocortical function and cortisol metabolism in old age. *J. Clin. Endocr.*, **21**: 1197–1207.
23. Wyllie, A. H., Kerr, J. F. R., and Currie, A. R. (1973): Cell death in the normal neonatal rat adrenal cortex. *J. Path.*, **11**: 255–261.

20

Cardiac and Coronary Pathology

Nobuhisa Baba, James J. Quattrochi, Peter B. Baker,
and Charles F. Mueller
Departments of Pathology and Radiology,
Ohio State University College of Medicine,
Columbus, Ohio

INTRODUCTION

Nonhuman primates have become the major animal model for atherosclerosis research because they are susceptible to atherosclerotic plaques that are not readily duplicated in other experimental animals. By using various primate species and dietary manipulations, several investigators have successfully produced advanced atherosclerosis even with myocardial infarction. Furthermore, the monkeys provide realistic models for studying the regression of atherosclerotic lesions upon dietary modulation, and are excellent subjects for lipid and lipoprotein metabolic studies relative to atherosclerosis. Recent papers have exhaustively reviewed the extent and scope of primate research in atherosclerosis (21, 25).

The monkeys in the present study were maintained for many years on a homogeneous low fat diet (Chapter 3, this volume) and at relatively low activity levels. Therefore, comparing their tissues with human tissue may provide some insight into the etiology of coronary and cardiac (myocardial and valvular) changes that are generally considered to be aging processes.

MATERIALS AND METHODS

Subjects were 26 pigtail macaques (*Macaca nemestrina*) and 2 longtail macaques (*M. fascicularis*), 20 females and 8 males, ranging in age from 4 to over 20 years.

Because there were no evident species or sex differences in our findings, the data from all animals were combined except where noted. Seven pigtail macaques had been exposed to high lipid diet for 5 to 12 months, and particular attention was given to evaluation of coronary arteries in these animals.

The heart was removed within 3 to 5 min of cardiorespiratory arrest in 22 cases, within 8 to 14 min in 5 cases, and after 40 min in 1 case. It was rinsed in saline, sealed in a plastic bag containing McDowell's fixative (Chapter 3, this volume) and shipped at ambient temperature. Nine hearts were intact. Their weight ranged from 14.4 to 67.3 gm; however, the heart/body weight ratio of these hearts was relatively constant, ranging from 0.43 to 0.46%. Multiple sections of tissue were excised from (a) the proximal 3 cm of the 3 major coronary arteries, (b) the left and right ventricular walls, (c) both anterior and posterior papillary muscles, (d) the sino-atrial and atrio-ventricular nodes, and (e) the tricuspid, mitral and aortic valves.

The coronary arteries were treated with 10% EDTA and 5% formic acid when decalcification was necessary. Sections were stained with hematoxylin-eosin. Selected arterial lesions were embedded in epoxy resin for transmission electron microscopy. The myocardial slides were stained with hematoxylin-eosin and hematoxylin-basic fuchsin-picric acid (5). Congo-red was used in one case of myocardial amyloidosis. The blocks containing the mitral and aortic valves and papillary muscles were placed in phosphate buffer, and x-ray films were taken using a mammography instrument to detect calcification. The mitral valve leaflets and aortic valves were stained for collagen, elastic tissue, mucopolysaccharides and calcium; they were also stained with hematoxylin-eosin.

For purposes of comparison with the human, similar examinations were made of coronary arteries and ventricular walls of hearts from 167 consecutive patients 25 to 65 years of age who died within 24 hr of acute onset of cardiac symptoms and were autopsied by the Franklin County Coroner's Office, Ohio State University College of Medicine, Columbus, Ohio.

RESULTS

Coronary Arteries

Both left and right coronary arteries were examined. In all of the monkeys the left circumflex was larger in diameter. The posterior descending branches arose from the right coronary arteries (right dominance) in 19 of 28 animals, and from the left coronary artery (left dominance) in 8 animals; the circulation was balanced in 1 animal. All coronary arteries exhibited a continuous endothelial layer and normally one cell layer in the intima between the endothelium and the internal elastic membrane (Figure 20-1).

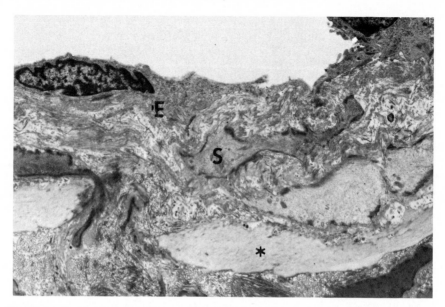

Fig. 20-1. Normal coronary artery. Endothelial cells (E) cover a thin intima with one cell layer of smooth muscle cells (S). The internal elastic membrane (*) borders the media and intima. Electron micrograph. ×12,000.

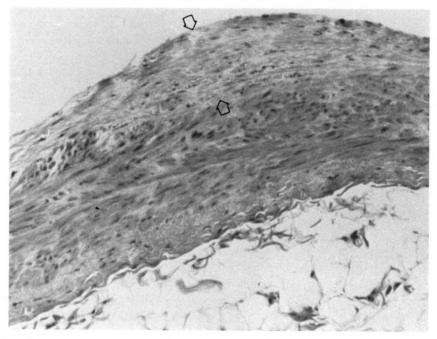

Fig. 20-2. Fibrous thickening of the intima (between arrows). Hematoxylin and eosin. ×400.

Table 20-1. Number of Macaques with Microscopic Coronary Arterial Lesions with Respect to Age Group, Arterial Segment, and Severity of Involvement.

Age (Years)	No. of Monkeys	Left Main Artery			Left Anterior Descending Branch			Right and Left Circumflex Branches			Right Coronary Artery			Total Lesions Total Segments		
		+	++	+++	+	++	+++	+	++	+++	+	++	+++	+	++	+++
4	3	0	0	0	1	0	0	1	0	0	0	0	0	.17	.00	.00
10	15	0	0	0	7	0	0	2	0	0	0	0	0	.15	.00	.00
20	10	1	0	1	3	1	1	2	0	1	4	0	0	.25	.03	.08
Total	28	2			13			6			4					
Percent of animals with lesions in given segment		7%			46%			21%			14%					

Key: + = 10% occlusion secondary to intimal fibrosis, ++ = 20% occlusion secondary to intimal fibrosis, +++ = 20% occlusion secondary to intimal fibrosis with focal calcification.

Intimal fibrosis (Figure 20-2) was noted in 13 cases, most prominently (46%) in the proximal 1 cm of the left anterior descending branch (Table 20-1). Similar intimal fibrosis was noted in 21% of the right and left circumflex branches. The cross-sectional narrowing of the arteries did not exceed 20%, even in the left anterior descending branch. The prevalence and severity increased with age and 1 20-y.o. female showed focal intimal calcification within the intimal fibrosis. Electron microscopy of typical areas of intimal fibrosis revealed proliferation of mature smooth muscle cells between the endothelial cells and the internal elastic membrane (Figure 20-3). These cells did not contain the large lipid vesicles that are characteristic of foam cells in human atherosclerotic lesions, with one exception: a small number of foam cells was found in a male that had been on a high

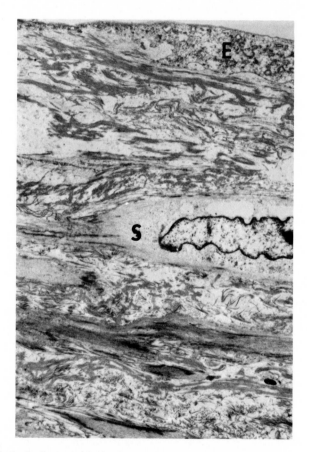

Fig. 20-3.   Markedly increased intimal smooth muscle cells (S) under the endothelium (E). ×4000.

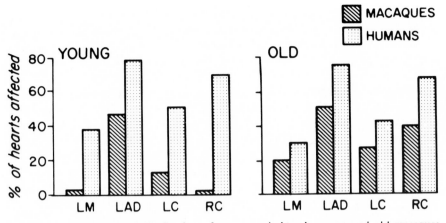

Fig. 20-4. Comparison of distribution of coronary lesions in young and old macaques and humans. LM = left main coronary, LAD = left anterior descending branch, LC = left circumflex, RC = right coronary.

fat diet for 12 months ending 24 months before sacrifice. In this animal the intima was fairly cellular with compact collagen fibers. The intimal fibrosis differed from that of human atherosclerosis in that it was focal rather than diffuse and lacked extracellular lipid deposition. Another male fed such a diet for 12 months had intimal fibrosis without foam cells. Of the 5 animals subjected to the diet for 6 months or less, only 1 10-y.o. female showed intimal fibrosis.

The degree of intimal fibrosis in 4 segments of the coronary vasculature is compared with the degree of atherosclerosis in humans in Figure 20-4. For this comparison, vascular segments in the human were classified as atherosclerotic if plaque formation obstructed the lumen by more than 75%. The young macaques included 15 animals in the 10-y.o. age group; the young humans included 105 patients 25 to 44 years old. The old macaques included 10 animals in the 20-y.o. group; the old humans were 62 patients 45 to 65 years old. The distribution of intimal fibrosis in the macaques of both age groups was similar to that in the corresponding human groups with the exception of very low involvement of the right coronary artery in the young macaques.

Myocardium

The myocardium in 19 of the 28 monkeys exhibited moderate ischemia. This probably reflected the delay between cardiorespiratory arrest and fixation of the myocardium, because little or no ischemic change was noted in 9 hearts obtained within 3 to 4 min of cardiorespiratory arrest.

Monkey myocardium, unlike human autopsy sections, presented a vesicular appearance of the nuclei as well as the sarcoplasm, which was more extensive in the subendocardial and central portions of the myocardium than in the sub-epicardium. Electron microscopy revealed no abnormalities. The sarcoplasm had normal appearance with abundant mitochondria and glycogen granules. No deposition of any pathologic material was present. The blood vessels within the interventricular septum were markedly dilated in 1 10- and 1 20-y.o. monkey, which probably constituted an increase in the collateral vasculature at the level of small arteries and arterioles between the anterior and posterior descending branches.

Focal interstitial fibrosis of the myocardium was noted in 13 macaques; the most common patterns involved the interventricular septum (n = 7) and the free wall (n = 4). Fibrosis was subendocardial in 9 monkeys and subepicardial and central in 1. The animals involved included 6 of 10 20-y.o.'s and 7 of 15 10-y.o.'s. Thus, no clear relation between prevalence and age was apparent in these 2 age groups.

A comparison of the distribution of focal intersitital fibrosis in different areas of the myocardium in macaques and humans is presented in Figure 20-5: the age

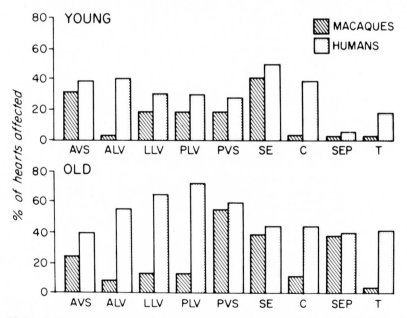

Fig. 20-5. Comparison of distribution of myocardial fibrosis in young and old macaques and humans. AVS = anterior ventricular septum, ALV = anterior left ventricle, LLV = lateral left ventricle, PLV = posterior left ventricle, PVS = posterior ventricular septum, SE = subendocardium, C = central, SEP = subepicardium, T = transmural.

classifications are the same as for Figure 20-4. The lesions represented were similar in the two species in that postinfarctional scarring was excluded in evaluating the human sample. Neither the macaque nor the human showed detectable fibrosis of the right ventricular wall. The pattern of distribution of lesions in the left ventricle was similar between species in the septal areas (septum, anterior ventricular septum, and posterior ventricular septum) and in the subendocardium. In the lateral ventricular walls (anterior, lateral, and posterior left ventricle), central, and transmural areas, however, the incidence of lesions in the human samples was relatively greater than in the macaques.

One 10-y.o. female showed a small focus of calcification, of undetermined nature, in the subepicardium of the right ventricle. A 20-y.o. female showed diffuse myocardial amyloidosis. This animal also showed amyloidosis in several

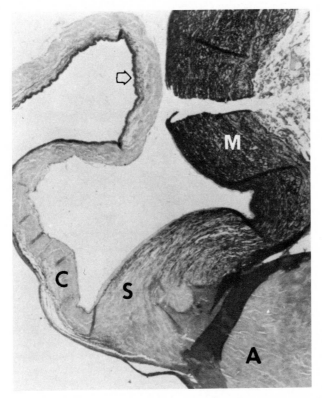

Fig. 20-6. Root of the aortic cusp (C). The aortic media (M) gradually loses its abundant elastic fibers as it reaches the aortic sinus wall (S). The annulus (A), sinus wall and cusp have a continuous collagenous tissue. Note the prominent elastic fibers over the surface of the cusp (arrow). Elastic-van Gieson stain. ×40.

other organs. The conduction system was normal in all animals with exceptions
of fibrosis in the sino-atrial nodes in 1 10-y.o. and 2 20-y.o. animals. Two monkeys (10 and 20 y.o.) showed persistent chronic pericarditis. One had rather
extensive myocardial inflammation with lymphocytic infiltration; the other did
not. Neither acute nor old myocardial infarction was present in these hearts.

Cardiac Valves

The aortic valves consisted of a collagenous lamella that was continuous with the
lateral wall of the aortic sinus but, in contrast to the sinus wall, contained few
elastic fibers. There were two elastic layers at the aortic and ventricular surfaces
of the cusp. One at the ventricular aspect was more pronounced and was continuous with the ventricular endocardial elastic tissue (Figure 20-6). Of 18 valves
histologically examined, 10 showed focal myxoid degeneration of the annulus
extending into the ventricular aspect of the valve (Figure 20-7). These repre-

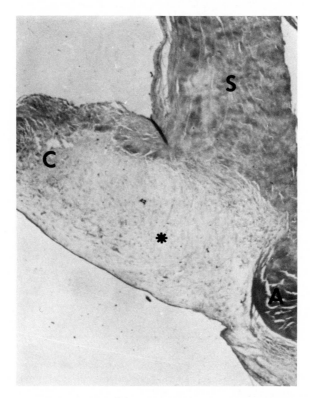

Fig. 20-7.   Root of the aortic cusp (C). S is the sinus wall. Note loose connective tissue
(*) on the ventricular aspect of the annulus (A). Elastic-van Gieson stain. ×40.

sented 1 of 6 20-y.o.'s, 6 of 11 10-y.o.'s, and 1 of 1 4-y.o. Ten-year-old monkeys showed most advanced myxoid degeneration of the valve. Two monkeys showed fibrous nodular thickening of the free edges, while 2 others showed minimal fibrosis at the base of the valve; all 4 animals were 10 to 20 y.o. Radiography and histologic preparations did not reveal calcification. All of the valves were tricuspid and no bicuspid anomaly was present.

Both anterior and posterior leaflets of the mitral valve showed a thick lamella of collagen fibers from their annular attachment to the insertion of the secondary chordae. Both the atrial and ventricular sides of the lamella were covered with layers of elastic fibers. Atrial muscle cells extended into the proximal (annular) portion of the leaflet on its atrial aspects. In the posterior leaflet a very prominent subendothelial elastic layer was present (Figure 20-8) above the collagen lamella and muscle cell layer and continuous with the prominent atrial endocardial elastic tissue. The distal portion of the valve from the line of closure to the free edge consisted of loose connective tissue with scattered elastic fibers. Abundant acid mucopolysaccharides stainable with colloidal iron filled this loose connective tissue. Mildly to moderately increased mucopolysaccharides in this area (Figure 20-9) were noted in 15 of 27 mitral valves examined. The finding

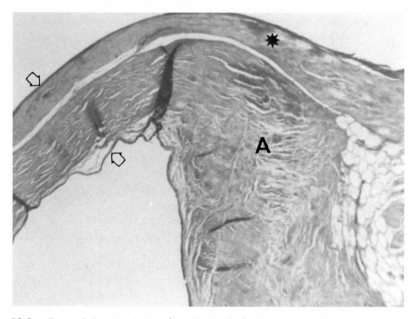

Fig. 20-8. Root of the mitral valve (anterior leaflet). Atrial myocardium continues on to the atrial surface of the valve (*). Dense collagen tissue of the annulus (A) extends into the ventricular aspect of the valve. Arrows indicate prominent elastic tissue on both endocardial surfaces. Elastic-van Gieson stain. ×40.

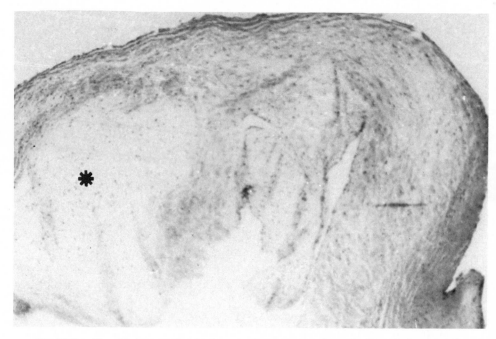

Fig. 20-9. Myxoid degeneration in the ventricular aspect, along the line of closure of the mitral valve (*). X150.

was proportionally equal in the 3 age groups, though the degree of myxoid change appeared more prominent in monkeys 10 or more years of age. Two 10-y.o. monkeys showed moderate fibrosis with increased collagen, a decrease of mucopolysaccharides, and fibroblastic proliferation and vascularization of the posterior leaflets of the mitral valve. Neither valvular deformities nor calcification were noted in any of the valves.

DISCUSSION

Compared with humans dying acute cardiac deaths, the aged macaques in this study had a strikingly lower incidence of coronary and cardiac lesions. No atherosclerosis comparable to the human disease was evident. However, one lesion, intimal fibrosis of the coronary arteries, seemed to increase in frequency and degree in the older age groups, and its distribution was similar to that of coronary atherosclerosis in humans. Interstitial fibrosis of the myocardium and myxoid degeneration of the mitral valves were observed in animals of all age groups.

Coronary Arteries

As in the human (18), right dominance of the coronary arteries was the most common pattern in these macaques. Lesions in the coronary arteries of the aged animals were local intimal fibrosis with proliferation of smooth muscle cells without lipids. Stary and Strong (20) observed left coronary arteries of rhesus macaques (*M. mulatta*) and classified the intimal lesions into intimal cushion lesions and diffuse intimal thickening. The former are padlike structures containing mucopolysaccharides and smooth muscle cells rich in endoplastic reticulum. The diffuse intimal thickening often presents a circumferential involvement of the internal wall and consists of myofilament-rich smooth muscle cells with the tissue being more dense than in intimal cushion lesions. Ultrastructural observations revealed some degenerative changes in the intimal smooth muscle cells and very few lipids in these cells. Foam cells were extremely rare. This diffuse intimal thickening was morphologically comparable to our findings of intimal fibrosis. Our observations are also similar to those reported by Lindsay *et al.* (6), but we did not observe disruption of the internal elastic membranes. Preservation of the internal elastic membrane has also been reported in the spontaneous coronary arterial lesions of rhesus macaques (2).

The paucity of coronary lesions was consistent with observations in other mammals (4). For a number of years, a similar low incidence of spontaneous atherosclerosis was reported in baboons (8), rhesus macaques (2, 11), and spider monkeys (11). Spontaneous severe coronary atherosclerosis was reported only in the squirrel monkey (9), which may reflect naturally high levels of serum cholesterol in this species. In recent years it has been found that the incidence of atherosclerosis in monkeys depends to a great degree on diet. The report of Lapin *et al.* (Chapter 2, this volume) that virtually all old baboons, macaques, and green monkeys autopsied at Sukhumi showed signs of atherosclerosis probably reflects the fact that animals at the Soviet primate center receive diets much more nearly approximating a modern human diet than do laboratory primates in the United States. Recent studies in this country have confirmed that some species of monkey placed on high cholesterol diets develop fatty streaks and atherosclerotic plaques similar to human lesions (3, 7, 22). The fact that the experimentally produced lesions regress when dietary cholesterol is reduced (1, 23) indicates that diet is a more critical factor in atherogenesis than aging *per se*. Diet-induced hypercholesterolemia can produce a markedly thickened intima containing numerous smooth muscle cells with lipid inclusions in the arteries of pigtail macaques if the endothelium is previously damaged mechanically (17).

This study showed that despite differences in the degree and morphology of coronary arterial lesions between macaques on laboratory diets and humans dying acute cardiac deaths, there was a similarity in their anatomical distribution. In both samples, the proximal left anterior descending branch of the coronary arteries showed the highest incidence of intimal thickening. However, a local intimal thickening was evident in the monkey compared to a more characteristic widespread diffuse intimal thickening in the human. The geographic similarity probably reflects similar hemodynamic influences on the coronary arterial segments in macaque and human. It is reasonable to postulate that the intimal thickening in the macaques represents a healing response to mechanical or hemodynamic wear-and-tear of the coronary arterial endothelium in the absence of dietary factors that predispose the average American to atherosclerosis. Chronic hyperlipidemia in humans seems to exert a complex effect on the initiation of the atherosclerotic process (17). The observation that the incidence of coronary atherosclerosis was similar in humans of the two age groups no doubt resulted from the selection for subjects with fatal cardiac disease. In the macaques, which represented a more random sample, the incidence of lesions was clearly age-related (Figure 20-4).

Myocardium

Diffuse or focal interstitial fibrosis is often noted in the human heart, even if the heart has not been affected by coronary disease (10), aortic stenosis, amyloid (senile) heart disease, or postrheumatic fever. The etiology is not well understood. Small areas of focal fibrosis were found in the left ventricular myocardium of 12 animals in this study, and there was no relation between this type of fibrosis and intimal thickening of the coronary arteries. No infarctions were found. The distribution of interstitial fibrosis in the macaques was similar to that of diffuse, nonpostinfarctional fibrosis in the human sample in that it was limited to the left ventricle. The finding that the pattern of distribution within the left ventricle differed somewhat, particularly in the older age group (Figure 20-5, bottom), may relate to the fact that, in this small sample, most of the animals with left dominance of the coronary arteries were in that group.

The presence or absence of interstitial fibrosis was not related to the presence of arterial lesions in the macaques of this study. Its incidence was similar to findings by Lapin *et al.* (Chapter 2) in 13 of 31 monkeys of various species at Sukhumi. Thus, unlike the arterial lesions, the myocardial lesions do not seem to relate strongly to dietary history. Though most of the Sukhumi animals showed signs of coronary atherosclerosis, they also showed no relation between the degree of atherosclerosis and interstitial fibrosis. The Soviet investigators postulate that interstitial fibrosis results from an interaction of episodes of neurogenic coronary insufficiency with a myocardium made vulnerable to ischemia by declining metabolic efficiency of cardiac muscle cells. Evidence in man and animals suggests that excessive activation of cardiac sympathetic nerve endings can produce myocardial fibrosis due to direct action of norepinephrine on the myocardium (14). Other possible mechanisms include viral or chemical injury.

Cardiac Valves

Aging disease of the human heart valve is frequently related to calcification. In the aortic valve, calcific stenosis is largely a sequel either to rheumatic fever or when combined with mitral stenosis, to congenital development of the bicuspid aortic valve (16). Severe stenosis with calcification has been observed most frequently in the human population (13, 16). Senile calcific change is also noted in the human mitral valve, frequently associated with regurgitation and senile aortic stenosis. This disease process primarily involves the annular region, particularly along the posterior leaflet. Although the exact site of calcification is the area below the insertion of the mitral valve involving the endocardium and myocardium, this disease is called annular calcification because of the characteristic radiographic findings (12).

In the present study no calcification was noted in either the aortic or mitral valves or ring. There is a morphologic suggestion that the calcific process of the human aortic valve is associated with focal deposition of lipids (19). Experimentally, monkeys fed with lipids can develop moderate calcification of the aortic and mitral valves (M. Bond, pers. comm.). Therefore, the lack of aortic valve calcification in aged macaques may simply be a further aspect of the low incidence of atherosclerosis. Another aortic valvular change that is often seen in humans, focal thickening of the free edges of the cusps, is expected to have no clinical manifestations in monkeys. Some mitral valves showed fibrosis in the posterior leaflet, but there was no deformation.

Although most severe myxoid degeneration of the heart valves occurs in the congenital metabolic disorders such as Marfan's syndrome and homocysteinemia in young humans, myxoid degeneration seen in the heart valves of old patients is considered to be due to the aging process (24). In monkeys, myxoid changes of the aortic and mitral valves seem to be prominent after 10 years of age.

ACKNOWLEDGMENTS

This investigation was supported in part by a grant from the Central Ohio Chapter of the American Heart Association to the Ohio State University College of Medicine and by National Institutes of Health grants RR00166, RR52177 and AG62145 to the University of Washington.

REFERENCES

1. Armstrong, M. L., Warner, E. D., and Connor, W. E. (1970): Regression of coronary atheromatosis in rhesus monkeys. *Circ. Res.*, **27**: 59–67.
2. Chakravarti, R. N., Mohan, A. P., and Komal, H. S. (1976): Atherosclerosis in *Macaca mulatta:* Histopathological, morphometric, and histochemical studies in aorta and coronary arteries of spontaneous and induced atherosclerosis. *Exp. Mol. Pathol.*, **25**: 390–401.
3. Clarkson, T. B., Lofland, H. B., Bullock, B. C., Lehner, N. D. M., St. Clair, R., and Prichard, R. W. (1969): Atherosclerosis in some species of New World monkeys. *Ann. N.Y. Acad. Sci.*, **162**: 103–109.
4. Fox, H. (1963): Arteriosclerosis in lower animals and birds. Its relation to the disease in man. Edited by E. V. Cowdry, pp. 153–193. New York; The Macmillan Co.
5. Lie, J. T., Hoolley, D. E., Kampa, W. R., and Titus, J. L. (1971): New histochemical method for morphologic diagnosis of early stages of myocardial ischemia. *Mayo Clin. Proc.*, **46**: 319–327.
6. Lindsay, S., and Chaikoff, I. L. (1966): Naturally occurring arteriosclerosis in non-human primates. *J. Atheroscler. Res.*, **6**: 36–61.
7. MacNintch, J. E., St. Clair, R. W., Lehner, N. D. M., Clarkson, T. B., and Lofland, H. B. (1967): Cholesterol metabolism and atherosclerosis in Cebus monkeys in relation to age. *Lab. Invest.*, **16**: 444–452.
8. McGill, H. C., Jr., Strong, J. P., Holman, R. L., and Werthessen, N. T. (1960): Arterial lesions in the Kenya baboon. *Circ. Res.*, **8**: 670–679.
9. Middleton, C. C., Clarkson, T. B., Lofland, H. B., and Prichard, R. W. (1964): Athero-sclerosis in the squirrel monkey. *Arch. Path.*, **78**: 16–23.
10. Mitchell, J. R. A., and Schwartz, C. J. (1965): *Arterial Disease*, pp. 118–120. Philadelphia; F. A. Davis.
11. Newman, W. P. III, Eggen, D. A., and Strong, J. P. (1974): Comparison of arterial lesions and serum lipids in spider and rhesus monkeys on an egg and butter diet. *Atherosclerosis*, **19**: 75–86.
12. Pomerance, A. (1970): Pathological and clinical study of calcification of the mitral valve ring. *J. Clin. Path.*, **23**: 354–361.
13. Pomerance, A. (1972): The pathogenesis of aortic stenosis and its relation to age. *Brit. Heart J.*, **4**: 569–574.
14. Reichenbach, D. D., and Benditt, E. P. (1970): Catecholamines and cardiomyopathy: the pathogenesis and potential importance of myofibrillar degeneration. *Human Path.* **1**: 125–150.
15. Roberts, W. C. (1970): Anatomically isolated aortic valvular disease. The case against its being of rheumatic etiology. *Amer. J. Med.*, **49**: 151–159.
16. Roberts, W. C., Perloff, J. K., and Constantino, T. (1971): Severe valvular aortic stenosis in patients over 65 years of age. A clinico-pathologic study. *Amer. J. Cardiol.*, **27**: 497–506.
17. Ross, R., and Harker, L. (1976): Hyperlipidemia and atherosclerosis. *Science*, **193**: 1094–1100.
18. Schlesinger, M. J. (1940): Relation of anatomic pattern to pathologic conditions of the coronary arteries. *Arch. Path.*, **30**: 403–415.
19. Sell, S., and Scully, R. E. (1965): Aging changes in the aortic and mitral valves. His-tologic and histochemical studies with observations on the pathogenesis of calcific aortic stenosis and calcification of the mitral annulus. *Amer. J. Path.*, **46**: 345–365.

20. Stary, H. C., and Strong, J. P. (1976): Coronary artery fine structure in rhesus monkeys: nonatherosclerotic intimal thickening. *Atherosclerosis in Primates*, edited by J. R. Strong, pp. 321–358. *Primates in Medicine*, Vol. 9. Basel: Karger.

21. Strong, J. P., editor (1976): *Atherosclerosis in Primates. Primates in Medicine*, Vol. 9. Basel; Karger.

22. Taylor, C. B., Cox, G. E., Manalo-Esterella, P., and Southworth, J. (1962): Atherosclerosis in rhesus monkeys. II. Arterial lesions associated with hypercholesteremia induced by dietary fat and cholesterol. *Arch. Path.*, **74**: 16–34.

23. Vesselinovitch, D., Wissler, R. W., Hughes, R., and Borensztajn, J. (1976): Reversal of advanced atherosclerosis in rhesus monkeys. I. Light-microscopic studies. *Atherosclerosis*, **23**: 155–176.

24. Whitney, J. C. (1975): The spontaneous cardiovascular diseases of animals. In: *The Pathology of the Heart*, edited by A. Pomerance and M. J. Davies, pp. 479–610. London; Blackwell.

25. Wissler, R. W., and Vesselinovitch, D. (1977): Regression of atherosclerosis in experimental animals and man. *Mod. Conc. Cardiov. Dis.*, **46**: 27–32.

21

Replicative Potential of Various Aortic Cell Types

Charles E. Ogburn, Beverly K. Kariya, Russell Ross, and George M. Martin

Department of Pathology, University of Washington
Seattle, Washington

INTRODUCTION

The finite replicative lifespan in cultures of human diploid fibroblastoid cells from skin (7) has provided a model for some aspects of cellular aging. With this in mind, we have investigated the replicative capabilities of other cell types, particularly vascular cells such as endothelial and smooth muscle cells of the thoracic and abdominal aorta. Such studies may be relevant to the cell proliferative changes involved in atherosclerotic vascular disease in man. We have tried to assess the ability of these cell types from human, monkey, rabbit, rat and mouse to synthesize DNA in organoid cultures (5, 6; Martin and Ogburn, unpublished). In these autoradiographic studies, we assumed that semiconservative DNA replication was being monitored. Other studies have involved cell cultures derived from aortic intimal-medial explants in which various parameters of cell growth were assessed (5, 6). In the present experiments, both approaches were applied to tissues from aging nonhuman primates. Such tissues are particularly valuable because postmortem specimens of human blood vessels, unlike those of skin (7), have proven unsatisfactory for such tissue culture experiments (Ogburn and Martin, unpublished).

In this study we tested three hypotheses: (a) that there is a decline in the replicative potential of various cell types with increasing age of donor; (b) that the distribution of cells capable of undergoing DNA synthesis within any given segment of aortic tissue was nonrandom; and (c) that cells from the abdominal aorta have a lesser replicative potential than cells from the thoracic aorta.

METHODS

Aortic specimens were collected from 20 pigtail macaques (*Macaca nemestrina*) and 2 longtail macaques (*M. fascicularis*), including 18 females and 4 males. The delay time after cardiorespiratory arrest (Chapter 3, this volume) was 3.8 ± 3.5 min for the thoracic aorta and 8.1 ± 2.8 min for the abdominal aorta. The thoracic segment was immediately subdivided for explant-derived cell cultures (investigators R. R. and B. K. K.) and organoid cultures (investigators G. M. M. and C. E. O.). The age of the donor remained unknown until all data were tabulated.

For explant-derived cultures, the proximal and distal thirds of the thoracic aorta were placed in Dulbecco-Vogt medium supplemented with 20 mM Tris-HCl (pH 7.4 at 37°C), 100 units/ml penicillin and 100 μg/ml streptomycin at 37°C, and cut into short (3 to 5 mm) cylindrical segments, which were cut open to expose the luminal surfaces. Intimal-medial strips were peeled from the segments under a dissecting scope using forceps and a scalpel blade (Bard-Parker #11). The peeled strips were cut into 1-mm^3 explants, washed 4 times and resuspended with fortified Dulbecco-Vogt medium with 27 mM sodium bicarbonate, 100 units/ml penicillin, 100 μg/ml streptomycin and 10% homologous serum. The homologous serum, obtained from pooled sera of 8 adult male pigtail macaques, was prepared by allowing whole blood to clot in syringes for 24 hr at 4°C. The resulting serum was separated from the clots and centrifuged at 22,000 × G for 15 min at 4°C. The centrifuged serum was filtered through a 0.22-μ filter (Millipore), heat-inactivated at 56°C for 30 min, and stored at -70°C.

The intimal-medial explants were dispensed into 75-cm^2 flasks, approximately 100 pieces in 2.5 ml of medium per flask. The flasks were turned on end for 1 hr to allow the explants to adhere to the surface of the flask. Approximately 1.0 ml of fresh medium (with 10% serum) was added 2 to 3 times in a 7- to 10-day period until outgrowth was observed and the explants were well anchored to the surface of the flask. Then the medium was replaced by increasing volumes of fresh medium with 5% serum up to a total of 12 ml in twice weekly feedings until confluency was reached, usually within 3 to 4 weeks. All flasks were incubated at 37°C in 5% CO_2.

Once confluency was reached, the cells were washed with a tris-buffered versene solution (2) and incubated for 10 min at 37°C with 5 ml of 0.05% trypsin in the same solution. At the end of the incubation, the cell suspension was mixed with a double volume of medium containing 10% fetal calf serum and centrifuged at $150 \times G$ for 7 min. The cells from one confluent flask were usually inoculated into 3 flasks at each trypsinization. Flasks maintained under such conditions typically yielded 2 to 3×10^6 cells at confluency.

For organoid cultures, the middle third of the thoracic aorta (3 to 4 cm long) and proximal two-thirds of the abdominal aorta (5 to 7 cm long) were placed in $4°C$ Hanks' balanced salt solution (BSS) with HEPES buffer (10) (33 mM, pH 7.4 at $37°C$), glucose (1 mg/ml), penicillin (200 units/ml) and streptomycin (200 μg/ml) (BSS).

After 10 to 15 min transit time to the tissue culture hood, the tissues were washed 3 times with 10 ml of Hanks' BSS and trimmed of excess adventitial fat and fascia. Each large segment was cut with a scalpel into 10 to 15 segments about 2 mm long. These were placed in 60-mm plastic dishes (Falcon, Los Angeles) with 5 ml of fortified Dulbecco-Vogt medium (4) containing 9% fetal calf serum (heat inactivated at $56°C \times 30$ min), penicillin (100 units/ml), streptomycin (100 μg/ml), HEPES buffer (33 mM, pH 7.4 at $37°C$) and sodium bicarbonate (9 mM). The dishes were incubated at $37°C$ in a humidified atmosphere of 1% CO_2 in air. The medium included 5 μCi/ml tritiated (^{3}H) thymidine (TdR) (New England Nuclear, S.A. 6.7 Ci/mM) for a 24-hr pulse period between days 3 and 4 or 4 and 5 of culture and, for a lesser number of cases, between days 2 and 3 of culture. "Day 1" commenced 20 to 24 hr after the initiation of the cultures.

After the ^{3}H TdR pulse, the aortic segments were rinsed 3 times with 0.1 M phosphate-buffered saline (pH 7.4 at $37°C$) and fixed in Bouin's fluid. The tissue was dehydrated, embedded in paraffin, and a series of step sections, 5 μm thick and 25 μm apart, was prepared. Mounted sections were rehydrated, dipped in photographic emulsion (Kodak NTB-2), diluted 1:1 with distilled water, and exposed in light-proof boxes at $4°C$ for 4 days. Slides were then developed (Kodak D-19), fixed (Kodak Rapidfix), and stained with hematoxylin and eosin.

All sections were evaluated with the light microscope (400X) for counting labeled and unlabeled intimal endothelial, medial smooth muscle and adventitial fibroblast nuclei. Because of the large number of sections and the comparatively low labeling indices, we estimated the average total numbers of endothelial and smooth muscle cells per microscopic cross section of abdominal and of thoracic aorta. Estimates were made by counting the total number of each of these cell types in one representative section from each site (abdominal or thoracic) for each animal and averaging the results. Student t-tests showed no significant differences in the total cell counts per section as a function of donor age (comparison of pooled data from 4- and 10-y.o. animals with data from 20-y.o. animals), so the data from all animals were pooled to obtain an estimate of the average total number of endothelial or smooth muscle cells per microscopic cross section of abdominal or thoracic aorta. These calculated averages were used in the determination of the labeling index for each segment, which involved 6 to 12 sections per segment. In the case of adventitial fibroblasts, overall averages were not used because there was significant variation in the amount of residual adventitia from segment to segment. Instead, the total number of cells was counted for each section evaluated, usually one section per segment, and used in the calculation of the labeling indices.

No differences were observed between animals of different sex or species on any of the experimental variables. Thus, the results of the entire sample were combined for analysis. Because of the nonrandom distribution of labeled cells, statistical analysis was done with a nonparametric test, the Kendall S test (1).

RESULTS

The explants from thoracic aorta were studied to determine the number of days required for culture growth to reach confluence. Suitable specimens were obtained from 18 pigtail macaques. Of these, 1 from a 10-y.o. animal failed to grow. The results from the remaining 17 are presented in the second column of Table 21-1 and in Figure 21-1. Because there were no apparent differences in findings with regard to species or sex, data from all animals are included in Tables 21-1 and 21-2. Explants from older animals, particularly of the 20-y.o. group, required more time to reach confluence than explants from the younger groups, i.e., time to first passage correlated positively with age ($r = 0.74$, $p < 0.001$). Indeed, explants from 4 of the 5 20-y.o. animals failed to reach confluence in time plotted. Explants from only 3 of the 12 animals in the younger groups failed to reach confluence. The cell type yielded by the explant culture was almost pure smooth muscle, since adventitia was minimized by the explantation procedure. Neither adventitial fibroblasts nor endothelial cells grow well under explant conditions and smooth muscle cells therefore have a selective advantage.

The organoid cultures from thoracic and abdominal aorta were studied to determine the percent of different cell types capable of supporting DNA synthesis as evidenced by incorporation of TdR. The results obtained using days 3 to 4 and days 4 to 5 of culture growth as pulse periods are presented in Table 21-1 and summarized in Table 21-2. All 3 cell types, endothelial, smooth muscle and adventitial, from the thoracic aorta showed greater incorporation of TdR than cells from the abdominal aorta (Table 21-2). There was no evidence in any of the cell types of a kinetic difference in the appearance of the labeled cells as a function of donor age. Experiments with aortic segments from subsets of these animals using pulse periods in days 2 to 3, 5 to 6, and 6 to 7 of culture produced similar results.

Labeled cells were distributed in a strikingly nonrandom fashion, appearing in "hot spots" and "cold spots" reflected in extremely heterogeneous labeling in-

Table 21-1. Results of Explant-Derived Cell Culture and Organoid Culture Analyses of Replicative Potentials of Various Aortic Cell Types in Macaques.

Age	Days to T1[a]	Pulse (day)[b]	Thoracic Aorta[c]			Abdominal Aorta[d]		
			Endothelium	% Labeled Cells S. Muscle	Adventitia	Endothelium	% Labeled Cells S. Muscle	Adventitia
4-y.o.	24	3–4	0.01–0.04	0.01–0.05	11.3–20.2	<0.01	<0.003	5.7–18.9
		4–5	<0.005	0.002–0.003	14.2–14.5	<0.01	<0.003	2.2–3.2
	24	3–4	0.02–0.38	0.17–0.35	16.1–30.9	<0.01–0.03	<0.003–0.003	<0.09–2.8
		4–5	<0.005	0.01	8.2–8.4	0.01–0.06	<0.003	4.9–13.0
	21	3–4	0.03–0.58	0.02–0.08	10.5–18.9	<0.01	<0.003–0.02	7.3–12.3
		4–5	0.08–0.27	0.01–0.22	10.6–16.4	0.01–0.09	<0.003–0.003	7.9–10.9
	–	3–4	0.05–0.14	0.02–0.05	3.0–16.3	0.04–0.82	0.01–0.09	7.0–11.6
		4–5	0.10–0.25	0.003–0.01	1.2–11.1	0.17–0.75	0.02–0.06	6.9–11.2
10-y.o.	20	3–4	0.06–0.28	0.003–0.04	8.5–14.4	<0.007	<0.002	12.3–13.3
		4–5	0.24–0.39	0.01–0.06	8.2–13.7	–	–	–
	–	3–4	0.05–0.09	<0.002	5.2–10.2	<0.01	<0.003	1.5–8.3
		4–5	0.11–0.90	<0.002–0.06	3.3–14.9	–	–	–
	20	3–4	0.01–0.03	<0.002–0.01	2.5–7.6	<0.01–0.40	<0.003	5.4–23.1
		4–5	0.01–0.03	<0.002	3.9–8.2	<0.01–0.01	<0.003	1.7–6.8
	21	3–4	<0.01	<0.002–0.01	18.1–26.1	<0.01–0.01	<0.003	0.7–2.6
		4–5	0.01–0.05	<0.002–0.005	18.4–24.0	<0.01–0.25	<0.002–0.01	2.5–9.7
	21	3–4	<0.01–0.02	<0.002	8.7–13.8	<0.01	<0.003	4.5–12.4
		4–5	<0.01–0.02	<0.002–0.002	7.1–19.4	<0.01–0.04	<0.003–0.02	2.9–6.5
	24	3–4	0.01–0.08	<0.002–0.01	0.2–18.2	<0.01–0.01	<0.003–0.01	1.2–5.0
		4–5	0.02–0.03	<0.002	4.1–13.6	<0.01–0.01	<0.003–0.003	0.3–12.5
	21	3–4	<0.005–0.01	0.003–0.02	10.8–20.7	<0.01–0.04	<0.002	6.2–11.6
		4–5	<0.005–0.005	<0.001–0.001	11.7–13.4	0.02	<0.002	7.6–7.8

21	3–4	0.03–0.39	<0.002–0.02	11.9–24.7	<0.01–0.07	<0.003–0.003	3.2–7.6
	4–5	<0.009–0.06	<0.002–0.009	2.7–5.8	<0.01–0.13	<0.003–0.003	2.7–5.9
28	3–4	<0.009–0.06	<0.002–0.007	0.3–15.4	<0.01	<0.003	3.1–7.5
	4–5	<0.009–0.06	<0.002–0.007	3.4–14.3	<0.01–0.09	<0.003	0.8–3.5
24	3–4	<0.009	<0.002–0.005	0.4–6.7	<0.01	<0.003	3.6–27.2
	4–5	<0.009–0.03	<0.002–0.009	2.0–16.4	<0.01	<0.003–0.003	2.7–6.4
20-y.o.							
—	3–4	<0.01–0.01	<0.002	0.3–1.4	<0.01–0.03	<0.003	0.5–3.0
	4–5	<0.01–0.09	<0.002–0.002	0.8–2.5	<0.03–0.06	<0.003	1.0–2.1
27	3–4	0.05–0.09	0.005–0.02	15.2–21.4	<0.01	<0.003–0.003	3.9–7.3
	4–5	0.16–0.51	0.01–0.51	14.5–21.8	<0.01	<0.003–0.003	0.5–3.8
31	3–4	0.11–0.44	0.002–0.01	10.8–27.2	<0.01–0.01	<0.003	5.4–8.8
	4–5	0.03–0.33	0.01–0.02	11.6–13.0	<0.01–0.38	<0.002–0.02	1.3–8.5
31	3–4	0.17–1.05	<0.002–0.17	11.2–17.3	<0.01–0.03	<0.003	7.4–22.3
	4–5	0.17–0.73	0.002–0.21	7.2–15.4	<0.007–0.01	<0.002	2.5–3.5
28	3–4	0.01–0.05	0.005–0.06	19.0–31.8	<0.01	<0.003	1.5–9.1
	4–5	<0.005	<0.001	11.8–17.4	<0.01–0.02	<0.002	6.8–9.0
31	3–4	0.01–0.08	0.27–0.31	11.2–17.6	<0.01–0.02	<0.002–0.003	7.2–11.8
	4–5	0.01–0.23	0.29–0.42	9.0–14.5	—	—	—
—	3–4	0.04–0.28	<0.002–0.03	<0.3–1.2	0.18–0.48	0.003–0.02	<0.1
	4–5	0.06–0.45	<0.002–0.05	<0.1–1.2	0.52–1.85	0.03	<0.2–4.7
—	3–4	<0.02	<0.005	7.1–25.4	<0.03	<0.006	10.3–12.6
	4–5	<0.02	<0.005	9.7–10.7	<0.03	<0.006	5.6–6.1

[a] Days between initiation of intimal-medical explant cultures from thoracic aorta and the first trypsinization (T1) of confluent cultures.
[b] 24-hr pulses of 5 μCi/ml ^{3}H thymidine (S.A. 6.7 Ci/mm) beginning on day 3 or day 4.
[c] Middle one-third of the thoracic aorta.
[d] Proximal two-thirds of abdominal aorta. Two to 4 independently cultured and processed segments (2 to 6 mm apart) were evaluated for each site and each pulse period; 24 5-μm sections were screened for each segment. Approximate number of cells screened per section for each cell type: thoracic aorta—endothelium, 1,800; smooth muscle, 7,200; adventitia, 1,200; abdominal aorta—endothelium, 1,200; smooth muscle, 5,000; adventitia, 500–2,000.

Table 21-2. Comparison of Labeling Indices as a Function of Donor Age (4, 10 or 20 years) and Location (T = thoracic aorta, A = abdominal aorta).

	Age Comparisons		Site Comparisons	
	Relationship	p	Relationship	p
Endothelium	4T < 20T	0.070	4T > 4A	0.013
	4A < 20A	0.310	10T > 10A	0.002
	10T < 20T	0.003	20T > 20A	<0.001
	10A > 20A	0.150		
Smooth Muscle	4T > 20T	0.050	4T > 4A	<0.001
	4A < 20A	0.240	10T > 10A	0.200
	10T < 20T	0.003	20T > 20A	<0.001
	10A < 20A	0.290		
Adventitia	4T > 20T	0.390	4T > 4A	<0.001
	4A < 20A	0.210	10T > 10A	<0.001
	10T < 20T	0.160	20T > 20A	<0.001
	10A > 20A	0.020		

p values determined by Kendall S test.

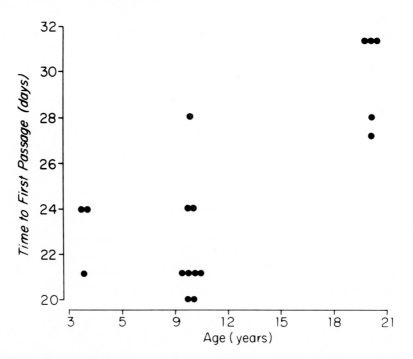

Fig. 21-1. Relationship between age of donor and time required for *in vitro* growth of thoracic aortic explants to reach confluence.

dices seen in different specimens from the same animal and the same specimen from different animals (Table 21-1). There was no consistent pattern of decline in cell labeling as a function of donor age. Although differences with significance levels of $p < 0.05$ were found in 4 of the 12 age comparisons (Table 21-2), in 2 instances they supported a *decline* in labeling while in 2 instances they supported a *rise* in labeling as a function of donor age. The latter was in fact more impressive statistically. We therefore reject the hypothesis of a systematic decline in cell labeling indices as a function of donor age using the sampling techniques of this study. The variability in labeling did not correlate with the length of time between cardiorespiratory arrest and specimen collection.

DISCUSSION

In the explant-derived cell culture study, the time interval from explantation to harvesting of confluent cultures gave clear evidence of correlation with age, longer time periods being required for establishing confluent cultures from older animals. This coincides with results on explant cultures from a variety of tissues in different species (11). The time to first passage was a more sensitive index of donor age than the autoradiographic analysis, presumably because the large numbers of individual explants pooled in initiating the culture reduced the sampling variance.

Unlike our previous studies in ICR mice (5), organoid culture assays failed to show a decline in the replicative potential of several vascular cell types as a function of age. There are several possible explanations. The labeling indices of these cells in primates may be so low and the sampling variance so great that a much larger number of animals and samples per animal may be required to discern age-related differences. This may especially be the case if there is genetic heterogeneity within the colony for factors influencing the propensity of such cells to undergo DNA synthesis in organoid culture. It is also possible that the kinetics of decline in these nonhuman primates are such that perceptible differences would be seen only in much older subjects. Finally, multifocal *increases* in the labeling indices of certain cell types (i.e., regional hyperplasias) may occur with aging (3), thus further compounding the sampling problems. In any event, it is clear that the organoid culture assay employed in this study does not provide a very useful marker for the assessment of the physiological age of the donor.

The nonrandom distribution of labeled cells is consistent with the clustering of labeled endothelial cells observed in Sprague-Dawley rats injected with ^{3}H thymidine (9). It is also comparable to the nonrandom distribution of labeled cells that we have observed in organoid cultures of the aortas of Fischer 344 rats (Ogburn and Martin, unpublished). In both the rat and monkey, the "hot spots" involve both endothelial and smooth muscle cells, but are less evident in the case of the adventitial fibroblasts, which have a higher and more uniform labeling index.

The lower labeling indices of the muscular cells of the monkey aorta compared with those we found in the mouse aorta (5) are of interest. There could be a variety of explanations for such differences, such as an intrinsic difference related to the genotype, or differential response to mitogens in calf serum. It is important, however, to rule out trivial explanations. In this connection, an outstanding methodological difference between the monkey and mouse studies involved the mode of sacrifice. The mice were killed by fracture of the cervical spine, whereas the monkeys were killed while anesthetized, in all but one case, by sodium "nembutal" [sodium 5-ethyl-5-(methylbutyl)-barbiturate]. Therefore, further studies are needed for valid interspecies comparison. It is also conceivable that nembutal could have depressed the labeling indices, and such depression combined with the sampling limitation could have obscured any consistent age regression in the labeling of organoid sections.

The finding that, for all cell types examined, there was a lower labeling index in the abdominal aorta than in the thoracic aorta, confirms our previous study with monkey tissues (6). That finding is of considerable interest in view of the fact that the abdominal aorta is a preferential site for atherosclerosis, whereas the thoracic aorta is a site of relative resistance (8). A potential role of such differential replicative potential in the pathogenesis of atherosclerosis has been discussed elsewhere (5).

ACKNOWLEDGMENTS

This work was supported by National Institutes of Health grants RR00166, RR52177, AG62145, AG00592, AG00299 and GM13543. We thank Ms. Krista Thie, Ms. Mary-Jane Rivest and Ms. Lynn Phillips for technical assistance.

REFERENCES

1. Armitage, P. (1971): *Statistical Methods in Medical Research*, pp. 398–403. New York; John Wiley.
2. Martin, G. M. (1964): Use of tris (hydroxymethyl) aminomethane buffers in cultures of diploid human fibroblasts. *Proc. Soc. Exp. Biol. Med.*, **116**: 167–171.
3. Martin, G. M. (1977): Cellular aging. A review. Part I: Clonal senescence. *Amer. J. Path.*, **89**: 484–511.
4. Martin, G. M., and Hoehn, H. (1974): Genetics and human disease. *Hum. Path.*, **5**: 387–404.
5. Martin, G. M., Ogburn, C., and Sprague, C. A. (1975): Senescence and vascular disease. In: *Explorations in Aging*, edited by V. J. Cristofalo and E. Holečková. *Adv. Exp. Med. Biol.*, **61**: 163–193.

6. Martin, G. M., and Sprague, C. A. (1973): Symposium on *in vitro* studies related to atherogenesis.   Life histories of hyperplastoid cell lines from aorta and skin. *Exp. Molec. Path.*, **18**: 125–141.

7. Martin, G. M., Sprague, C. A., and Epstein, C. J. (1970): Replicative life-span of cultivated human cells.   Effects of donor's age, tissue and genotype. *Lab. Invest.*, **23**: 86–92.

8. Roberts, J., Jr., Moses, C., and Wilkins, R. H. (1959): Autopsy studies in atherosclerosis.   I. Distribution and severity of atherosclerosis in patients dying without morphologic evidence of atherosclerotic catastrophe. *Circulation*, **20**: 511–519.

9. Schwartz, S. M., and Benditt, E. P. (1976): Clustering of replicating cells in aortic endothelium. *Proc. Nat. Acad. Sci. (Wash.)*, **73**: 651–653.

10. Shipman, C., Jr. (1969): Evaluation of 4- (2-hydroxyethyl)-1-piperazinethane sulfonic acid (HEPES) as a tissue culture buffer. *Proc. Soc. Exp. Biol. Med.*, **130**: 305–313.

11. Soukupova, M., Holečková, E., and Hnevkovsky, P. (1970): Changes of the latent period of explanted tissues during ontogenesis. In: *Aging in Cell and Tissue Culture*, edited by E. Holečková and V. J. Cristofalo, pp. 41–56. New York; Plenum Press.

22

Plasma Lipid, Lipoproteins and Lecithin:Cholesterol Acyltransferase (LCAT)

Andras G. Lacko and William R. Hazzard

Department of Biochemistry, Texas College of Osteopathic Medicine and
Center for Studies in Aging, North Texas State University,
Denton, Texas and
Department of Medicine and Northwest Lipid Research Clinic
University of Washington School of Medicine
Seattle, Washington

INTRODUCTION

The variability of genetic makeup and the difficulty in controlling experimental variables such as diet in human populations necessitates the development of suitable animal models for the study of aging. Whether one is interested in the environmental contribution to chronic diseases later in life or in the genetically predetermined factors that promote the deterioration of physiological events during senescence, a uniform and well controlled sample population is essential for a thorough investigation. In recent years, there has been a growing acceptance of the laboratory rat as a suitable model for aging studies. Two strains, the Sprague-Dawley and Fischer rats, have been extensively used for the study of many age dependent parameters (11, 14, 15). Atherosclerosis and its cardiovascular complications, however, represent an area in which rats do not appear to be adequate models. Although plasma lipoprotein structure, composition, and function in the rat appear similar to those in man, the distribution of lipoproteins among their principal classes differs from that in man, especially with regard to the low levels of low-density lipoproteins (LDL). In addition, the rat is notoriously resistant to atherosclerosis.

Primates have long been considered the best models for many biomedical studies, because *in vivo* findings can commonly be extrapolated to the human

274

system. We have thus taken the opportunity to study the plasma lipoproteins from three age groups of pigtail macaque (*Macaca nemestrina*), focusing on the plasma lipids and their distribution among the lipoprotein fractions and the measurement of lecithin:cholesterol acyltransferase (LCAT). Particular emphasis was placed on the cholesterol content of LDL, which is thought to promote atherosclerosis (12), and of high density lipoprotein (HDL), which is thought to retard it (7).

MATERIALS AND METHODS

The subjects were 15 female pigtail macaques (3 4-y.o., 7 10-y.o., 5 20-y.o.), whose care, diet, and life history are described in Chapter 3. A venous blood sample, drawn into tubes containing EDTA (1 mg/ml), was obtained from each animal before sacrifice. Samples of plasma were separated by low speed centrifugation and immediately delivered on ice to the Northwest Lipid Research Clinic of the University of Washington for a battery of lipid and lipoprotein analyses and to the Lipid Research Laboratory of the Texas College of Osteopathic Medicine in Denton, Texas via air and ground transportation for LCAT and free cholesterol determinations.

Lipid and lipoprotein determinations reported here were done by the methods of the Northwest Lipid Research Clinic (9) with the exception of the unesterified cholesterol determination, which was done by the method of Parekh and Young (10). LCAT determinations were performed by a slightly modified version (4) of the method described by Stokke and Norum (17).

RESULTS

Neither cholesterol nor triglyceride in whole plasma varied significantly with age (Table 22-1), though a correlation coefficient of +0.49 suggested some increase in triglyceride. Lipoprotein lipid analysis localized this increase to a significant (p < 0.001) rise in HDL triglyceride (Figure 22-1, left), which was weakly intercorrelated (r = 0.51) with a parallel increase in HDL cholesterol (Figure 22-1, center). LDL cholesterol displayed an opposite trend (Figure 22-1, right), accounting for the failure of whole plasma cholesterol to vary with age in these animals. A relatively sharp increase of LCAT activity with age (Table 22-2) was probably related to the increase in free cholesterol (Figure 22-2), an important determinant of the rate of esterification of plasma cholesterol. Because ages were in most instances estimated and the animals were grouped into 3 age categories, these changes with age must be interpreted cautiously, especially the results of regression analyses, in which age was entered in stepwise fashion (4, 10, or 20 years) rather than as a continuum of age between these extremes.

Table 22-1. Plasma Lipid and Lipoprotein Lipid Levels in Female *Macaca nemestrina* of Three Age Groups.

Age Group (yr.)	Wgt. (kg)	Plasma		Very Low Density Lipoproteins		Low Density Lipoproteins		High Density Lipoproteins	
		Cholesterol mg/dl	Triglyceride mg/dl	Cholesterol mg/dl	Triglyceride mg/dl	Cholesterol mg/dl	Triglyceride mg/dl	Cholesterol mg/dl	Triglyceride mg/dl
4	3.3	129	46	8	16	55	18	66	12
4	3.6	116	42	1	6	55	22	60	14
4	5.0	133	51	6	13	62	24	65	14
Mean ± S.D.		126 ± 9	46 ± 5	5 ± 4	11 ± 5	57 ± 4	21 ± 3	65 ± 3	13 ± 1
10	7.7	133	75	1	21	75	33	60	21
10	7.3	97	124	17	53	37	36	43	35
10	4.8	122	57	6	18	48	16	68	23
10	8.4	118	65	2	15	46	16	70	24
10	4.8	110	60	2	18	52	19	56	23
10	7.2	112	60	3	17	35	15	74	28
10	6.1	92	115	9	44	35	30	48	41
Mean ± S.D.		112 ± 14	79 ± 28	6 ± 6	27 ± 15	39 ± 20	31 ± 13	60 ± 12	28 ± 7
20	6.1	103	81	6	4	45	42	65	35
20	5.5	114	98	8	36	19	22	87	40
20	3.5	122	64	3	14	42	23	77	27
20	4.9	102	94	11	36	8	15	83	43
20	6.2	143	92	4	16	33	17	106	59
Mean ± S.D.		117 ± 17	86 ± 14	21 ± 14	29 ± 16	29 ± 16	24 ± 11	84 ± 15	41 ± 12
Correlation with age Group		r −.12	0.49	0.12	0.13	−0.65	0.09	0.61	0.77
		p NS	NS	NS	NS	<.01	NS	<.02	<.001

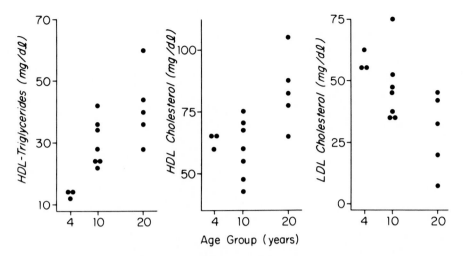

Fig. 22-1. Relation of age to HDL triglyceride, HDL cholesterol, and LDL cholesterol in 15 female pigtail macaques. Each circle represents 1 animal.

Table 22-2. Free Cholesterol and LCAT Activity in Plasma Samples from 14 Female *M. nemestrina*.

Age (years)	Free Cholesterol (mg/dl)	LCAT	
		% Cholesterol Esterified/hr	nM/ml/hr
4	41	6.3	72
4	50	6.3	81
4	53	7.1	97
x̄ ± s.d.	48 ± 6.2	6.6 ± 0.5	83 ± 13
10	66	7.3	125
10	51	8.3	109
10	28	6.1	44
10	64	7.7	127
10	44	5.6	64
10	59	5.5	84
10	57	7.4	109
x̄ ± s.d.	47 ± 16	6.3 ± 1.3	78 ± 37
20	73	8.63	163
20	59	8.25	147
20	40	6.78	70
20	58	6.63	99
x̄ ± s.d.	58 ± 14	7.6 ± 1.0	120 ± 43

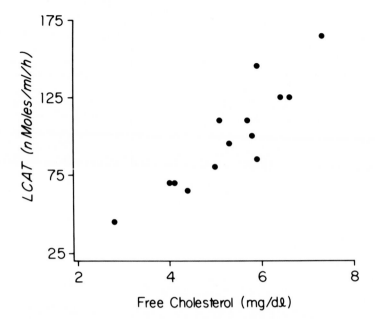

Fig. 22-2. Relation of LCAT activity (rate of cholesterol esterification) to free cholesterol in female pigtail macaques. Regression coefficient R = 0.92, p < 0.001.

DISCUSSION

Age dependent changes of certain plasma lipids are well documented in human populations; the gradual increase of plasma cholesterol to middle age is perhaps the best example (6). The literature to date has been less explicit on age dependent changes in the other plasma lipid parameters reported in this communication. At least two papers report no age dependent trends in LCAT activity as shown by either rate of cholesterol esterification (5) or levels of LCAT enzyme (1, 3).

One of the early studies of age dependent changes in the lipoprotein compartments of the plasma was done by Searcy *et al.* (12), who proposed the designation "atherolipid number" which was proportional to the beta/alpha lipoprotein cholesterol ratio. They found that atherolipid numbers in human populations increased with age due to the increasing levels of beta lipoprotein cholesterol (LDL cholesterol), while alpha lipoprotein cholesterol (HDL cholesterol) levels remained unchanged. Recent information indicates that HDL and LDL cholesterol may best be treated as independent variables, and the percentage of total cholesterol residing in HDL may be a useful parameter of the "anti-atherogenic" potential of an individual (3).

A potentially important feature of the present study is the apparent increase in HDL cholesterol with age in the pigtail macaque (1.7 mg/dl/yr). Whether this represents a true feature of aging in this species or the selection by survivorship of animals in the older age group for this small, cross-sectional study is not clear. Also, whether the age-related changes are confined to females is uncertain. However, a high level of HDL cholesterol may permit unusual longevity in the monkey, as has been reported in the human (2). If so, this change in HDL cholesterol and the parallel decrease in LDL cholesterol may explain the remarkable resistance to coronary atherosclerosis (Chapter 20) and the lack of corneal lipid deposits (Chapter 13). The significance of the increased HDL triglyceride levels in the older age groups is unclear.

A recent report indicates that an atherogenic diet fed to rhesus monkeys selectively increased the LDL cholesterol portion, while there was little change in HDL cholesterol (8). The macaque model may thus be capable of reflecting the powerful dietary influences on plasma lipids which have a cumulative clinical effect in some elderly human populations. While genetic factors are bound to affect individual resistance to atherosclerosis as it relates to the clearance of plasma lipids, the macaque may serve as an excellent model to study the effects of nutritional factors on cardiovascular risk.

ACKNOWLEDGMENTS

Supported in part by grants from the Administration on Aging 90-A1050101, American Heart Association, Texas Affiliate, and National Heart, Lung, and Blood Institute (Northwest Lipid Research Clinic NIH V12157A), and by National Institutes of Health grants RR00166, RR52177 and AG62145 to the University of Washington. Dr. Hazzard is an investigator of the Howard Hughes Medical Institute. The dedicated technical assistance of the staff of the Care Laboratory of the Northwest Lipid Clinic is gratefully acknowledged.

REFERENCES

1. Akanuma, Y., Kuzuya, T., Hayashi, J., Ide, T., and Kuzuya, N. (1973): Positive correlation of serum lecithin:cholesterol acyltransferase activity with relative body weight. *Eur. J. Clin. Invest.*, **3**: 136–141.
2. Glueck, C. J., Fallat, R. W., Millett, F., Gartside, P., Elston, R. C., and Go, R. C. P. (1975): Familial hyper-alpha-lipoproteinemia: studies in eighteen kindreds. *Metabolism*, **24**: 1243–1265.
3. Gordon, T., Castelli, W. P., Hjortland, M. C., Kannel, W. B., and Dawber, T. R. (1977): High density lipoprotein as a protective factor against coronary heart disease. *Am. J. Med.*, **62**: 707–714.
4. Lacko, A. G., Rutenberg, H. L., and Soloff, L. A. (1973): Measurement of the initial rate of serum cholesterol esterification. *Biochem. Med.*, **7**: 173–183.

5. Lacko, A. G., Rutenberg, H. L., and Soloff, L. A. (1977): The influence of age and sex on the esterification of human serum cholesterol. *Biochem. Med.*, 17: 275–283.

6. Lopez-S, A., Krehl, A., and Hodges, R. E. (1967): Relationship between total cholesterol and cholesteryl esters with age in human blood plasma. *Am. J. Clin. Nutr.*, 20: 808–815.

7. Miller, G. J., and Miller, N.E. (1975): Plasma-high-density-lipoprotein concentration and development of ischaemic heart-disease. *Lancet*, 1: 16–19.

8. Nelson, C. A., and Morris, M. D. (1977): Effects of cholesterol feeding on primate serum lipoproteins. II. Low density lipoprotein characterization from rhesus monkeys with a moderate rise in serum cholesterol. *Biochem. Med.*, 17: 320–332.

9. Northwest Lipid Research Clinic (1974): *Manual of Laboratory Operations*, Vol. I. DHEW publication No. NIH75628.

10. Parekh, A. C., and Jung, D. H. (1970: Cholesterol determination with ferric acetate-uranium acetate and sulfuric acid-ferrous sulfate reagents. *Anal. Chem.*, 42: 1423–1427.

11. Schmucker, D. L., and Jones, A. L. (1975): Hepatic fine structure in young and aging rats treated with oxandrolone: a morphometric study. *J. Lipid Res.*, 16: 143–150.

12. Searcy, R. L., Carroll, V. P. II, Davis, W. H., and Bergquist, L. M. (1960): "Atherolipid numbers": an expression of serum-cholesterol and serum-lipoprotein relationships. *Lancet*, 2: 1196.

13. Stokke, K. T., and Norum, K. R. (1971): Determination of lecithin:cholesterol acyl-transfer in human blood plasma. *Scand. J. Lab. Clin. Invest.*, 27: 21–27.

14. Story, J. A., Tepper, S. A., and Kritchevsky, D. (1976): Age-related changes in the lipid metabolism of Fisher 344 rats. *Lipids*, 11: 623–627.

15. Takeuchi, N., Yamamura, Y., Katayama, Y., Hayashi, C., and Uchida, K. (1976): Impairment of feed back control and induction of cholesterol synthesis in rats by aging. *Exp. Gerontol.*, 11: 121–126.

23

The Effect of Digitalis on Sodium, Potassium-ATPase of Myocardial and Neural Tissue

Steven I. Baskin, Zebulon V. Kendrick, Tai Akera,
Satoshi Yamamoto, and Theodore M. Brody
Departments of Pharmacology, Medical College of Pennsylvania,
Philadelphia, Pennsylvania; and Michigan State University,
East Lansing, Michigan

INTRODUCTION

The incidence of digitalis toxicity, characterized by cardiac arrhythmias (22), increases with increasing age in humans (11, 16, 23, 29). The increased sensitivity may be caused by changes in pharmacokinetics of the drug with age or by physiologic changes that alter its influence on heart rate, blood pressure, or sympathetic tone. The physiology and biochemistry of the aging cardiovascular system undergo subtle yet profound changes with age. For example, the electrocardiogram shows a prolonged P-R interval and QRS complex duration, and the left ventricular ejection time is increased in older normal human subjects (12, 36). Thus, changes in the heart may predispose the myocardium to increased cardiotoxicity of the drug. Cardiac glycosides acting on the autonomic nervous system may also contribute to the toxic actions on the myocardium. For example, digitalis may act on multiple sites of the sympathetic-adrenal axis (27). Cardiac arrhythmias can be induced by applying digitalis to the brain (9), and ouabain exerts a central action resulting in increased adrenergic activity innervating the heart (13).

Na^+, K^+-stimulated, Mg^{2+}-dependent adenosine triphosphatase, E.C. 3.6.1.3. (Na^+, K^+-ATPase) is a membrane-bound enzyme found in animal tissues (10) that is responsible, in part, for maintaining Na^+ and K^+ gradients across cell membranes (32). It is probably the therapeutic as well as a toxic site of action for cardiac glycosides (2, 24, 30). Glycoside binding, enzyme inhibition, electrophysiologic and physiologic studies suggest that this enzyme is a site for some of the pharmacologic activities of digitalis compounds (2, 13, 14, 21, 25, 26, 32). It remains to be established, however, which tissues, as well as interactions among tissues *in vivo* (i.e., the central and peripheral nervous systems, adrenal gland and/or the myocardium), are responsible for digitalis-induced cardiac arrhythmias. In the rat brain, Na^+, K^+-ATPase activity increases from birth to 20 days of age (1), and decreases (in senescent Fischer 344 rats) between 12 and 28 months of age (8). Spinal cord Na^+, K^+-ATPase is more resistant to cardiac glycoside inhibition in 3-month-old than in 12-, 24-, or 28-month old rats. The enzyme inhibition in the central nervous system, at least in the rat, may contribute to the arrhythmias produced by the digitalis glycosides.

In the present study, we examined cardiac tissue and the thoracic spinal cord of a nonhuman primate, the pigtail macaque (*Macaca nemestrina*). Our goals were threefold: (a) to determine age-related differences in ouabain binding kinetics of Na^+, K^+-ATPase in the heart of a nonhuman primate (authors T. A., S. Y., T. M. B.); (b) to determine age-related differences in inhibition of Na^+, K^+-ATPase activity by ouabain in the thoracic spinal cord of these animals (authors S. I. B., Z. V. K.); and (c) to contribute to the search for appropriate animal models of age-related glycoside toxicity by comparing characteristics of the primate model with those of other animal models.

MATERIALS AND METHODS

The apex of the heart and the thoracic spinal cord of 4-, 10-, and 20-y.o. *M. nemestrina* were taken within 14 min (heart) and 30 min (spinal cord) of cardiopulmonary arrest (Chapter 3, this volume). Each specimen was placed in an individual plastic bag, frozen, and shipped on dry ice. The cardiac tissue was analyzed upon arrival; the thoracic spinal cords were frozen at $-20°C$ for 50 to 70 days and then analyzed. No relations were found between the specific activity of the enzyme and either the time from cardiopulmonary arrest to specimen excision, or the length of frozen storage.

Tritiated Ouabain Binding to Cardiac Muscle

The cardiac muscle was thawed, immediately minced with scissors, and homogenized in 9 vol of a 50-mM Tris HCl buffer solution (pH 7.5) using a motor-driven Potter Elvehjem homogenizer with a Teflon pestle (A. H. Thomas Scientific Company, Philadelphia, PA; Type A). The homogenate was kept at $0°C$ for 10 min, then passed through gauze mesh to remove the tissue debris. The filtered homogenate was used without further purification.

Filtered homogenates (1.0 mg protein/ml) were incubated with 10 nM tritiated (^{3}H) ouabain[1] in the presence of 100 mM NaCl, 5 mM MgCl$_2$, 5 mM Tris ATP and 50 mM Tris HCl buffer (pH 7.5) at 37°C. At 1, 3, 5 and 10 min a 1.0-ml aliquot of the incubation mixture was removed and immediately filtered through a nitrocellulose filter (Selectron^R membrane filter, Schleicher and Schuell, Inc., Keene, NH, type B-6, pore size 0.45 μM) under vacuum. The filter was rinsed twice with 5 ml of ouabain-free incubation medium. The filter was dissolved in ethylene glycol monomethyl ether and the radioactivity of the bound ouabain retained on the filter was estimated using a liquid scintillation spectrometer (6). Tritiated ouabain binds to the Na$^+$, K$^+$-ATPase in the homogenate preparation under these conditions, causing inhibition of that enzyme (3, 7, 15, 31). Nonspecific binding of ouabain was estimated concurrently in the absence of ATP and the presence of 0.1 mM nonlabeled ouabain which was added to suppress the saturable binding of ^{3}H-ouabain to Na$^+$, K$^+$-ATPase. Ouabain was selected as the cardiac glycoside because of its relatively high water solubility and resultant low nonspecific binding.

After a 10-min incubation at 37°C for the ^{3}H-ouabain binding reaction, an excess of nonlabeled ouabain (final concentration, 0.1 mM) was added to terminate the saturable binding of ^{3}H-ouabain. The subsequent release of the labeled ouabain from Na$^+$, K$^+$-ATPase was monitored following addition of unlabeled ouabain by taking aliquots at indicated times and estimating the amount of enzyme-bound ouabain as described above.

Protein concentration in cardiac tissue was assayed (20) with bovine serum albumin as the standard.

Ouabain Inhibition of Na$^+$, K$^+$-ATPase of Thoracic Spinal Cord

Approximately 1.5 g of thoracic spinal cord was homogenized with 6 vol of ice cold solution containing 0.25 M sucrose, 5 mM histidine, 5 mM EDTA, and 0.2% deoxycholate (pH 7.0). The homogenate was centrifuged at 12,000 × g for 30 min. The supernatant was centrifuged at 35,000 × g for 30 min and the pellet was suspended in a solution containing 0.25 M sucrose, 5 mM histidine and 1.0 mM EDTA (pH 7.0). The suspension was centrifuged again at 100,000 × g for 30 min. The final residue was suspended in a medium containing 0.25 M sucrose, 5.0 mM histidine HCl, and 1.0 mM tris-EDTA (pH 7.0) and microsomal protein was assayed (20).

The Na$^+$, K$^+$-ATPase activity of the microsomal fraction was assayed at 37°C in a total volume of 1.0 ml containing 50 mM Tris-HCl buffer (pH 7.5), 5 mM

---

[1] ^{3}H-ouabain (generally labeled; specific activity, 19 Ci/mM) was purchased from Amersham/Searle Corp., Arlington Heights, IL. Tris ATP and ouabain octahydrate were obtained from Sigma Chemical Co., St. Louis, MO. Other chemicals used were reagent grade.

MgCl$_2$ and 5.0 mM Tris-ATP, with or without 100 mM NaCl and 15 mM KCl. The reaction was started by adding Tris-ATP after a 5-min incubation period of the assay and was terminated 10 min later by adding 1.0 ml of ice cold 15% trichloroacetic acid. The mixture was centrifuged at 600 X g for 15 min and the organic phosphate liberated from ATP was determined in a 1.0-ml aliquot of the supernatant solution (3).

RESULTS

^{3}H-Ouabain Binding to Cardiac Muscle

The time course of the binding of ^{3}H-ouabain to Na$^+$, K$^+$-ATPase in cardiac homogenates was studied first. As in dog, cat, rabbit and guinea pig, the binding of ouabain to Na$^+$, K$^+$-ATPase in homogenates obtained from pigtail macaques was a slow process, and did not attain equilibrium within the 10-min incubation period at 37°C (Figure 23-1a). Longer incubations were not attempted because of significant hydrolysis of ATP under these experimental conditions. The amount of specifically bound ^{3}H-ouabain formed in the presence of 10 nM ^{3}H-ouabain was greatest with cardiac homogenates obtained from 20-y.o. macaques and lowest with those from 4-y.o. macaques. These results, however, do not necessarily indicate an age-dependent difference in Na$^+$, K$^+$-ATPase concentrations in cardiac homogenates, since the ouabain binding at 5 and 10 min seems to approach equilibrium in 10- and 20-y.o. animals, whereas in 4-y.o. animals it seems still to be increasing at 10 min. If the incubation period were longer, the ouabain binding to cardiac homogenates in 4-y.o. macaques might

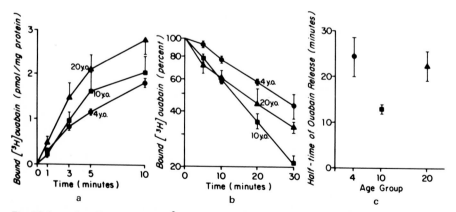

Fig. 23.1. a, Specific binding of ^{3}H-ouabain to cardiac homogenates. Mean of 3 4-y.o., 10 10-y.o. and 5 20-y.o. animals. Vertical line indicates S.E.M. b, Time course of the release of specifically bound ^{3}H-ouabain from cardiac homogenates. Vertical line indicates S.E.M. c, Half-time (S.E.M.) for the release of specifically bound ^{3}H-ouabain from cardiac homogenates. Values corresponding to 0 min in Fig. 23-1b were omitted from the calculation.

reach a higher level. In addition, the concentration of bound ouabain formed in the presence of a fixed concentration of ^{3}H-ouabain depends on two variables— the binding site concentration and the affinity of each binding site for ouabain. Thus, the data in Figure 23-1a indicate that there are age-related differences in the time course of ^{3}H-ouabain binding to cardiac Na$^+$, K$^+$-ATPase, and that either the enzyme concentration in the homogenate or the affinity of the enzyme for ouabain, or both, are different. The time course of ^{3}H-ouabain binding to cardiac Na$^+$, K$^+$-ATPase in pigtail macaques was quite different from that in Sprague-Dawley rats, in which the binding reaction reaches equilibrium within a few minutes (18).

After termination of ^{3}H-ouabain binding, the bound ouabain was released gradually from cardiac Na$^+$, K$^+$-ATPase (Figure 23-1b). As indicated by the nearly straight line on a semilogarithmic plot, the release of ouabain from the enzyme roughly followed first-order kinetics. The time course of the ouabain release was fastest in cardiac Na$^+$, K$^+$-ATPase obtained from 10-y.o. macaques and significantly slower in those obtained from 4- and 20-y.o. macaques. From the slope of a linear regression line fitted to data obtained from individual animals, the half-time for the release of specifically bound ^{3}H-ouabain was calculated for each animal. The half-life of the complex of cardiac Na$^+$, K$^+$-ATPase with ouabain was significantly shorter in 10-y.o. animals than in the other age groups (Figure 23-1c).

Ouabain Inhibition of Na$^+$, K$^+$-ATPase of Thoracic Spinal Cord

The microsomal protein concentration (mg protein/gm wet tissue) of the thoracic spinal cord increased as a function of age (Figure 23-2). The Na$^+$,

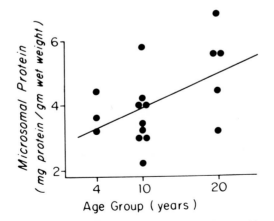

Fig. 23-2. Microsomal protein determination for thoracic spinal cord in macaques of different age groups. Each circle represents one animal. Solid line represents linear regression (p < 0.05).

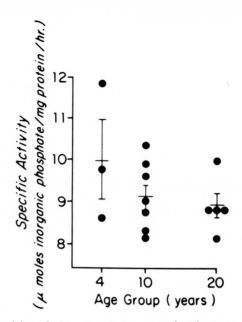

Fig. 23-3. Specific activity of thoracic spinal cord Na^+, K^+-stimulated, Mg^{2+}-dependent ATPase of macaques of different age groups. Each circle represents one animal. Horizontal bar represents the mean and the vertical line, the S.E.M. for each group.

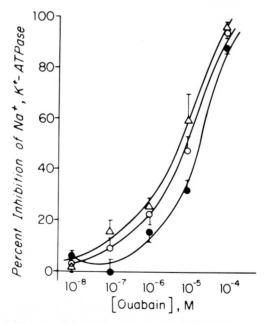

Fig. 23-4. Percent inhibition of thoracic spinal cord Na^+, K^+-ATPase activity by ouabain in macaques of different age groups: ●, 4-y.o. (n = 3); o, 10-y.o. (n = 8); △, 20-y.o. (n = 5). Symbols represent the mean values of inhibition of Na^+, K^+-ATPase for each age group for each molar concentration of ouabain.

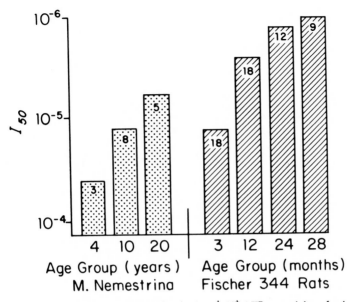

Fig. 23-5. Age-related ouabain inhibition (I_{50}) of Na^+, K^+-ATPase activity of spinal cord in a macaque and rat (Fischer 344). Numbers at tops of bars indicate the number of animals contributing to the determinations.

K^+-ATPase specific activity (μmoles inorganic phosphate/mg protein/hour) did not change as a function of age (Figure 23-3). No marked change with aging was observed in either the Na^+, K^+-stimulated component or in the Mg^{2+}-dependent portion of the enzyme in the thoracic spinal cord (data not shown).

The inhibitory effect of 10^{-8} to 10^{-4} M ouabain on the activity of Na^+, K^+-ATPase purified from the thoracic spinal cord indicated that the enzyme from 10- and 20-y.o. macaques was more sensitive ($p < 0.05$) than that from 4-y.o. animals (Figure 23-4). At the ouabain concentration of 10^{-5} M, the enzymatic activity was inhibited 59% in 20-y.o. macaques and 48% in 10-y.o. animals, but only 32% in the 4-y.o. group. At ouabain concentrations of 10^{-4} M, enzymatic activity was inhibited by 90% or more for all groups. I_{50}, the concentration of ouabain that inhibits the enzyme by 50%, was 2.07×10^{-5}, 1.15×10^{-5} and 5.50×10^{-6} for the 4-, 10- and 20-y.o. animals, respectively (Figure 23-5).

DISCUSSION

Ouabain inhibition of Na^+, K^+-ATPase is of interest because ouabain belongs to the group of compounds that may exert their therapeutic and/or toxic effects through the inhibition of this enzyme (2, 4, 24, 30). The myocardium is the site of action of the drug's therapeutic effects. The question regarding site or sites of action for its toxic effects is unsettled.

One determinant of digitalis sensitivity is the response of cardiac Na^+, K^+-ATPase to the inhibitory action of this agent (2, 5, 25), or more specifically, the stability of the enzyme-digitalis complex (3, 7, 34). In the present study, the ouabain-enzyme complex was more stable in 4-y.o. and 20-y.o. macaque hearts than in the 10-y.o. hearts. Our study also suggests age-related differences either in the concentration of Na^+, K^+-ATPase in cardiac tissue or in the affinity of the enzyme for ouabain. One or a combination of these changes in cardiac Na^+, K^+-ATPase could account for some of the differences in the heart's sensitivity to digitalis *in vivo*.

The central nervous system has been proposed as a possible site of action leading to toxic arrhythmias (13, 27, 35). There are no direct human data on the effects of cardiac glycosides on Na^+, K^+-ATPase activity in the central nervous system. However, in enzyme preparations obtained from the brains of elderly patients after death, alcohol exerted a greater inhibition of Na^+, K^+-ATPase (33). In the present study, Na^+, K^+-ATPase in the spinal cord was more sensitive to ouabain (10^{-7}–10^{-4}M) in 10- and 20-y.o. macaques than in the 4-y.o. animals, paralleling recent observations in rat spinal cord (8). The age-related ouabain inhibition of macaque thoracic spinal cord Na^+, K^+-ATPase supports the hypothesis that a neural site may be partly responsible for increased digitalis toxicity with increasing age.

The biochemical basis for the age-differences in ouabain's effect on the enzyme in nerve tissue is unknown. It may, for instance, result from shifts in the lipid composition of neural tissue which predispose to increased accumulation of fat soluble digitalis compounds in certain parts of the central nervous system. Regardless of the mechanism, a marked change in Na^+, K^+-ATPase activity occurring nonuniformly in the central nervous system could distort the pattern of sympathetic-parasympathetic control of the heart in such a way as to increase vulnerability to cardiac arrhythmia (27, 28).

The microsomal protein (mg protein/gm wet weight) of the thoracic spinal cord increased significantly with age. However, this observation should be interpreted with care, owing to considerable overlap of the data points from different age groups (Figure 23-2). For example, monkey 72399 had the lowest protein concentration for 10-y.o. animals, and had many other characteristics that made her seem older (see Chapter 3 of this book). If she were grouped with the 20-y.o. animals, there would not be a significant difference in microsomal protein concentration of the thoracic spinal cord preparation. Certainly, more definitive insight for the increased protein concentration might have been obtained if a more extensive chemical or histochemical analysis for specific proteins had been performed on this tissue. The enzyme specific activity (μmoles inorganic phosphate/mg protein/hr), as well as the Na^+, K^+-stimulated and the Mg^{2+}-dependent components of the enzyme, did not change as a function of age.

Any interpretation of these data must consider the effects of ketamine and sodium pentobarbital, which were used as the anesthestic agents (10 mg/kg and 10-12 mg/kg, respectively), on Na$^+$, K$^+$-ATPase and on the ouabain inhibition of the enzyme. Depending on the concentration of sodium pentobarbital (19), the specific activity of the enzyme can be either stimulated or inhibited. Further research is needed on the effect of barbituates to establish their effects on ouabain inhibition of Na$^+$, K$^+$-ATPase.

Experiments on the relation between the changes in cardiac and thoracic spinal cord Na$^+$, K$^+$-ATPase and digitalis sensitivity have not been done in human subjects because they involve life-threatening digitalis toxicity. Systematic studies on age-related changes of the cardiac cell membrane and ion fluxes have been performed in rats (14). However, the kinetics of the interaction between digitalis and cardiac Na$^+$, K$^+$-ATPase are markedly different in the rat from those in more digitalis-sensitive species such as guinea pig, rabbit, cat, and dog (7, 18, 34). For example, the half-time of the release of ouabain from cardiac Na$^+$, K$^+$-ATPase ranges from 5 to 90 min in those species, whereas in rats it is estimated to be several seconds (34). Furthermore, the basic biochemistry and physiology of the rat heart seem to be unique among mammals, as indicated by an unusual force-frequency relationship in this species (17, 18). Results of the present study support the view that the cardiac enzyme response in primates is more similar to that of the other species than of the rat.

The apparent increase in sensitivity of the CNS enzyme to ouabain in the older macaques of this study suggests that Na$^+$, K$^+$-ATPase in the primate nervous system becomes more sensitive to cardiac glycosides with age. Further studies of the binding, distribution, pharmacokinetics and pharmacodynamics of these drugs in various species are necessary to identify the optimal animal model for determining the mechanism of increased digitalis toxicity with age in man.

ACKNOWLEDGMENTS

This work was supported by National Institutes of Health grants AG00003 to the Medical College of Pennsylvania, HL16052 to Michigan State University, and RR00166, RR52177 and AG62145 to the University of Washington, and by a grant from the PMA Foundation. We thank Mrs. Linda Hurley, Ms. Ann Pollack and Mr. Randy Lipschutz for technical assistance, and Ms. Betty Floyd for secretarial assistance.

REFERENCES

1. Abdel-Latif, A. A., Yamaguchi, M., Smith, J., and Yamaguchi, T. (1968): Studies on the effect of ouabain on sodium and phosphate uptake into nerve ending of developing rat brain. *Life Sci.*, **7**: 1325–1338.

2. Akera, T. (1977): Membrane adenosine triphosphatase: a digitalis receptor? *Science*, 198: 569–574.
3. Akera, T. (1961): Quantitative aspects of the interaction between ouabain and the Na$^+$, K$^+$-ATPase. *Biochem. Biophys. Acta.*, 259: 53–62.
4. Akera, T., and Brody, T. M. (1976): Inotropic action of digitalis and ion transport. *Life Sci.*, 18: 135–142.
5. Akera, T., Larsen, F. S., and Brody, T. M. (1969): The effect of ouabain on sodium- and potassium-activated adenosine triphosphatase from the hearts of several mammalian species. *J. Pharmacol. Exp. Ther.*, 170: 17–26.
6. Akera, T., Tobin, T., Gatti, A., Shieh, J., and Brody, T. M. (1974): Effect of potassium on the conformational state of the complex of ouabain with sodium- and potassium-dependent adenosine triphosphatase. *Mol. Pharmacol.*, 10: 509–518.
7. Allen, J. C., and Schwartz, H. (1969): A possible biochemical explanation for the insensitivity of the rat to cardiac glycosides. *J. Pharmacol. Exp. Ther.*, 168: 42–46.
8. Baskin, S. I., Roberts, J., and de Sousa, B. N. (1977): Na$^+$, K$^+$-ATPase and age dependent digitalis toxicity. *Pharmacologist*, 19: 132.
9. Bircher, R. P., Kanai, T., and Wang, S. C. (1963): Mechanism of cardiac arrhythmias and blood pressure changes induced in dogs by pentylenetetrazol, picrotoxin and deslanoside. *J. Pharmacol. Exp. Ther.*, 141: 6–14.
10. Bonting, S. L., and Caravaggio, L. L. (1963): Studies on sodium-potassium activated adenosine triphosphatase. V. Correlation of enzyme activity with cation flux in six tissues. *Arch. Biochem.*, 101: 37–55.
11. Burch, G. E. (1973): The practice of cardiology today. *Amer. Heart J.*, 85: 291–293.
12. Cheraskin, E., and Ringsdorf, W. M. (1971): Younger at heart: a study of the P-R interval. *J. Amer. Geriatric Soc.*, 19: 271–275.
13. Gillis, R. A. (1971): Role of the nervous system in the arrhythmias produced by coronary occlusion in the cat. *Amer. Heart J.*, 81: 677–684.
14. Goldberg, P. B., and Roberts, J. (1976): Influence of age on the pharmacology and physiology of the cardiovascular system. In: *Special Review of Experimental Aging Research, Progress in Biology*, edited by M. F. Elias, B. F. Eleftherion and P. K. Elias, pp. 71–103. Bar Harbor; Experimental Aging Research.
15. Hansen, O., Jensen, J., and Norby, J. G. (1971): Mutual exclusion of ATP, ADP and g-strophantin binding to NaK-ATPase. *Nature New Biol.*, 234: 122–124.
16. Herrmann, G. R. (1966): Digitoxicity in the aged: recognition, frequency and management. *Geriatrics*, 21: 109.
17. Koch-Weser, J., and Blinks, J. R. (1963): The influence of the interval between beats on myocardial contractility. *Pharmacol. Rev.*, 15: 601–652.
18. Ku, D. D., Akera, T., Tobin, T., and Brody, T. M. (1976): Comparative species studies on the effect of monovalent cations and ouabain on cardiac Na$^+$, K$^+$-adenosine triphosphatase and contractile force. *J. Pharmacol. Exp. Ther.*, 197: 458–469.
19. Larsen, E. R., Van Dyke, R. A., and Chenowith, M. B. (1968): Mechanisms of narcosis. In: *Drugs Affecting the Central Nervous System, Vol. 2*, edited by A. Burger, pp. 1–24. New York: Marcel Dekker.
20. Lowry, O. H., Rosebrough, N. J., Farr, A. L., and Randall, R. J. (1951): Protein measurement with Folin phenol reagent. *J. Biol. Chem.*, 193: 265–275.
21. Marks, B. H., and Weissler, A. M., eds. (1972): *Basic and Clinical Pharmacology of Digitalis*, p. 328. Springfield, Ill.; Thomas.
22. Mason, D. T., and Braunwald, E. (1968): Digitalis and related preparation. In: *Cardiovascular Disorders*, edited by A. M. Brest and J. H. Moyer, pp. 383–397. Philadelphia. F. A. Davis Co.

23. Raisbeck, M. J. (1952): The use of digitalis in the aged. *Geriatrics*, **7**: 12–19.
24. Repke, K. R. H. (1963): Metabolism of cardiac glycosides. In: *New Aspects of Cardiac Glycosides, Vol. III*, edited by W. Wilbrandt, pp. 47–73. London; Pergamon Press.
25. Repke, K., Est, M., and Portius, H. J. (1965): Über die ursache der speciesunterschiede in der digitalisempfindlichkeit. *Biochem. Pharmacol.*, **14**: 1785–1802.
26. Roberts, J., and Kelliher, G. J. (1972): The mechanism of digitalis at the subcellular level. *Seminars in Drug Treatment*, **2**: 203–220.
27. Roberts, J., Kelliher, G. J., and Lathers, C. M. (1976): Role of adrenergic influences in digitalis-induced ventricular arrhythmia. *Life Sci.*, **18**: 665–678.
28. Saunders, B. A., and Jenkins, L. C. (1973): Cardiac arrhythmias of central nervous system origin: possible mechanism and suppression. *Canad. Anaesth. Soc. J.*, **20**: 617–628.
29. Schott, A. (1964): Observations of digitalis intoxication—a plea. *Postgrad. Med. J.*, **40**: 628–643.
30. Schwartz, A., Lindenmayer, G. E., and Allen, J. C. (1975): The sodium-potassium adenosine triphosphatase: pharmacological, physiological and biochemical aspects. *Pharmacol. Rev.*, **27**: 3–134.
31. Schwartz, A., Matsui, H., and Laughter, A. H. (1968): Tritiated digoxin binding to Na^+, K^+-activated adenosine-triphosphatase: Possible allosteric site. *Science*, **160**: 323–325.
32. Skou, J. C. (1975): The $(Na^+ + K^+)$ activated enzyme system and its relationship to transport of sodium and potassium. *Quart. Rev. Biophys.*, **7**: 401–434.
33. Sun, A. Y., and Samorajski, T. (1975): The effects of age and alcohol on $(Na^+ + K^+)$–ATPase activity of whole homogenate and synaptosomes prepared from mouse and human brain. *J. Neurochem.*, **24**: 161–164.
34. Tobin, T., and Brody, T. M. (1972): Rates of dissociation of enzyme-ouabain complexes and $K_{0.5}$ values in $(Na^+ + K^+)$ adenosine triphosphatase from different species. *Biochem. Pharmacol.*, **21**: 1553–1560.
35. Weaver, L. C., Akera, T., and Brody, T. M. (1976): Digoxin toxicity: primary sites of drug action on the sympathetic nervous system. *J. Pharmacol. Exp. Ther.*, **197**: 1–9.
36. Willems, J. L., Roelandt, J., DeGeest, H., Kesteloot, H., and Joossens, J. V. (1970): The left ventricular time in elderly subjects. *Circulation*, **42**: 37–42.

24

Pulmonary Function, Morphology and Morphometrics

E. S. Boatman, P. Arce, D. Luchtel, K. K. Pump, and C. J. Martin

Department of Environmental Health, University of Washington,
Seattle, Washington; and
Department of Respiratory Physiology,
Virginia Mason Research Center, Seattle, Washington

INTRODUCTION

Morphometric and structural changes in the aging lung have not been well documented in either man or nonhuman primate, although morphometric techniques have been widely used to obtain a variety of quantitative data from both normal and diseased lungs in man and in laboratory animals (1, 11, 26). This chapter describes lung structure and function in pigtail macaques (*Macaca nemestrina*) of three age groups. To compare these observations with those in man, one must bear in mind that the macaque's life span is one-third that of man, and that the macaque lung has 7 lobes instead of 5, i.e., upper, middle and lower on each side and an infracardiac lobe. Other differences in anatomy and development have been described elsewhere (4).

MATERIALS AND METHODS

Subjects were 12 female and 2 male pigtail macaques (*M. nemestrina*) aged 4 to 22 years. All were of the subspecies *M. n. nemestrina* except for 2 females of the subspecies *M. n. leonina*. The lungs were removed under general anesthesia within 5 min of cardiorespiratory arrest and inspected grossly for evidence of lung mites. The left lung was removed, weighed, and cannulated. The right upper lobe was used for pressure-volume and length-tension studies, the left upper and middle lobes for resin casting, and the left lower lobe for morphometry and microscopy. Because of the frequency of mite infestation whole lungs from additional animals in the younger age groups were obtained for the pressure volume studies.

Pressure-Volume Measurements

Following aspiration of gross secretions, the right upper lobe was degassed and its volume measured by water displacement. The main bronchus was connected to a Krogh spirometer and placed in a plethysmograph. Pressure within the plethysmograph was lowered relative to ambient pressure. The differential pressures between airway and plethysmograph were measured. A distending pressure of 30 cm H_2O cleared the lobe of atelectasis, after which the pressure was raised and lowered slowly (~1.5 ml/sec) to the same pressure for 3 inflations. The fourth inflation was compared with the fifth, in which filling and emptying were interrupted by a 15-sec pause 8 or more times. The minimum lobe volume after 2 min at zero transpulmonary pressure was recorded and the total volume again was measured by volume displacement. The pressure-volume data were discarded if the plethysmographic and displacement volumes differed by more than 10% (14).

Length-Tension Measurements

Subpleural slips of parenchyma (n = 4-8) were removed from each right upper lobe, reduced to 25 X 25 X 150 μm by microdissection and extended in a buffered saline bath at 37°C (32). The clamps holding the tissue were attached to force and length transducers mounted vertically above and below the bath. The output of the force and length transducers was fed into an XY plotter and recorded on magnetic tape. Two binocular dissecting microscopes with eyepiece graticules were mounted at right angles to one another and used to measure the tissue diameters. The maximum extensibility of the tissue ($\lambda m = L_{max}/L_0$) was calculated from the maximum tissue extension (L_{max}) defined as the vertical asymptote of the length-tension curve. Resting tissue length (L_0) was defined as the greatest tissue length that could be attained without force. The energy loss in length-tension cycling was measured as a hysteresis ratio (HR), i.e., the area within the length-tension loop divided by the total area beneath the extension curve. With progressive increase in tissue extension there is deformation of the length-force relationship (yield) and eventually the tissue breaks. Yield strain and force, and breaking strain and force, were determined from these curves.

Lung Corrosion Casting

Casts of the left upper lobes were prepared (36) using general purpose polyester resin or by infiltration with latex (28). In resin casts, penetration down the bronchial tree was stopped in the region of the alveolar ducts, whereas in latex casts the material was allowed to fill the alveoli. Tissue was removed from the casts by immersion in concentrated hydrochloric acid. Casts were trimmed under a dissecting microscope, and airway diameters, interbranch distances, and dissected acini were measured with a micrometer eyepiece.

Lung Fixation and Processing

Fixation was accomplished by bronchial instillation of 0.1 M sodium cacodylate buffered 1.5% glutaraldehyde (pH 7.4, osmolality 320 mOsm) maintained at a pressure of 20 cm H_2O with the lung (i.e., left lung) immersed in a beaker containing buffered fixative. After 18 to 20 hr fixation at 21°, the bronchus was clamped and the volume of the lung (V_L) was estimated by displacement.

The upper and middle lobes were removed for resin casting and the lower lobe was cut transversely into slices 5.0 mm thick. Slices were arranged in order, submerged in saline, and examined for evidence of lung mites (cavities) and signs of gross emphysematous changes.

Samples of glutaraldehyde-fixed lung for scanning electron microscopy (SEM) containing mostly central airways, peripheral airways, or parenchyma were dehydrated in alcohol and dried by the Freon "critical-point" method, mounted on metal stubs and coated with gold-palladium. In some instances, fragments of the distal portions of acini from resin casts were attached to stubs and observed after gold-palladium coating. Specimens were observed by a JEOL JSM35 scanning electron microscope.

Light Microscope Morphometry

For estimates of the volume density of nonparenchyma (V_{np}), glutaraldehyde-fixed 5.0-mm thick slices of left lower lobe superimposed by a plastic grid consisting of rows of points 2.0 mm apart (10) were observed under a dissecting microscope at 10X magnification and point "hits" falling on airways, blood vessels and parenchyma were counted using both sides of the tissue slice. The volume densities of various components of the parenchyma were determined from 1.0-μm resin sections stained with azure II-methylene blue using either photography or video-imaging. In the first method 3 1-μm stained sections from each left lower lobe were photographed (Zeiss Ultraphot II) at 35X magnification on 35 mm film taking 15 random fields/section. The films were analyzed on a multipurpose test screen (38) consisting of 84 lines and 168 test points for point and intersection counting. The second method used a television camera and monitor that had a built-in variable point counting grid (Quartz crystal dot-bar generator) consisting of points, horizontal lines or vertical lines. By either method, 500 point hits were counted from which we determined the relative volume densities of alveolar air space (V_{va}), septal tissue (V_{vt}) and alveolar ducts (V_{vad}). The surface density of air space (S_{va}) and the mean linear intercept (L_m) were estimated by intersection counts (35). Since the mean linear intercept measurements included both alveolar and duct air spaces, measurements of 20 individual alveolar profiles per tissue slice were made by direct projection and tracings. The alveolar density (NA_a) was calculated from the number of alveoli in 10 random fields of a standard area as determined on each film strip (10).

The total number of alveoli per lung (N_{AT}) was calculated by the formula of Weibel and Gomez (39) modified by Burri et al. (7):

$$N_{AT} = N_{va} \times V_{vp} \times V_L$$

where

$$N_{va} = \frac{1}{\beta} \frac{NA_a^{3/2}}{\sqrt{V_{va}}};$$

$$V_{vp} = 100 - V_{np};$$

and

$$\beta = 1.55.$$

The total air space of the left lung (S_a) was obtained by use of the surface density of air space (S_{va}) multiplied by the volume of lung parenchyma, i.e., S_a = lung volume (V_L) $\times$ percentage of lung parenchyma (V_{vp}).

Electron Microscope Morphometry

Three or 4 glutaraldehyde-fixed slices of lung were post-fixed in cacodylate buffered 1% osmium tetroxide, dehydrated and embedded in Epon 812. Ultrathin sections were cut from random blocks of tissue, mounted on 200 mesh carbon-coated grids and photographed in a random manner with a JEOL 100 S electron microscope (37). About 40 to 50 pictures were taken per left lower lobe on 35mm film at a magnification of 1,120X. Film positives were analyzed on the same multipurpose test screen (38) as for light microscopy, but at a final magnification of 10,500X. The parameter estimated was the arithmetic mean thickness of the air-blood barrier (38).

RESULTS

The dry-wet ratio of the pigtail macaque lung (0.189 ± 0.008) showed no significant change with age. Pressure volume studies showed, likewise, that the compliance of the filling curve, if one accepts the volume at 30 cm H_2O as total lung capacity (TLC), is 13.7 ± 2.6 ml per g of tissue with no age-related change. The minimum lung volume per g lung weight, or the lung volume at zero transpulmonary pressure per g lung weight, was 1.72 ± 0.53 ml. This increased with age ($r = 0.87$).

On the deflation curve, the transpulmonary pressure (P_{tp}) at 80 and 60% of TLC increased with age (Figure 24-1). At 80% TLC, the slope of the regression line as plotted is increased by including data from 3 right upper lobe preparations in which there were lung mites. Disregarding these data, there is nevertheless a significant increase in elastic recoil to 11 years at 80% TLC ($r = 0.81$). The regression equation (Ptp (80% TLC) = 4.8 + 0.23 age) shows the intercept and coefficient for age to be greater than that for the change in elastic recoil at 60% TLC (Ptp (60% TLC) = 1.99 + 0.13 age). The relation between age and transpulmonary pressure at 60% TLC ($r = 0.65$) and 40% TLC ($r = 0.58$) was not significant.

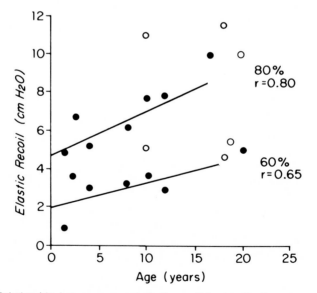

Fig. 24-1. Relationship between age and elastic recoil in the pigtail macaque at 80% and 60% TLC (volume at 30 cm H_2O). ● = right or left lungs; ○ = right upper lobes (mite infested).

Comparison of the length-tension properties (L-T) of mite-infested and non-infested lungs showed no significant difference in any tissue sampled 5 mm or more from sites of mite infestation in animals matched for age and sex. The L-T properties of *M.n. nemestrina* and *M.n. leonina* were also compared in matched (age and sex) animals, and no significant difference was found. Thus, for these measurements, the data for the two subspecies were pooled and the results of the mite-infested lungs were included.

The maximum extensibility of parenchymal walls ($\lambda_m = L_{max}/L_0$ was not significantly different from the extensibility at which yield occurred ($r = 0.90$); λ_m fell with age ($r = -0.56$) as did yield strain ($r = -0.55$). The slope of the regression of λ_m upon age is more marked than that in man (Figure 24-2). The data suggest a greater fall with age in the male than in the female macaque but the difference was not significant with the few male tissues available.

The energy loss in length-tension cycling (HR) did not change significantly with age ($r = 0.19$), nor did the breaking force of parenchymal walls ($r = -0.03$). No relation was found between the breaking strain of these tissues and age, nor were measures of Eulerian stress at specific extensions of the tissue related to age.

The gross anatomy of the left lungs showed substantial variation in respect to lobular demarcation. In one 4-y.o. monkey, the upper lobe included 3 incomplete intralobular fissures. Lung volume corresponded closely to body weight, chest dimensions and lung wet weight. The lung volume/wet weight ratio was fairly constant at 16.5 ± 1.7 ml/g in lungs filled with fixative at 20 cm

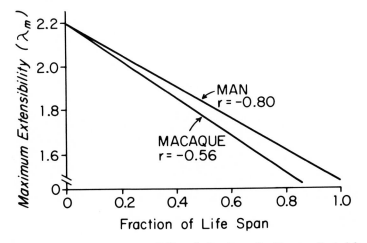

Fig. 24-2. Change in maximum extensibility of alveolar wall with age adjusted for maximum life span of the macaque (40 years) and man (115 years).

Table 24-1. Body Measurements and Gross Anatomy of the Left Lungs of Two Subspecies of *M. nemestrina* According to Age (mean ± standard deviation).

Age Group (yrs)	Sex	Number of Animals	Body Weight (kg)	Trunk Height (cm)	Left Lung Wet Weight (gm)	Left Lung Vol. (ml)	Animals With Abnormal Air Spaces Left Lung	Animals With Mite Cavities Left Lung
M.n. nemestrina								
4	F	3	4.6 ± 0.8	31.5 ± 0.2	9.0 ± 1.2	150 ± 20.0	None seen	None seen
10	F	5	6.9 ± 1.1	31.8 ± 2.2	13.0 ± 2.7	213 ± 42.6	2	
	M	1	15.9	39.0	28.2	465		4
20	F	2	6.9 ± 1.1	29.4 ± 0.2	13.8 ± 0.5	232 ± 10.6	1	
	M	1	12.2	36.6	20.2	333		2
M.n. leonina								
20	F	2	5.2 ± 0.4	27.1 ± 0.2	14.5 ± 0.1	237 ± 0.5	2	2

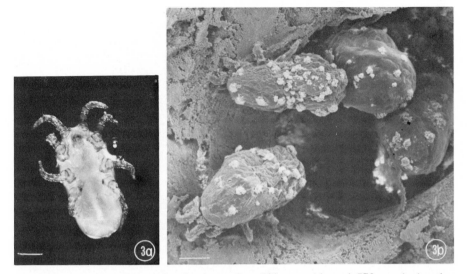

Fig. 24-3. a, light micrograph of a lung mite, 300 μm wide and 550 μm in length. Marker = 0.1 mm (81×). b, SEM showing lung mites in a burrowed out cavity of lung parenchyma. Granular appearance of the cavity surface is due to red blood cells which coat such lung surfaces. Marker = 0.1 mm (100×).

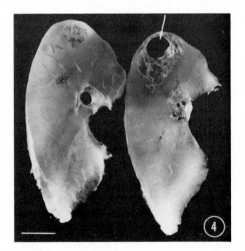

Fig. 24-4. Adjacent slices of distended (20 cm H$_2$O) and fixed lower lobe showing superficial (left) and severe (right) destruction of tissue by lung mites. Arrow shows large cavity about 7.5 mm dia. Marker = 10 mm (1.2×).

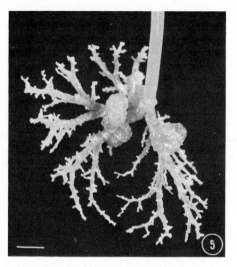

Fig. 24-5.   Portion of a resin bronchial cast of the left upper lobe showing negative profiles of 4 cavities arising from major bronchi of 2 and 3 mm in dia. Marker = 10 mm (1×).

H_2O, or slightly above that of air-filled lungs. In the 20-y.o. group, a significant decrease in trunk height was seen. The ratio of chest breadth to depth was relatively constant at about 0.9 for all 3 age groups. Data concerning these and other measurements are shown in Table 24-1.

Gross examination of 5.0-mm slices of lung for infestation and tissue destruction due to the mite *Pneumonyssus simicola* (Figure 24-3, 24-4) showed that 8 of 14 left lungs were infested. The amount of involvement ranged from 1 to 7% in the lower lobes, and 16 to 38% in the upper lobes; 8 of 11 lungs had evidence of mite infestation at the pleural surface. An idea of the size and location of these fibrotic cavities is shown in Figure 24-5.

Focal areas of enlarged air spaces resembling centrilobular emphysema were found in 5 of 14 animals; the extent of emphysema in the more affected upper

Table 24-2.   Data from Latex Casts of the Lingular Lobes of 3 Female
***M. n. nemestrina* from Different Age Groups.**

Age Group (years)	4	10	20
Length of axial bronchus of lingular lobe	1.4 cm	4.2 cm	5.0 cm
Number of generations	35	26	30
Number of branches on acinus	155	172	119
Number of alveoli/acinus	5778	4586	4103
Average size of alveoli (diameter)	132 μm	183 μm	179 μm
Number of acini/cm^3 (calculated)	36.3 × 10^3	32.7 × 10^3	39.0 × 10^3

Fig. 24-6. Portion of resin bronchial cast distal to a small bronchus. Part of the central airway and many lateral branches show small protuberances (all or some of which may be alveoli) over the airway surface (arrows). Profiles of muscle bundles or elastic tissue spiral around the airways (lines). Alveolar ducts (d) arise from branches of the central respiratory bronchiole of about 0.7 mm dia. Marker = 1 mm (10X).

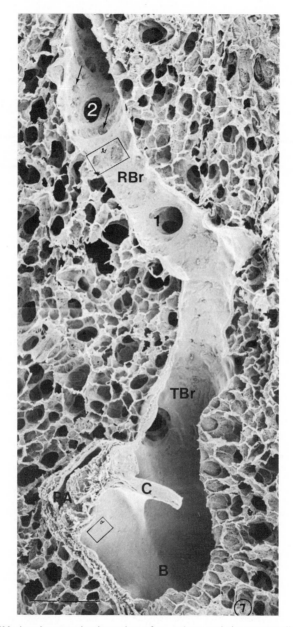

Fig. 24-7.   SEM showing proximal portion of an acinus and the surrounding alveoli. B = bronchus; C = cartilage; PA = pulmonary artery accompanying the bronchus; TBr = terminal bronchiole; RBr = respiratory bronchiole. Arrows show alveoli at the lumen surface, and 2 respiratory bronchioles or, perhaps, alveolar ducts (1 and 2) branch from the airway. The squares in the airway indicate two areas further magnified in Fig. 24-8.   * = junction of terminal bronchiole with respiratory bronchiolar portion. Marker = 1 mm (30X).

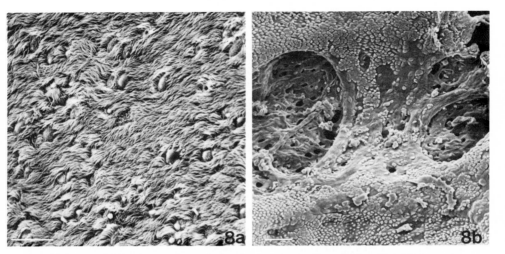

Fig. 24-8. A, SEM of a portion of bronchial surface, enlarged from Fig. 24-7, square "a." Dome-shaped nonciliated cells (Clara cells) are interspersed among the ciliated cells. Marker = 20 μm (800X). B, SEM of the respiratory bronchiolar area (Fig. 24-7, square "b"). Clara cells are the predominant cell type at the airway surface. The two circular areas are alveoli extending from the surface of the bronchiole. Marker = 50 μm (200X).

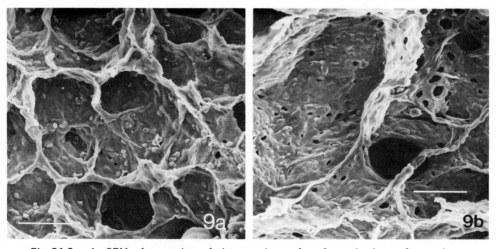

Fig. 24-9. A, SEM of a portion of the saccular surface from the lung of a newborn macaque. The majority of the saccules do not have pores of Kohn. Marker = 50 μm (400X). B, SEM of a portion of the alveolar surface from the lung of a 20-y.o. macaque. Almost every alveolus shows many pores of Kohn of various diameters. Marker = 50 μm (400X).

lobes was 18 to 39%. The 4-y.o. macaques, which were all raised in captivity, showed neither mite involvement nor enlarged air spaces in the left lung.

Limited data from casts of latex-filled lingular lobes of 3 pigtail macaques matched for subspecies, sex, and body weight at maturity are shown in Table 24-2. Age-related differences were found in the length of the axial bronchi, the size of the acini and in the size and number of alveoli per acinus. In some areas of acini, profuse branchings of alveolar ducts closely aligned in the limited space arose directly from the sides of respiratory bronchioles.

The alveoli of all 3 lungs showed no departure from the norm in contour, variations in size and their proximity to each other. Terminal bronchioles were very short and difficult to identify, but always showed dichotomous division. Acini showed up to 5 generations of respiratory bronchioles. The alveoli in the latex casts were remarkably even in size and in distribution over the surfaces of bronchioles, alveolar ducts and sacs. Figure 24-6 shows a portion of a resin cast distal to a small bronchus, illustrating small protuberances (all or some of which may be alveoli) distributed over the surfaces of the airways in a manner similar to that seen in latex casts. Cast profiles of what were probably muscle bundles or elastic tissue were also seen spiralling around the airways.

A scanning electron micrograph of the proximal portion of an acinus and the surrounding alveoli in a 20-y.o. macaque is shown in Figure 24-7. This portion was 7 mm long before dehydration and drying. The terminal bronchiole (TBr) is 0.7 mm in diameter and 3.2 mm long. It extends from a small bronchus and ends where the respiratory bronchiolar portion starts at about the point indi-

Table 24-3. Morphometric Measurements by Light Microscopy of the Left Lungs of Two Subspecies of *M. nemestrina* According to Age. V_{va} = volume density of alveolar air-space; V_{vt} = volume density of alveolar tissue; V_{ad} = volume density of alveolar duct air-space (mean ± standard deviation).

Age Group (yrs)	Sex	Number of Animals	% Non-Parenchyma	$V_{va}\%$	$V_{vt}\%$	$V_{vad}\%$
			M. n. nemestrina			
4	F	3	9.3 ± 1.3	57 ± 1.0	10.0 ± 0.6	33 ± 1.2
10	F	5	10.0 ± 1.7	48 ± 2.9	9.5 ± 0.9	42 ± 3.3
	M	1				
20	F	2	10.0 ± 1.5	46 ± 1.9	9.7 ± 1.4	43 ± 2.6
	M	1				
			M. n. leonina			
20	F	2	11.7 ± 2.5	35.5 ± 1.1	9.8 ± 0.2	54.7 ± 1.0

Table 24-4. Morphometric Measurements of the Left Lungs of Two Subspecies of *M. nemestrina* According to Age. L_M = mean linear intercept; $\bar{\tau}$ = arithmetic thickness of air-blood barrier; N_a = number of alveoli; N_{AT} = absolute number of alveoli for left and right lung (calculated) (mean ± standard deviation).

Age Group (yrs)	Sex	Number of Animals	L_M (μm)	Alv. Size (μm)	$\bar{\tau}$ (μm)	N_a cm³ × 10⁻⁵	N_{AT} × 10⁻⁶
M. n. nemestrina							
4	F	3	191 ± 8.9	180 ± 3.4	1.94 ± 0.25	2.1 ± 0.09	71 ± 8.1
10	F	5	224 ± 11.8	202 ± 4.3	1.67 ± 0.10	1.5 ± 0.18	73 ± 17.4
	M	1					154
20	F	2	215 ± 7.0	206 ± 4.8	1.25 ± 0.7	1.6 ± 0.18	85 ± 7.0
	M	1					125
M. n. leonina							
20	F	2	230 ± 2.4	206.7 ± 3.5	1.36 ± 0.1	1.9 ± 0.1	76 ± 0.1

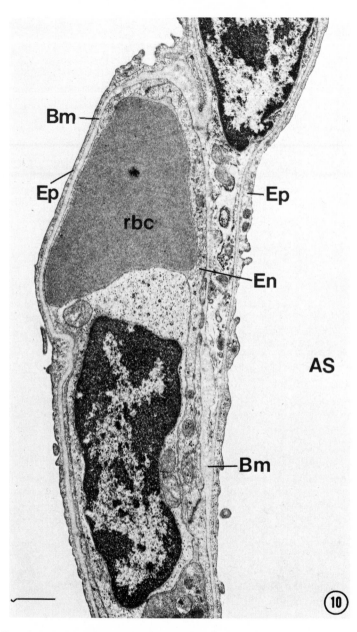

Fig. 24-10.   An electron micrograph of a portion of an alveolar wall from the left lobe of a 10-y.o. monkey showing normal ultrastructure. Ep = surface epithelium, En = capillary endothelium, Bm = basement membrane, rbc = red blood cell, AS = air space. Marker = 1 μm (15,120×).

cated by the asterisk. The beginning of the TBr contains large numbers of ciliated cells and secreting (Clara) cells (Figure 24-8a). Figure 24-8b shows 2 alveoli in the respiratory region surrounded by cuboidal cells. Parenchyma from the lung of a newborn obtained from another study and a 20-y.o. macaque were compared in respect to the numbers of pores present/alveolar profile and their size range. The younger animal had fewer and smaller pores (Figure 24-9).

Light and electron microscopic morphometry showed that the percentage of nonparenchymous tissue was approximately the same for animals in all 3 age groups (Table 24-3). Estimates of the volume densities of various components of parenchymous tissue for the left lower lobes of the 3 groups are also shown. The volume density of alveolar air space is significantly decreased in the 10- and 20-y.o. animals compared with that in the 4-y.o. macaques. The volume density of alveolar tissue did not differ according to age, whereas that of alveolar ducts increased significantly.

Further morphometric parameters of the left lower lobes are shown in Table 24-4. Both the mean linear intercept and alveolar size, measured individually by direct measurement of profiles, increased in the 10- and 20-y.o. groups compared with the 4-y.o. group. The mean width of the air-blood barrier was significantly and progressively reduced as the age of the animals increased. The mean number of alveoli/cm^3 was lower in the 10- and 20-y.o.'s than the 4-y.o.'s. The total number of alveoli was the same for females of all ages. Because of a marked difference in body size and lung volume, males had nearly twice as many total alveoli as females.

A comparison of the ultrastructure of random alveolar septa from the lungs of monkeys of different ages revealed no marked differences that could be attributed to age alone. An electron micrograph of a portion of an alveolar wall showing ultrastructure typical of this tissue is shown in Figure 24-10. Small amounts of collagen and elastic tissue are invariably present on one side or the other of the capillary space. In appropriate sections, alveolar macrophages and type II cells are attached to the alveolar wall.

DISCUSSION

The objectives and limitations of the overall study in respect to the sample size should be borne in mind in assessing these data. Although some observations may be statistically inappropriate, the data may serve as a basis of comparison for later studies. Furthermore, an age of 20 years is by no means an indication of senescence in a species whose life span is in the 30s.

A problem, particularly in the functional studies, was the use of lungs infested by mites (*P. simicola*). Monkey lungs are commonly infested with parasites and those of the macaques are no exception; 57% of the animals in the present study were affected. Blood counts and hemoglobin estimations were not abnormal for infested monkeys in spite of the fact that both immature and mature mites are believed to utilize hemoglobin and parenchymal tissue for growth and maturation. Previous studies have shown 100% incidence of infestation (12) except for laboratory reared animals removed from their mothers at birth (20). The pathology of the pulmonary lesions due to mites has been well documented (21, 31); we, too, found both pleural and bronchial lesions, with the latter predominantly in large airways. Because the walls of these cavities are fibrotic, only 3 mite-infested lungs, as noted in Figure 24-1, were included in the pressure-volume studies. In these, the infested upper lobes showed greater elastic recoil than expected (Figure 24-1).

Pressure-volume calculations were compiled on whole lungs of 1.5- to 20-y.o. animals. The mean ratio of total lung volume to body weight for 12 macaques of different ages was 64 ml/kg. In man, the total lung volume to body weight ratio is 63 ml/kg (25).

The maximum lung volume increased slightly with age. As in man (14), the gas volume of the lung increased as tissue weight increased. The relatively constant maximum lung volume per unit of lung weight suggests that the maximum length of the parenchymal tissue changes little with age. The maximum extensibility of the tissue, however, falls with age (Figure 24-2), indicating a progressive increase in resting tissue length (L_0). This change in L_0 predicts the increase in minimum lung volume and the increase in mean linear intercept measured in these animals. It also suggests a loss of elastic recoil will occur over this age span.

The maximum extensibility of lung parenchyma (λ_m) and the strain at which "yield" occurs in the macaque are similar to those in man. In both species, λ_m falls with age (Figure 24-2) although the relationship is better in man (r = -0.80) than in the macaque (r = -0.56). The slope of the change in λ_m with age is steeper in the macaque. When adjusted for the differences in life expectancy, however, the regression equations in man (λ_m = 2.19-0.72 (age/115)) and the macaque (λ_m = 2.2-0.84 (age/40)) have similar slopes and intercepts. While the intercept and slope of λ_m with age are greater in the male than in the female human, this could not be confirmed in the macaque because of the few males available. The intercept did not appear to be different, but the slope of λ_m may be more rapid in the male.

Elastic recoil in the macaque increases to at least age 12. That this occurs in spite of the increase of L_0 must mean that there is an increase in the number of elastic elements. Lung weight increases as does the nonparenchymal tissue and the absolute number of alveoli (Table 24-4). The increase in number of elastic elements exceeds the effect of the progressive change in L_0. In man, lung growth continues to at least age 12, during which time elastic recoil increases

(24, 30). Beyond 12 years, these data are insufficient to determine whether or at what point senescence occurs in the macaque. Man, in later years, shows a fall in lung elastic recoil when lung weight is presumably stable (3), but there is a progressive increase in L_0 (22).

In man, the viscoelastic properties of lung parenchymal tissue change with age, i.e., the energy loss with length-tension cycling or hysteresis ratio (HR) increases. In the macaque no relation between HR and age ($r = 0.19$) was found. Mean values for HR, however, were similar to that seen in man. This finding is in sharp contrast to the change in hysteresis with age in the rat and rabbit, whose energy loss in HR decreases significantly over their short life span (22).

As in man and horse (22), macaque lung parenchymal walls reduced to the same dimensions do not show a relation between breaking force and age ($r = -0.03$). The male rat and female rabbit do show an increase in the breaking force of lung parenchymal walls, and in other tissues such as the skin. Tissue integrity must be largely a function of collagen, which would suggest that the amount of collagen, its cross-linkage and its organization within the tissue do not change appreciably with age in man, macaque and horse.

Resin casts of normal human bronchial trees have revealed both symmetric and asymmetric branching patterns; whereas branching distal to airways of 0.7 mm dia. down to the respiratory bronchioles occurred by symmetric dichotomy, alveolar ducts branched in an asymmetric dichotomous fashion (17, 18, 27). The distal respiratory bronchioles (order 1) were taken to be those branches about 0.40 mm in dia. and 0.48 mm long. Staub (29) considered the terminal bronchioles in the human to be 0.5 mm in dia. at 75% TLC and the respiratory bronchioles to measure about 0.4 mm in dia. with 4 orders. Hilsop *et al.* (16) measured terminal bronchioles in lungs from humans ranging from 1 to 18 y.o., and although the lengths of the terminal bronchioles varied widely from 0.3 to 1.1 mm over this age span, the diameter of the bronchioles progressively increased from 0.3 to 0.7 mm. In our study the average terminal bronchiole (i.e., the last bronchiole without alveoli) in a 10-y.o. pigtail macaque was 0.7 mm in dia. and 3.0 mm in total length, and the respiratory bronchiole was 0.5 mm in dia. and 10.0 mm in total length. Although the terminal bronchiole in the macaque is reported to be shorter than in man (9), the length of the respiratory bronchiole with 3 to 5 orders, as measured in latex casts, is comparable. Overall, apart from the 2 additional lobes in the macaque lung, and bearing in mind the errors inherent in preparing and measuring the casts and in deciding the beginning and end of a particular branch, the monkey lung is similar to that of the human in respect to the size of the respiratory unit. The precise location of a terminal bronchiole, respiratory bronchiole, or alveolar duct can be settled only from reconstructions of histologic sections.

Measurements derived from negative resin casts of the lung can be, to some extent, supplemented by measurements from lung slices with which we have to deal and an interpretation of where one species of distal airway begins and ends is not easy. On one hand, in the development of the monkey lung, like that of man, canalization of the bronchopulmonary segments begins simultaneously at the peripheral portion of each segment that is destined to be an alveolar duct and progresses centralwards (5). On the other hand, the presence in the adult monkey of pseudorespiratory bronchioles which are lined on one side by pseudostratified ciliated epithelium and on the other by squamous epithelium represents a marked departure from the human lung (6).

Castleman *et al.* (9) studied 3 species of macaque and concluded that there is a general similarity in the mucosal structure of bronchi and respiratory bronchioles of monkey and man, but there are specific differences in the number of generations and types of epithelial lining of the terminal bronchioles. Our findings support this statement. Furthermore, in respect to the species of macaque, the morphology of the terminal bronchioles of *M. nemestrina* (Figure 24-6, 7) would fit more closely with that of *M. mulatta* and *M. arctoides* than that of *M. radiata*. The number of generations and the dimensions of branches, both diameter and length, before the alveolus is reached vary markedly according to the space available (Figure 24-6). During the growth of the lung, not only do alveoli increase in size and number, but elongation and distortion of existing airways occur in the competition for space.

As in the human, the pores of Kohn are evident in the alveoli of the monkey lung. As might be expected, they are less numerous in newborn lungs than in adult lungs. Martin (23) estimated the number and size of the pores in the lungs of dogs from 3 days to 10 years old. At 3 days pores were absent, but during the first year of life they increased in number to an average of 10 per alveolus and then remained steady thereafter. The size of the pores (av. 4.5 μm) did not increase after the first year. Preliminary studies suggest this may also be true for *M. nemestrina*. A more comprehensive study of the pores of Kohn in this species is currently underway.

In the human, lung volume doubles between 8 and 25 years, while the number of alveoli remains constant ($\sim$290 $\times$ 10^6) and alveolar linear dimensions increase from 230 μm to 280 μm, or 26% (10). In the macaque, a 15% increase in linear dimensions occurs between 4 and 20 years. Extrapolation at the same rate of change to the newborn would give a 25% increase in linear dimension, similar to that of man. The number of alveoli/cm^3 declines with age in the macaque (Table 24-4) and in man (34).

Measurement of alveolar diameter is subject to considerable error because of the varied planes of section and the methods used. We compared 3 methods: measurement from latex casts (Table 24-2), from mean linear intercept (histologic section), and by projection and measurement of alveolar profiles (Table

24-4).   By the latex method alveolar diameters are underestimated due to shrinkage, while by the linear intercept method they are overestimated due to inclusion of some alveolar duct space.   Direct measurement, however, gave a mean of 204 μm for the adult macaque in lung near TLC.   Smaller alveoli may accompany higher metabolic rates (33) making the energy needs of the macaque greater per unit weight than in man.

In aging man, alveolar tissue diminishes by 21% between 60 and 90 years of age (19).   Part of this loss is due to a reduction in the thickness of the alveolar wall (15).   In the monkey the dimensions of the air-blood barrier progressively decreased 35%, from 1.95 μm to 1.25 μm (Table 24-4).   This may have been due to a progressive dilatation of the alveoli from 180 μm to 206 μm, a phenomenon also seen in man (34).   For the human lung, Cassan *et al.* (8) have found the arithmetic thickness of the air-blood barrier in biopsy material to be 1.66 μm.   Weibel found 1.30 μm for the human (37) and 1.64 μm for the rhesus macaque (40).   For our group of 10-y.o. pigtail macaques we obtained a mean of 1.67 μm. The dimensions of the air-blood barrier also vary according to the degree of inflation during fixation (13).   Thus, in most respects, including the fine structural aspects, the alveoli of man and monkey seem to be comparable.

ACKNOWLEDGMENTS

This study was supported by National Institutes of Health grants RR00166, RR52177, AG62145 and ES01049 to the University of Washington.

REFERENCES

1. Bignon, J., Khoury, F., Even, P., Andre, J., and Brouet, G.   (1969): Morphometric study in chronic obstructive broncho-pulmonary disease. *Amer. Rev. Resp. Dis.*, **99**: 669-695.
2. Boatman, E. S., and Lowe, D.   (1971): Photographic mapping of a tissue surface to locate fields for electron microscopy: mouse lung. *Stain Technol.*, **46**: 63-69.
3. Bode, F. R., Dosman, J., Martin, R. R., Bluzzo, H., and Macklem, P. T. (1976): Age and sex differences in lung elasticity and in closing capacity in nonsmokers. *J. Appl. Physiol.*, **41**: 129-135.
4. Boyden, E. A.   (1975): Development of the human lung. In: *Brennemann's Practice of Pediatrics, vol. IV.*, Chap. 64. Hagerstown, Maryland; W. F. Prior Co.
5. Boyden, E. A.   (1976): The programming of canalization in fetal lungs of man and monkey. *Amer. J. Anat.*, **145**: 125-126.
6. Boyden, E. A.   (1976): The development of the lung in the pig-tail monkey (*Macaca nemestrina, L.*). *Anat. Rec.*, **186**: 15-38.
7. Burri, P. H., Dbaly, J., and Weibel, E. R.   (1974): The postnatal growth of the rat lung. 1. Morphometry. *Anat. Rec.*, **178**: 711-730.
8. Cassan, S. M., Divertie, M. B., and Brown, A. L.   (1974): Fine structural morphometry on biopsy specimens of human lung. 1. Normal lung. *Chest*, **65**: 269-274.

9. Castleman, W. L., Dungworth, D. L., and Tyler, W. S. (1975): Intrapulmonary airway morphology in three species of monkeys: a correlated scanning and transmission electron microscopic study. *Amer. J. Anat.*, **142**: 107–122.

10. Dunnill, M. (1962): Quantitative methods in the study of pulmonary pathology. *Thorax*, **17**: 320–328.

11. Dunnill, M. (1975): Quantitative assessment of chronic non-specific lung disease at necropsy. Report by M.R.C. committee on research into chronic bronchitis, April 1972. *Thorax*, **30**: 241–251.

12. Finegold, M. J., Seaquist, M. E., and Doherty, M. J. (1968): Treatment of pulmonary acariasis in rhesus monkeys with an organic phosphate. *Lab. Anim. Care*, **18**: 27–30.

13. Forrest, J. B. (1976): Lung tissue plasticity: morphometric analysis of anisotropic strain in liquid filled lungs. *Resp. Physiol.*, **27**: 223–239.

14. Frank, R., Brain, J. D., and Yokohama, E. (1973): Compression atelectasis: a method for unilateral ventilation of the lung. *J. Appl. Physiol.*, **34**: 704–707.

15. Freeman, E. (1973): In: *Textbook of Geriatric Medicine and Gerontology*, edited by J. C. Brocklehurst, p. 405. Edinburgh, Churchill, Livingstone.

16. Hilsop, A., Muir, D. C. F., Jacobsen, M., Simon, G., and Reid, L. (1972): Postnatal growth and function of the pre-acinar airways. *Thorax*, **27**: 265–274.

17. Horsfield, K., and Cumming, G. (1967): Angles of branching and diameters of branches in the human bronchial tree. *Bull. Math. Biophys.*, **29**: 245–259.

18. Horsfield, K., Dart, G., Olson, D., Filley, G. F., and Cumming, G. (1971): Models of the human bronchial tree. *J. Appl. Physiol.*, **31**: 207–217.

19. Howell, T. H. (1970): *A Students Guide to Geriatrics.* London; Staples Press.

20. Innes, J. R. M. (1969): In: *Using Primates in Medical Research, Vol. 2*, edited by W. I. B. Beveridge, p. 36. New York; S. Karger.

21. Innes, J. R. M., Colton, M. W., Yerich, P. P., and Smith, C. L. (1954): Pulmonary acariasis as an enzootic disease caused by *Pneumoyssus simicola* in imported monkeys. *Amer. J. Pathol.*, **30**: 813–835.

22. Martin, C. J., Chihara, S., and Chang, D. B. (1977): A comparative study of the mechanical properties in aging alveolar wall. *Amer. Rev. Resp. Dis.*, **115**: 981–988.

23. Martin, H. B. (1963): The effect of aging on the alveolar pores of Kohn in the dog. *Amer. Rev. Resp. Dis.*, **88**: 773–778.

24. Murray, J. F. (1976): *The Normal Lung*, pp. 334. Philadelphia; W. B. Saunders.

25. Nelson, N. M. (1966): Neonatal pulmonary function. *Ped. Clin. N. Amer.*, **13**: 769–799.

26. Niewoehner, D., and Kleinerman, J. (1973): Effects of experimental emphysema and bronchiolitis on lung mechanics and morphometry. *J. Appl. Physiol.*, **35**: 25–31.

27. Parker, H., Horsfield, K., and Cumming, G. (1971): Morphology of distal airways in the human lung. *J. Appl. Physiol.*, **31**: 386–391.

28. Pump, K. K. (1969): Morphology of the acinus of the human lung. *Dis. Chest*, **56**: 126–133.

29. Staub, N. C. (1963): The interdependence of pulmonary structure and function. *Anesthesiology*, **24**: 831–854.

30. Stigol, L. C., Vawter, G. F., and Mead, J. (1972): Studies on Elastic recoil of the lung in a pediatric population. *Amer. Rev. Resp. Dis.*, **105**: 552–563.

31. Stone, W. B., and Hughes, J. A. (1969): Massive pulmonary acariasis in the pig-tail macaque. *Bull. Wildlife Dis. Ass.*, **5**: 20–22.

32. Sugihara, T., Martin, C. J., and Hilderbrandt, J. (1971): Length tension properties of alveolar wall in man. *J. Appl. Physiol.*, **30**: 874–878.

33. Tenney, S. M., and Remmers, J. E. (1963): Comparative quantitative morphology of the mammalian lung: diffusing area. *Nature*, **197**: 54–56.
34. Thurlbeck, W. M. (1975): Postnatal growth and development of the lung. *Amer. Rev. Resp. Dis.*, **111**: 803–844.
35. Tomkeieff, S. I. (1945): Linear intercepts, areas and volumes. *Nature*, **155**: 24.
36. Tompsett, D. H. (1970): *Anatomical Techniques*, 2nd edition, p. 123. Edinburgh; Livingstone.
37. Weibel, E. R. (1963): *Morphometry of the Human Lung*. New York; Academic Press.
38. Weibel, E. R. (1970): Morphometric estimation of pulmonary diffusion capacity. 1. Model and method. *Resp. Physiol.*, **11**: 54–75.
39. Weibel, E. R., and Gomez, D. M. (1962): A principle for counting tissue structures on random sections. *J. Appl. Physiol.*, **17**: 343–348.
40. Weibel, E. R., Lewerenz, M., and Kaplan, H. P. (1968): Electron microscopic and morphometric study of rat, monkey and dog lungs exposed to 68% O_2 and 32% N_2 at 258 Torr for eight months. *U.S.A.F. Aerospace Med. Res. Lab.*, **68**: 189–212.

25

Pulmonary Extravascular Albumin

Bryan E. Marshall, Ralph T. Geer, Lisa A. Litvin, and
Gordon R. Neufeld

Department of Anesthesia, University of Pennsylvania School of Medicine,
Philadelphia, Pennsylvania

INTRODUCTION

The factors governing transcapillary fluid exchange and lymph flow were clearly recognized by Starling (5) in 1896. The movement of water between the vascular and extravascular space in the normal lung is primarily dependent on the balance between the hydrostatic and protein (principally albumin) oncotic pressures in both the pulmonary capillary plasma and the interstitial tissue space. The normal lung does not show gross evidence of pulmonary edema until, for example, the capillary hydrostatic pressure is substantially increased. This physiologic safety factor used to be regarded as dependent solely on the opposing plasma oncotic pressure. More recent studies suggesting negative interstitial hydrostatic pressures, differentially permeable capillary endothelium, and variable lymph flow have provided several additional hypothetical explanations for this safety factor (2, 6).

Central to the resolution of these controversies is the assignment of a value for the pulmonary interstitial oncotic pressure. Precise measurement of pulmonary extravascular albumin in health and during the course of edema would provide an appropriate index by which to test some of these hypotheses. The best estimates currently available are based on analysis of lymph, which seems certain to provide an underestimate (6).

There have been no definitive studies comparing the magnitude of the safety factor for edema in the lungs of animals of different ages. A systematic change in the extravascular albumin with age in adults would suggest that the safety factor is altered. The purpose of this study was, therefore, to calculate the quantity of extravascular albumin in nonhuman primate lungs and to examine the influence of age.

METHODS

Subjects were 16 pigtail macaques (*M. nemestrina*), 3 4-y.o., 8 10-y.o. and 5 20-y.o., whose history and care are described in Chapter 3 of this volume. The animals were anesthetized, 5-ml samples of whole blood were obtained and the plasma was anticoagulated with EDTA. Then the thorax was opened, the trachea was clamped, and the lungs were removed within 5 min after death. Slices of lung tissue from different regions of one lung (mean sample weight 2.20 g) were removed and placed in a tightly closed container. Lung and plasma samples were shipped in dry ice, and whole blood at ambient temperature.

Upon arrival (usually within 24 hr), the lung specimen was weighed. Distilled water (10 ml) was added, the mixture was homogenized (Willems Polytron) for 15 min with a jacket of iced water to prevent heating, and was kept overnight at 4°C. The following day, aliquots were prepared as follows:

Half the homogenate was removed and weighed. It was frozen in vials immersed in an alcohol/solid carbon dioxide mixture, freeze-dried under vacuum (Virtis Freeze Dryer), and reweighed. The fractional water content of the homogenate was thereby determined. The remainder of the homogenate was centrifuged at 30,000 g for 60 min (International B-20 centrifuge). A thin layer of lipid at the surface was removed and the supernatant decanted and divided for analysis. A weighed, precise volume (2 ml) was freeze-dried and reweighed to determine its fractional water content. Duplicate 1-ml volumes were mixed with Drabkins solution, and the hemoglobin concentration determined spectrophotometrically. Duplicate samples of supernatant were analyzed for total protein concentration spectrophotometrically by the biuret reaction. The fraction of albumin in the supernatant proteins was measured by standard electrophoretic separation in cellulose acetate plates. The bands were stained with Ponceau-S, and the relative concentrations determined by densitometric scanning and recording. The fraction was adjusted for the optical density of the albumin band. The sodium (Na^+) and potassium (K^+) concentrations in the supernatant were measured by flame photometry.

Samples of blood and plasma were analyzed as follows: The fractional water contents were calculated by weighing, freeze-drying, and reweighing 2-ml aliquots of plasma and whole blood. Whole blood hematocrit was measured in triplicate (microhematocrit). Whole blood hemoglobin concentration was measured spectrophotometrically using Drabkins solution. Plasma total proteins were measured spectrophotometrically by the biuret technique. The albumin fraction of the plasma protein was measured by cellulose acetate electrophoresis. The sodium and potassium concentrations in plasma and lysed, whole blood were measured by flame photometry.

CALCULATIONS

The following symbols are used in the equations below.

$$L_w = \text{lung sample weight (g)}$$
$$S_{Hb} \text{ and } B_{Hb} = \text{supernatant and whole blood hemoglobin (g/ml)}$$
$$S_{fw} \text{ and } B_{fw} = \text{supernatant and whole blood fractional water content (ml/ml)}$$
$$H_{fw} = \text{homogenate water fraction (ml/g)}$$
$$B_{Ht} = \text{hematocrit of whole blood}$$
$$P_A \text{ and } S_A = \text{plasma and supernatant albumin concentration (mg/ml)}$$
$$0.76 = \text{ratio of large vessel hematocrit to lung hematocrit}$$
$$0.41 = \text{fractional interstitial volume of extravascular space}$$

Lung Blood Volume (LBV): $\dfrac{(L_w + 10)\, S_{Hb}}{S_{fw} \times B_{Hb} \times 0.76}$

Extravascular Lung Water Volume (ELWV): $H_{fw}(L_w + 10) - (LBV \times B_{fw}) - 10$

Extravascular Lung Albumin (ELA):

$$(S_A \times H_{fw})(L_w + 10) - [LBV \times P_A(1 - [B_{Ht} \times 0.76])]$$

Interstitial Albumin Concentration: $\dfrac{ELA}{0.41(ELWV)}$

For purposes of comparison, the absolute measurements were normalized, so that the lung blood volume is expressed per 100 g of wet lung; the lung water volume per g of dry, blood-free lung and per g of wet, blood-free lung; and the extravascular albumin per g dry, bloodless lung.

Differences of the results between age groups were tested by Student's t-tests for unpaired data and by linear regression analysis with significance identified for P values less than 0.05.

RESULTS

The means and standard errors of the essential data are presented in Table 25-1. The first two lines of data were calculated from the combined data of Boatman et al. (Chapter 24, this volume) and those presented here.

Table 25-1. Lung Blood, Water, and Albumin Contents (mean ± SE).

Age (Years)	4	10	20
N	3	5	4
Left Lung Wet Weight (g/kg body weight)	1.72** ±.07	1.70* ±.09	2.63 ±.31
Left Lung Dry Weight (g/kg body weight)	0.38** ±.04	0.42* ±.05	0.65 ±.09
N	3	8	5
Total Lung Water Volume (ml/g total dry lung)	4.64 ±.44	4.28 ±.25	3.93 ±.13
Total Lung Albumin (mg/g total dry lung)	69.8 ±10.3	67.2 ±3.7	57.1 ±4.7
Lung Blood Volume (ml/100 g)	25.07** ±1.25	20.09 ±1.92	15.56 ±1.26
Hematocrit (large vessel) (%)	34.9 ±0.6	36.6 ±2.1	38.3 ±1.2
Plasma Albumin (mg/ml)	32.7 ±0.7	34.0 ±1.3	33.2 ±2.4
Extravascular Lung Water Volume (ml/g dry bloodless lung)	4.38 ±.54	4.04 ±.26	3.80 ±.17
Extravascular Albumin (mg/g dry bloodless lung)	51.4 ±6.7	52.3 ±5.3	44.0 ±3.1
Interstitial Albumin (mg/ml)	25.2 ±7.4	32.3 ±3.8	28.3 ±1.8
Interstitial/Plasma Albumin Ratio	0.78 ±0.23	0.96 ±0.13	0.86 ±0.04
Extravascular Na^+/K^+	±1.69 ±0.12	1.68 ±0.10	1.70 ±0.13

Difference between mean significant at 0.05 level from unpaired Student's t-test is indicated by: *10 vs. 20 and **4 vs. 20.

Left lung wet weight (g/kg body weight) increased significantly with age (left lung wet weight = 0.064 age + 1.3; r = 0.73). However, the left lung dry weight (g/kg body weight) also increased continuously with age (left lung dry weight = 0.079 age + 0.28; r = 0.73) to such an extent that total lung water volume (ml/g total dry lung) tended to decrease continuously with age (Figure 25-1). The observations that total lung albumin (mg/g total dry lung) tended to decrease with age (Figure 25-2) and that lung blood volume (ml/100 g lung) decreased significantly with age (lung blood volume = 26.2–0.55 age; r = −0.63) (Figure 25-3) suggested that the increased dry weight was due to changes in the lung

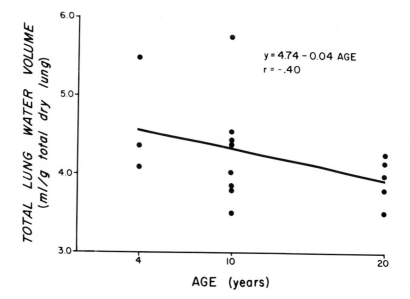

Fig. 25-1.   Relation of age and total lung water volume (mg/g total dry lung).

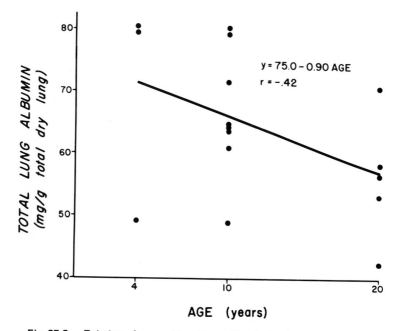

Fig. 25-2.   Relation of age and total lung albumin (mg/g total dry lung).

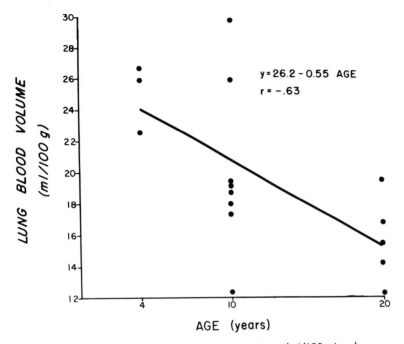

Fig. 25-3. Relation of age and lung blood volume (ml/100 g lung).

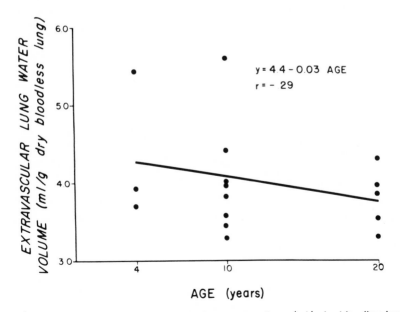

Fig. 25-4. Relation of age and extravascular lung water volume (ml/g dry bloodless lung).

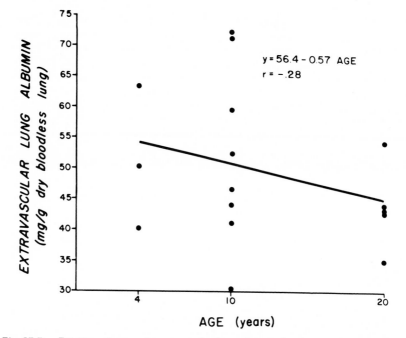

Fig. 25-5.   Relation of age and extravascular lung albumin (mg/g dry bloodless lung).

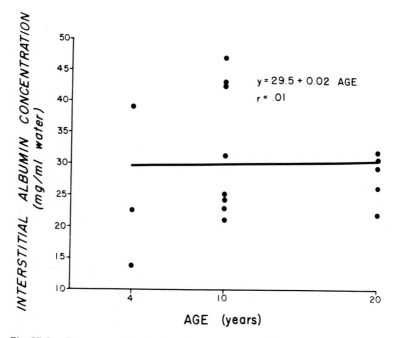

Fig. 25-6.   Relation of age and interstitial albumin concentration (mg/ml water).

parenchyma. The hematocrit and plasma albumin concentration were essentially unrelated to age group.

The volume of extravascular lung water (ml/g dry bloodless lung) decreased with age (Figure 25-4), suggesting a decreased interstitial protein oncotic activity, and this was supported by the tendency for extravascular lung albumin (mg/g dry bloodless lung) to decrease with age (Figure 25-5). Since both the extravascular water volume and extravascular albumin content decreased proportionally with age, it follows that interstitial albumin concentration (mg/ml water) remained unchanged (Figure 25-6).

The constancy of the extravascular Na^+/K^+ ratio confirmed that no gross changes occurred with age in intra- and extracellular fractions of the extravascular space.

DISCUSSION

These observations indicate that in the macaque, lung water volumes and lung albumin contents decrease continuously with age when calculated with reference to the lung dry weight. However, the finding that the left lung weight increases with age indicates that the primary change is in the lung dry weight. That lung water volumes remain fundamentally unchanged is supported by the constancy of the interstitial albumin concentration and the interstitial/plasma albumin ratio. Before speculating as to the mechanism underlying these changes, it is necessary to consider some of the assumptions and to compare these results with those obtained in other species.

The direct measurements of total lung water volume, total lung albumin content, and lung blood volume are made under the assumption that the samples of lung are comparable. Since the lungs were removed some minutes after the death of the animal and blood was allowed to drain from the samples, it is likely that fluid shifts occurred, but these are assumed to be similar in extent at all ages. There have been numerous published measurements of total lung water volume and lung blood volume from a variety of species, using several different techniques. Therefore, it is of interest that the values obtained in these monkeys were similar to those obtained in man, sheep, dog, rabbit, and rat (6). Previous studies have not demonstrated the effects of age noted here, although an examination of collected data (i.e., Table 11 in Ref. 6) supports the trends described.

The importance of correcting for blood content has been stressed before, but the present finding that the volume varies with age re-emphasizes this factor. Ideally, the red cell and plasma volumes should be measured independently; but in the present studies, the plasma volume was calculated utilizing the measured red cell volume and a hematocrit correction factor, 0.76. The latter factor is a composite, correcting for both the difference between large and small lung vessel hematocrit and for the effects of gravity drainage of blood from the specimen postmortem. This factor was obtained from studies in rabbits and dogs in this laboratory, and was assumed to be the same for monkeys and not to vary with age. The latter assumption is partially supported by observations that the whole body hematocrit is not altered by age in man (1).

The interstitial albumin concentration and, hence, the interstitial/plasma albumin concentration ratio are critically dependent on the fraction of extra-vascular water that is interstitial (i.e., extracellular). For these calculations a value of 0.41 was used, based on measurements in this and other laboratories in man, sheep, dog, rabbit, and rat (6). No studies of the effects of age on this fraction have been located. However, it was hypothesized that substantial error in this assumption would be indicated by a change in the calculated extravascular Na^+/K^+ ratio. The constancy of this ratio in the three age groups, therefore, suggests a constant interstitial fraction.

The pulmonary interstitial/plasma albumin ratio of approximately 0.9 observed in this study was very similar to the value obtained in rabbits, dogs, and man in this laboratory and is compatible with the current estimates based on lymph/plasma concentration (6). We are not aware of any previous studies that have compared the systematic effects of age on these values.

Despite the uncertainties associated with some of these assumptions, it may be useful to speculate as to causes of the changes observed. A decreased lung blood volume with advancing years was suggested by the observations of decreased diffusing capacity with age and decreased density of the alveolar capillary network (4). It has been suggested that these changes result indirectly from the progressive replacement by collagen (3) and, therefore, our observation of decreasing lung blood volume was not unexpected. The trend for both interstitial lung water volume and interstitial albumin content to decrease with age, when related to dry bloodless lung weight, is similarly explained if the functional interstitial space is progressively replaced by connective tissue. The constancy of both interstitial albumin concentration and interstitial/plasma albumin concentration ratios suggest that no fundamental changes in the regulation of lung water volume occur with increasing age.

In summary, this study has suggested the following four conclusions: 1) For interpretation of lung wet/dry weight ratios, the age of the subjects should be considered. 2) The parenchymal dry weight increases with age. 3) In considering compartmental water volumes, correction for blood content is mandatory. 4) There are no progressive changes in the interstitial albumin concentration, which remains at approximately 0.9 of the plasma concentration at all ages.

ACKNOWLEDGMENTS

This work was supported by National Institutes of Health grants HL16916 to the University of Pennsylvania and RR00166, RR52177 and AG62145 to the University of Washington.

REFERENCES

1. Cohn, J. E., and Shock, N. W. (1949): Blood volume studies in middle-aged and elderly males. *Am. J. Med. Sci.*, **217**:388–392.
2. Guyton, A. C., Taylor, A. E., and Granger, H. J. (1975): *Circulatory Physiology. II. Dynamics and Control of the Body Fluids.* Philadelphia; W. B. Saunders.
3. Kohn, R. R. (1964): Changes in connective tissue–biochemical and structural changes in aging tissue. In: *Aging of the Lung–Perspectives*, edited by L. Cander and J. H. Moyer, New York; Grune and Stratton.
4. Reid, L. (1967): Embryology of the lung. In: *Development of the Lung*, Ciba Foundation Symposium. Boston; Little, Brown.
5. Starling, E. H. (1896): On the absorption of fluids from the connective tissue spaces. *J. Physiol. (London)*, **19**:312–326.
6. Staub, N. E. (1974): Pulmonary edema. *Physiol. Rev.*, **54**:678–811.

26

Renal Disease

W. E. Giddens, Jr., R. A. Seifert, and J. T. Boyce

Regional Primate Research Center and Department of Pathology
University of Washington, Seattle, Washington

INTRODUCTION

It is well recognized that in aging humans the kidney declines in size and in renal blood flow and glomerular filtration rate (see Ref. 6 for review). The most striking anatomical finding in this regard is an increase in the incidence of hyalinized or "obsolescent" glomeruli, a finding closely correlated with age (10, 13).

One of the best documented examples of age-related glomerular disease is in the rat (7), in which proteinuria and focal glomerular sclerosis are closely correlated with age. The data of Couser and Stilmant (4) support the view that mesangial deposits of immunoglobulin-M (IgM) precede and probably lead to the glomerular lesions, whereas those of Bolton et al. (1) indicate that IgM deposition is independent of glomerular sclerosis.

Among nonhuman primates, spontaneous glomerulonephritis associated with the deposition of glomerular immune complexes has been documented in *Galago sp.* (3), owl monkeys (*Aotus trivirgatus*) (9, 12) and longtail macaques (*Macaca fascicularis*) (14). In studies of these species, little attempt was made to correlate renal lesions with age. The macaque study (14) is interesting because it documents a high incidence of renal immunoglobulin deposition in the absence of any functional abnormalities and only minimal evidence of glomerulonephritis.

Our experience with histopathologic examination of necropsy material indicates that subclinical and clinical cases of glomerular disease in pigtail macaques (*M. nemestrina*) are relatively common (5). The purpose of this study was to examine blood, urine and kidney tissues from apparently normal pigtail and longtail macaques of known age in an effort to determine (a) whether there was chemical or histopathologic evidence of renal disease or dysfunction, (b) whether immune complexes were present in renal glomeruli, (c) whether these complexes were associated with morphological or functional evidence of disease, and (d) whether any of these findings were related to age.

MATERIALS AND METHODS

Subjects were 21 pigtail macaques and 2 longtail macaques as described in Table 26-1. At the time of euthanasia the monkeys were anesthetized and blood was collected. After laparotomy, if the bladder contained urine, a sample was collected by aspiration. The left kidney was removed before cardiorespiratory arrest and samples were collected for electron microscopy, immunofluorescence, and histopathology.

Urine was examined for specific gravity with a hydrometer and for proteinuria and pH with clinical dip sticks (Labstix, The Ames Co., Elkhart, IN 46514). Renal cortex was frozen in 5-mm cubes on glass plates chilled with dry ice, placed in airtight containers, and stored at $-70°C$ until sectioning. Tissue sections, 4 μm thick, were collected on untreated glass slides and allowed to air dry at least 2 hr at room temperature before being placed in plastic slide boxes. The boxes were sealed with tape, and the tissues were stored at $-20°C$ for up to a month before they were stained.

For immunofluorescence, 5 20-y.o. monkeys were selected on the basis of availability of tissue, serum chemistries and urinalysis. Five 10-y.o. monkeys matched for species and sex were selected for comparison. Tissues were stained for immunoglobulins (Ig) and complement (C) by the following method. Fluorescein isothiocyanate-conjugated antihuman IgG, IgM, IgA and C_3 (Behring Diagnostics, Inc., Somerville, NJ 08876) were reconstituted with distilled water and further diluted 1:4 with phosphate-buffered saline (PBS) containing 0.1% sodium azide. The diluted fluorescent antisera were kept in capped, foil-covered Coplin jars and stored in a refrigerator between uses. These dilutions were stable for up to 6 months. Slides were thawed, labeled and washed in PBS for 15 min, drained, then stained in the appropriate solution for 30 min. They were protected from light and kept at room temperature. The slides were then rapidly dehydrated in ethanol, cleared in xylene, and coverslipped with Pro-Tex mounting medium. They were examined with a Zeiss photomicroscope using an HBO 200 mercury bulb, and FITC exciter filter and No. 44 and 50 barrier filters.

Table 26-1. Laboratory Findings.

| Age/Sex | Species | Proteinuria | Blood Chemistry | | | |
			BUN mg/dl	Creatinine mg/dl	Protein g/dl	Albumen g/dl
20-M*	Mf	+5	150	8.0	4.9	3.1
20-F*	Mn	+3	19	0.8	6.5	2.9
20-F*	Mn	−	24	0.8	8.0	3.7
20-F*	Mn	+3	16	0.8	7.6	4.1
20-F*	Mn	+4	15	0.9	7.7	4.1
20-M	Mn	+4	19	1.0	7.9	4.4
20-F	Mn	−	67	1.4	8.2	3.8
20-F	Mn	−	−	−	−	−
20-F	Mn	+2	−	−	−	−
20-F	Mn	−	−	−	−	−
10-M*	Mf	−	−	−	−	−
10-F*	Mn	−	22	0.6	7.5	3.8
10-F*	Mn	+4	12	1.3	8.2	4.2
10-F*	Mn	+4	9	0.9	7.2	3.8
10-F*	Mn	+3	8	0.7	7.7	3.8
10-F	Mn	+2	20	0.8	7.5	3.8
10-F	Mn	+5	8	0.9	7.4	3.7
10-M	Mn	+2	32	1.8	8.2	4.2
10-F	Mn	+2	11	0.8	8.0	4.5
10-F	Mn	−	−	−	−	−
4-F	Mn	+2	23	1.1	8.3	4.2
4-F	Mn	+3	31	1.0	7.6	4.3
4-F	Mn	+3	16	0.9	7.5	4.1

Mn = *Macaca nemestrina*; Mf = *Macaca fascicularis*. M = male; F = female.
Proteinuria: +1 = negative; +2 = trace; +3 = 30 mg%; +4 = 200 mg%; +5 = 300 mg%.
*Monkeys selected for immunofluorescent studies.

The degree of glomerular immune complex deposition was assayed by the following procedure. Ten glomeruli, observed while systematically scanning the section, were scored for intensity of fluorescence and percentage of glomerular involvement. Intensity of fluorescence was rated on a subjective scale of 0 to ++++, with ++++ indicating maximal fluorescence of the type seen in severe renal disease in humans. The pattern of fluorescence was also categorized as pinpoint, granular, or linear. The scores were averaged for the 10 glomeruli to give a score for the subject.

Tissue for histopathology was fixed in a formaldehyde-glutaraldehyde fixative (Chapter 3), washed in alcohol, cleared in xylene, and embedded in paraffin.

Renal Histopathological Observations					
Mesangioproliferative Glomerulonephritis	Hyalinized Glomeruli	Tubular Degeneration	Tubular Casts	Interstitial Fibrosis	Interstitial Lymphycytes
+++	++	++	++	++	+
+++	+++	+++	+++	++	++
+	0	++	++	++	0
0	0	0	0	0	0
0	0	0	0	0	0
++	++	++	++	++	+
0	0	+	+	0	0
0	+	+	+	0	0
0	0	0	+	0	0
0	0	0	+	0	0
+	+	+	++	++	+
0	+	+	+	0	+
0	0	0	0	0	0
+	0	+	+	+	0
+	0	+	+	0	0
+	0	+	+	0	0
0	0	0	0	0	0
+	+	+	++	+	+
+	0	0	++	0	0
0	0	0	0	0	0
+	+	++	++	+	+
0	0	0	+	0	0

0 = absent; + = minimal; ++ = slight; +++ = moderate; ++++ = severe.

Sections of paraffin-embedded tissue, 4 μm thick, were stained with hematoxylin and eosin, periodic acid-methenamine silver, and Gomori's trichrome. The observations on presence and severity of renal lesions were made without knowledge of the animal's age or its blood or urinalysis values.

RESULTS

The results of clinical chemistry and urinalysis, and summary of the histopathology, are shown in Table 26-1.

There was a high incidence of proteinuria; 11 of 19 monkeys had > 30 mg/dl protein in urine, and another 5 had traces. A 20-y.o. longtail male seemed to be in renal failure (blood urea nitrogen was 150 mg/dl, and creatinine was 8.0 mg/dl). This and a 20-y.o. pigtail female had hypoalbuminemia (albumen <3.5 g/dl). These 2 monkeys had the most severe glomerulonephritis of any in the study. The latter may also have had hypoalbuminemia for extrarenal causes since it also had severe hepatic amyloidosis. This must have compromised hepatic function and may have resulted in decreased synthesis of albumen.

Histopathologic examination was complicated because the tissues were brittle and in most sections of the glomeruli seemed swollen, particularly in subcapsular locations, obliterating Bowman's space and making accurate characterization of glomerular capillary loops difficult. This may have been caused by the fixative (see Chapter 3). The periodic acid-methenamine silver stain did not clearly delineate glomerular basement membranes, possibly because of excessive crosslinking of proteins due to the glutaraldehyde in the fixative.

The normal glomerulus of the pigtail macaque, as in most mammals, consists of patent capillary loops and minimal amounts of mesangial cells and matrix (Figure 26-1). Bowman's space is prominent.

Eleven of 22 monkeys had varying degrees of mesangioproliferative glomerulonephritis with minimal to moderate proliferation of mesangial cells and

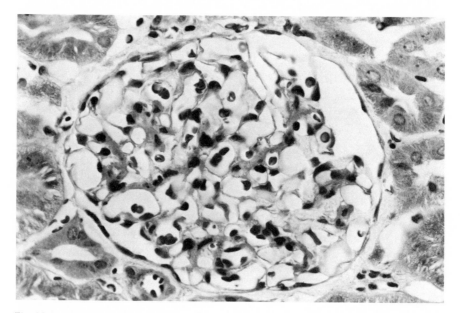

Fig. 26-1. Normal glomerulus from a 20-y.o. female pigtail macaque (#76199). Glomerular capillaries are patent. H & E. X640.

mesangial matrix. The lobular architecture of the glomerulus seemed accentuated. In the more severe of these, capillary lumens were narrowed. In 2 of the oldest monkeys these changes were particularly advanced (Figure 26-2).

Hyalinized, obsolescent glomeruli were seen in 8 of 22 monkeys, and seemed to correlate well with the more severe cases of glomerulonephritis. Tubular degeneration (13/22) was characterized by atrophy of proximal or distal convoluted tubules and by cytoplasmic vacuolation. It was usually accompanied by tubular casts in the cortex or medulla (17/22), and, occasionally, by interstitial fibrosis (8/22), and interstitial lymphocytic infiltration (7/22). These lesions were more severe in the 2 monkeys with more severe glomerulonephritis (Figure 26-2), and were interpreted as being secondary to decreased blood flow through the hypercellular glomeruli.

One 20-y.o. pigtail macaque had a microscopic nodule of neoplastic tubular epithelial cells in the renal cortex. The nodule had expanded to press on adjacent normal cortical tissue. It consisted of enlarged cells with slightly vesicular nuclei which formed acini, tubules, and cysts, the latter often containing papillary projections. This lesion was diagnosed by the Armed Forces Institute of Pathol-

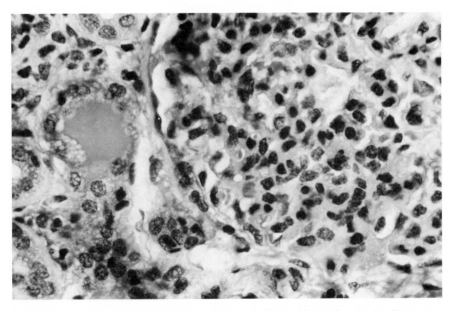

Fig. 26-2. Mesangioproliferative glomerulonephritis from a 20-y.o. female pigtail macaque (#57240), with proliferation of mesangial cells and matrix, and general glomerular hypercellularity. In adjacent tissue there is interstitial fibrosis, and convoluted tubules are atrophied and contain proteinaceous material in their lumens. H & E. X640.

ogy as a renal tubular adenocarcinoma, and is described in detail elsewhere (11). The nature and intensity of immunoglobulin deposition in renal glomeruli are presented in Table 26-2.

Sections stained with IgA exhibited a relatively low degree of background fluorescence, with the exception of some proximal tubular basement membranes which were stained. Of the 10 animals studied, 1 had glomeruli containing slight deposits of IgA in a granular pattern in the mesangial stalk region, 3 had only trace amounts of glomerular IgA staining, and 6 were completely negative. IgG-stained frozen sections also had a low degree of background fluorescence. Specific granular staining of the glomerular mesangial stalk region was observed to a slight degree (++) in 4 of 10 monkeys, with trace amounts in 5 others. The most intense staining of immunoglobulins was with IgM: moderate (+++) amounts were observed in 3 of 10 animals (Figure 26-3), slight amounts in 5 of 10 and minimal amounts in 1 of 10. One animal was completely negative. The degree of background staining with IgM was negligible. Sections stained with C_3 were hard to interpret, owing to intense background staining of the tubules. Short bright linear bands of fluorescence were seen on the epithelial surface of glomerular tufts, but could not with certainty be distinguished from similar patterns in the tubules. The tubular staining patterns also consisted of broad bands which were primarily on the apical surfaces of tubular epithelial cells. This pattern was seen to a minimal or slight degree in 8 of 10 animals.

There was no apparent correlation between intensity of immunoglobulin deposition and either age or severity of renal disease, as determined by either laboratory values (proteinuria, hypoalbuminemia, uremia) or histopathology.

Table 26-2. Immunoglobulin Deposition in Renal Glomeruli of *Macaca spp.*

Age-Sex	Species	IgA	IgG	IgM	Glomerulonephritis
20-M	Mf	+	++	++	+++
20-F	Mn	0	0	++	+++
20-F	Mn	+	+	+++	+
20-F	Mn	0	+	+	0
20-F	Mn	0	++	++	0
10-M	Mf	++	+	+++	0
10-F	Mn	+	++	+++	+
10-F	Mn	0	+	++	0
10-F	Mn	0	+	++	0
10-F	Mn	0	++	0	+
Total (slight or above)		1/10	4/10	8/10	6/10

Mf = *Macaca fascicularis*; Mn = *Macaca nemestrina*; 0 = absent; + = minimal; ++ = slight; +++ = moderate; ++++ = severe.

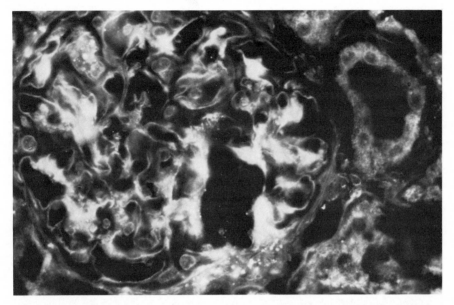

Fig. 26-3. Immunofluoresent micrograph of frozen section of renal glomerulus from a 10-y.o. female pigtail macaque (#76203) stained with anti-human IgM. There are granular deposits of IgM, scored as +++, in the mesangial regions, and linear and granular deposits in the glomerular basement membranes.

DISCUSSION

This study indicates that renal disease in varying degrees of severity is a common finding in pigtail macaques of all age groups. We have no good explanation why the incidence of proteinuria was so high. It cannot be attributed to contamination during collection because it was obtained by bladder aspiration following laparotomy. The degree of proteinuria did not correlate well with other parameters of renal disease, or with renal immunoglobulin deposition. Abnormal blood urea nitrogen and albumen did correlate well with the more severe forms of glomerulonephritis.

Our immunofluorescent observations indicate that a majority of 10- and 20-y.o. pigtail macaques have slight to moderate amounts of granular IgM depositions in their glomeruli; a smaller number also have IgG and IgA deposits. It is interesting to compare our results with those of Poskitt *et al.* (14), who found that 72% of adult longtail macaques had granular deposits. They also found no correlation between deposition of glomerular immunoglobulins and clinical or morphologic evidence of renal abnormality. While they reported considerably heavier immunoglobulin deposits in longtail macaques than we observed in pigtail macaques, the immunofluorescent results of the two studies cannot be quantitatively compared because of differences in technique. They, for example, used fluorescein-labeled antisera prepared from longtail immunoglobulins, whereas we used commerically produced antisera against human immunoglobulins. This probably resulted in a higher specificity and intensity of staining in their sections. Pigtail macaques in our study seemed to have more functional and histopathologic evidence of glomerular disease, but this may have been due to the older age of our animals (none of their subjects was over 8 years old).

The histopathologic observations summarized in Table 26-1 indicate some of the variety of tissue alterations a pathologist might encounter in so-called "normal control" pigtail macaques. Most of the morphological alterations that we observed are reported here, even if they were only minimal in severity (e.g., only 1 tubule with a cast in the entire tissue section). Even in the 2 most severe cases, the kidneys did not exhibit glomerulonephritis of the severity we have described in other monkeys with naturally occurring (2) or experiment-related (8) renal disease.

The glomerulonephritis in pigtail macaques is basically a proliferation of mesangial cells and matrix, forming thick mesangial stalks around which compressed capillary lumens are organized (2). In view of the fundamental significance of immune mechanisms in initiating diffuse glomerulonephritis, we believe one pathogenic mechanism of this lesion to be the recurrent deposition of immune complexes in glomeruli and their "processing" by the mesangium. Most of the immune complexes we saw were located in the mesangial regions of glomeruli. There was not, however, a high degree of correlation between immune complex deposition and glomerulonephritis. This suggests two possibilities. One is that glomerular immune complexes produce little acute disease in pigtail macaques and are continuously cleared from glomeruli, resulting in a population of "activated" mesangial cells which produce the mesangioproliferative glomerulonephritis. The second possibility is that other pathogenic mechanisms are at work, such as activation of complement through the alternate pathway or activation of other chemical mediators of inflammation such as bradykinin.

Four of 9 monkeys in the 20-y.o. group, 6 of 10 in the 10-y.o. group and 1 of 3 in the 4-y.o. group had glomerulonephritis. However, if one excludes those with only minimal lesions, then 3 of 9 aged monkeys were affected whereas none of the 10 adult or 3 young monkeys were involved.

This raises a question of what constitutes an age-related disease. If a person cuts his hand badly, he is usually left with a permanent scar. If a sample of 1000 randomly selected people is examined carefully, it would seem reasonable to assume that (all other things being equal) the older people would have more scars on their hands since they have had more opportunities to cut themselves.

Can one then say that the severity of scarring of the hands is an age-related disease? Similarly, if one assumes that glomerulonephritis in pigtail macaques is the result of a continuous or intermittent series of injuries to the glomerulus, all of which have some permanent effect, is the glomerulonephritis age-related?

In summary, we have described a mesangioproliferative glomerulonephritis of slight to moderate severity in a large percentage of adult pigtail macaques. In its more severe forms it is associated with hypoproteinemia and uremia. The more advanced cases of glomerulonephritis were found in the oldest monkeys, suggesting that some association exists between this disease and aging. Deposition of slight to moderate amounts of immunoglobulins, particularly IgM, is common in renal glomeruli and does not seem to correlate with age or glomerular disease.

ACKNOWLEDGMENTS

This study was supported by National Institutes of Health grants RR00166, RR00489, RR52177, AG62145, AG76029 and GM00100 to the University of Washington.

REFERENCES

1. Bolton, W. K., Benton, F. R., Maclay, J. G. and Sturgill, B. C. (1976): Spontaneous glomerular sclerosis in aging Sprague-Dawley rats. *Amer. J. Path.*, **85**: 277–302.
2. Boyce, J. T., Giddens, W. E., Jr., and Seifert, R. (1978): Glomerulonephritis in the pigtail macaque (*Macaca nemestrina*). In: *The Renal Pathology of Nonhuman Primates*, edited by W. E. Giddens, Jr. *Veterinary Pathology*. In press.
3. Burkholder, P. M., and Bergeron, J. A. (1970): Spontaneous glomerulonephritis in the prosimian primate *Galago*. A correlative light, immunofluorescence and electron microscopic study. *Amer. J. Path.*, **61**: 437–456.
4. Couser, W. G., and Stilmant, M. N. (1975): Mesangial lesions and focal glomerular sclerosis in the aging rat. *Lab. Invest.*, **33**: 491–501.
5. Giddens, W. E., Jr., Boyce, J. T., Blakley, G., and Seifert, R. (1978): Renal pathology in the pigtail macaque (*Macaca nemestrina*). In: *The Renal Pathology of Nonhuman Primates*, edited by W. E. Giddens, Jr. *Veterinary Pathology*. In press.
6. Goldman, R. (1977): Aging and the excretory system: kidney and bladder. In: *Handbook of the Biology of Aging*, edited by C. E. Finch and L. Hayflick. New York; Van Nostrand Reinhold.
7. Guttman, P. H., and Kohn, H. I. (1960): Progressive intercapillary glomerulosclerosis in the mouse, rat and chinese hamster, associated with aging and x-ray exposure. *Amer. J. Path.*, **37**: 293–307.
8. Heidel, J., Giddens, W. E., Jr., and Boyce, J. T. (1978): Renal pathology in catheterized baboons (*Papio cynocephalus*). In: *The Renal Pathology of Nonhuman Primates*, edited by W. E. Giddens, Jr. *Veterinary Pathology*. In press.
9. Hunt, R. D., Van Zwieten, M. J., Baggs, B. R., Sehgal, P. K., King, N. W., Roach, S. M., and Blake, B. J. (1976): Glomerulonephritis in the owl monkey (*Aotus trivirgatus*). *Lab. Anim. Sci.*, **26**: 1088–1092.

10. Kaplan, C., Pasternack, B., Shah, H., and Gallo, G. (1975): Age-related incidence of sclerotic glomeruli in human kidneys. *Amer. J. Path.*, **80**: 227–234.
11. Jones, S. R., and Casey, H. W. (1978): Primary renal neoplasms in nonhuman primates. In: *The Renal Pathology of Nonhuman Primates*, edited by W. E. Giddens, Jr. *Veterinary Pathology*. In press.
12. King, N. W., Jr., Baggs, R. B., Hunt, R. D., Van Zwieten, J. L., and MacKey, J. J. (1976): Glomerulonephritis in the owl monkey (*Aotus trivirgatus*). Ultrastructural observations. *Lab. Anim. Sci.*, **26**: 1093–1103.
13. McLachlan, M. S. F., Guthrie, J. C., Anderson, C. J., and Fulker, M. J. (1977): Vascular and glomerular changes in the aging kidney. *J. Pathol.*, **121**: 65–78.
14. Poskitt, T. R., Fortwengler, H. P., Jr., Bobrow, J. C., and Roth, G. J. (1974): Naturally occurring immune complex glomerulonephritis in monkeys (*Macaca iris*). I. Light, immunofluorescence, and electron microscopic studies. *Amer. J. Path.*, **76**: 145–164.

27

Long Bone Calcification and Morphology

Douglas M. Bowden, Cheryl Teets, Joan Witkin, and David M. Young

Department of Psychiatry and Behavioral Sciences and
Regional Primate Research Center, University of Washington,
Seattle, Washington;
Department of Anthropology, Columbia University,
New York, New York; and
Department of Veterinary Science, Montana State University,
Bozeman, Montana

INTRODUCTION

Reviewing indices of biological aging in man, Alex Comfort (2) found that, of 25 variables for which correlation coefficients were available, the metacarpal osteoporotic index (3) had the strongest correlation with chronological age. In recent decades osteoporosis of aging has assumed increasing clinical importance, due to the numbers of individuals with longer lifespan who have become vulnerable to skeletal fractures and their life-threatening sequelae. In the human, the decline in cortical bone thickness with age seems to result from a reduction in the ratio of hydroxyapatite apposition rate to resorption rate at the endosteal surface (4). While a number of phenomena have been demonstrated to correlate with downward shifts in the apposition:resorption ratio, e.g., nutritional deficits, severe restriction of activity, and menopause, the pathophysiological mechanisms underlying osteoporosis of aging remain to be elucidated.

The purpose of this study was (a) to determine whether the radiographic technique most commonly used to assess osteoporosis in human populations, *viz.*, cortical thickness in the second metacarpal, would detect evidence of a comparable process in the macaque, and (b) to explore correlations between this measurement and potentially related physiological, morphological, and biochemical characteristics of bone in the aging primate. The variables studied included the rate of apposition of new bone and the density and degree of remodeling of osteons in the femur, and the mineral composition of cortical and trabecular bone in the tibial shaft (Chapter 28, this volume).

METHODS

Osteoporosis was evaluated by radiographs of the hands and feet from 20 pigtail macaques (*Macaca nemestrina*) and 2 longtail macaques (*M. fascicularis*). They included 3 4-y.o., 11 10-y.o. and 8 20-y.o. animals; 18 were females, 4 were males.

Percent cortical area (PCA) was calculated for the second and third metacarpals of the right hand, second metacarpal of the left hand, and second metatarsal of the right foot. Two calculations of PCA were made, one comparing the cortical area with total area in a longitudinal section of the bone (PCA–L), the other comparing cortical area with total area in a cross section of the bone at midshaft (PCA–C). The measurements for PCA–L were obtained by projecting the radiograph onto a sheet of paper to produce an 8X enlargement. The outlines of the entire bone and of the marrow space were traced, and the length of the bone was measured (Figure 27-1). Two lines were constructed perpendicular to the long axis of the bone and one-quarter of the length from each end. The drawing was then mounted on a GRAF-PEN digitizer and the perimeters of the total area (TA) and marrow area (MA) were traced with the sonic pen. The output of the digitizer went to an IMSAI 8080 microprocessor which calculated the areas of the enclosed spaces. PCA–L was calculated by the formula: PCA–L = 100(TA – MA)/TA. The reliability of the measure, based on repeated

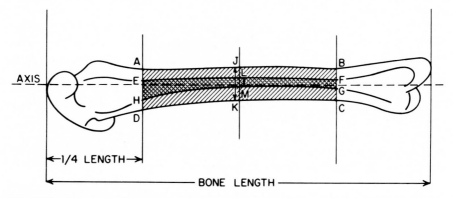

Fig. 27-1. Schematic diagram of right second metacarpal showing the areas and lengths used to calculate PCA-L and PCA-C. TA = area bounded by ABCD; MA = area bounded by EFGH; TD = JK; MD = LM.

digitizer tablet measurements from the same tracing in different orientations on the digitizer table, was ±2.4% (normalized root mean square of the error × 100).

The second method was identical to that used by Garn (4) in human studies. Three independent measurements of total diameter (TD) and marrow diameter (MD) were taken at midshaft (Figure 27-1) using a Helios dial caliper with needle points and a 2× viewer magnification. PCA–C was calculated from the means of the values ($\overline{TD}$ and $\overline{MD}$) by the formula: PCA–C = $100(\overline{TD}^2 - \overline{MD}^2)/\overline{TD}^2$. PCA–L was determined for all four bones in each animal; PCA–C, a standard index of cortical thickness in human studies (4), was determined only for the right second metacarpal.

Histologic evidence of remodeling was evaluated by tetracycline labeling in the femoral diaphysis of 16 macaques. Tetracycline (25 mg/kg in lactated Ringer's solution) was administered intravenously on 2 consecutive days 3 weeks before sacrifice and again 1 week before sacrifice. At sacrifice two 5-mm-wide blocks were taken from the midshaft of the femur. One was placed in 70% ethanol, the other in Bouin's fixative for routine histologic preparation and hematoxylin and eosin (H & E) staining. Specimens were shipped at ambient temperature. The bone samples in ethanol were sectioned on a Gillings-Hamco thin sectioning machine. The sections of bone were ground under glass using waterproof fine-grained sandpaper to obtain a uniform thickness of 80 μm. The sections were evaluated via fluorescence microscopy. The distance between the tetracycline labels of an osteon was measured with an ocular micrometer. After fluorescence studies, sections were mounted for microradiography on Kodak High Resolution Plates in a simple vacuum cassette. The cassette was placed in a self-contained x-ray unit (Faxitron) and exposed at 20 KV for 75 min. The plates were developed using routine procedures and evaluated under the light microscope.

Sections of iliac crest, mandible, vertebrae, rib and distal radius were fixed in Bouins, processed and stained with H & E and evaluated histologically.

All measurements of all characteristics were made without knowing the ages of the animals.

RESULTS

PCA–L of the second metacarpal of the right hand varied with age as illustrated in the left scatterplot of Figure 27-2. While mean PCA–L was less in older age groups than in younger age groups for all bones measured (Table 27-1), the differences were significant only for the second metacarpals of the 2 hands. Of the 2 animals with the lowest PCA–L values, both were females in the 20-y.o. age groups. One was postmenopausal by several indices (#75026, see Chapter 16, this volume); no information regarding reproductive status of the other was

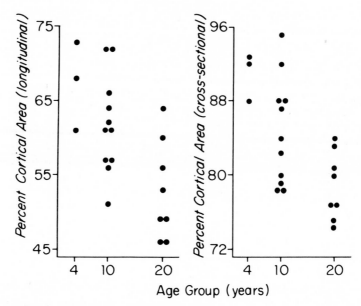

Fig. 27-2. Distributions of two measures of percent cortical area by age-group. Left: PCA-L; right: PCA-C.

Table 27-1. Mean Percent Cortical Area for 4 Long Bones of the Hands and Foot of 20 *M. nemestrina* and 2 *M. fascicularis*.

Age Group (Years)	n	Bone			
		Second Metacarpal Right Hand	Second Metacarpal Left Hand	Third Metacarpal Right Hand	Second Metatarsal Right Foot
PCA—L					
4	3	67.6[a]	68.7[a]	57.3[a]	69.2[a]
10	11	61.6[a]	65.6[ab]	52.6[a]	64.1[a]
20+	8	53.1[b]	60.3[b]	45.8[a]	61.2[a]
PCA—C					
4	3	90.7[a]			
10	11	84.7[b]			
20+	8	78.8[c]			

[a,b,c]Any two means not followed by a common letter differ significantly p < 0.03; two-tailed t-test).

available. Measurements from an earlier radiograph of one 20-y.o. female showed a decline from 74.1% at age 14 years to 70.9% at the time of sacrifice.

Most of the 10-y.o. and 20-y.o. females had been members of breeding colonies for much of their lives. To evaluate the relation of PCA to parity, they were divided into two groups on the basis of high or low parity, i.e., as being above or below the median for parity. In both age groups, mean PCA–L was greater for high-parity females than for low-parity females (Table 27-2). The difference in mean PCA–L was significant for animals in the 10-y.o. group ($p < 0.05$; one-tailed t-test).

A 10-y.o. male and a 20-y.o. male *M. nemestrina* showed PCA–L's of the second right metacarpal equal to 71.6% and 49.3%, respectively. Those in a 10-y.o. and 20-y.o. male *M. fascicularis* were 60.0% and 56.1%, respectively. Thus, the direction of differences in the males of both species was similar to that in the female *M. nemestrina*.

The correlation between PCA–L and PCA–C was high ($R = 0.93$; $p < 0.001$). Both showed an inverse correlation with age ($R = -0.64$; $p < 0.001$) and significant age group differences by analysis of variance. Tests for differences between the mean values for the three age groups taken two at a time (Table 27-1) suggested that PCA–C may be a more sensitive index of age than PCA–L. Whereas both indices differentiated between the 20-y.o. groups and the younger groups, only PCA–C differentiated between the 4-y.o. and 10-y.o. groups.

To evaluate the correspondence of variation in metacarpal findings to variation in other long bones, tests were made for correlations between PCA of the second metacarpal of the right hand and analysis of mineral content of the left tibia (Chapter 28, this volume). For purposes of correlation in these and sub-

Table 27-2. Relation of Percent Cortical Area in Female *M. nemestrina* to Parity and Age Group (each entry represents 1 animal).

Age Group	10 y.o.		20 y.o.	
Parity	Low	High	Low	High
PCA–L	50.9	60.7	46.3	53.1
	63.6	72.0	49.1	60.4
	56.5	62.3		
	56.9	65.8		
Mean ± s.d.	57.0 ± 5.2	65.2 ± 5.0	47.7 ± 2.0	56.8 ± 5.2

Parity = live births + caesarian section deliveries + still births + 0.5 × spontaneous abortions; Low < 3.0; High > 3.0.

Table 27-3. Correlations between Metacarpal PCA—L and Several Indices of Mineral Metabolism (Chapter 28 this volume); Combined Data from Female *M. nemestrina* of All Age Groups.

	Index	n	R	p
Cortical Bone	Ca	16	0.07	NS
(left tibia)	Mg	16	0.25	NS
	Zn	16	−0.26	NS
	Ca/Zn	16	0.54	0.03
	Mg/Zn	16	0.42	NS
Trabecular Bone	Ca	16	0.61	0.01
(left tibia)	Mg	16	0.63	0.01
	Zn	16	0.40	NS
	Ca/Zn	16	0.45	0.08
	Mg/Zn	16	0.67	0.01
Serum	Ca	14	0.45	NS
	Cu	16	−0.65	<0.01
	Zn	16	−0.43	0.10

R = linear regression coefficient; p = significance level; NS = not significant (p > 0.10).

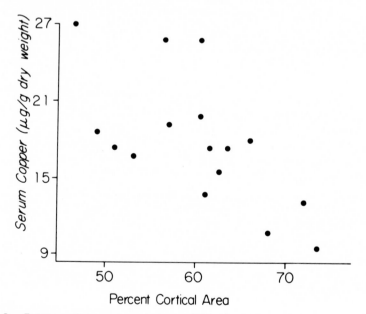

Fig. 27-3. Relation of percent cortical area (PCL-L) of the right second metacarpal to serum copper.

sequent analyses, PCA refers to PCA—L of the second metacarpal of the right hand. The calcium:zinc ratio (Ca/Zn) in tibial cortex correlated with PCA of the metacarpal (Table 27-3). A similar trend was seen in the trabecular bone. The magnesium:zinc ratio (Mg/Zn), calcium (Ca), and magnesium (Mg) levels in trabecular bone also correlated with the metacarpal PCA. Finally, serum copper (Cu) showed an inverse correlation with metacarpal PCA (Table 27-3; Figure 27-3).

Nine of 16 animals showed evidence of tetracycline labeling in the femoral diaphysis (Table 27-4). All of these were in the 4-y.o. and 10-y.o. groups. Scheduling constraints and problems with carrying out repeated intravenous injections in the oldest animals limited the number of 20-y.o. animals in this part of the study to 3; of these none showed labeling of osteons in the femoral

Table 27-4. Skeletal Indices.

Age Group (Years)	Sex	Femoral Cortex Label	Femoral Microradiography OS/cm^2	OSR
4	F	+	1625	13
4	F	+	1375	12
4	F	0	1250	8
Mean ± s.d. or proportion		2 of 3	1425 ± 200	11 ± 3
10	F	+	1025	120
10	F	+	975	6
10	F	+	1000	1
10	F	+	900	20
10	F	+	850	14
10	F	+	–	–
10	F	0	1525	36
10	F	0	1925	6
10	F	0	–	–
10	M	+	–	–
Mean ± s.d. or proportion		7 of 10	1175 ± 400	29 ± 42
20	F	0	1025	6
20	F	0	1175	3
20	F	0	1100	8
20	F	–	1250	260
20	F	–	2300	3
20	F	–	1100	139
20	M	–	1725	36
Mean ± s.d. or proportion		0 of 3	1382 ± 467	65 ± 99

+ = labeled osteons found; 0 = no labeled osteons found; – = no measurement; OS/cm^2 = osteons per cm^2; OSR = osteon remodeling evident.

diaphysis. The small number of 20-y.o. subjects and the fact that about one-third of the younger animals also failed to show labeling precluded statistical demonstration of a difference in labeling frequency as a function of age. Among the 9 animals in which labeling occurred, 6 showed a measurable distance between the labels corresponding to the 2 pairs of injections. These included both 4-y.o. animals and 4 of the 10-y.o. animals. The rate of bone formation was calculated as the distance between labels (μm) divided by the number of days (10 to 14) between injections. The rate ranged from 1.4 to 2.7 μm/day; there was no evidence that age influenced this measure of bone formation.

Possible relationships between osteonal labeling in the femoral diaphysis and other indices of skeletal status were explored by dividing the subjects into 2 groups, 9 that exhibited labeling and 7 that did not, regardless of age. These groups were compared with regard to metacarpal PCA and all of the tibial mineralization indices in Table 27-3. None of the comparisons yielded significant differences using two-tailed t-tests for difference of the means.

The number of primary osteons per cm^2 of cortex of the femoral diaphysis did not vary significantly with age (Table 27-4). There was also no consistent relation between the degree of osteonal remodeling and age (Table 27-4). The variation in degree of remodeling (Figures 27-4 and 27-5), however, clearly

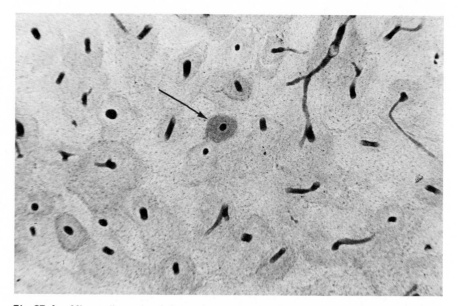

Fig. 27-4. Microradiograph of femoral cross section from a 4-y.o. macaque. Note the regular distribution of osteons. One osteon (arrow) appears to be partially mineralized, whereas the majority appear to be well mineralized.

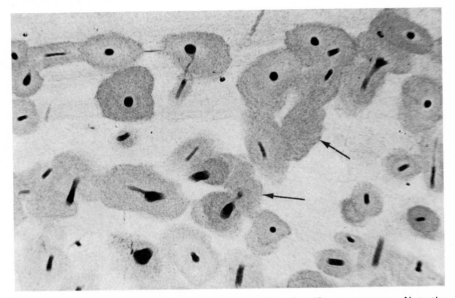

Fig. 27-5. Microradiograph of a femoral cross section of a 20-y.o. macaque. Note the irregular distribution of osteons and the large number that are partially mineralized (arrows). Many osteons have irregular borders giving the impression of extensive remodeling.

increased in the older age groups as reflected in the fact that individual animals in the 10-y.o. and 20-y.o. groups showed values 8 to 30 times the median values for their groups.

Attempts to relate the quantitative data on the density and remodeling of osteonal bone in the femoral diaphysis to metacarpal PCA, tibial mineralization, and labeling activity of the femur revealed no correlation. Only 1 of 18 linear regressions yielded a statistically significant result, *viz.*, osteons per cm^2 vs. serum copper (R = -0.53; p = 0.04). (Approximately one significant result in 20 regression analyses would be expected by chance.)

Histologic evaluation of sections of bone prepared from various sampling sites revealed no significant changes. In addition, evaluation of microradiographs of cross sections of femoral diaphyses revealed insignificant variations in densities of osteons.

DISCUSSION

In man, the osteoporotic index is among the physical measures that correlate most strongly with chronological age (2). This study shows change in a similar measure, percent cortical area, to be characteristic of macaques. We prefer Garn's

(4) term "percent cortical area" to "osteoporotic index" because the direction of change in the index should correspond to direction of change in the underlying phenomenon. High values of the various osteoporotic indices proposed to date reflect greater cortical thickness, not cortical thinning. Thus, they are not properly "osteoporotic" indices. For clarity of exposition, percent cortical area is a preferable term.

Results of this study indicated that in the macaque, as in man, PCA of the second metacarpal of the right hand correlated more strongly with chronological age than that of several other bones in the hands and feet. They also indicated that, in the monkey at least, calculations of PCA based on triplicate measures of midshaft diameters of total width and width of the marrow space (PCA–C) yield values more strongly correlated with chronological age than calculations based on longitudinal areas taken in the mid-half of the bone (PCA–L). If confirmed on a larger number of animals, this observation would suggest that osteoporosis of aging is more pronounced in the center of the diaphysis than at its extremes.

The age-group differences in PCA observed in this study indicated a change in the same direction as the osteoporosis of aging in man. Furthermore, the magnitude of the difference between the 10-y.o. and 20-y.o. groups (12%) was comparable to the decline seen in human females between the fourth and seventh decades of life (ref. 4, p. 135). The generality of the process to other parts of the skeletal system was suggested by the finding of enlarged medullary spaces in the cranial bones of the older animals (Chapter 29, this volume), and various indices from other bones discussed below.

A question of considerable geriatric interest concerns the relation of cortical thinning to hormonal aspects of reproductive function in the female. In human females of a given age, the diameter of the medullary space in the metacarpal is inversely proportional to parity, i.e., women who have experienced many pregnancies show less evidence of cortical bone resorption in later life than women who have experienced few pregnancies. Though the number of female pigtail macaques of known parity in this study was small, a similar trend was observed. Higher parity was associated with less osteoporosis.

The maximal rate of decline in PCA occurs in women during the sixth decade and coincides with the first years of complete cessation of menses. This observation has led to the general concept of a close relationship between menopause and osteoporosis of aging. Because the skeletal change begins in the fourth decade, however, some investigators have questioned whether there is a direct functional relationship between menopause and the osteoporosis of aging. They may be independent processes that happen to overlap in time course. As noted above, the difference in mean PCA of the 10-y.o. and 20-y.o. females was of the same magnitude as that seen between premenopausal and postmenopausal women. This was true whether the 20-y.o. group was limited to premenopausal females or not (age-group difference of 11% and 12%, respectively). This observation suggests that in the macaque, the osteoporosis of aging proceeds relatively independently of cessation in ovarian function. Whereas current evidence (5) indicates that menopause occurs later in the lifespan of the macaque than of the human female, the results of this study indicate that the onset of osteoporosis occurs at a comparable period in the lifespan of the two species, and is not closely associated with the menopause.

In the human there is a marked sex difference in the rate and end point of the osteoporosis of aging. The small number of male subjects in this study precluded addressing this question in the macaque. The data were consistent, however, with the concept that the direction of change in cortical bone thickness in males is the same as in female pigtail macaques, and that it occurs in other macaque species (longtail macaques) as well.

The same mineralization indices determined from tibial bone that correlated well with age (Chapter 28) also correlated well with metacarpal PCA (Table 27-3). This was to be expected, given that age and metacarpal PCA were inversely correlated (Figure 27-1). The strong correlation of cortical thickness with the Ca and Mg content of trabecular bone may indicate that, as the cortex decreases in thickness, the proportion of marrow dry weight represented by bone declines as well. This is consistent with the notion that the factors responsible for a decrease in the apposition:resorption ratio at the endosteal surface also decrease the ratio at the surface of trabecular bone. The reduced Ca/Zn and Mg/Zn ratios with decreasing cortical thickness suggest a change in the mineral composition of the remaining bone with age.

Assuming that the negative correlation between cortical thickness and serum copper level (Table 27-3; Figure 27-2) is not a statistical artifact, its functional significance is unclear. Copper deficiency produces osteoporotic changes in some animals (1). The fact that thinning of the metacarpal cortex and decreased numbers of osteons per unit area in the femoral shaft were associated with increased serum copper levels makes it highly improbable that osteoporosis of aging in the macaque is secondary to copper deficiency. Elevated copper levels in the more osteoporotic animals may reflect an inability to use copper in endosteal bone apposition or the vain engagement of a homeostatic mechanism to counteract an osteoporotic process based on other factors.

The thinning of cortical bone in later life is attributed to a decline in the ratio of apposition rate to resorption rate at the endosteal surface (4). Osteons are remodeled and new bone is formed by a continuous process in which osteoclasts tunnel into existing bone, resorbing hydroxyapatite crystals and matrix, and osteoblasts follow, laying down new osteoid in which amorphous calcium phosphate crystallizes to form new hydroxyapatite. When this process is active, tetracycline is incorporated into the new calcium phosphate crystals and is identifiable by its fluorescence under ultraviolet light (7). If the remodeling process is dormant no tetracycline is incorporated. In this study, none of 3 animals in the 20-y.o. group showed evidence of tetracycline incorporation in femoral cortex, and one-third of animals in the 4-y.o. and 10-y.o. groups failed to show such evidence. Furthermore, not all animals that showed labeling exhibited two distinct bands corresponding to the two periods of administration, 10 to 14 days apart. In those animals in which labeling occurred on both administrations, the rate of apposition, as judged by the distance between the labels, was within the range seen in humans (6).

The lack of labeling did not correlate with any other skeletal measure. This lack of correlation could reflect problems in laboratory technique, but more likely it reflects the small sample size. Remodeling and new bone formation occur at different times, at different rates, and in response to different stimuli in different parts of the skeleton. Thus, the midshaft of the femur in sedentary macaques may not be an appropriate site to look for changes in bone formation that correlate with metacarpal osteoporosis. Or, in the temporal sphere, a single 2-week assessment of remodeling activity of any bone may not accurately represent the rate of activity over months and years that is reflected in reduced thinning of metacarpal PCA and changes in tibial mineralization. If the process alternates between active and dormant states, a measure of the proportion of time spent in each state would be expected to correlate much better with the radiographic and biochemical indices than an evaluation of the state of activity at one point in time.

The fact that the various measures of mineralization in the tibia correlated better than femoral microstructure with metacarpal PCA would suggest that changes in the mineral composition of bone may be more closely related to the osteoporosis of aging and less susceptible to individual variation than the tetracycline labeling and microstructural indices. The decline in bone content of Ca and Mg and their individual ratios to Zn are consistent with findings in the aging human skeleton (Chapter 28).

Despite the relatively small number of animals studied and the fact that few of them were well into the third trimester of life, it is clear by several indices that macaques exhibit osteoporosis of aging. At the present time, the data on this and other species are inadequate to determine whether the mechanism of the process is more similar to that in the human than mechanisms of osteoporosis in nonprimates.

ACKNOWLEDGMENTS

This research was supported in part by National Institutes of Health grants RR00166, RR52177, and AG62145 to the University of Washington.

REFERENCES

1. Adelstein, S. J., and Vallee, B. L. (1962): Copper. In: *Mineral Metabolism*, edited by C. L. Comar and F. Bronner. New York; Academic Press.
2. Comfort, A. (1969): Test-battery to measure ageing-rate in man. *Lancet*, **2**: 1411–1415.
3. Dequeker, J. V., Baeyenos, J. P., and Claessens, J. (1969): The significance of stature as a clinical measurement of ageing. *J. Am. Geriat.*, **17**: 169–179.
4. Garn, S. M. (1970): *The Earlier Gain and Later Loss of Cortical Bone*. Springfield, Ill.; Thomas.
5. Hodgen, G. D., Goodman, A. L., O'Connor, A., and Johnson, D. K. (1977): Menopause in rhesus monkeys: model for study of disorders in the human climacteric. *Am. J. Obstet. Gynec.*, **127**: 581–584.
6. Lacroix, P. (1971): The internal remodeling of bones. In: *The Biochemistry and Physiology of Bone*, Vol. 3, edited by G. H. Bourne, pp. 119–144. New York; Academic Press.
7. Rasmussen, H., and Bordier, P. (1974): *The Physiological and Cellular Basis of Metabolic Bone Disease*. Baltimore; Williams and Wilkins.

28

Mineral Content of Bone and Other Tissues

K. Y. Lei and L. C. Young

Nutrition Program, College of Agriculture and Home Economics
Agricultural and Forestry Experiment Station
Mississippi State University, Mississippi State, Mississippi

INTRODUCTION

The demineralization of bone with age is universal and is initiated at about age 30 in humans. This has been attributed to such factors as decline in endocrine function, decrease in physical activity, and nutritional deficiency which are characteristics of many older people (6). The major mineral component of cortical bone is calcium, which comprises approximately 39% by ashed weight. Other important components are magnesium and zinc, which amount to 0.49 and 0.02% by ashed weight respectively (1). An average adult male body contains about 2 g of zinc, and most of this is located in the bone (1). Based on a calcium content of 1500 g, Aitken (1) calculated the zinc content in the skeleton of an average man to be 0.68 to 0.96 g. Skeletal calcium can decline with age, without a similar fall in skeletal zinc. Thus, the calcium:zinc ratio of the human femur is inversely related to age. Copper is a fourth mineral that has been shown to play a role in osteoporosis in some animals. Dogs, cattle, pigs, and sheep reared on copper deficient diets show several signs of deficient bone mineralization (15).

There is little quantitative data on the precise distribution of these and other minerals in the skeleton and soft tissues of human or nonhuman primates, or on how these may vary with age. This study was designed to examine the distribution of selected minerals in bone and various soft tissues collected from 4-, 10-, and 20-y.o. groups of macaques.

METHODS

The subjects were 18 macaques, 16 *Macaca nemestrina* and 2 *Macaca fascicularis*; the majority (14) were females. The age distribution included three 4-y.o., ten 10-y.o. and five 20-y.o. animals. Their diet was a commercial monkey chow (Chapter 3, this volume) adequate in all nutrients known to be essential for good health. Specimens were taken of bone, serum, liver, pancreas, skeletal muscle, kidney, and esophagus. The tissue samples were excised from animals with stainless steel instruments at sacrifice, packaged in plastic containers, stored in dry ice, and shipped by air freight.

Two discs of bone, 1 to 2 cm wide, were cut from the middle and distal parts of the tibia. The cortical bone from the midshaft disc was cleaned of periosteum, endosteal bone, and debris, and split into two halves to give a sample of about 600 mg. The trabecular bone embedded in fatty marrow was separated from the cortical bone, and about 0.5 cm^3 was removed from the distal-shaft. The samples were dried in a drying oven at 80°C for 4 days and the dry weights were determined. The samples were wet-digested by the same method described for soft tissues below. Lanthanum chloride was used as the suppressant for phosphate interference in calcium determinations in the tibia. The concentration of the lanthanum salt in the test solution was 0.75%.

Triplicate or duplicate samples of approximately equal wet weight were excised from each soft tissue specimen. The tissue samples were dried and the dry weights determined. Three ml of nitric acid were used for the wet-digestion of the samples in polypropylene test tubes. Digestion was carried out at 100°C for 4 hours. The samples were then diluted to suitable volume for trace mineral determinations by atomic absorption spectrophotometry (10). The minerals assayed in bone included calcium, magnesium and zinc; those assayed in serum and soft tissues included zinc, copper and iron. Blood hemoglobin content was determined by Laboratory Medicine, University Hospital, at the University of Washington.

The specimens had been coded by animal number and the age code was not broken until complete data on all animals were recorded. The data were analyzed statistically by least squares analysis of variance, and means were ranked by Duncan's new multiple range test (16).

RESULTS

The calcium, magnesium, and zinc contents of cortical and trabecular bone are presented in Table 28-1. The absolute contents of the three minerals in cortical

Table 28-1. Mean Contents and Proportions of Calcium, Magnesium, and Zinc in Cortical and Trabecular Bone from the Tibias of Macaques in Three Age Groups.

Age Group (Years)	Number of Subjects	Calcium mg/g D.M.	Magnesium mg/g D.M.	Zinc µg/g D.M.	Ca:Zn mg/µg	Mg:Zn µg/µg	Ca:Mg mg/mg
				Cortical Bone			
4	3	[a]228 ± 15	[a]3.54 ± 0.09	[a]86.0 ± 8.0	[a]2.66 ± 0.09	[a]41.5 ± 5.1	[a]64.5 ± 5.3
10	10	[a]248 ± 59	[ab]3.19 ± 0.32	[a]100.0 ± 29.0	[a]2.52 ± 0.29	[ab]33.7 ± 7.8	[a]77.9 ± 18.1
20	5	[a]228 ± 15	[b]3.08 ± 0.16	[a]110.0 ± 14.0	[b]2.09 ± 0.25	[b]28.5 ± 4.7	[a]74.1 ± 6.5
				Trabecular Bone			
4	3	[a]130 ± 19	[a]2.04 ± 0.44	[a]75.5 ± 18.2	[a]1.76 ± 0.27	[a]27.1 ± 0.88	[a]64.8 ± 7.7
10	10	[b]72 ± 16	[b]0.96 ± 0.20	[b]46.3 ± 4.9	[ab]1.56 ± 0.30	[b]20.7 ± 3.00	[a]75.3 ± 10.4
20	5	[b]61 ± 15	[b]0.74 ± 0.06	[b]48.2 ± 14.0	[b]1.30 ± 0.23	[b]16.9 ± 5.56	[a]79.9 ± 16.5

Values are means ± standard deviations.

[a,b]Duncan's new multiple range test: for a given bone type (cortical or trabecular), means preceded by a different superscript in a column differ from one another (p < 0.05).

bone either declined (as in the case of magnesium), or did not differ significantly among the age groups. In trabecular bone, the content of each of the three minerals was greater in the 4-y.o. group than in the 10- and 20-y.o. groups. The ratio of calcium to zinc (Ca:Zn) and of magnesium to zinc (Mg:Zn), however, declined significantly with increasing age in both cortical and trabecular bone. Scattergrams of Ca:Zn, Mg:Zn, and Ca:Mg ratios are presented in Fig. 28-1. With the exception of the zinc content of trabecular bone in the 4-y.o. group, the significant age differences in Ca:Zn and Mg:Zn resulted from a decline in calcium and magnesium content and an increase in zinc content with age. There were no significant differences in the Ca:Mg ratio among the three age groups.

The contents of zinc, copper, and iron found in a variety of nonskeletal tissues are presented in Table 28-2. The nonsignificant trend toward increased zinc levels noted in cortical bone was seen in most of the tissues studied and reached statistical significance in the pancreas and skeletal muscle (gastrocnemius). Serum copper was significantly higher in the 10- and 20-y.o. groups than in the 4-y.o. group, but no relation between age and copper level was detected in any of the soft tissues studied. Iron content increased with age in all tissues studied except the esophagus. This relation to age was significant in skeletal muscle and renal cortex. A similar but nonsignificant trend was seen in blood hemoglobin content. Mean ± standard deviations were 9.8 ± 0.6 g%, 10.8 ± 2.3 g%, and 12.4 ± 3.1 g% for the 4-, 10- and 20-y.o. groups respectively.

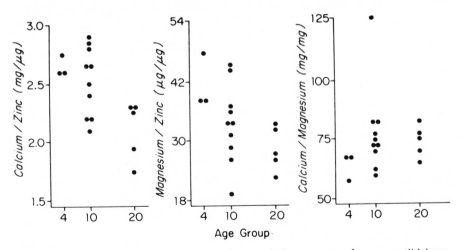

Fig. 28.1.   Interrelations of calcium, magnesium, and zinc contents of macaque tibial cortex with age.

Table 28-2. Mean Zinc, Copper, and Iron Contents of Soft Tissues from Three Age Groups of Macaques. Tissue Content, μg/g dry wt.

Age Group (Years)	Number of Subjects	Serum	Liver	Pancreas	Muscle Gastrocnemius	Kidney Cortex	Kidney Medulla	Esophagus
				Zinc				
4	3	[a]63.0 ± 2.0	[a]153 ± 15	[a]107.6 ± 14.7	[a]149 ± 10	[a]197 ± 21	[a]121 ± 27	[a]124 ± 16
10	10	[a]87.5 ± 24.5	[a]177 ± 37	[b]197.1 ± 47.4	[ab]186 ± 44	[a]230 ± 74	[a]155 ± 49	[a]114 ± 25
20	5	[a]82.7 ± 18.4	[a]177 ± 44	[b]185.7 ± 44.3	[b]220 ± 40	[a]229 ± 52	[a]135 ± 34	[a]88 ± 27
				Copper				
4	3	[a]114 ± 23	[a]18.6 ± 2.1	[a]7.67 ± 0.7	—	[a]22.6 ± 1.3	[a]16.0 ± 2.2	—
10	10	[b]181 ± 47	[a]16.5 ± 1.9	[a]8.46 ± 1.0	—	[a]23.2 ± 4.1	[a]18.9 ± 3.2	—
20	5	[b]191 ± 50	[a]15.9 ± 3.1	[a]8.22 ± 1.5	—	[a]23.2 ± 2.4	[a]16.9 ± 1.5	—
				Iron				
4	3	—	[a]526 ± 131	[a]89 ± 11	[a]114 ± 29	[a]182 ± 19	[a]200 ± 40	[a]149 ± 46
10	10	—	[a]1019 ± 1328	[a]146 ± 29	[ab]159 ± 41	[ab]268 ± 88	[a]277 ± 69	[a]113 ± 26
20	5	—	[a]2035 ± 2374	[a]328 ± 324	[b]202 ± 57	[b]382 ± 165	[a]344 ± 152	[a]127 ± 46

Values are means ± standard deviations; −, value not determined.

[a,b]Duncan's new multiple range test: for a given mineral, means preceded by a different superscript in a column differ from one another ($p < 0.05$).

DISCUSSION

The findings of reduced Ca:Zn and Mg:Zn ratios in older macaques agree with Aitken's (1) finding of reduced Ca:Zn ratio in the cortical bone of the human femur with increasing age. For the most part, age-related differences in the mineralization of bone cortex followed a steady trend across the age groups. This was not the case in the trabecular bone, where the contents of calcium, magnesium, and zinc were all significantly higher in the 4-y.o. group than in the 10- and 20-y.o. groups. The fact that 4-y.o. macaques are in a very active growth phase may account for the relatively intense mineralization of trabecular bone in this age group. Magnesium accumulates about twice as fast in the bones of young rats as in the bones of old rats (8) and humans show marked reduction in calcium content of trabecular bone between 30 and 50 years of age (1).

A common postulate based on human studies is that nutritional factors or exercise differences may account for the differences in bone composition seen in young vs. older individuals. Those factors were controlled for in the present study in the sense that animals in all age groups had received the same diet and most of them had been housed in single cages for most of their adult lives. The pattern of demineralization with age seen in this sample of macaques was similar to that in man, thus lending credence to the contrasting view, based on some epidemiological studies in man (5), that the osteoporosis of aging does not derive primarily from nutritional or activity factors.

The tendency for zinc content to be higher in several different kinds of tissue from 10- and 20-y.o. than from 4-y.o. animals in this study is consistent with findings in rodents and man. Bergman *et al.* (2), studying female rats from 3 to 32 weeks of age, found that the zinc levels of pancreas and serum were correlated and that alterations with age consisted primarily of a drop during the 8th to 12th weeks of age and a later return to a constant level. This period coincides with the sexual maturation of female rats and may be similar to the adolescent period of the monkey. Thus, the lower levels noted in muscle and pancreatic zinc in the 4-y.o. macaques may be related to the period of life when tissue mineral levels are adjusting to the influence of the hormonal changes and the rapid growth of adolescence. This interpretation is consistent with reports that, while zinc levels may be lower in the adolescent age group, intestinal absorption of [65]zinc is greater in young rats than in older ones (9). Zinc metabolism also changes with age in man (12): zinc balances reported for children (4) and young adults (13) are higher than for older people. The concentrations of zinc and other trace elements of the human brain remain essentially constant from 31 to 80 years of age, and the regional differences within the brain persist throughout life (14). Still, the pattern of change varies with the tissue studied. In humans, the concentration of zinc increases in the prostate but decreases in the uterus with age (11). In the kidney, the zinc content reaches a peak in the 40–50 decade and declines thereafter. Similarly, the zinc content of the aorta declines slowly with age after reaching a peak between 20 and 30 years of age.

Previous studies of changes in copper content with age have, for the most part, concentrated on the liver. In most species, including man and the rat, the liver copper concentrations are higher in newborns than in adults (7, 15). However, in sheep, liver copper concentration rises continuously from birth; and in cows, it changes little from birth to old age (3). The monkeys in this study demonstrated no differences in liver copper level with age. It seemed to be slightly higher in the 4-y.o. group than in the others but the difference was not statistically significant. Perhaps by the age of 4 years, the decline in whole liver copper in the monkey has been completed. The levels of copper in the serum were significantly higher in the older age groups than in the 4-y.o. group. This is of interest in view of the fact that cortical bone thickness was found to correlate positively with serum copper level (see Chapter 27, this volume).

The mechanism responsible for the increasing tissue zinc and iron and higher serum copper concentrations observed in the older monkeys remains to be elucidated. Dietary trace mineral intake may be marginally deficient and thus account for some of the difference between the rapidly growing 4-y.o. group and the 10-y.o. group. The levels per unit weight of tissue may remain low in the younger group until growth ceases and "normal" stores can accumulate. This explanation cannot, however, explain the continuing increases seen in many tissues between the 10-y.o. and 20-y.o. groups. The mechanisms underlying these differences remain to be elucidated.

ACKNOWLEDGMENTS

We gratefully acknowledge the technical assistance of Ms. Rita C. Y. Tsai. This study was aided by the Mississippi Agricultural and Forestry Experiment Station and is published as journal article No. *3728.* It was also supported in part by National Institutes of Health grants RR00166, RR52177 and AG62145 to the University of Washington.

REFERENCES

1. Aitken, J. M. (1976): Factors affecting the distribution of zinc in the human skeleton. *Calcif. Tiss. Res.*, **20**: 23–30.
2. Bergman, B., Sjöström, R., and Wing, K. R. (1974): The variation with age of tissue zinc concentrations in albino rats determined by atomic absorption spectrophotometry. *Acta Physiol. Scand.*, **92**: 440–450.

3. Cunningham, I. J. (1931): Some biochemical and physiological aspects of copper in animal nutrition. *Biochem. J.*, **25**: 1267–1294.
4. Engel, R. W., Miller, R. F., and Price, N. O. (1966): Metabolic patterns in preadolescent children. XIII. Zinc balance. In: *Zinc Metabolism*, edited by A. S. Prasad, pp. 326–338. Springfield, Ill.; Thomas.
5. Garn, S. M. (1970): *The Earlier Gain and the Later Loss of Cortical Bone*. Springfield, Ill.; Thomas.
6. Garn, S. M. (1975): Bone-loss and aging. In: *The Physiology and Pathology of Human Aging*, edited by R. Goldman and M. Rockstein, pp. 39–57. New York; Academic Press.
7. Gregoriadis, G., and Sourkes, T. L. (1967): Intracellular distribution of copper in the liver of the rat. *Can. J. Biochem.*, **45**: 1841–1851.
8. Lengemann, F. W. (1959): The metabolism of magnesium and calcium by the rat. *Arch. Biochem.*, **84**: 278–285.
9. Methfessel, A. H., and Spencer, H. (1970): Effect of age and protein intake on [65]Zn excretion and tissue distribution in the rat. *Radiat. Res.*, **43**: 237.
10. Prasad, A. S., Oberleas, D., and Halsted, J. A. (1966): Determination of zinc in biological fluids by atomic absorption spectrophotometry. In: *Zinc Metabolism*, edited by A. S. Prasad, pp. 27–37. Springfield, Ill.; Thomas.
11. Schroeder, H. A., Nason, A. P., Tipton, I. H., and Balassa, J. J. (1967): Essential trace metals in man: Zinc. Relation to environmental cadmium. *J. Chron. Dis.*, **20**: 179–210.
12. Spencer, H., Osis, D., Kramer, L., and Norris, C. (1976): Intake, excretion, and retention of zinc in man. In: *Trace Elements in Human Health and Disease*, edited by A. S. Prasad, pp. 345–361. New York; Academic Press.
13. Tribble, H. M., and Scoular, F. I. (1954): Zinc metabolism of young college women on self-selected diets. *J. Nutr.*, **52**: 209–216.
14. Ule, G., Volkl, A., and Berlet, H. (1974): Trace elements in human brain. II. Copper, zinc, calcium and magnesium of 13 brain areas compared to iron during the 4th to 8th life decade. *Zeitchrift Für Neurologie*, **206**: 117–128.
15. Underwood, E. J. (1977): *Trace Elements in Human and Animal Nutrition*. New York; Academic Press.
16. Winer, B. J. (1962): *Statistical Principles in Experimental Design*. New York: McGraw Hill.

29

Craniofacial Sutures

Vincent G. Kokich, Peter A. Shapiro, Benjamin C. Moffett

Department of Orthodontics, School of Dentistry,
University of Washington, Seattle, Washington

Ernest W. Retzlaff

Department of Biomechanics, College of Osteopathic Medicine,
Michigan State University, East Lansing, Michigan

INTRODUCTION

Sutures provide the fibrous interconnection between the skeletal components of the craniofacial complex. The soft tissue in the sutures supplies the cellular reserve that responds to functional demands during growth by initiating deposition or resorption of bone at the sutural margin. The suture is therefore a highly adaptive and responsive articulation. If, however, bony union, or synostosis, occurs across the suture its adaptability ceases. A basic description of craniofacial skeletal growth and development is therefore incomplete without a clear understanding of the morphologic and histologic changes that occur in the sutural ligament with age.

Fusion of human and nonhuman primate cranial sutures has been studied by several investigators. The majority of the earlier studies evaluated dry skulls of unknown or estimated age by gross inspection of the ectocranial and endocranial surfaces of intact sutures (1, 5, 19, 20). In general, these studies showed that sutural fusion commenced during early adulthood; however, the internal portions of the sutures were not examined for possible areas of initial fusion, nor were histologic aging changes noted.

Recently methods have been established to evaluate external and internal surfaces of sutures in human autopsy specimens (4, 10). These methods have permitted documentation of the age-related changes in the human facial sutures, showing that in man the frontonasal, frontomaxillary, zygomaticotemporal, frontozygomatic, and zygomaticomaxillary sutures do not fuse before the seventh or eighth decade (4, 10). The human facial sutures are therefore potentially responsive to extrinsic functional demands until late in life. There are age-related changes, however, including an increase in morphologic sutural irregularity, a decrease in the number of collagen fibers, and an increase in the size of the medullary cavity of the facial bones adjacent to the sutures (4, 10).

While the age changes in human facial sutures have been clearly elucidated in recent years, little is known about the aging of nonhuman primate sutures. Since nonhuman primates are widely used as experimental models to test treatments for the correction of skeletal malrelation of the craniofacial complex, it is essential that the life cycle of their sutures be explored in detail.

METHODS

Facial sutures of 23 pigtail macaques (*Macaca nemestrina*) ranging in age from 4 years to 20+ years, were examined by histologic, radiographic and gross techniques (investigators V. K., P. S., and B. M.) to determine the aging changes in the sutures and the status of sutural patency. The frontozygomatic suture was examined in all 23 animals, and 6 (2 4-y.o., 2 10-y.o. and 2 20-y.o.) were selected for additional analysis of the zygomaticomaxillary, zygomaticotemporal and intermaxillary sutures. The frontozygomatic, zygomaticomaxillary and zygomaticotemporal sutures are bilateral, so the left suture from each specimen was used for radiographic and gross examination for fusion, and the right side for histologic analysis. The intermaxillary suture was divided into thirds; the anterior and posterior thirds were analyzed for sutural fusion and the middle third was prepared for histologic analysis (4, 10).

Histologic sections were obtained by removing and decalcifying a block of bone containing the suture (Figure 29-1). The decalcified block was embedded in paraffin, and 7-μm sections were cut across the suture in a plane perpendicular to the external surface of the bone. The intermaxillary suture was sectioned perpendicularly to its oral surface. The sections were stained with hematoxylin and eosin, Verhoeff's elastic stain, alcian blue-periodic acid Schiff, and Mallory's aniline blue collagen stain.

To document synostosis a tissue block containing the entire suture was removed from each specimen. The tissue blocks were placed in a presoak commercial enzyme solution (Biz[R]) for 1 to 2 weeks. The enzyme solution removes the remaining soft tissue without affecting the dimensional integrity of bone (4). The suture was then embedded in Ward's Bioplastic* (Figure 29-2), and 250-μm

*Ward's Natural Science Establishment, Inc., Rochester, New York.

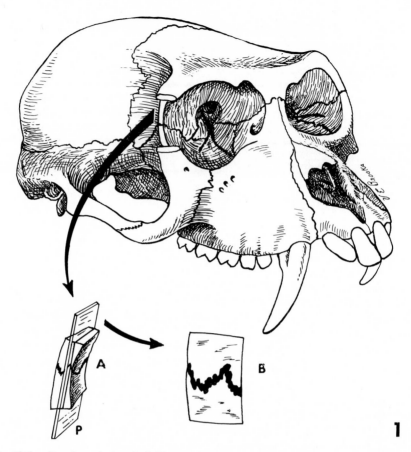

Fig. 29-1. Drawing of the skull illustrating the orientation of the sections through the frontozygomatic suture. A, the suture removed intact from the skull, showing the plane of sections (P); B, a representative section of the frontozygomatic suture.

Fig. 29-2. Bioplastic block containing the frontozygomatic suture. The suture is placed in Bioplastic for orientation and support during ground sectioning. The plastic stage provides fixation to the thin sectioning machine.

Fig. 29-3. Bioplastic section of the frontozygomatic suture, 250 μm. The suture is rigidly supported by the Bioplastic during and after the sectioning procedure, eliminating accidental fracture of the section. (×3)

sections were cut on a Gillings-Hamco Thin Sectioning Machine (Figure 29-3). Each section was radiographed with a Picker industrial x-ray machine. The radiographs were viewed at 10x magnification and those sections that exhibited unquestionable radiolucency of the sutural space were recorded as patent (Figure 29-4). If sutural patency was questionable on the radiograph (Figure 29-5a), the corresponding bioplastic section was placed in Ward's Bioplastic Solvent for 3 weeks. Specimens that separated at the suture during that time were regarded as

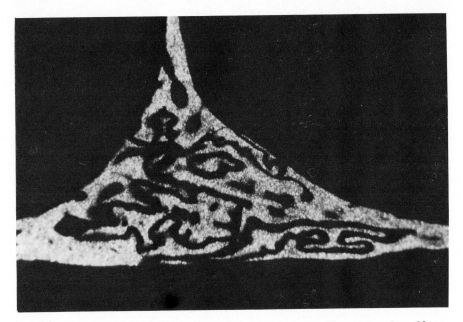

Fig. 29-4. Radiograph of a Bioplastic section of the intermaxillary suture in a 20-y.o. macaque. No radiopaque areas are found in the suture, indicating that this section of the suture is not fused. (×10)

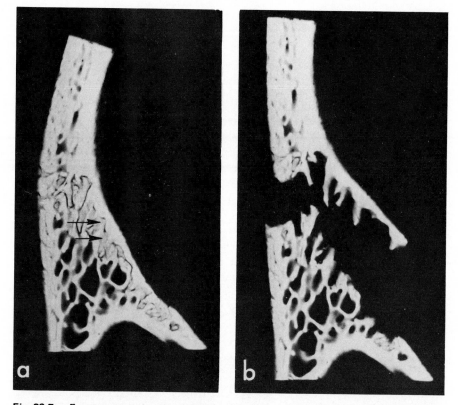

Fig. 29-5. Frontozygomatic suture, 20-y.o. macaque. a, radiograph of a Bioplastic section exhibiting several radiopaque areas (arrows) of questionable synostosis within the suture. b, separation at the suture following treatment with Bioplastic solvent indicating that the suture was not fused. (×6)

not fused (Figure 29-5b), and those that did not, as fused. At no time were the sections mechanically manipulated.

The calvaria of 3 females of each age group matched for subspecies and body weight at maturity were used to study age-related changes in sutural collagen patterns and innervation (investigator E. R.). They were processed by the method of Popevec *et al.* (15). A 5-cm tissue block including the parietotemporal suture was removed from the calvarium and trimmed so that the width did not exceed 1 cm. Care was taken to preserve the inner and outer periosteum. Before decalcification, the bone segment was divided into 3 equal portions. The center third, used in the study, was cut into segments 1 to 2 mm wide. Decalcification was accomplished with 5% formic acid in 70% ethanol changed at 12-hour intervals. The process was complete when no precipitate appeared in 5 ml of the used acid-alcohol upon the addition of 1 ml of 5% ammonium oxalate. The tissues were embedded in paraffin and sectioned at 7 μm using a rotary microtome, affixed to 1 × 3 inch glass slides, and stored for staining. The protargol silver-gelatine method of Retzlaff and Fontaine (16) demonstrated both the sutural connective tissue and the nerve fibers. The sutural tissue with the adjacent parietal and temporal bones, stained by the protargol method, were viewed with a Zeiss photomicroscope using a lens combination that provided a field 0.56 mm in diameter. Sharpey's fiber bundles of collagenous connective tissue were counted in areas where they passed from the sutural tissue into the adjacent cranial bone. These bundles were counted in every fifth section to minimize counting the same bundle more than once. Ten fields were counted from each specimen and the mean number of fibers per field was calculated.

All evaluations of suture specimens were performed without knowledge of the ages of the animals from which they were taken.

OBSERVATIONS

Examination of bioplastic sections of the intermaxillary, zygomaticomaxillary, frontozygomatic, and zygomaticotemporal sutures revealed complete patency in these sutures through 20 years of age. The histologic age changes in these sutures

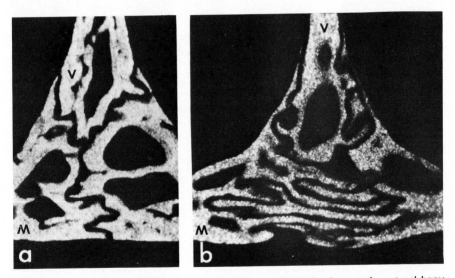

Fig. 29-6. a, intermaxillary suture, 4-y.o. macaque. The projections at the sutural bony margin are short, so the suture exhibits minimal morphologic irregularity at this age. (×6) b, intermaxillary suture, 20-y.o. macaque, showing increased length and number of bony spicules which produce an extremely irregular morphology. (×6) V, vomer; M, maxilla.

in general were similar, so the following observations will refer to all sutures studied unless otherwise stated.

Initially, the bony surfaces comprising a suture exist as two flat plates separated by the immature sutural ligament (Figure 29-6a, 7a). With advancing age, these surfaces become irregular due to the formation of bony spicules extending into the sutural space (Figure 29-6b). Spicules begin as a localized thickening or accumulation of unremodeled nonlamellar bone at the sutural surface. With advancing age, they increase in length by accretions of nonlamellar bone at their tips (Figure 29-7b). The previously deposited bone then undergoes remodeling to form osteons at the base of each projection (Figure 29-7c). This process recurs numerous times during the life cycle of a suture, resulting in a progressive increase in the number of projections (Figure 29-6b). The orientation of the bony projections remains constant with age, paralleling the external or internal surfaces of the bones that form the suture (Figures 29-6b and 29-7b). Although

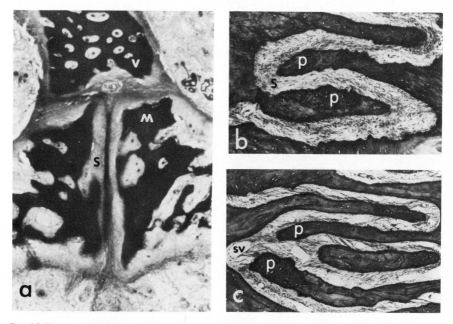

Fig. 29-7. a, intermaxillary suture, neonatal macaque. At birth, the intermaxillary suture is composed of two flat plates of bone separated by the immature sutural ligament. (×16) V, vomer; M, maxilla; S, sutural ligament. b, intermaxillary suture, 4-y.o. macaque. The bony projections (p) at this age consist predominantly of unremodeled nonlamellar bone. The collagen fibers are evenly distributed throughout the suture (S). (×24) c, intermaxillary suture, 20-y.o. macaque. At this age, the bony projections (p) consist largely of secondary osteons, with nonlamellar bone located at the suture surface. Several sinusoidal vessels (SV) are evident. (×32)

Table 29-1. Sharpey's Fibers in the Parietotemporal Suture in 3 Age Groups of Female *M. nemestrina*. Each Entry Represents the Mean Number of Sharpey's Fibers per Microscopic Field for One Animal.

	Age Group (Years)		
	4	10	20
Number of Fibers	24	21	16
	25	20	15
	23	19	14
Range	24 ± 1	20 ± 1	15 ± 1

the number of bony projections increases with age, the degree of morphologic irregularity varies according to suture. In the oldest specimens, the intermaxillary suture is the most convoluted, followed by the zygomaticomaxillary, frontozygomatic, and zygomaticotemporal sutures.

The sutural ligament consists of an orderly arrangement of cells, blood vessels, and collagen fibers, which change in volumetric proportion with advancing age. At younger ages, the sutural ligament is predominantly composed of evenly distributed collagen fibers coursing between and into the surfaces of the 2 bones comprising the suture (Figure 29-7b). At this age, fibroblasts are randomly dis-

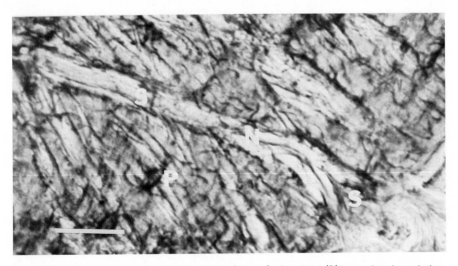

Fig. 29-8. Photomicrograph of thick section (25 mμ) of parietal (P) bone showing relation of Sharpey's Fiber (S) and the Golgi Type IV nerve fibers (N) in 20-y.o. macaque. Protargol-silver gelatine stain. (Scale 100 mμ.)

persed within the collagen fiber network while osteoblasts are located at the bony surfaces. Arterioles and venules are also found in small numbers within the fiber system. The concentration of collagen fibers decreases with age. By 20 years of age they are sparse, and those that remain form bundles associated with localized areas of bony deposition (Figure 29-7c). The number of Sharpey's fibers in the parietotemporal suture decreases with age (Table 29-1). At all ages studied, however, one or more Golgi type IV nerve fibers accompany each Sharpey's fiber into the bone (Figure 29-8).

The cellularity of the sutures decreases with advancing age (Figure 29-7b, c). By 20 years of age, the number of fibroblasts decreases significantly and osteoblasts are found only in isolated areas of bony deposition. Although localized

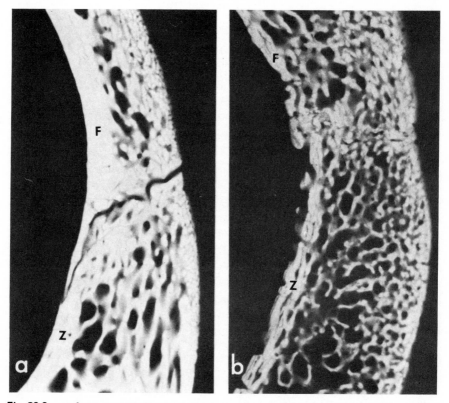

Fig. 29-9. a, frontozygomatic suture, 4-y.o. macaque, showing size of the medullary cavity in the frontal (F) and zygomatic (Z) bones adjacent to the suture. (×7) b, frontozygomatic suture, 20-y.o. macaque, showing large increase in the size of the medullary cavity in the frontal (F) and zygomatic (Z) bones. (×7)

areas of bony deposition and resorption were found at the sutural surfaces at all ages, the number of depository areas decreased with advancing age.

The number of large blood vessels within the sutural ligament increases with age. By 20 years of age, these large, thin-walled, sinusoidal vessels are dispersed randomly within the sutural ligament (Figure 29-7c). These vessels often communicate with the medullary cavity.

Age changes were also observed in the internal architecture of the bones that form the sutures. With advancing age, the medullary cavity increases in size (Figure 29-9).

DISCUSSION

The results of the present study clearly indicate that the frontozygomatic, zygomaticotemporal, and zygomaticomaxillary sutures do not undergo bony synostosis, but remain patent at least through 20 years of age in the pigtail macaque. This finding contradicts Krogman's (5) report that the facial sutures fuse shortly after eruption of the third molar teeth in Old World primates, but is consistent with the finding that these sutures in humans do not fuse until the seventh decade (4, 10). The finding that the intermaxillary suture does not fuse by age 20 in the macaque is not compatible with human findings (6, 10, 13). Intermaxillary sutural fusion in humans can occur by as early as 18 years of age, although patency has been reported in some specimens up to 28 years of age (14). Little is known about what stimulates bony union across sutural surfaces. Further studies comparing the physiologic and functional milieu associated with the human and nonhuman primate intermaxillary sutures may provide a clue to the species difference in the age at which sutural synostosis begins.

The present investigation shows a tendency toward enlargement of the medullary cavity of the bones that border the facial sutures. This finding is in agreement with the radiographic, biochemical, and histologic study of long bones of the same animals reported by Bowden et al. (Chapter 27, this volume). In humans, similar enlargement of the medullary cavity occurs in facial bones (4, 10), mandible (7), and rib (2, 17). A physiologic osteoporosis seems to occur with increasing age, as in humans, owing to an enlargement of the marrow cavity at the expense of the cortical plate. A greater surface area of bone undergoes resorption than formation during old age (18), so that a net loss of bone occurs and results in osteoporosis.

In man, the medullary spaces of the facial bones increase in number and size and progressively expand toward the suture until fatty marrow communicates with and finally replaces the sutural ligament at older ages (4, 10). Replacement of the sutural ligament by fatty marrow was not observed in nonhuman primate sutures in the present study. There are two possible explanations for this difference: 1) the nonhuman primate facial sutures are continually active through-out life and are not replaced by fatty marrow; or 2) the replacement of the non-human primate sutural ligament by fatty marrow occurs after 20 years of age. To evaluate the validity of the second hypothesis, the histologic sections of human and nonhuman primate facial sutures were compared to develop a direct age correlation between man and monkey. The results indicated that the 20-y.o. macaque exhibits the same histologic sutural aging characteristics as a 50- to 65-y.o. human. Since the dissolution of the sutural ligament and replacement by fatty marrow occur after age 65 in human facial sutures, they should be investi-gated in macaques older than 20 years of age.

The present study demonstrates an increase in the morphologic irregularity of the bony sutural surface due to an age related increase in the number and length of the bony projections or interdigitations. This change is similar to that ob-served in human facial sutures (4, 10). Washburn (21) and Moss (11, 12) suggest that a relationship exists between the development of interdigitations at the sutural surface and the extrinsic functional milieu affecting a particular suture. They believe that the fine details of sutural morphology, such as interdigitations, are secondary responses to the extrinsic forces imposed on the bones. This is consistent with the view that the degree of development of sutural serrations is related to the length of time the suture is patent; sutures that do not undergo bony synostosis until old age are more highly serrated than those that fuse earlier (8). The results of the present study substantiate this finding, since the human intermaxillary suture, which fuses during the second to third decade of life, is less serrated than the macaque intermaxillary suture, which remains patent until at least 20 years of age.

The present investigation documents fewer collagen fibers in the sutural liga-ment with advancing age, which agrees with findings in human facial sutures (4, 10). Age changes in collagen have also been demonstrated in other areas of the human body, such as a decrease in the ratio of ground substance to collagen and a decrease in the amount of soluble collagen with increasing age (3, 9). It is therefore reasonable to assume that similar age changes in collagen may also occur in the nonhuman primate sutural ligament.

In summary, the results of this study suggest a close similarity between the human and nonhuman primate with respect to several histologic aging charac-teristics. Of perhaps greater biologic importance, however, are the dissimilarities, which open new questions regarding human growth, development, and aging that should be explored in the nonhuman primate model: What are the extrinsic func-tional influences that prolong the onset of fusion in the nonhuman primate inter-maxillary suture? Are these influences lacking in humans, and if so, does this suggest any clues about what stimulates normal sutural fusion in man? Are the same stimuli operative in human cases involving abnormally premature sutural synostosis? Clearly, extensive investigation of the sutural articulations in the nonhuman primate can be a vital factor in understanding the normal and abnormal development of the human craniofacial complex.

ACKNOWLEDGMENTS

This study was supported by National Institutes of Health grants RR00166, RR52177, AG62145, DE02918 and DE02931, by the University of Washington Orthodontic Memorial Fund, and by The Cranial Academy.

REFERENCES

1. Dwight, T. (1890): The closure of the sutures as a sign of age. *Boston Med. Surg. J.*, **123**: 389–392.
2. Epker, B. N., Kelin, M., and Frost, H. M. (1965): Magnitude and location of cortical bone loss in human rib with aging. *Clin. Orthoped.*, **41**: 198–202.
3. Gross, J. (1961): Aging of connective tissue; the extracellular components. In: *Structural Aspects of Aging*, edited by G. H. Bourne, pp. 177–195. New York; Hafner.
4. Kokich, V. G. (1976): Age changes in the human frontozygomatic suture from 20 to 95 years. *Am. J. Orthod.*, **69**: 411–430.
5. Krogman, W. M. (1930): Studies in growth changes in the skull and face of anthropoids and old world apes. *Am. J. Anat.*, **46**: 315–353.
6. Latham, R. A., and Burston, W. R. (1966): The postnatal pattern of growth at the sutures of the human skull. *Dent. Pract.*, **17**: 61–67.
7. Manson, J. D., and Lucas, R. B. (1962): A microradiographic study of the age changes in the human mandible. *Arch. Oral Biol.*, **7**: 761–769.
8. Massler, M., and Schour, I. (1951): The growth pattern of the cranial vault in the albino rat as measured by vital staining with alizarin red S. *Anat. Rec.*, **119**: 83–101.
9. Milch, R. A. (1966): Aging of connective tissues. In: *Perspectives in Experimental Gerontology*, edited by N. W. Schock, pp. 109–124. Springfield, Ill.; Thomas.
10. Miroue, M., and Rosenberg, L. (1975): The human facial sutures: A morphologic and histologic study of age changes from 20 to 95 years. M.S.D. Thesis, University of Washington.
11. Moss, M. L. (1957): Experimental alteration of sutural morphology. *Anat. Rec.*, **127**: 569–590.
12. Moss, M. L. (1961): Extrinsic determination of sutural area morphology in the rat calvaria. *Acta Anat.*, **44**: 263–272.
13. Persson, M. (1973): Structure and growth of facial sutures. *Odontol. Revy*, 24, Suppl. 6.
14. Persson, M., and Thilander, B. (1977): Palatal suture closure in man from 15 to 35 years of age. *Am. J. Orthod.*, **72**: 42–52.
15. Popevec, J. P., Biggert, T. P., and Retzlaff, E. W. (1976): Histological techniques for cranial bone studies. *J. Am. Osteopath. Assoc.*, **75**: 606–607.
16. Retzlaff, E. W., and Fontaine, J. (1960): Reciprocal inhibition as indicated by a differential staining reaction. *Science*, **131**: 104–105.
17. Stoker, N. G., and Epker, B. N. (1971): Age changes in endosteal bone remodeling and balance in the rabbit. *J. Dent. Res.*, **50**: 1570–1574.

18. Storey, E. (1972): Growth and remodeling of bone and bones. *Am. J. Orthod.*, **62:** 142–165.
19. Todd, T. W., and Lyon, D. W. (1924): Endocranial suture closure I. Adult males of white stock. *Am. J. Phys. Anthrop.*, 7: 325–384.
20. Todd, T. W., and Lyon, D. W. (1925): Cranial suture closure—its progress and age relationship II. Ectocranial closure in adult males of white stock. *Am. J. Phys. Anthrop.*, 8: 23–45.
21. Washburn, S. L. (1947): The relation of the temporal muscle to the form of the skull. *Anat. Rec.*, 99: 239–248.

30

Modeling of the Cranial Base

Robert N. Moore

Departments of Orthodontics and Anatomy,
West Virginia University Medical Center,
Morgantown, West Virginia

Pete E. Lestrel

School of Dentistry, University of California, Los Angeles, California;
and Dental Research Unit, Veterans Administration Hospital,
Sepulveda, California

INTRODUCTION

The cranial base in man and nonhuman primates is the postnatal derivative of the fetal chondrocranium and its intramembranously ossified lateral extensions. In fetal and neonatal life the cranial base is comprised of the frontal, ethmoid, presphenoid, basisphenoid, and basioccipital bones. With age there is progressive fusion of their midline articulations, the sphenofrontal suture and the spheno-ethmoidal, midsphenoidal, and spheno-occipital synchondroses, such that in the adult the cranial base is essentially one structure.

In man the cranial base completes slightly more than half of its anteroposterior linear growth during the first 7 to 8 years of life. While the angulation of the cranial base (basion-sella-nasion; Ba-S-N) generally remains stable from 12 to 20 years of age (2, 8), there is marked individual variation. Numerous investigators have described this as an increased or decreased "bending" of the cranial base structures (5), but recent studies have shown that bending probably does not occur, and instead two separate mechanisms are responsible for this angular change: osseous remodeling along the cranial base and angular change at sutures and/or synchondroses (10). Because of the progressive fusion at the articulations, the influence of the second mechanism decreases so that after the first decade, only the spheno-occipital synchondrosis exhibits any appreciable growth activity.

Although the cranial base angle has been used to describe changes in angulation, this is not correct anatomically since the foramen caecum, not the nasofrontal suture (nasion), is the anterior limit of the cranial base. Further, the position of nasion relative to foramen caecum changes with age in the same individual and varies between individuals. Another factor frequently overlooked is that the cranial base itself does not grow as one structure, but has multiple components (3). Individual segments tend to follow either a neural (sella-foramen caecum, opisthion-basion) or a skeletal (foramen caecum-nasion, basion-sella) pattern of growth, but not an intermediate one. Thus, the elongation of the anterior cranial base (sella-nasion) includes an appreciable amount of remodeling of the frontal sinus with a negligible longitudinal structural increase in the anterior cranial fossa (2, 16).

The cranial base angle in nonhuman primates, unlike that in man, increases to adulthood (1) and the midsphenoidal synchondrosis remains patent at least up to age $4\frac{1}{2}$ years in *M. mulatta* (6). Using tetracycline labeling in 20 *M. mulatta* females from term to 24 months, Michejda (11) concluded that the change in shape of the hypophyseal fossa and the delayed fusion of the midsphenoidal synchondrosis were both associated with cranial base flattening and this area was the main site of cranial base flexion. The spheno-occipital synchondrosis was considered to have a secondary role in the flattening process. Using Ba-S-N, no significant angular change was observed in the infantile period (14 to 30 weeks), while in the juvenile period (76 to 132 weeks) the angle increased about 7° (12). Swindler *et al.* (17) have shown that in *M. nemestrina* there is also a gradual increase in the cranial base angle during early postnatal ontogenesis (3 months to 3 years), but could not confirm the considerable rate of increase in the cranial base angle observed in the older juvenile *M. mulatta* by Michejda and Lamey (12).

In a cephalometric study of *M. mulatta* aged 9 to 39 months, the sella turcica moved dorsally within the body of the sphenoid bone after the age of 15 months (9). From age 9 to 27 months, clival length and the cranial base angle increased with growth at the spheno-occipital synchondrosis and apposition in the area of basion. After the age of 27 months, the remodeling of the dorsal clivus counteracted the increase in the cranial base angle caused by synchondrosal growth. Riolo and McNamara (15) found no growth at any synchondroses and no change in linear measurements in adult *M. mulatta*, although the cranial base angle increased slightly due to remodeling.

These studies have demonstrated that the usual metric and angular measurements of cranial base growth do not adequately represent the anatomical structures in either man or nonhuman primates. Since most of these measurements traverse long distances between structures, they are not sensitive enough to detect the subtle changes in shape that occur with osseous remodeling, the primary mechanism of change in the aging adult.

A more precise measurement of the midsagittal cranial base in fetal *M. nemestrina* has been obtained using Fourier analysis (7). This mathematical analysis permits accurate measurement of the irregular form of the endocranial profile by minimizing the effects of size and maximizing shape differences, thus adding a quantitative dimension to the descriptive analysis of shape change using a combined histologic and cephalometric approach (13). The development of a precise analysis of the cranial base profile has potential usefulness as a noninvasive, relatively disease and nutrition resistant index of biological age, sex, and subspecies in the nonhuman primate. Clinically, such an analysis may be useful to examine changes in anatomical relationships in children with craniofacial anomalies and malocclusions (4). In the present investigation we modified our Fourier analysis technique to quantify the changes in cranial base shape in a sample of aging *M. nemestrina* and to evaluate remodeling patterns in the adult.

MATERIALS AND METHODS

Subjects were 16 *M. nemestrina* aged 4 (n = 3), 10 (n = 9), and 20 (n = 4) years. The animals were anesthetized, positioned in a primate headholder and laterally radiographed. The cephalograms (Figure 30-1) were enlarged onto 8 × 10 inch Kodalith sheets to retain stable dimensions and facilitate visualization of craniofacial morphology. The endocranial profile of the cranial base from foramen caecum to basion was then traced using 0.003-inch matte acetate sheets.

The geometric framework used for Fourier analysis was modified from that previously published (7) by eliminating the basion-opisthion plane and adopting a more mathematically suitable intersection with the extremities of the cranial base. These changes improve the fit of the Fourier functions to the cranial base and allow comparisons between macaque, gorilla, and man.

To describe the data in polar coordinates (ranges and angles) a radial geometric framework was required. A radial pattern template with 1° intervals was made by attaching a self-stick Letraset LT 196 sheet to a sheet of 20-ml clear acetate. Each cranial base tracing was prepared for measuring in two steps. First, 3 lines were drawn (Figure 30-2a): (a) a line intersecting basion, ba, and tangent to the most anteroinferior border of the pituitary fossa, ipf; (b) a line perpendicular to ba-ipf at ba; and (c) a line parallel to ba-ipf and tangent to the anterior aspect of the cranial base, acb. Points ba and acb marked the extremes of the cranial base. Second, the tracing was superimposed on the radial template so that the line perpendicular to ba-ipf coincided with the 0° line of the template and the 36° line on the template intersected acb. The 36° line was drawn from acb to its intersection with the 0° line, thus defining point c. Two points were marked on the cranial base, one, ba', 2° in from ba and the other, acb', 6° in from acb (Figure 30-2b). Points ba' and acb' defined the limits of the cranial base profile used for analysis. Two new lines were drawn through ba' and acb' parallel to

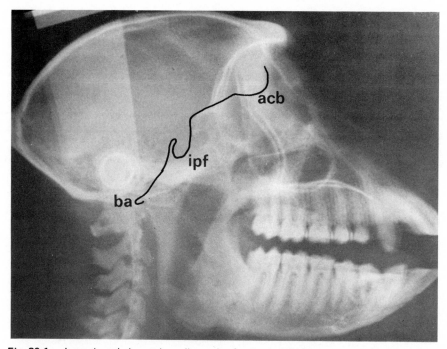

Fig. 30-1. Lateral cephalometric radiograph of animal #75282, a 4-y.o. female *M. nemestrina*. See text for definition of abbreviations.

ba'C and acb'C, respectively (Figure 30-2c). These two lines intersected at point VCTR, the origin of the vectors serving as raw data for Fourier analysis.

The anatomical cranial base from basion to foramen caecum was not used in this investigation because of goodness-of-fit considerations. It is imperative that the starting vector (ba') and the ending vector (acb') be approximately perpendicular to the endocranial profile to avoid loss of fit due to discontinuities (Figure 30-2c). The loss is slight at the end of the dorsal clivus (ba) since the length is decreased by only 2°. At the anterior aspect, the length was decreased by 6° because of the curvature of the cribriform plate.

With the geometry defined, 73 ranges at 0.5° intervals between the ba' and acb' limits (0 and 72) were drawn from VCTR to the endocranial outline of the cranial base (Figure 30-2d). The vectors were measured using a Helios dial caliper direct reading to 0.1 mm and submitted as data to a specially written Fourier analysis program (13). This program calculates the coefficients of the Fourier equation which quantitatively describe the entire midsagittal cranial base profile. This equation $f(\theta) = a_o + \sum_{i=1}^{n} a_i \cdot \cos i\theta$ effectively reduces the 73 ranges or variables to a more manageable function (15 Fourier coefficients and the con-

RESULTS AND DISCUSSION

The size-standardized cranial base Fourier coefficients for the three age groups are shown in Table 30-1. A major consideration of the Fourier function is how accurately it fits the morphology of the structure being examined. Since the Fourier equation is a series solution, the curve-fit improves as the number of series terms increases. This improvement in fit can be calculated as the mean residual or difference between the observed data points and predicted data points using the Fourier function. With respect to the present cranial base data, the mean residuals and their associated standard deviations ranged from 0.13 ± 0.03 mm to 0.18 ± 0.08 mm with 15 coefficients. This marks an improvement over the residual of approximately 0.30 mm published earlier (7) and is a consequence of the modified geometric framework described. The fit, as measured by this average residual, is satisfactory for the cranial base as a whole. However, because of the pronounced curvature of the posterosuperior portion of dorsum sellae, there remains a local discontinuity in this region which results in a double-valued function. In such a case, the vector is measured only to sella and not to the dorsum sella (Figure 30-2d). Even with this discontinuity, the loss in fit of the most superior aspect of the dorsum sellae is minor with respect to the entire cranial base region being measured.

Cranial Base Variance

By averaging the vectors that define a specific anatomical region of the cranial base, it is possible to establish an estimate of the variability for that region. Vectors 0 to 20 represented the dorsal clivus, 30 to 55 the hypophyseal fossa region, and 60 to 70 the anterior cranial base (Table 30-2). These vector ranges were selected because in the entire sample they included only the anatomical structure under consideration. The average sample variances (s^2) based on a sample of 16 are: dorsal clivus, $s^2 = 0.50$; hypophyseal fossa $s^2 = 7.57$; and anterior cranial base, $s^2 = 2.96$. These values suggest that the pituitary area is

Table 30-2. Age Distribution of Cranial Base Vectors and Ba-S-N Angle (mean ± standard deviation).

Anatomical Region	Vector Range	Age Groups (yrs)		
		4 n = 3	10 n = 9	20 n = 4
Dorsal Clivus	0–20	100.4 ± 0.7 mm	101.0 ± 0.9 mm	101.4 ± 1.0 mm
Hypophyseal Fossa Area	30–55	99.3 ± 4.0 mm	98.4 ± 3.2 mm	97.8 ± 3.8 mm
Anterior Cranial Base	60–70	100.6 ± 1.1 mm	101.5 ± 0.8 mm	102.2 ± 0.6 mm
Cranial Base Angle (Ba-S-N)		157.8 ± 8.6°	154.6 ± 2.9°	158.2 ± 4.0°

the most variable structure. However, more definitive examination of the fossa discloses that the variability of the posterior border ($s^2 = 9.67$) is less than that of the anterior border ($s^2 = 11.76$). In the region of the inferior border of sella the variability decreases ($s^2 = 2.34$).

The preceding variance estimates were derived by superimposition of the cranial base profile on the geometry formed by the $36°$ angle (ba'-VCTR-acb') in Figure 30-2c. If the cranial base profile is superimposed on a line from the center of the hypophyseal fossa (sella) to VCTR, and the vector along this line from VCTR to the inferior border of the fossa is measured, the variability decreases even more ($s^2 = 1.72$). Regardless of superimposition techniques, the inferior border of the hypophyseal fossa appears to be relatively stable, but not as stable as the dorsal clivus region. While these results show a pattern in the variability of the cranial base profile, they are dependent upon the sample size of 16, and cannot be considered definitive.

Cranial Base Shape Changes

When the mean cranial base vectors were examined in the different age groups (Table 30-2), both the dorsal clivus (vectors 0 to 20) and the anterior cranial base (vectors 60 to 70) showed an increase with age. In the intermediate area around the pituitary, a decreasing trend was evident, suggesting a slight increase in the angular relationship of the dorsal clivus and the anterior cranial base. The cranial base angle (Ba-S-N) was measured on all specimens (Table 30-2) and by subspecies. These data did not show an increase in the angular relationship of the cranial base corresponding to the change in profile demonstrated by Fourier analysis. The differences may be due in part to the fact that the entire cranial base was not measured by the Fourier method, while the angular measurement most likely reflects the inclusion of the nasofrontal area. The latter may contribute an appreciable amount of variability which does not reflect any changes in the anterior cranial base (2). Because of the limited sample size and the unavailability of specimens for histologic analysis, the present results cannot indicate the precise anatomical site(s) of bony remodeling. However, the results are in agreement with those of Riolo and McNamara (15) who reported a slight increase in the cranial base angle due to bony remodeling changes in adult *M. mulatta*.

ACKNOWLEDGMENTS

This study was supported in part by National Institutes of Health grants RR05304 to the University of California and RR00166, RR52177 and AG62145 to the University of Washington.

REFERENCES

1. Ashton, E. H. (1957): Age changes in the basicranial axis of the anthropoidea. *Proc. Zool. Soc. London*, **129**: 61–74.
2. Bjork, A. (1955): Cranial base development. *Am. J. Orthodont.*, **41**: 198–226.
3. Ford, E. H. R. (1958): Growth of the human cranial base. *Am. J. Orthodont.*, **44**: 498–506.
4. Hopkin, G. B., Houston, W. J. B., and James, G. A. (1968): The cranial base as an aetiological factor in malocclusion. *Angle Orthodont.*, **38**: 250–255.
5. Hoyte, D. A. N. (1975): A critical analysis of the growth in length of the cranial base. *Birth Defects:* Original Article Series, **11**: 255–282.
6. Latham, R. A. (1958): Skull growth in the rhesus monkey. *J. Anat.*, **92**: 654.
7. Lestrel, P. E., and Moore, R. N. (1978): The cranial base in fetal *Macaca nemestrina*. A quantiative analysis of size and shape. *J. Dent. Res.*, **57**: 395–401; Erratum in *J. Dent. Res.*, **57**: 947.
8. Lewis, A. B., and Roche, A. F. (1977): The saddle angle: Constancy or change? *Angle Orthodont.*, **47**: 46–54.
9. Melsen, B. (1971): The postnatal growth of the cranial base in *Macaca* rhesus analyzed by the implant method. *Tandlaegebladet*, **75**: 1320–1329.
10. Melsen, B. (1974): The cranial base: The postnatal development of the cranial base studied histologically on human autopsy material. *Acta Odont. Scand.*, 32: Suppl. 62.
11. Michejda, M. (1972): The role of basicranial synchondroses in flexure processes and ontogenetic development of the skull base. *Am. J. Phys. Anthrop.*, **37**: 143–150.
12. Michejda, M., and Lamey, D. (1971): Flexion and metric age changes of the cranial base in the *Macaca mulatta*. *Folia Primat.*, **14**: 84–94.
13. Moore, R. N. (1978): A cephalometric and histologic study of the cranial base in foetal monkeys, *Macaca nemestrina*. *Arch. Oral Biol.*, **23**: 57–67.
14. Parnell, J. N., and Lestrel, P. E. (1977): A computer program for fitting irregular two-dimensional forms. *Computer Programs in Biomedicine*, 7: 145–161.
15. Riolo, M. L., and McNamara, J. A., Jr. (1973): Cranial base growth in the rhesus monkey from infancy to adulthood. *J. Dent. Res.*, **52**: 249.
16. Roche, A. F., and Lewis, A. B. (1976): Late growth changes in the cranial base. In: *Symposium on Development of the Basicranium*, edited by J. F. Bosma, pp. 221–239. DHEW Publication no. (NIH) 76–989. Bethesda, Md.; U.S. Department of Health, Education, and Welfare, NIH.
17. Swindler, D. R., Sirianni, J. E., and Tarrant, L. H. (1973): A longitudinal study of cephalofacial growth in *Papio cynocephalus* and *Macaca nemestrina* from three months to three years. *Proc. 4th Int. Congr. Primat.*, **3**: 227–240.

Index

Reproductive organs, 198; method of study, 185–186; weights, 186; histology, 187, 188–196

Reproductive senescence: in human, 183–184, 197–199; in *Pan*, 199–200; in Old World monkeys, 17, 30–32, 36; in *M. mulatta*, 198; in *M. nemestrina*, 184, 185–200; in nonprimates, 199–200. *See also* Reproductive organs: histology

Respiratory system. *See* Lung

Response: inhibition, 49–52; latency, 48, 51. *See also* Cognition

Restraint stress, 230. *See also* Cortisol: response to stress

Reticular formation: brainstem, 83; lateral, 82; pontine, 85; lipofuscin in, 89

Rhesus monkey. *See Macaca mulatta*

RNA: coding vs. noncoding sequences in brain, 77; diversity in brain, 71–79 (*see also* Gene expression in brain); tissue specific messenger, 78; in adrenal cortex, 232–233

RNA, heterogeneous nuclear: in *M. nemestrina* brain, 71–79; yield, 73; influence of proteinase K and SDS on yield, 74–75; influence of post-mortem interval on, 76; in chimpanzee and human, 77; influence of age on, 76–77

RNA-DNA hybridization: sensitivity of technique, 77–78; and age in mice, 77. *See also* RNA; Gene expression in brain.

Rodents: degree of genetic homology to man, 72; as cognition model, 54; cerebellum, 134, 138; mammary development, 207–208; alpha-lactalbumin in, 203; adrenal, 230, 245; trace elements, 353–354; mentioned, 11. *See also* Guinea pig; Mouse; Rat

Role: social, 56

Sacrifice procedure, 43–46

Saguinus (tamarin): maximum lifespan, 2; longevity related to DNA repair, 6, mentioned, 4, 11

Saimiri (squirrel monkey): maximum lifespan, 2; social organization, 57; atherosclerosis in, 259; lipofuscin in cerebellum, 134; adrenal, 245

ScDNA. *See* DNA: single copy

Senile plaques, 32

Serotonin: location of cells in brain, 82–83; relation to age, 89–92; brain synaptosome uptake, 100–104; platelet uptake, 8, 100–104; mentioned, 110

Sharpey's fiber bundles, 361, 363. *See also* Collagen: in craniofacial sutures

Sheep: lung, 321–322; osteoporosis, 348; trace minerals, 354

Short-lived species identification, 11–12

Sleep: monoamines and, 96

Smooth muscle: proliferation in coronary artery, 252 (*see also* Coronary artery: lesions); antibodies against (*see* Antibodies: test panel)

SN. *See* Substantia nigra

Social behavior: in *M. nemestrina*, 61–68; in aged, 62–69; in postmenopausal female, 68; coalitions, 57, 58; disengagement, 69; influencing survival in the wild, 60. *See also* Affinity ties; Dominance; Kinship ties; Aged role; Social Roles

Social organization: culture free models, 56; five types, 56–59

Social roles: in evolutionary context, 59–60; comparison of nonhuman and human primates, 61; change with age in individual, 61–62

Socioemotional behavior: relevance of nonhuman primate models, 9

Sodium, potassium ATPase (Na$^+$, K$^+$ATPase): description, 281–282; species differences in kinetics with cardiac glycosides, 289; mentioned, 8. *See also* Cardiac glycosides

Solitary: males, 57; species, 57

Somatic mutation theory of aging, 72

Somatotrophs: defined, 172; described, 173–175, 177

Specimen preservation shipping, 45

Sperm: antisperm antibodies, 120

Spider monkey. *See Ateles*

Spinal cord: acetylcholinesterase activity in, 139

Spleen, 32

Squirrel monkey. *See Saimiri*

Statistical analyses, 46–47

Status, social, 56, 59–61; determinants of, 57–61